Verbal Reasoning

for

NTSE, Olympiads & Competitive Exams

Jaya Ghosh
B.Sc. (Maths), MCA, MBA (HR)

V&S PUBLISHERS

Published by:

F-2/16, Ansari road, Daryaganj, New Delhi-110002
☎ 23240026, 23240027 • *Fax:* 011-23240028
✉ info@vspublishers.com • www.vspublishers.com

Online Brandstore: amazon.in/vspublishers

Regional Office : Hyderabad
5-1-707/1, Brij Bhawan (Beside Central Bank of India Lane)
Bank Street, Koti, Hyderabad - 500 095
☎ 040-24737290
✉ vspublishershyd@gmail.com

Follow us on:   

BUY OUR BOOKS FROM: AMAZON FLIPKART

ISBN 978-93-505792-2-0
New Edition

Printed at : Param Offsetters, Okhla, New Delhi–110020

Publisher's Note

With a view to strengthen the career aspirations of student community, V&S Publishers has published this book **VERBAL REASONING for NTSE, Olympiads & Competitive Examinations** under its Gen X Series (Generating Xcellence in Generation X). While the books under Gen X Series are published to propel school students into higher learning orbit, this particular book is intended to boost the success rate of school students appearing or intending to write these research-based and other competitive examinations for higher studies or jobs.

The importance of NTSE and Olympiad examinations lies in the fact that on the basis of its result, a student can win scholarship for five years or more years and succeed in building a bright career. And hence we are giving details of this examination right at the start of the book.

This book covers the Verbal Reasoning part of the MAT (Mental Aptitude Test) question paper, one of the three papers which the students write in each of the Stages-I and II of the National Talent Search Examination (NTSE). Stage-I is conducted by States and Union Territories whereas NCERT conducts Stage-II examination.

This examination is organised to award scholarship to students currently studying at the Class X level. Scholarships are awarded up to Ph.D. in Sciences, Social Sciences, Humanities, Languages, Commerce, Vocational Studies and Fine arts. And up to second degree level for professional courses in medicines, engineering, technology, management and law. NTSE consists of Mental Ability Test (MAT), Language Test (LT) and Scholastic Aptitude Test (SAT) having multiple choice questions. Every year about 1000 scholarships are awarded - Rs.1250/- per month for Class XI & XII and Rs.2000/- at Graduation and Post-graduation level. Scholarship at Ph.D. level is governed by UGC norms.

All students studying in Class X in any recognized school are eligible to appear in Stage-I exam. For Stage-II, there is a quota for each State and Union Territory based on Student enrollment at secondary level.

There are 3 papers in both stages–

1. Mental Ability Test (MAT)
2. Language Test (LT) and
3. Scholastic Ability Test (SAT).

Questions are in the form of multiple choices with negative marking deducting 1/3 marks only at the Stage II (National level). The tests are conducted in Asamiya, Bangla, English, Gujarati, Hindi, Kannada, Marathi, Malyalam, Odia, Punjabi, Tamil, Telugu and Urdu. However, language test is available in two languages – English & Hindi.

Test	No. of Questions	Maximum Marks	Time
Mental Ability Test (MAT)	50	50	45 minutes
Language Test	50	50	45 minutes
Scholastic Ability Test (SAT)	100	100	90 minutes

The concepts have been explained through various solved examples and multiple choice questions with answer key besides hints for solving the problems and use of everyday language hopefully enable students to master the subject with relative ease.

V&S Publishers has your welfare in mind, be assured!

Preface

To go through the NTSE examination a student must have a dedicated and serious approach. Students are often misled by the casual approach and the wrong notion that Objective Type Questions are easy to solve but in fact they require an extensive understanding of each prescribed subject or topic. Therefore, only hard work and diligent study can help the candidates crack the exam successfully.

This book provides a brief **Theory** on each topic, **Solved Examples** followed by **Fully Solved Exercises**.

The book contains questions very similar to what have been asked in the previous NTSE examinations of class 10th. I ask students ***Do all the Exercises***, not missing even one of them. Make an attempt to answer the question first, and then read the given answer. I hope, on second reading, students would be able to do that on their own, without looking at the answers. In short, the condidates have to make an honest effort to achieve the goal.

Wish you a grand success in your examination, and a very bright future. I am sure the students will find this book most useful. I will be happy to receive constructive feedback and suggestions.

How to Read This Book

- The book in your hand is a unidirectional effort to guide and prepare students for NTSE/ Olympiad examinations.
- The book covers Verbal Reasoning. It consists of *Key Concepts* followed by *Solved Examples, Multiple Choice Questions* and *Answer Key and Hints and Solution.* The solutions to the MCQ's are provided at the end of each chapter.
- This book will really prove to be an asset for Class 7th, 8th, 9th and 10th students as they hardly find any material which can help them in building a strong foundation.
- The contents of this book have been developed as per the needs of the students *i.e.* the simple approach, conceptual clarity and exhaustive coverage in each section. Questions incorporated in the book conform to the latest pattern of NTSE making this book an exhaustive study material.
- *Previous Years Questions* have been given at the end of each chapter for clear cut understanding of the papers. Hint and Explanations of most of the questions have been provided so that the students could know how the correct answer has been reached at.
- A unique approach has been adopted to explain and illustrate methodology in Mathematics and Logical Reasoning, which is considered to be the key chapter to get an overall good score.
- Last, but not the least, four Mock Test Papers and two Solved Papers have been incorporated for the real exam – time feel.

Happy Reading.......

NTSE : An Introduction

The National Talent Search Examination for students studying in Class X is meant to identify and nurture talent. The examination is conducted every year at two levels: Stage – I (State Level) and Stage – II (National Level). National Talent Search Examination (NTSE) is an annual examination conducted by NCERT at national level. It is one of the most reputed talent search exams in India. It was started in the year 1963 and has grown in prestige and scope ever since. The objective of the exam is to identify students who have potential to excel in Science, Social Science, Engineering, Medicine, Management and Law. The successful students, called NTSE Scholars, receive financial support / scholarships from NCERT till the time they continue to study.

The NTSE not only provides scholarship to the good students but also highlights the students with good aptitude and knowledge.

Scholarships: About One thousand scholarships are awarded for different stages of education as follows:

(a) Scholarship of Rs. 1250/- per month for Class-XI to XII.

(b) Scholarship of Rs. 2000/- per month for Undergraduates and Post-graduates.

(c) Amount of Scholarship for Ph.D. be fixed in accordance with the UGC norms.

Reservation: 15% for students belonging to the SC category, 7.5% for students belonging to the ST category and 3% for Physically Challenged Group of Students.

Selection: Stage-I, selection will be done by States/UTs and those who qualify Stage- I, will be eligible to appear for Stage-II examination, conducted by NCERT.

Qualifying Marks: Qualifying marks for candidates from General category is 40% in each paper and for candidates from SC, ST, PH is 35% in each paper.

Language Test Qualifying in nature and marks obtained for Language Test will not be counted for final merit.

Important Dates: Dates for submission of application form and conduct of examination, are given below:

Stage	Area	Tentative Dates
Stage-I (State)	Last Date for Submission of Application Form	To be notified by the respective State and it may vary from state to state
	Examination in Mizoram, Meghalaya, Nagaland and Andaman and Nicobar Islands	7th November, 2015 (Saturday)
	Examination in All other States and Union Territories	8th November, 2015 (Sunday)
Stage-II (National)	Examination in All States and Union Territories	8th May, 2016 (Sunday)

Eligibility: All students of Class X studying in recognized schools are eligible to appear for the Stage -I examination, conducted by the States/UTs, in which the schools are located. There will be no domicile restriction.

Students registered under Open Distance Learning (ODL) will also be eligible for scholarship, provided the student is below the age of 18 years (as on 1st July of the particular year), the student is not employed and s/he is appearing in class X examination for the first time.

Examination: The pattern of written examination will be as follows:

- Stage I examination at the State/UT level will comprise three parts, namely (a) Mental Ability Test (MAT) (b) Language Test (LT) and (c) Scholastic Aptitude Test (SAT).
- **Qualifying Marks:** Qualifying marks for candidates from General category is 40% in each paper and for candidates from SC, ST, PH is 35% in each paper.
- **Lanuage Test** Qualifying in nature and marks obtained for Language Test will not be counted for final merit.

♦ The pattern of stage I will be as under:

Test		No. of Questions	No. of Marks	Duration (in minutes)
Mental Ability Test (MAT)		50	50	50
Scholastic Test	Language Comprehensive Test	40	40	40
	Aptitude Test	90	90	90
Total		**180**	**180**	**180**

♦ The pattern of stage II will be as under:

Test	No. of Questions	No. of Marks	Duration (in minutes)
(i) Mental Ability Test (MAT)	50	50	45
(ii) Language Test (LT) English/Hindi	50	50	45
(iii) Scholastic Aptitude Test (SAT)	100	100	90

At Stage – II (National Level), there will be negative marking in each paper. For each wrong answer 1/3 marks will be deducted. No marks will be deducted for unattempted questions.

Application Form: You may contact the State/UT Liaison officer for procuring application form.

The completed application form should be signed by the Principal of the school much before the last date of submission. The candidate as well as the Principal of the school must adhere to the last date for submission of the Application Form. **Different states may have different last dates for submission. Please confirm from the liaison officer of your state, the address at which the completed forms are to be submitted.** The State-wise contacts of the liaison officers are given in the CD and are also available on the NCERT website www.ncert.nic.in. **All queries related to application form should be directed to the State Liaison Officers (LOs). No application should be sent to NCERT.**

Fees: States and Union Territories may notify the fee required which will be paid for the Stage-I examination. Therefore, before submitting the application form, you may find out the fees charged for Stage-I Examination and also the mode of payment from the respective State"Liaison Officers (LOs). However, NCERT does not charge any fee for Stage-II examination.

Indian Students Studying Abroad in Class X can appear directly for Stage II NTS Examination under conditions prescribed in the NTS brochure which is available on the NCERT website. Candidates may fill up the Application Form, available on the NCERT website and send to the undersigned along with a photocopy of the mark sheet of previous examination, **latest by February 28th, 2016. Application Form for students study abroad will be uploaded on NCERT website in the month of October, 2015. Announcement for Indian Students Studying Abroad will be announced separately.**

How to Prepare for NTSE

Here are some tips on how to prepare for NTSE :

- **Start your preparation with last year's NTSE papers:** The objective is understood the type of questions asked and your current level. You should take last year's paper or NTSE sample questions and just write the exam once with all seriousness. It does not matter if you have not prepared or never heard of it before. Just sit down and write the test. This will help you gain a knowledge of NTSE and also give you a fair idea of the exam.
- **Analyze your performance:** Make sure to minutely assess what you could do and what you had a hard time with. Is it the knowledge of subject matter that you lacked? Or did you miss out because you made some silly mistakes? Or is it that mental ability questions that took a long time for you to crack? Whatever it is, just analyze your performance very minutely and critically
- **Make a plan:** Once you know your weak points, make a plan. You will definitely need to study and revise the subject matter. That is required not just for NTSE but also for your school. So there is no letting up on that front. You will also need to practice more mental ability questions. But the allocation of time will depend upon your analysis of how weak or strong you are in that particular aspect
- **Practice, practice and practice:** These are the only 3 steps that can lead to success. Get exposed to more questions of mental ability so that you are not shocked on the exam day, solve more papers and then analyze each one in detail. Take help from seniors. As you practice, you can also get confident of your speed, subject knowledge and accuracy.

Tips on How to Write Examination

The written examination (NTSE II stage) comprises two tests namely, MAT (Mental Ability Test) and SAT (Scholastic Ability Test). Each test comprises 100 multiple choice type questions which are attempted in 90 minutes. Thus on an average, the examinee will get around 54 seconds to answer a question. Therefore, both speed and accuracy are essential.

- In the MAT section, questions of the same type are grouped together. Since the instructions for all these questions are the same, read them carefully and answer all the questions.
- Use your time wisely. If you are doubtful at a particular question, omit it and move ahead without wasting much time on it. Do not let yourself get stuck on a tough question and lose time. You can always return to questions that you have omitted before the time is up.
- Do easy questions first because you earn as much credit for correctly answering those questions as you do for correctly answering a difficult question.

Do's for Answering Multiple Choice Questions in NTSE

- If the question is 'conceptual', i.e., if the answer it seeks is a statement, begin by covering the alternatives with a ruler or piece of paper. Then, carefully read and understand the stem of the question before looking at the alternatives.
- Circle or underline key words in the stem, paying special attention to qualifying words such as 'always,' 'major,' 'increase,' etc.
- Use your knowledge of headings from where lecture notes, lab, etc. is drawn. Recall a few salient points about the information. If necessary, jot down any relevant facts you need to process the alternatives. This does not have to take much time but this recall is an essential step.
- Predict an answer, if possible.
- Think over all of the alternatives and check the format of the question. Is only one of the alternatives correct, or can several or all of the alternatives be correct?

- If you know the answer, carefully mark the correct answer on your answer sheet.
- If you do not know the answer, re-check the question. Narrow your choices by eliminating any alternative that you know is incorrect. If two options still look equally appealing, compare each to the stem of the question, making sure that the one you eventually choose answers what is asked.
- If you are unable to make a choice and need to spend more time with the question, put a big question mark beside that question, and move on to the next.
- Don't stick to one question in the exam. It is much better to move on and finish all of those questions that you can answer and then to come back to the problematic questions.
- If the answer that you have calculated, is not one of the given options, check your procedure again, making any necessary changes, and recalculate your answer.
- If you still do not arrive at one of the given options, put a big question mark on that question, and go on to the next. When you get to the end of the exam, go back to any questions that you did not answer the first time.

Don'ts for Answering Multiple-Choice Questions

- Don't guess any choice as the correct answer because there is negative marking.
- Don't select an alternative just because you remember learning the information in the course; it may be a 'true' statement in its own right, but you have to make sure that it is the 'correct' answer to the question.
- Don't pick an answer just because it seems to make sense. You must answer from your knowledge of the course content, not just from your general knowledge and logic.
- Don't dismiss an alternative because it seems too obvious and simple. If you are well prepared for the exam, some of the questions will appear very straight forward to you.

❒

CONTENTS

Verbal Reasoning

Verbal Reasoning

- ✓ Verbal Classification
- ✓ Coding-Decoding
- ✓ Series Completion Test
- ✓ Number Puzzles
- ✓ Blood Relations
- ✓ Logical Sequence of Words
- ✓ Analytical Reasoning
- ✓ Number, Ranking and Time Sequence Tests
- ✓ Verbal Analogy
- ✓ Direction Sense Test
- ✓ Arithmetical Reasoning Test
- ✓ Logical Venn Diagrams
- ✓ Sitting Arrangements
- ✓ Verification of Truth of Statement
- ✓ Problems on Calendar and Clocks
- ✓ Logical Reasoning

UNIT 1
Verbal Classification

Classification is the process of grouping various objects on the basis of their common properties. Classification, therefore, helps to make a homogeneous group from a heterogeneous one. Questions on classification are designed to test a candidate's ability to classify given objects and find the object which does not share the common property with the rest objects of the group. Classification can be divided into different forms. Some forms of classification are given below.

❐ Forms of Classification

1. **Words Classification:** Different objects are classified on the basis of common features or properties such as name, place, uses, situations, origin etc.
2. **Alphabet Classification:** Alphabets are classified into a group using a particular method or rule. Rules or methods applied for such classification are often simple and hence can easily be understood.
3. **Miscellaneous Classification:** Any rule other than that described above can be used for classification or grouping. Questions on such pattern do not necessarily use the alphabets and words. Here the numeric and other mathematical symbols can also be used.

Solved Examples

All possible classifications have been explained through the following examples.

☛ ***Direction to solve (1 to 3) :*** *In each of the following questions, a group of five items is given. Four of them share common features whereas one doesn't. Choose the word which is different from the rest.*

1. Choose the item which is different from others.
   (a) Milk (b) Syrup
   (c) Squash (d) Tea
   (e) Cake
   Solution: Option (e) is correct.
   Explanation: All others are drinks.
2. Choose the item which is different from others.
   (a) Moon (b) Football
   (c) Earth (d) Bangle
   (e) Watermelon
   Solution: Option (d) is correct.
   Explanation: All other items are three dimensional figures.
3. Choose the item which is different from others.
   (a) Gold (b) Silver
   (c) Bronze (d) Iron
   (e) Zinc
   Solution: Option (c) is correct.
   Explanation: 'Bronze' is an alloy (alloy is a combination of two or more metals).

☛ ***Direction to solve (4 to 7) :*** *In each of the following questions, four out of five alternatives contain alphabet placed in a particular form. Find the one that does not belong to the group.*

4. Choose the odd one out.
   (a) BEA (b) PSO
   (c) WZV (d) JMI
   (e) RTQ
   Solution: Option (e) is correct.
   Explanation: In all other groups there is a gap of two letters between the first and the second letters.
5. Choose the odd one out.
   (a) ELS (b) HOV
   (c) CJQ (d) KRX
   (e) GNU
   Solution: Option (d) is correct.
   Explanation: In all other groups, letters adjacent to the middle one are equidistant from it in the alphabet.
6. Choose the odd one out.
   (a) ZYAB (b) TSGH
   (c) ONLM (d) UTFH
   (e) QPKL
   Solution: Option (e) is correct.
   Explanation: In all other groups first, second and third, fourth letters are the consecutive alphabet.

7. Choose the odd one out.
   (a) YDWB (b) TKRI
   (c) QNOM (d) HLFJ
   (e) WFUD

   Solution: Option (c) is correct.

   Explanation: In all other groups, first and second letters are moved two steps backward to obtain third and fourth letters respectively.

☛ ***Direction to solve: (8 to 10) :** In each of the following questions, certain pairs of words are given, out of which the words in all pairs except one bear a certain common relationship. Choose the pair in which the words are differently related.*

8. Choose the pair in which the words are differently related from the rest.
   (a) Car : Road
   (b) Ship : Sea
   (c) Rocket : Space
   (d) Aeroplane : Pilot

   Solution: Option (d) is correct.

   Explanation: In all other pairs, first is the means of transport on the medium denoted by the second.

9. Choose the pair in which the words are differently related from the rest.
   (a) Steel : Utensils
   (b) Bronze : Statue
   (c) Duralumin : Aircraft
   (d) Iron : Rails

   Solution: Option (d) is correct.

   Explanation: In all other pairs, first is the alloy used to make the second. (Iron is not an alloy but a metal.)

10. Choose the pair in which the words are differently related from the rest.
    (a) Class : Students
    (b) Sentence : Words
    (c) Tree : Forest
    (d) Hour : Minutes

    Solution: Option (c) is correct.

    Explanation: In all other pairs, second is a unit of the first.

Multiple Choice Questions

☛ ***Direction to solve: (1 to 65) :** In each of the following questions, five words have been given, out of which four are alike in some manner, while the fifth one is different. Choose the word which is different from the rest.*

1. Choose the word which is different from the rest.
   (a) Bajra (b) Mustard
   (c) Rice (d) Wheat
   (e) Barley
2. Choose the word which is different from the rest.
   (a) Cot (b) Sheet
   (c) Quilt (d) Pillow
   (e) Blanket
3. Choose the word which is different from the rest.
   (a) Assassinate (b) Kill
   (c) Kidnap (d) Stab
   (e) Murder
4. Choose the word which is different from the rest.
   (a) Doe (b) Bitch
   (c) Sorceress (d) Drone
   (e) Mare
5. Choose the word which is different from the rest.
   (a) Physics (b) Chemistry
   (c) Geography (d) Botany
   (e) Zoology
6. Choose the word which is different from the rest.
   (a) Football (b) Volleyball
   (c) Cricket (d) Chess
   (e) Hockey
7. Choose the word which is different from the rest.
   (a) Trunk (b) Tree
   (c) Fruit (d) Leaf
   (e) Flower
8. Choose the word which is different from the rest.
   (a) Giraffe (b) Hyena
   (c) Deer (d) Rhinoceros
   (e) Zebra
9. Choose the word which is different from the rest.
   (a) Poland (b) Greece
   (c) Spain (d) Italy
   (e) Korea
10. Choose the word which is different from the rest.
    (a) Reader (b) Writer
    (c) Printer (d) Publisher
    (e) Reporter
11. Choose the word which is different from the rest.
    (a) Arrow (b) Axe
    (c) Knife (d) Dagger
    (e) Sword
12. Choose the word which is different from the rest.
    (a) Feathers (b) Tentacles
    (c) Scales (d) Pseudopodia
    (e) Flagella
13. Choose the word which is different from the rest.
    (a) Flood (b) Hurricane
    (c) Avalanche (d) Earthquakes
    (e) Explosion
14. Choose the word which is different from the rest.
    (a) Gangtok (b) Singhbhum
    (c) Hyderabad (d) Chennai
    (e) Bhubaneswar
15. Choose the word which is different from the rest.
    (a) Turtle (b) Lamb
    (c) Colt (d) Bitch
    (e) Farrow

16. Choose the word which is different from the rest.
(a) Raid (b) Attack
(c) Assault (d) Defence
(e) Ambush

17. Choose the word which is different from the rest.
(a) Guava (b) Litchi
(c) Papaya (d) Watermelon
(e) Jackfruit

18. Choose the word which is different from the rest.
(a) Cabbage (b) Papaya
(c) Gourd (d) Cucumber
(e) Brinjal

19. Choose the word which is different from the rest.
(a) Jordan (b) Bhutan
(c) Turkey (d) Norway
(e) Spain

20. Choose the word which is different from the rest.
(a) Engineer (b) Architect
(c) Mechanic (d) Mason
(e) Blacksmith

21. Choose the word which is different from the rest.
(a) Sleet (b) Fog
(c) Hailstone (d) Vapour
(e) Mist

22. Choose the word which is different from the rest.
(a) Trigger (b) Muzzle
(c) Pallets (d) Barrel
(e) Bullet

23. Choose the word which is different from the rest.
(a) Cigar (b) Cigarette
(c) Tobacco (d) Pipe
(e) Hookah

24. Choose the word which is different from the rest.
(a) Sun (b) Moon
(c) Star (d) Planets
(e) Universe

25. Choose the word which is different from the rest.
(a) Month (b) Year
(c) Fortnight (d) Season
(e) Week

26. Choose the word which is different from the rest.
(a) Decantation (b) Filtration
(c) Centrifugation (d) Sublimation
(e) Condensation

27. Choose the word which is different from the rest.
(a) Fern (b) Moss
(c) Algae (d) Fungi
(e) Grass

28. Choose the word which is different from the rest.
(a) Sparrow (b) Eagle
(c) Hawk (d) Vulture
(e) Owl

29. Choose the word which is different from the rest.
(a) Mahavir (b) Buddha
(c) Marx (d) Jesus
(e) Gandhi

30. Choose the word which is different from the rest.
(a) Seminar (b) Semicolon
(c) Semi-final (d) Semicircle
(e) Semitone

31. Choose the word which is different from the rest.
(a) Nephrology (b) Entomology
(c) Astrology (d) Mycology
(e) Pathology

32. Choose the word which is different from the rest.
(a) Tulsidas (b) Sheridan
(c) Kalidas (d) Shakespeare
(e) Bernard Shaw

33. Choose the word which is different from the rest.
(a) Arrow (b) Missile
(c) Sword (d) Bullet
(e) Spear

34. Choose the word which is different from the rest.
(a) Madagascar (b) Thailand
(c) Cuba (d) Greenland
(e) Tasmania

35. Choose the word which is different from the rest.
(a) Grasslands (b) Pampas
(c) Downs (d) Prairies
(e) Savanna

36. Choose the word which is different from the rest.
(a) Sesame (b) Corn
(c) Olive (d) Onion

37. Choose the word which is different from the rest.
(a) Radium (b) Thorium
(c) Sodium (d) Polonium
(e) Uranium

38. Choose the word which is different from the rest.
(a) Moth (b) Bee
(c) Lizard (d) Aphid
(e) Cockroach

39. Choose the word which is different from the rest.
(a) Tuberculosis (b) Small pox
(c) Cholera (d) Typhoid
(e) Tetanus

40. Choose the word which is different from the rest.
(a) Sambhar (b) Dal
(c) Baikal (d) Siachen
(e) Chilka

41. Choose the word which is different from the rest.
(a) Manure (b) Nitrogen
(c) Ammonia (d) Urea
(e) Potash

42. Choose the word which is different from the rest.
(a) Write (b) Read
(c) Knowledge (d) Learn
(e) Study

43. Choose the word which is different from the rest.
(a) Cataract (b) Hypermetropia
(c) Trachoma (d) Eczema
(e) Glaucoma

44. Choose the word which is different from the rest.
(a) Pupil (b) Iris
(c) Cornea (d) Medulla
(e) Retina

45. Choose the word which is different from the rest.
(a) Dog (b) Lion
(c) Jackal (d) Tiger
(e) Cheetah

46. Choose the word which is different from the rest.
(a) Hindi (b) Sindhi
(c) Oriya (d) Urdu
(e) Gujarati

47. Choose the word which is different from the rest.
(a) Table (b) Cupboard
(c) Chair (d) Sofa
(e) Paper weight

48. Choose the word which is different from the rest.
(a) Mandible (b) Rib
(c) Sternum (d) Ulna
(e) Pinna

49. Choose the word which is different from the rest.
(a) Volume (b) Size
(c) Large (d) Shape
(e) Weight

50. Choose the word which is different from the rest.
(a) Antelope (b) Kangaroo
(c) Hippopotamus (d) Unicorn
(e) Rhinoceros

51. Choose the word which is different from the rest.
(a) Gasoline (b) Methane
(c) Asphalt (d) Paraffin wax
(e) Diesel

52. Choose the word which is different from the rest.
(a) Cancel (b) Change
(c) Repeal (d) Revoke
(e) Rescind

53. Choose the word which is different from the rest.
(a) Gorges (b) Bars
(c) Canyons (d) Meanders
(e) Rapids

54. Choose the word which is different from the rest.
(a) Ghosts (b) Spirits
(c) Phantoms (d) Skeletons
(e) Apparitions

55. Choose the word which is different from the rest.
(a) Mussoorie (b) Pahalgam
(c) Jaipur (d) Darjeeling
(e) Manali

56. Choose the word which is different from the rest.
(a) Swimming (b) Diving
(c) Driving (d) Sailing
(e) Fishing

57. Choose the word which is different from the rest.
(a) Baboon (b) Gibbon
(c) Chimpanzee (d) Gorilla
(e) Jaguar

58. Choose the word which is different from the rest.
(a) Confucius (b) Prophet
(c) Guru Gobind (d) Moses
(e) Lao Tse

59. Choose the word which is different from the rest.
(a) Spiracles (b) Gills
(c) Lungs (d) Trachea
(e) Stomata

60. Choose the word which is different from the rest.
(a) Sucrose (b) Ptyalin
(c) Amylase (d) Pepsin
(e) Lipase

61. Choose the word which is different from the rest.
(a) Hepatitis (b) Tetanus
(c) Cancer (d) Conjunctivitis
(e) Measles

62. Choose the word which is different from the rest.
(a) Plassey (b) Haldighati
(c) Panipat (d) Sarnath
(e) Kurukshetra

63. Choose the word which is different from the rest.
(a) Faraday (b) Newton
(c) Addison (d) Marconi
(e) Beethovan

64. Choose the word which is different from the rest.
(a) Valley (b) Sea
(c) Tower (d) Mountain
(e) River

65. Choose the word which is different from the rest.
(a) Madagascar (b) Cuba
(c) Greenland (d) Hawaii
(e) Chile

☛ ***Direction to solve: (66 to 75) :*** *In each of the following questions, certain pairs of words are given, out of which the words in all pairs except one bear a certain common relationship. Choose the pair in which the words are differently related.*

66. Choose the pair in which the words are differently related from the rest.
(a) Shirt : Dress (b) Boy : Girl
(c) Mango: Fruit (d) Table: Furniture

67. Choose the pair in which the words are differently related from the rest.
(a) Scalpel : Surgeon (b) Chisel : Soldier
(c) Awl : Cobbler (d) Knife : Chef

68. Choose the pair in which the words are differently related from the rest.
(a) Tree : Stem (b) Face : Eye
(c) Chair : Sofa (d) Plant: Flower

69. Choose the pair in which the words are differently related from the rest.
(a) Book : Page (b) Table : Drawer
(c) Loom : Cloth (d) Car : Wheel

70. Choose the pair in which the words are differently related from the rest.
(a) Beans : Pulses (b) Rice : Cereals
(c) Tea : Beverages (d) Legumes : Nodules

71. Choose the pair in which the words are differently related from the rest.
(a) Whale : Mammal
(b) Salamander : Insect
(c) Snake : Reptile
(d) Frog : Amphibian

72. Choose the pair in which the words are differently related from the rest.
(a) Broad : Wide (b) Light: Heavy
(c) Tiny : Small (d) Big : Large

73. Choose the pair in which the words are differently related from the rest.
(a) Army : General
(b) Team : Captain
(c) Crèche : Infant
(d) Meeting : Chairman

74. Choose the pair in which the words are differently related from the rest.
(a) Petrol : Car (b) Ink : Pen
(c) Garbage : Dustbin (d) Lead : Pencil

75. Choose the pair in which the words are differently related from the rest.
(a) Sky : Cloud
(b) Purse : Wallet
(c) Cupboard : Almirah
(d) Chair : Stool

☛ ***Direction to solve: (76 to 90) :*** *In each of the following questions, some groups of letters are given, all of which except one share a common similarity while one is different. Choose the odd one out.*

76. Choose the odd one out.
(a) OTP (b) ABA
(c) SZX (d) UVB
(e) YQR

77. Choose the odd one out.
(a) FAA (b) OFF
(c) ATT (d) IFF
(e) EPP

78. Choose the odd one out.
(a) DW (b) HS
(c) MN (d) GT
(e) KO

79. Choose the odd one out.
(a) BYX (b) LPO
(c) EVU (d) FUT
(e) IRQ

80. Choose the odd one out.
(a) AOT (b) CPA
(c) REB (d) TIW
(e) QUD

81. Choose the odd one out.
(a) XW (b) FG
(c) ML (d) PO
(e) TS

82. Choose the odd one out.
(a) RTW (b) QOM
(c) IKG (d) IKM
(e) BDF

83. Choose the odd one out.
(a) HGF (b) XWV
(c) NML (d) OPQ
(e) UTS

84. Choose the odd one out.
(a) GDA (b) OLI
(c) VSP (d) KHE
(e) WYZ

85. Choose the odd one out.
(a) NPM (b) IJL
(c) QSZ (d) BHK
(e) XGT

86. Choose the odd one out.
(a) XUW (b) DAC
(c) PMN (d) HEG
(e) TQS

87. Choose the odd one out.
(a) RNJ (b) XTP
(c) MIE (d) ZWR
(e) YBE

88. Choose the odd one out.
(a) RUX (b) GJM
(c) YBE (d) ZCF
(e) NPS

89. Choose the odd one out.
(a) HJN (b) JLP
(c) PRU (d) QSW
(e) DAC

90. Choose the odd one out.
(a) HSRI (b) MVUN
(c) OLKP (d) PJQX
(e) WDCX

Answer Key

1. (b)	**16.** (d)	**31.** (c)	**46.** (d)	**61.** (b)	**76.** (b)
2. (a)	**17.** (d)	**32.** (a)	**47.** (e)	**62.** (d)	**77.** (a)
3. (c)	**18.** (b)	**33.** (c)	**48.** (e)	**63.** (e)	**78.** (e)
4. (d)	**19.** (c)	**34.** (b)	**49.** (c)	**64.** (c)	**79.** (b)
5. (c)	**20.** (c)	**35.** (a)	**50.** (d)	**65.** (e)	**80.** (b)
6. (d)	**21.** (d)	**36.** (d)	**51.** (b)	**66.** (b)	**81.** (b)
7. (b)	**22.** (c)	**37.** (c)	**52.** (b)	**67.** (b)	**82.** (a)
8. (b)	**23.** (c)	**38.** (c)	**53.** (b)	**68.** (c)	**83.** (d)
9. (e)	**24.** (e)	**39.** (b)	**54.** (d)	**69.** (c)	**84.** (e)
10. (a)	**25.** (d)	**40.** (d)	**55.** (c)	**70.** (d)	**85.** (b)
11. (a)	**26.** (e)	**41.** (b)	**56.** (c)	**71.** (b)	**86.** (c)
12. (a)	**27.** (e)	**42.** (c)	**57.** (e)	**72.** (b)	**87.** (d)
13. (e)	**28.** (a)	**43.** (d)	**58.** (c)	**73.** (c)	**88.** (e)
14. (b)	**29.** (c)	**44.** (d)	**59.** (e)	**74.** (c)	**89.** (c)
15. (d)	**30.** (a)	**45.** (a)	**60.** (a)	**75.** (a)	**90.** (d)

Explanatory Notes

1. (b)
All except Mustard are food grains, while mustard is an oilseed.

2. (a)
All except Cot are parts of bedspread.

3. (c)
All except Kidnap are actions of killing.

4. (d)
All except Drone are females.

5. (c)
All except Geography are branches of Science.

6. (d)
All except Chess are outdoor games.

7. (b)
All others are parts of a tree.

8. (b)
Hyena is the only flesh-eating animal in the group.

9. (e)
All except Korea are European countries, while Korea is an Asian country.

10. (a)
All except Reader are the persons involved in the preparation of a journal, newspaper or magazine.

11. (a)
All except Arrow are used holding in hand.

12. (a)
All except Feathers are organs for movement in different organisms.

13. (e)
All except Explosion are natural calamities.

14. (b)
All except Singhbhum are capitals of states of India.

15. (d)
All except Bitch are young ones of animals, while bitch is a female dog.

16. (d)
All except Defence are forms of attack.

17. (d)
All except Watermelon grow on trees while watermelon grows on creepers.

18. (b)
All except Papaya are vegetables while papaya is a fruit.

19. (c)
All except Turkey are countries ruled by kings.

20. (c)
All except Mechanic help in building a house.

21. (d)
All except Vapour are different forms of precipitation.

22. (c)
All except Pallets are parts of a gun.

23. (c)
All except Tobacco are means of smoking.

24. (e)
All except Universe form a part of the universe.

25. (d)
All except Season are precise measurements for days.

26. (e)
All except Condensation are methods employed for separation of mixtures.

27. (e)
All except Grass are non-flowering plants.

28. (a)
All except Sparrow are flesh-eating birds.

29. (c)
All except Marx propagated non-violence.
30. (a)
In all except Seminar, 'semi' indicates 'half.
31. (c)
All except Astrology are branches of Biology.
32. (a)
All except Tulsidas are names of famous dramatists.
33. (c)
All except Sword strike the target at a distance.
34. (b)
All except Thailand are islands.
35. (a)
All except Grasslands are types of grasslands.
36. (d)
All except Onion are used to extract oil.
37. (c)
All except Sodium are radio-isotopes, while sodium is a metal.
38. (c)
All except Lizard are insects, while lizard is a reptile.
39. (b)
All except Small pox are diseases caused by bacteria, while small pox is caused by virus.
40. (d)
All except Siachen are lakes, while Siachen is a glacier.
41. (b)
All except Nitrogen are used as fertilizers.
42. (c)
All others are resorted to by one to acquire knowledge.
43. (d)
All except Eczema are eye infections, while eczema is a skin infection.
44. (d)
All except Medulla are parts of the eye, while medulla is a part of the brain.
45. (a)
All except Dog are wild animals.
46. (d)
All except Urdu are Indo-Aryan languages.
47. (e)
All except Paper weight are items of furniture.
48. (e)
All except Pinna are bones, while Pinna is the external part of an ear.
49. (c)
All except Large are general physical properties of matter.
50. (d)
All except Unicorn are animals, while unicorn is an imaginary creature.
51. (b)
All except Methane are products obtained from petroleum.
52. (b)
All except Change are synonyms.
53. (b)
All except Bars are structures formed by rivers, while bars are formed by sea.
54. (d)
All except Skeletons are synonyms and are concerned with superstitions.
55. (c)
All except Jaipur are hill stations.
56. (c)
All except Driving are activities performed in water.
57. (e)
All except Jaguar are different species of monkeys or apes, while Jaguar belongs to cat family.
58. (c)
All except Guru Gobind founded one or the other religion.
59. (e)
All except Stomata are respiratory organs in animals.
60. (a)
All except Sucrose are enzymes, while sucrose is a type of sugar.
61. (b)
All except Tetanus are diseases caused by virus, while tetanus is caused by bacteria.
62. (d)
All except Sarnath are famous battlefields.
63. (e)
All except Beethovan were scientists, while Beethovan was a musician.
64. (c)
All except Tower are natural geographical features, while tower is man-made.
65. (e)
All except Chile are islands.
66. (b)
In all other pairs, second denotes the class to which the first belongs.
67. (b)
In all other pairs, first is a tool used by the second.
68. (c)
In all other pairs, second is a part of the first.
69. (c)
In all other pairs, second is a part of the first.
70. (d)
In all other pairs, second denotes the class to which the first belongs.
71. (b)
In all other pairs, second is the class of animals to which the first belongs.
72. (b)
The words in all other pairs are synonyms.
73. (c)
In all other pairs, second is the head of the first.

74. (c)
In all other pairs, first is required by the second for its functioning.

75. (a)
In all other pairs, the two words denote things which serve the same purpose.

76. (b)
There is no repetition of any letter in any other group.

77. (a)
In all other groups, a vowel is followed by a consonant repeated twice.

78. (e)
In all other groups, the first letter occupies the same position from A onward as the second letter occupies from Z backward e.g. D is the fourth letter from the beginning and W is the fourth letter from the end of the alphabet.

79. (b)
In all other groups, the first and second letters occupy the same position (from the beginning and the end respectively. The second letter is moved one step backward to obtain the third letter.)

80. (b)
In all other groups, the middle letter is a vowel.

81. (b)
All other groups contain two consecutive letters in reverse order.

82. (a)
All other groups contain alternate letters of the alphabet.

83. (d)
In all other groups, the three letters are consecutive but in reverse order.

84. (e)
In all other groups, the second and first letters are three steps ahead of third and second letters respectively.

85. (b)
No other group contains a vowel.

86. (c)
In all other groups, the second letter is moved two steps forward to obtain the third letter which is then moved one step forward to obtain the first.

87. (d)
In all other groups, the first and second letters are moved four steps backward to obtain second and third letters respectively.

88. (e)
In all other groups, first and second letters are moved three steps forward to obtain second and third letters respectively.

89. (c)
In all other groups, the third letter is four steps ahead of the second letter which, in turn, is two steps ahead of the first letter.

90. (d)
In all other groups, first and fourth letters are consecutive, while second and third letters are in reverse alphabetical order.

❐

Previous Year Questions

☛ ***Direction to solve: (1 to 3) :*** *In each of the following questions, five words have been given, out of which four are alike in some manner, while the fifth one is different. Choose the word which is different from the rest.*

1. Choose the word which is different from the rest.
[NTSE 2003 – Arunachal Pradesh second stage paper]
(a) December (b) February
(c) March (d) July
(e) May

2. Choose the word which is different from the rest.
[NTSE 2005 – Delhi second stage paper]
(a) Courteous (b) Humble
(c) Civil (d) Polite
(e) Honest

3. Choose the word which is different from the rest.
[NTSE 2001 – Uttar Pradesh second stage paper]
(a) Magnalium (b) Germanium
(c) Duralumin (d) Bronze
(e) Brass

☛ ***Direction to solve: (4 to 5) :*** *In each of the following questions, certain pairs of words are given, out of which the words in all pairs except one bear a certain common relationship. Choose the pair in which the words are differently related.*

4. Choose the pair in which the words are differently related from the rest.
[NTSE 2003 – Orissa second stage paper]
(a) Mercury: Sun (b) Moon : Earth
(c) Star : Galaxy (d) Wheel: Axle

5. Choose the pair in which the words are differently related from the rest.
[NTSE 2012 – Punjab second stage paper]
(a) Apple : Jam
(b) Lemon : Citrus
(c) Orange : Squash
(d) Tomato : Puree

☛ ***Direction to solve: (6 to 10) :*** *In each of the following questions, some groups of letters are given, all of which, except one, share a common similarity while one is different. Choose the odd one out.*

6. Choose the odd one out.
[NTSE 2001 – Chandigarh second stage paper]
(a) BdEg (b) KmNp
(c) PrSu (d) TwXz

7. Choose the odd one out.
[NTSE 2012- Assam second stage paper]
(a) OUSF (b) PIGS
(c) TEPJ (d) XLPA

8. Choose the odd one out.
[NTSE 2002 – Manipur first stage paper]
(a) ABDG (b) IJLO
(c) MNPS (d) RSUY

9. Choose the odd one out.
[NTSE 2004 – Punjab Bihar first stage paper]
(a) JIHG (b) OPNM
(c) SRQP (d) ZYXW

10. Choose the odd one out.
[NTSE 2003 – Haryana Second stage paper]
(a) UAZF (b) SCXH
(c) RDWJ (d) KBPG

❒

Answer Key

1. (b)	2. (c)	3. (b)	4. (c)	5. (d)	6. (d)	7. (a)	8. (d)	9. (b)	10. (c)

Explanatory Notes

1. (b)
   All except February are months with 31 days, while February has 28 or 29 days.
2. (c)
   All except Civil are related to human nature.
3. (b)
   All except Germanium are alloys, while germanium is a metal.
4. (c)
   In all other pairs, first moves around the second.
5. (b)
   In all other pairs, second is the form in which the first is preserved.
6. (d)
   In all other groups, second, third and fourth letters are two, one and two steps ahead of the first, second and third letters respectively.
7. (a)
   This is the only group containing two vowels.
8. (d)
   In all other groups, the first, second and third letters move one, two and three steps forward respectively to give the second, third and fourth letters respectively.
9. (b)
   All other groups contain four consecutive letters in reverse alphabetical order.
10. (c)
    In all other groups, the third and fourth letters each are five steps ahead of the first and second letters respectively.

❐

UNIT 2

Verbal Analogy Test

Analogy means similarity. Two objects related to each other in some way are given and a third object with four or five alternatives below is also given. You have to find out which one of the alternatives bears the same relation with the third object as the first and second objects.

The questions on analogy cover all types of relationship that one can think of. The most common ways of establishing a relationship are given here.

Solved Examples

Example 1:

Curd : Milk :: Shoe : ?

(a) Leather (b) Cloth
(c) Jute (d) Silver

Solution: Option (a) is correct.

Explanation: As curd is made from milk, similarly shoe is made from leather.

Example 2:

Calf : Piglet :: Shed : ?

(a) Prison (b) Nest
(c) Pigsty (d) Den

Solution: Option (c) is correct.

Explanation: Calf is the young one of cow and piglet is the young one of Pig. Shed is the dwelling place of cow. Similarly Pigsty is the dwelling place of pig.

Example 3:

Malaria : Mosquito :: ? : ?

(a) Poison : Death
(b) Cholera : Water
(c) Rat : Plague
(d) Medicine : Disease

Solution: Option (b) is correct.

Explanation: As malaria is caused due to mosquito, similarly cholera is caused due to water.

Example 4:

ABC : ZYX :: CBA : ?

(a) XYZ (b) BCA
(c) YZX (d) ZXY

Solution: Option (a) is correct.

Explanation:

CBA is the reverse of ABC, similarly, XYZ is the reverse of ZYX.

Example 5:

4 : 18 :: 6 : ?

(a) 32 (b) 38
(c) 11 (d) 37

Solution: Option (b) is correct.

Explanation:

As, $(4)^2 + 2 = 18$

Similarly, $(6)^2 + 2 = 38$

☛ ***Direction to solve: (6 to 10) :*** *Each of the following questions has a group. Find out which one of the given alternatives will be another member of the group of that class.*

Example 6:

'Kathak' is related to 'U.P' in the same way as 'Odyssey' is related to:

(a) Assam (b) Kerala
(c) Orissa (d) Gujarat

Solution: Option (c) is correct.

Explanation: As 'Kathak' is common in 'U.P', in the same way 'Odyssey' is common in 'Orissa'.

Example 7:

'Metal' is related to 'Conduction' in the same way as 'Plastic' is related to:

(a) Ground oil chemistry
(b) Industry
(c) In-flammability
(d) Insulation

Solution: Option (c) is correct.

Explanation: As 'Conduction' is the property found in 'Metal', in the same way 'In-flammability' is the property found in 'Plastic'.

Example 8:

'Sea' is related to 'Ship' in the same way as 'Road' is related to:

(a) Traffic (b) Travellers
(c) Journey (d) Bus

Solution: Option (d) is correct.

Explanation: As the means of transport in 'Sea' is 'Ship', similarly the means of transport on 'Road' is 'Bus'.

Example 9:

'Rabbit' is related to 'Burrow' in the same way as 'Lunatic' is related to:

(a) Prison (b) Cell
(c) Barrack (d) Asylum

Solution: Option (d) is correct.

Explanation: As the dwelling place of 'Rabbit' is 'Burrow', in the same way the dwelling place of 'Lunatic' is 'Asylum'.

Example 10:

'Much' is related to 'Many' in the same way as 'Measure' is related to:

(a) Count (b) Measures
(c) Calculate (d) Weigh

Solution: Option (a) is correct.

Explanation: As 'Much' corresponds to 'Many', in the same way 'Measure' corresponds to 'counting'.

Multiple Choice Questions

☛ ***Direction to Solve: (1 to 20)*** *In each of the following questions find out the alternative which will replace the question mark.*

1. Ice : Coldness :: Earth : ?
(a) Weight (b) Jungle
(c) Gravitation (d) Sea

2. Parts : Strap :: Wolf : ?
(a) Fox (b) Animal
(c) Wood (d) Flow

3. Physician : Treatment :: Judge : ?
(a) Punishment (b) Judgement
(c) Lawyer (d) Court

4. Race : Fatigue :: Fast : ?
(a) Food (b) Laziness
(c) Hunger (d) Race

5. Peace : Chaos :: Creation : ?
(a) Build (b) Construction
(c) Destruction (d) Manufacture

6. Tiger : Forest :: Otter : ?
(a) Cage (b) Sky
(c) Nest (d) Water

7. Poles : Magnet :: ? : Battery
(a) Cells (b) Power
(c) Terminals (d) Energy

8. Cassock : Priest :: ? : Graduate
(a) Cap (b) Tie
(c) Coat (d) Gown

9. College : Student :: Hospital : ?
(a) Nurse (b) Doctor
(c) Treatment (d) Patient

10. Tree : Forest :: Grass : ?
(a) Lawn (b) Garden
(c) Park (d) Field

11. South : North-West :: West : ?
(a) North (b) South-West
(c) North-East (d) East

12. Cloth : Mill :: Newspaper : ?
(a) Editor (b) Reader
(c) Paper (d) Press

13. Country : President :: State : ?
(a) Governor (b) M.P
(c) Legislator (d) Minister

14. Conference : Chairman :: Newspaper : ?
(a) Reporter (b) Distributor
(c) Printer (d) Editor

15. Safe : Secure :: Protect : ?
(a) Lock (b) Sure
(c) Guard (d) Conserve

16. Master : OCUVGT :: LABOUR : ?
(a) NCDQWT (b) NDERWT
(c) NBERWT (d) NEDRWT

17. Microphone : Loud :: Microscope : ?
(a) Elongate (b) Investigate
(c) Magnify (d) Examine

18. Melt : Liquid :: Freeze : ?
(a) Ice (b) Condense
(c) Solid (d) Force

19. Carbon : Diamond :: Corundum : ?
(a) Garnet (b) Ruby
(c) Pukhraj (d) Pearl

20. Architect : Building :: Sculptor : ?
(a) Museum (b) Stone
(c) Chisel (d) Statue

☛ ***Direction to solve: (21 to 30) :*** *In each of the following questions find out the alternative which will replace the question mark.*

21. REASON : SFBTPO :: THINK : ?
(a) SGHMJ (b) UIJOL
(c) UHNKI (d) UJKPM

22. PSQR : CFED :: JMKL : ?
(a) UVXZ (b) YVZX
(c) YXZW (d) WZYX

23. FIELD : GJFME :: SICKLE : ?
(a) RHBJKD (b) RHJBKD
(c) TJLDMF (d) TJDLMF

24. ? : QEHMDF :: WIDELY : HVCDXK
(a) FRINGE (b) STRING
(c) FRANCE (d) DEMAND

25. ACFJ : ZXUQ :: EGIN : ?
(a) VUSQ (b) UTRP
(c) VRPM (d) VTRM

26. ABCD : WXYZ :: EFGH : ?
(a) STUV (b) ZYXW
(c) VUTS (d) WXZY

27. QIOK : MMKO :: YAWC : ?
(a) UESG (b) USGA
(c) VUES (d) SUEG

28. PASS : QBTT :: FAIL : ?
(a) GJBM (b) GBJM
(c) MBJG (d) MJBG

29. BLOCKED : YOLXPVW :: ? : OZFMXS
(a) DEBATE (b) RESULT
(c) LABOR (d) LAUNCH

30. CEDH : HDEC :: ? : PNRV
(a) VRNP (b) RNPV
(c) NRVP (d) VNRP

☛ ***Direction to solve: (31 to 45) :*** *In each of the following questions find out the alternative which will replace the question mark.*

31. 25 : 37 :: 49 : ?
(a) 41 (b) 65
(c) 56 (d) 60

32. K/T : 11/20 :: J/R : ?
(a) 10/18 (b) 11/19
(c) 10/8 (d) 9/10

33. 68 : 130 :: ? : 350
(a) 220 (b) 224
(c) 222 (d) 226

34. 61 : 121 :: ? : 337
(a) 211 (b) 222
(c) 220 (d) 240

35. 27 : 125 :: 64 : ?
(a) 162 (b) 216
(c) 517 (d) 273

36. 10 : 99 :: 9 : ?
(a) 69 (b) 80
(c) 97 (d) 49

37. 8 : 24 :: ? : 32
(a) 5 (b) 6
(c) 10 (d) 8

38. 144 : 10 :: 169 : ?
(a) 14 (b) 11
(c) 13 (d) 12

39. 9 : 8 :: 16 : ?
(a) 27 (b) 17
(c) 16 (d) 18

40. MXN : 13 × 14 :: FXR : ?
(a) 14 × 15 (b) 5 × 17
(c) 6 × 18 (d) 7 × 19

41. 6 : 56 :: 32 : ?
(a) 96 (b) 112
(c) 120 (d) 128

42. 4 : 19 :: 7 : ?
(a) 52 (b) 49
(c) 28 (d) 68

43. 24 : 60 :: 120 : ?
(a) 160 (b) 220
(c) 300 (d) 108

44. 335 : 216 :: 987 : ?
(a) 868 (b) 867
(c) 872 (d) 888

45. 123 : 13^2 :: 235 : ?
(a) 23^2 (b) 35^2
(c) 25^3 (d) 25^2

☛ ***Direction to solve: (46 to 60) :*** *Each of the following questions consists of a pair of words bearing a relationship between them, from amongst the alternatives, pick up the pair that best illustrates a similar relationship.*

46. Thermometer : Temperature
(a) Millimetre : Scale
(b) Length : Breadth
(c) Solar Energy : Sun
(d) Cardiograph : Heart rate

47. Border : Country
(a) Pen : Cap (b) Book : Cover
(c) Handle : Shade (d) Frame : Picture

48. River : Ocean
(a) Child : School (b) Book : Library
(c) Lane : Road (d) Cloth : Body

49. Arc : Circle
(a) Number : Count
(b) Fraction : Percentage
(c) Pie : Slice
(d) Segment : Line

50. Sound : Muffled
(a) Moisture : Humid
(b) Colour : Faded
(c) Despair : Anger
(d) Odour : Pungent

51. Platform : Train
(a) Aeroplane : Aerodrome
(b) Hotel : Tourist
(c) Quay : Ship
(d) Footpath : Traveller

52. Train : Track
(a) Water : Boat (b) Bullet : Barrel
(c) Idea : Brain (d) Fame : Television

53. Chalk : Blackboard
(a) Type : Point (b) Table : Chair
(c) Door : Handle (d) Ink : Paper

54. Rectangle : Pentagon
    (a) Side : Angle
    (b) Diagonal : Perimeter
    (c) Triangle : Rectangle
    (d) Circle : Square
55. Kick : Football
    (a) Wash : Dishes (b) Dust : Rage
    (c) Mop : Sweep (d) Throw : Ring
56. Scales : Fish
    (a) Bear : Fur (b) Woman : Dress
    (c) Skin : Man (d) Tree : Leaves
57. Numismatist : Coins
    (a) Jeweller : Jewels
    (b) Cartographer : Maps
    (c) Philatelist : Stamps
    (d) Geneticist : Chromosomes
58. Sunrise : Sunset
    (a) Dawn : Twilight (b) Noon : Midnight
    (c) Morning : Night (d) Energetic : Lazy
59. Candle : Wick
    (a) Hammer : Nail (b) Light : Bulb
    (c) Oven : Fire (d) Bicycle : Wheel
60. Glove : Hand
    (a) Neck : Collar (b) Tie : Shirt
    (c) Socks : Feet (d) Coat : Pocket

☛ ***Direction to solve: (61 to 75) :*** *Each of the following questions has a group. Find out which one of the given alternatives will be another member of the group or of that class.*

61. Tamilian, Gujarati, Punjabi
    (a) Aryan (b) Dravidan
    (c) Indian (d) Barbarian
62. Clutch, Brake, Horn
    (a) Car (b) Scooter
    (c) Accident (d) Steering
63. Wrestling, Karate, Boxing
    (a) Pole-vault (b) Swimming
    (c) Judo (d) Polo
64. Newspaper, Hoarding, Television
    (a) Press (b) Media
    (c) Rumour (d) Broadcast
65. Arid, Parched, Droughty
    (a) Draft (b) Earth
    (c) Dry (d) Cow
66. Carpenter, Plumber, Electrician
    (a) Doctor (b) Blacksmith
    (c) Professor (d) Lawyer
67. Mars, Earth, Jupiter
    (a) Planets (b) Cosmos
    (c) Orbits (d) Astronauts
68. Lungs, Liver, Kidney
    (a) Neck (b) Testis
    (c) Heart (d) Nose
69. Basic, Pascal, Fortran
    (a) Cobol (b) Bhopal
    (c) Calculator (d) Cyclotron
70. Root, Stem, Branch
    (a) Fertilizer (b) Leaf
    (c) Tree (d) Wood
71. Volleyball, Hockey, Football
    (a) Aquatics (b) Baseball
    (c) Athletes (d) Sports
72. Pathology, Cardiology, Radiology, Ophthalmology
    (a) Biology (b) Haematology
    (c) Zoology (d) Geology
73. Wheat, Barley, Rice
    (a) Food (b) Agriculture
    (c) Farm (d) Gram
74. Lock, Shut, Fasten
    (a) Window (b) Door
    (c) Iron (d) Block
75. Lucknow, Patna, Bhopal, Jaipur
    (a) Shimla (b) Mysore
    (c) Pune (d) Indore

❒

Answer Key

1. (c)	**11.** (c)	**21.** (b)	**31.** (b)	**41.** (b)	**51.** (c)	**61.** (c)	**71.** (b)
2. (d)	**12.** (d)	**22.** (d)	**32.** (a)	**42.** (a)	**52.** (b)	**62.** (d)	**72.** (b)
3. (b)	**13.** (a)	**23.** (d)	**33.** (c)	**43.** (c)	**53.** (d)	**63.** (c)	**73.** (d)
4. (c)	**14.** (d)	**24.** (a)	**34.** (a)	**44.** (a)	**54.** (c)	**64.** (d)	**74.** (d)
5. (c)	**15.** (c)	**25.** (d)	**35.** (b)	**45.** (c)	**55.** (d)	**65.** (c)	**75.** (a)
6. (d)	**16.** (a)	**26.** (a)	**36.** (b)	**46.** (d)	**56.** (c)	**66.** (b)	
7. (c)	**17.** (c)	**27.** (a)	**37.** (b)	**47.** (d)	**57.** (c)	**67.** (a)	
8. (d)	**18.** (c)	**28.** (b)	**38.** (b)	**48.** (c)	**58.** (c)	**68.** (c)	
9. (d)	**19.** (b)	**29.** (d)	**39.** (a)	**49.** (d)	**59.** (d)	**69.** (a)	
10. (a)	**20.** (d)	**30.** (a)	**40.** (c)	**50.** (b)	**60.** (c)	**70.** (b)	

Explanatory Notes

1. (c)
As the effect of Ice is cold, similarly the effect of Earth is gravitation.

2. (d)

As

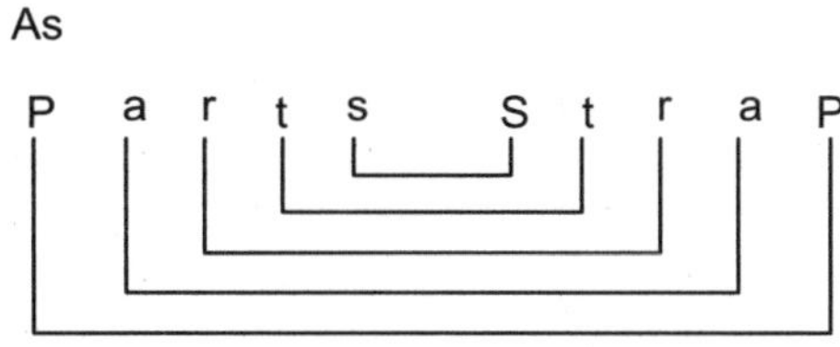

Similarly,

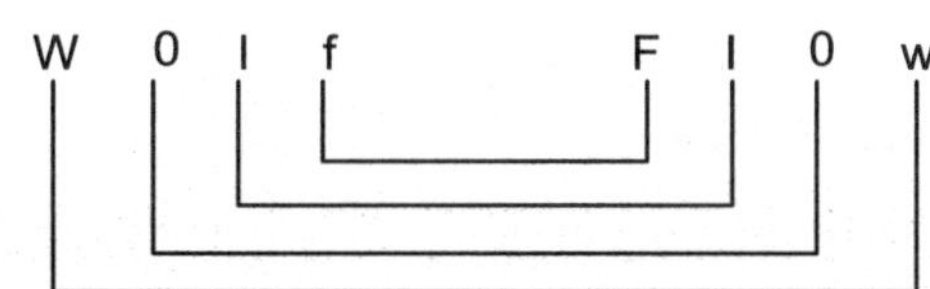

3. (b)
As a Physician does the treatment, similarly a Judge delivers the judgement.

4. (c)
As the result of Race is Fatigue, similarly the result of Fast is Hunger.

5. (c)
As opposite meaning of peace is chaos, similarly opposite meaning of creation is destruction.

6. (d)
As Tiger is found in Forest, similarly Otter is found in the water.

7. (c)
As magnet has poles, similarly battery has terminals.

8. (d)
A Priest wears cassock while a Graduate wears gown.

9. (d)
As Students read in College, similarly Patients are treated in Hospital.

10. (a)
As Tree is found in Forest, similarly Grass is found in Lawn.

11. (c)

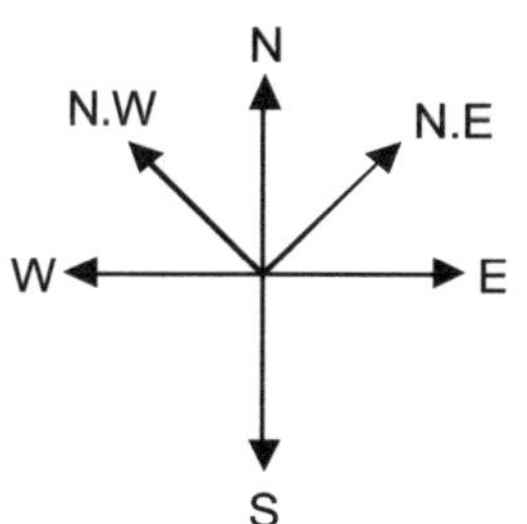

As North-West is 135° clockwise from South, in the same way North-East is 135°clockwise from the West.

12. (d)
As Cloth is made in a Mill, similarly Newspaper is printed in a Press.

13. (a)
As President is the nominal head of a country, similarly Governor is the nominal head of a State.

14. (d)
As Chairman is the highest authority in a conference, similarly Editor holds the same position for a Newspaper.

15. (c)
As safe and secure have same meaning, in the same way protect and guard have same meaning.

16. (a)

As	Similarly
M —(+2)→ O	L —(+2)→ N
A —(+2)→ C	A —(+2)→ C
S —(+2)→ U	B —(+2)→ D
T —(+2)→ V	O —(+2)→ Q
E —(+2)→ G	U —(+2)→ W
R —(+2)→ T	R —(+2)→ T

17. (c)
As Microphone makes sound louder, similarly Microscope makes the object magnified.

18. (c)
As on melting the liquid is formed, similarly on freezing the solid is formed.

19. (b)
As Diamond is made of Carbon, similarly Ruby is made of Corundum.

20. (d)
As 'Architect' makes 'Building', similarly 'Sculptor' makes 'Statue'.

21. (b)

As	Similarly
R —+1→ S	T —+1→ U
E —+1→ F	H —+1→ I
A —+1→ B	I —+1→ J
S —+1→ T	N —+1→ O
O —+1→ P	K —+1→ L
N —+1→ O	

22. (d)

As,

P S Q R : C F E D

(S to R: −1; P to Q: +1; Q to R: +1) : (F to E: −1; E to D: −1; C to D: +1)

Similarly

J M K L : W Z Y X

(M to L: −1; J to K: +1; K to L: +1) : (Z to Y: −1; Y to X: −1; W to X: +1)

23. (d)

As	Similarly
F —+1→ G	S —+1→ T
I —+1→ J	I —+1→ J
E —+1→ F	C —+1→ D
L —+1→ M	K —+1→ L
D —+1→ E	L —+1→ M
	E —+1→ F

24. (a)

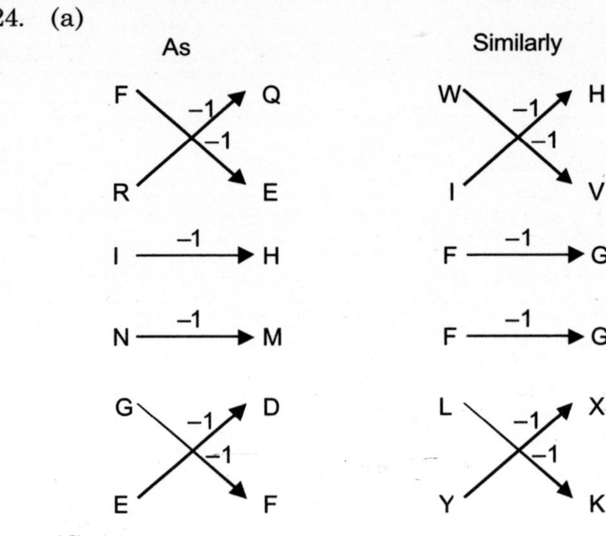

25. (d)

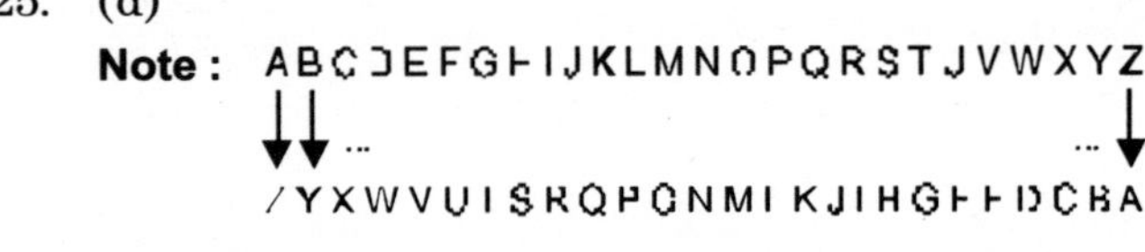

As,

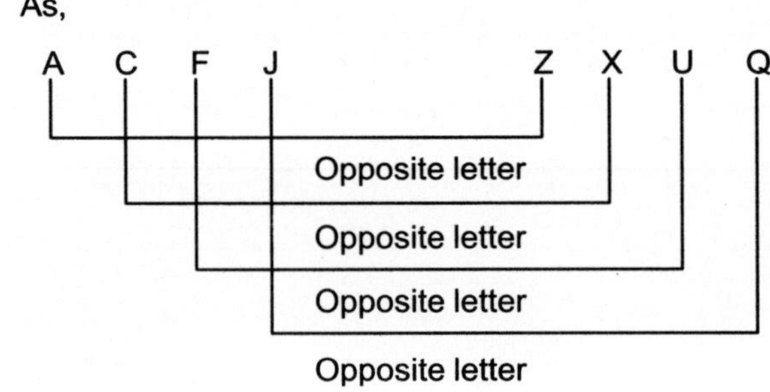

Similarly,

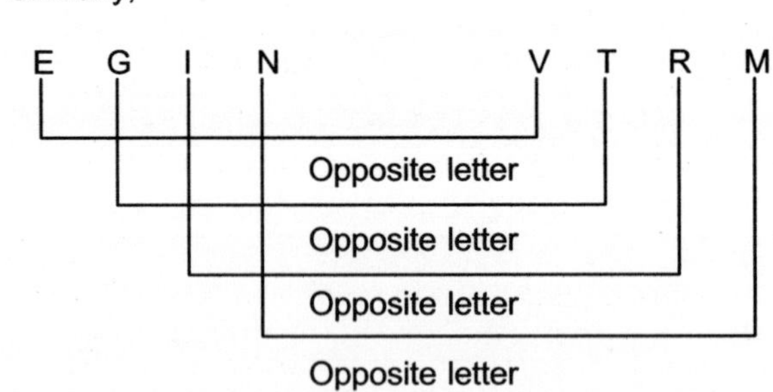

26. (a)

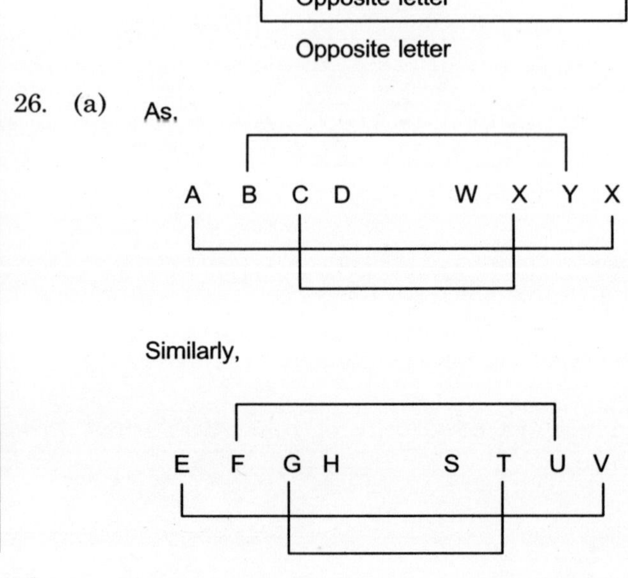

27. (a)

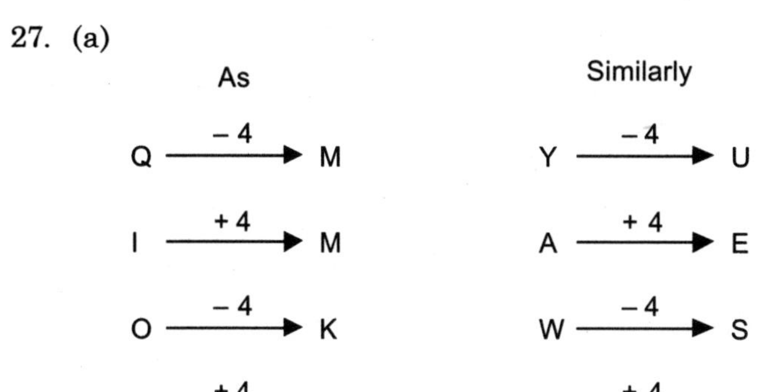

28. (b)

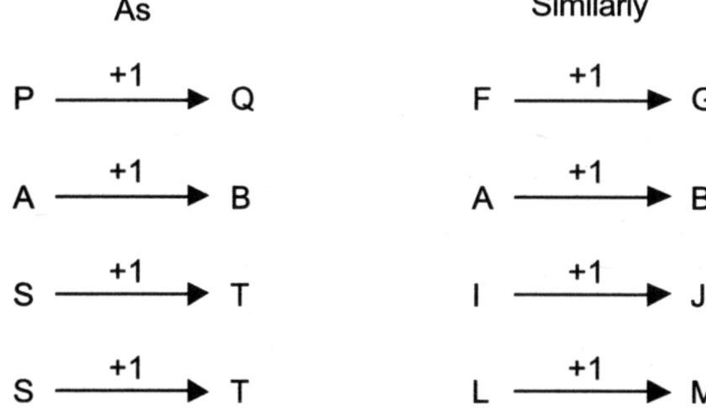

29. (d)

ABCDEFGH JKLMNOPQRSTUVWXYZ

↓↓ ... ... ↓

ZYXWVUTSRQPONMLKJ HGFEDCBA

As	Similarly
B → Y	L → O
L → O	A → Z
O → L	U → F
C → X	N → M
K → P	C → X
E → V	H → S
D → W	

30. (a)

CEDH — Reverse it → HDEC

VRNP — Reverse it → PNRV

Therefore, VRNP is the answer

31. (b)

As $25 = (5)^2 \rightarrow (5 + 1)^2 + 1 = 37$

As $49 = (7)^2 \rightarrow (7 + 1)^2 + 1 = 65$

32. (a)

Alphabetical positions of K and T are 11 and 20 respectively.

Similarly the positions of J and R are 10 and 18 respectively.

33. (c)

As, $68 = (4)^3 + 4$

$130 = (5)^3 + 5$

and $350 = (7)^3 + 7$

Therefore, $? = (6)^3 + 6 = 222$

34. (a)

As, $61 = (4)^3 - 3$

$121 = (5)^3 - 4$

and $337 = (7)^3 - 6$

Therefore, $? = (6)^3 - 5 = 211$

35. (b)

$27 \rightarrow 3^3, 125 \rightarrow 5^3, 64 \rightarrow 4^3$

Therefore, $? = 6^3 = 216$.

36. (b)

As, 10 : 99 — $(10)^2 - 1$ Similarly 10 : 80 — $(9)^2 - 1$

37. (b)

$24 \rightarrow 2 \times 4 = 8$

$32 \rightarrow 3 \times 2 = 6$

38. (b)

As 144 : 10 — $\sqrt{144} - 2$ Similarly, 169 : 11 — $\sqrt{169} - 2$

39. (a)

$9 = (3)^2$

$8 = (3 - 1)^3$

and $16 = (4)^2$

$? = (4 - 1)^3 = 27$

40. (c)

As position of M and N in Eq. alphabets are 13 and 14 respectively.

41. (b)

As, 16:56 = (2/7)

Similarly, 32.112 = (2/7)

42. (a)

As, $(4)^2 + 3 = 19$

Similarly, $(7)^2 + 3 = 52$

43. (c)

As 24:60 = (2/5)

Similarly, 120/300 = (2/5)

44. (a)

As 335 – 216 = 119

Similarly, 987 – X = 119

Therefore, X = 987 – 119 = 868

45. (c)

As $123 \rightarrow 13^2$

Similarly, $235 \rightarrow 25^3$

46. (d)

As temperature is measured from a ther-mometer, in the same way heart rate is measured with cardiograph.

47. (d)
First is the boundary of the second.

48. (c)
As River joints to Ocean, similarly Lane joints to Road.

49. (d)
As Arc is a part of Circle, similarly segment is a part of line.

50. (b)
Second is the process of gradual disappearances of the first.

51. (c)
Second is the place where the first stops.

52. (b)
As Train is guided by the track, similarly Bullet is guided by the barrel.

53. (d)
As chalk is used to write on the blackboard, similarly the Ink is used to write on the paper.

54. (c)
The Second has one more side than the first.

55. (d)
As Kick is in the game of Football, similarly Throw is used in the game of Ring.

56. (c)
As scales form an outer layer of fish, similarly skin form an outer layer of man.

57. (c)
As Numismatist collects coins, similarly Philatelist collects stamps.

58. (c)
At sunrise the morning begins, similarly at sunset the night begins.

59. (d)
As Wick is a part of Candle, similarly Wheel is a part of Bicycle.

60. (c)
As Glove is worn in Hands, similarly Socks are worn on feet.

61. (c)
All these words represent the inhabitants of India.

62. (d)
All these are part of a vehicle.

63. (c)
All these are defensive games.

64. (d)
All these are used for broadcast.

65. (c)
The synonym of arid, parched and droughty is dry.

66. (b)
Carpenter, Plumber, Electrician and Blacksmith are in same working category.

67. (a)
All these are planets.

68. (c)
As Lungs, Liver and Kidney are internal part of the body, in the same way 'heart' is also an internal organ.

69. (a)
All these are languages of computer.

70. (b)
All these are the parts of a tree.

71. (b)
Baseball is like volleyball, Hockey and Football.

72. (b)
All the terms are medical terms and Haematology is medical term also.

73. (d)
All the terms are cereals and gram is one of the cereals also.

74. (d)
The synonym of Lock, Shut and Fasten is Block.

75. (a)
All the cities are state capitals, similarly Shimla is also a capital.

❐

Previous Year Questions

☛ ***Direction to solve: (1 to 10) :*** *Each of the following questions has a group. Find out which one of the given alternatives will be another member of the group or of that class.*

1. 'Calf' is related to 'Cow' in the same way as 'Kitten' is related to: ***[NTSE 2005 - UP first stage paper]***
   (a) Deer (b) Bear
   (c) Cat (d) Duck
2. 'Smoke' is related to 'Pollution' in the same way as 'War' is related to: ***[NTSE 2003 - Assam first stage paper]***
   (a) Victory (b) Treaty
   (c) Defeat (d) Destruction
3. 'Mountain' is related to 'Hill' in the same way as 'River' is related to: ***[NTSE 2001 - Goa first stage paper]***
   (a) Path (b) Swimming
   (c) Flowing (d) Tank
4. 'Dogs' is related to 'Bark' in the same way as 'Goats' is related to: ***[NTSE 2002 - Chandigarh second stage paper]***
   (a) Bleat (b) Crow
   (c) Grunt (d) Howl
5. 'Cat' is related to 'Kitten' in the same way as 'Woman' is related to: ***[NTSE 2005 - Delhi first stage paper]***
   (a) Puppy (b) Colt
   (c) Calf (d) Baby
6. 'Horse' is related to 'Hoof' in the same way as 'Eagle' is related to: ***[NTSE 2003 - Bihar second stage paper]***
   (a) Clutch (b) Leg
   (c) Foot (d) Claw
7. 'Forest' is related to 'Viviparium' in the same way as 'sea' is related to: ***[NTSE 2000 – Haryana first stage paper]***
   (a) Port site (b) Water
   (c) Fishery (d) Aquarium
8. 'Walk' is related to 'Run' in the same way as 'Breeze' is related to: ***[NTSE 2000 – Delhi first stage paper]***
   (a) Cold (b) Dust
   (c) Wind (d) Air
9. 'Wax' is related to 'Grease' in the same way as 'Milk' is related to: ***[NTSE 2002 – Himachal Pradesh first stage paper]***
   (a) Drink (b) Ghee
   (c) Protein (d) Curd
10. 'College' is related to 'Teachers' in the same way as 'Hospital' is related to: ***[NTSE 2004 – Karnataka first stage paper]***
    (a) Doctors (b) Patients
    (c) Medicine (d) Beds

❐

Answer Key

1. (c)	2. (d)	3. (d)	4. (a)	5. (d)	6. (d)	7. (d)	8. (c)	9. (d)	10. (a)

Explanatory Notes

1. (c)
As 'Calf' is the young one of 'Cow', similarly 'Kitten' is the young one of 'Cat'.

2. (d)
As 'smoke' leads to 'pollution', in the same way "War" leads to 'destruction'.

3. (d)
As the short form of 'Mountain' is 'Hill', similarly 'Tank' is the short form of 'River'.

4. (a)
As the cry of 'Dog' is called 'Bark', in the same way the cry of 'Goat' is called 'Bleat'.

5. (d)
As the young one of a 'cat' is 'kitten', in the same way the young one of 'woman' is 'baby'.

6. (d)
As the foot of the 'Horse' is called 'Hoof', in the same way the foot of the 'Eagle' is called 'Claw'.

7. (d)
As 'Forest' and 'Viviparium' have the same meaning, in the same way 'Sea' and 'Aquarium' have the same meaning.

8. (c)
As the fast mode of 'Walk' is 'Run', in the same way the fast mode of 'Breeze' is 'Wind'.

9. (d)
As 'Grease' is prepared from 'Wax', in the same way 'Curd' is prepared from 'Milk'.

10. (a)
As teaching is done by 'Teachers' in the 'College', similarly treatment is done by 'Doctors' in the 'Hospital'.

UNIT 3

Coding – Decoding

'Coding' is a system used to hide actual message of a word or a group of words. 'Decoding, on the other hand, means trying to find out actual message from the given code.

In this test, the candidate has to decipher or decode the given message identifying the pattern or principal. Each question follows different patterns. Each type of questions requires a lot of understanding, judgement, imagination and concluding skills.

There are numerous methods of coding and decoding a particular message. For the convenience of students these methods have been classified as follows:

(i) Letter Coding : Certain letters of alphabet stand for certain others letters of alphabet.

(ii) Number Coding : Letters are changed by the numbers in a certain pattern.

Solved Examples

1. If in a certain language, MADRAS is coded as NBESBT, how is BOMBAY coded in that code?
   (a) CPNCBX (b) CPNCBZ
   (c) CPOCBZ (d) CQOCBZ
   (e) None of these
   Solution: Option (b) is correct.
   Explanation: Each letter in the word is moved one step forward to obtain the corresponding letter of the code.

2. In a certain code, TRIPPLE is written as SQHOOKD. How is DISPOSE written in that code?
   (a) CHRONRD (b) DSOESPI
   (c) ESJTPTF (d) ESOPSID
   (e) None of these
   Solution: Option (a) is correct.
   Explanation: Each letter in the word is moved one step backward to obtain the corresponding letter of the code.

3. If DELHI is coded as 73541 and CALCUTTA as 82589662, how can CALICUT be coded?
   (a) 5279431 (b) 5978213
   (c) 8251896 (d) 8543691
   (e) None of these
   Solution: Option (c) is correct.
   Explanation:
   In CALICUT,
   C is coded as 8,
   A as 2, L as 5,
   I as 1, U as 9 and
   T as 6.
   Thus, the code for CALICUT is 8251896.

4. In a certain code, RIPPLE is written as 613382 and LIFE is written as 8192. How is PILLER written in that code?
   (a) 318826 (b) 318286
   (c) 618826 (d) 338816
   (e) None of these
   Solution: Option (a) is correct.
   Explanation:
   In PILLER,
   P is coded as 3,
   I as 1,
   L as 8,
   E as 2 and
   R as 6.
   Thus, the code for PILLER is 318826

5. In as a certain code, 15789 is written as EGKPT and 2346 is written ALUR. How is 23549 written in that code?
   (a) ALEUT (b) ALGTU
   (c) ALGUT (d) ALGRT
   (e) None of these
   Solution: Option (c) is correct.
   Explanation:
   In ALGUT
   2 is coded as A,
   3 as L,
   5 as G,
   4 as U and
   9 as T.
   So, 23549 is coded as ALGUT.

6. The number in each question below is to be codified in the following code:

Digit	7	2	1	5	3	9	8	6	4
Letter	W	L	M	S	I	N	D	J	B

What is the code for 184632?

(a) MDJBSI (b) MDJBIL
(c) MDJBWL (d) MDBJIL
(e) None of these

Solution: Option (d) is correct.

Explanation:

As given, 1 is coded as M,
8 as D,
4 as B,
6 as J,
3 as I and
2 as L.
So, 184632 is coded as MDBJIL.

7. The number in each question below is to be codified in the following code:

Digit	7	2	1	5	3	9	8	6	4
Letter	W	L	M	S	I	N	D	J	B

What is the code for 879341?

(a) DWNIBS (b) DWNBIM
(c) DWNIBM (d) NDWBIM
(e) None of these

Solution: Option (c) is correct.

Explanation:

As given, 8 is coded as D,
7 as W,
9 as N,
3 as I,
4 as B and
1 as M.
So, 879341 is coded as DWNIBM.

8. In a certain code, '289' means 'read from paper'; '276' means 'tea from field' and '85' means 'wall paper'. Which of the following is the code for 'paper'?

(a) 2 (b) 8
(c) 9 (d) Can't be determined
(e) None of these

Solution: Option (b) is correct.

Explanation: In the first and second statements, the common digit is '2' and the common word is 'from'.
So, '2' is the code for 'from'.
In the first and third statements, the common code digit is '8' and the common word is 'paper'.
So, '8' is the code for 'paper'.
As shown above, '8' is the code for 'paper'.

Multiple Choice Questions

1. If in a code language, COULD is written as BNTKC and MARGIN is written as LZQFHM, how will MOULDING be written in that code?
(a) CHMFINTK (b) LNKTCHMF
(c) LNTKCHMF (d) NITKHCMF

2. In a certain code, MONKEY is written as XDJMNL. How is TIGER written in that code?
(a) QDFHS (b) SDFHS
(c) SHFDQ (d) UJHFS

3. In a certain code, COMPUTER is written as RFUVQNPC. How is MEDICINE written in the same code?
(a) EOJDJEFM (b) EOJDEJFM
(c) MFEJDJOE (d) MFEDJJOE

4. If VICTORY is coded as YLFWRUB, how can SUCCESS be coded?
(a) VXEEIVV (b) VXFFHVV
(c) VYEEHVV (d) VYEFIVV

5. In a certain code, TOGETHER is written as RQEGRJCT. In the same code, PAROLE will be written as:
(a) NCPQJG (b) NCQPJG
(c) RCPQJK (d) RCTQNC

6. If BOMBAY is written as MYMYMY, how will TAMIL NADU be written in that code?
(a) TIATIATIA (b) MNUMNUMNU
(c) IATIATIAT (d) ALDALDALD

7. If FRIEND is coded as HUMJTK, how is CANDLE written in that code?
(a) EDRIRL (b) DCQHQK
(c) ESJFME (d) FYOBOC

8. If in a certain language, COUNSEL is coded as BITIRAK, how is GUIDANCE written in that code?
(a) EOHYZKBB (b) FOHYZJBB
(c) FPHZZKAB (d) HOHYBJBA

9. If ROSE is coded as 6821, CHAIR is coded as 73456 and PREACH is coded as 961473, what will be the code for SEARCH?
(a) 246173 (b) 214673
(c) 214763 (d) 216473

10. If in a certain code, TWENTY is written as 863985 and ELEVEN is written as 323039, how is TWELVE written in that code?
(a) 863203 (b) 863584
(c) 863903 (d) 863063

11. If the letters in PRABA are coded as 27595, and that in THILAK are coded as 368451, how can BHARATHI be coded?
(a) 37536689 (b) 57686535
(c) 96575368 (d) 96855368

12. If GIVE is coded as 5137 and BAT is coded as 924, how is GATE coded?
    (a) 5427 (b) 5724
    (c) 5247 (d) 2547
13. If PALE is coded as 2134, EARTH is coded as 41590, how is PEARL coded in that code?
    (a) 29530 (b) 24153
    (c) 25413 (d) 25430
14. In a certain language if ENTRY is coded as 12345 and STEADY is coded as 931785, then state which the correct code is for TENANT.
    (a) 956169 (b) 196247
    (c) 352123 (d) 312723
15. In a certain language if ENTRY is coded as 12345 and STEADY is coded as 931785, then state which the correct code is for NEATNESS.
    (a) 25196577 (b) 21732199
    (c) 21362199 (d) 21823698
16. In a certain language if ENTRY is coded as 12345 and STEADY is coded as 931785, then state which the correct code is for SEDATE?
    (a) 918731 (b) 954185
    (c) 814195 (d) 614781
17. In a certain language if ENTRY is coded as 12345 and STEADY is coded as 931785, then state which the correct code is for ARREST?
    (a) 744589 (b) 744193
    (c) 166479 (d) 745194
18. In a certain language if ENTRY is coded as 12345 and STEADY is coded as 931785, then state which the correct code is for ENDEAR?
    (a) 524519 (b) 174189
    (c) 128174 (d) 124179
19. If ENGLAND is written as 1234526 and FRANCE is written as 785291, how is GREECE coded?
    (a) 381171 (b) 381191
    (c) 832252 (d) 835545
20. In a certain code, a number 13479 is written as AQFJL and 5268 is written as DMPN. How is 396824 written in that code?
    (a) QLPNKJ (b) QLPNMF
    (c) QLPMNF (d) QLPNDF
21. The number in each question below is to be codified in the following code:

Digit	7	2	1	5	3	9	8	6	4
Letter	W	L	M	S	I	N	D	J	B

    What is the code for 64928?
    (a) JBNLD (b) JBLND
    (c) BJNLD (d) DBNLS
22. If white is called blue, blue is called red, red is called yellow, yellow is called green, green is called black, black is called violet and violet is called orange, what would be the colour of human blood?
    (a) Red (b) Green
    (c) Yellow (d) Violet
23. If orange is called butter, butter is called soap, soap is called ink, ink is called honey and honey is called orange, which of the following is used for washing clothes?
    (a) Honey (b) Butter
    (c) Orange (d) Ink
24. If the animals which can walk are called swimmers, the animals that crawl are called flying, those living in water are called snakes and those which fly in the sky are called hunters, then what will a lizard be called?
    (a) Swimmers (b) Snakes
    (c) Flying (d) Hunters
25. If air is called green, green is called blue, blue is called sky, sky is called yellow, yellow is called water and water is called pink, then what is the colour of clear sky?
    (a) Blue (b) Sky
    (c) Yellow (d) Water
26. If sky is called sea, sea is called water, water is called air, air is called cloud and cloud is called river, then what do we drink when thirsty?
    (a) Sky (b) Air
    (c) Water (d) Sea
27. If man is called girl, girl is called woman, woman is called boy, boy is called butler and butler is called rogue, who will serve in a restaurant?
    (a) Butler (b) Girl
    (c) Man (d) Rogue
28. If train is called bus, bus is called tractor, tractor is called car, car is called scooter, scooter is called bicycle, bicycle is called moped, which is used to plough a field?
    (a) Train (b) Bus
    (c) Tractor (d) Car
29. If lead is called stick, stick is called nib, nib is called needle, needle is called rope and rope is called thread, what will be fitted in a pen to write with it?
    (a) Stick (b) Lead
    (c) Needle (d) Nib
30. If rose is called popy, popy is called lily, lily is called lotus and lotus is called glandiola, which is the king of flowers?
    (a) Rose (b) Lotus
    (c) Popy (d) Gladiola

❐

Answer Key

1. (c)	**2.** (a)	**3.** (a)	**4.** (b)	**5.** (a)	**6.** (b)	**7.** (a)	**8.** (b)
9. (b)	**10.** (a)	**11.** (c)	**12.** (c)	**13.** (b)	**14.** (d)	**15.** (b)	**16.** (a)
17. (b)	**18.** (c)	**19.** (a)	**20.** (b)	**21.** (a)	**22.** (c)	**23.** (d)	**24.** (c)
25. (b)	**26.** (b)	**27.** (d)	**28.** (d)	**29.** (c)	**30.** (d)		

Explanatory Notes

1. (c)
Each letter in the word is moved one step backward to obtain the corresponding letter of the code.

2. (a)
The letters of the word are written in a reverse order and then each letter is moved one step backward to obtain the code.

3. (a)
The letters of the word are written in reverse order and each letter, except the first and the last one, is moved one step forward to obtain the code.

4. (b)
Each letter of the word is moved three steps forward to obtain the code.

5. (a)
Each of the letters at odd positions is moved two steps backward and each of the letters at even positions is moved two steps forward to obtain the corresponding letters of the code.

6. (b)
The letters at the third and sixth places are repeated thrice to code BOMBAY as MYMYMY.
Similarly, the letters at the third, sixth and ninth places are repeated thrice to code TAMIL NADU as MNUMNUMNU.

7. (a)
The first, second, third, fourth, fifth and sixth letters of the word are respectively moved two, three, four, five, six and seven steps forward to obtain the corresponding letters of the code.

8. (b)
Each of the letters at odd positions is moved one step backward, while the letters at even positions are moved six, five, four, three, two,... steps backward respectively to obtain the corresponding letters of the code.

9. (b)
In SEARCH,
S is coded as 2, E as 1,
A as 4, R as 6,
C as 7, H as 3.
Thus, the code for SEARCH is 214673.

10. (a)
In TWELVE ,
T is coded as 8,
W as 6, E as 3,
L as 2, V as 0.
Thus, the code for TWELVE is 863203.

11. (c)
In BHARATHI,
B is coded as 9,
H as 6, A as 5,
R as 7, T as 3 and,
I as 8.
Thus, the code for BHARATHI is 96575368.

12. (c)
In GATE,
G is coded as 5,
A as 2, T as 4 and E as 7
Thus, the code for GATE is 5247.

13. (b)
In PEARL,
P is coded as 2,
E as 4, A as 1,
R as 5 and L as 3.
Thus, the code for PEARL is 24153.

14. (d)
In TENANT,
T is coded as 3
E as 1, N as 2
and A as 7.
So, TENANT is coded as 312723.

15. (b)
In NEATNESS,
N is coded as 2,
E as 1, A as 7,
T as 3 and S as 9.
So, NEATNESS is coded as 21732199.

16. (a)
In SEDATE,
S is coded as 9,
E as 1, D as 8,
A as 7 and T as 3.
So, SEDATE is coded as 918731.

17. (b)
In ARREST,
A is coded as 7,
R as 4, E as 1,
S as 9 and T as 3.
So, ARREST is coded as 744193.

18. (c)
In ENDEAR,
E is coded as 1,
N as 2, D as 8,
A as 7 and R as 4
So, ENDEAR is coded as 128174.

19. (a)
In GREECE,
G is coded as 3,
R as 8, E as 1
and C as 9.
Thus, GREECE is coded as 381191.

20. (b)
In the number 396824
3 is coded as Q,
9 as L, 6 as P,
8 as N, 2 as M and
4 as F
So, 396824 is coded as QLPNMF.

21. (a)
In the number 64928
6 is coded as J,
4 as B, 9 as N,
2 as L and 8 as D.
So, 64928 is coded as JBNLD.

22. (c)
The colour of the human blood is 'red' and as given, 'red' is called 'yellow'.
So, the colour of human blood is 'yellow'.

23. (d)
Clearly, 'soap' is used for washing the clothes. But, 'soap' is called 'ink'.
So, 'ink' is used for washing the clothes.

24. (c)
Clearly, a lizard crawls and the animals that crawl are called 'flying'.
So, 'lizard' is called 'flying'.

25. (b)
The colour of clear sky is 'blue' and as given, 'blue' is called 'sky'.
So, the colour of clear sky is 'sky'.

26. (b)
One drinks 'water' when thirsty and as given; 'water' is called 'air'.
So, we drink 'air' when thirsty.

27. (d)
A 'butler' serves in a restaurant but 'butler' is called 'rogue'.
So 'rouge' will serve in the restaurant.

28. (d)
A 'tractor' is used to plough a field. But a 'tractor' is called 'car'.
So, a 'car' is used to plough the field.

29. (c)
Clearly, a 'nib' is fitted into the pen to write with it. But a 'nib' is called 'needle'.
So, a 'needle' is fitted into the pen.

30. (d)
The king of flowers is the 'lotus'. But 'lotus' is called 'glandiola'.
So, 'glandiola' is the king of flowers.

❐

Previous Year Questions

1. In a certain code, '37' means 'which class' and '583' means 'caste and class'. What is the code for 'caste'?
[NTSE 2012 - Punjab first stage paper]
(a) 3 (b) 7
(c) 8 (d) Either 5 or 3
(e) Either 5 or 8

2. In a certain code language, '743' means 'mangoes are good'; '657' means 'eat good food' and '934' means 'mangoes are ripe'. Which digit means 'ripe' in that language?
[NTSE 2002 - Maharashtra first stage paper]
(a) 9 (b) 4
(c) 5 (d) 7
(e) None of these

3. In a certain code, '247' means 'spread red carpet'; '256' means 'dust one carpet' and '234' means 'one red carpet'. Which digit in that code means 'dust'?
[NTSE 2012 - UP first stage paper]
(a) 2 (b) 3
(c) 5 (d) 6
(e) Can't say

4. In a certain code, '256' means 'you are good'; '637' means 'we are bad' and '358' means 'good and bad'. Which of the following represents 'and' in that code?
[NTSE 2012 - Delhi first stage paper]
(a) 2 (b) 5
(c) 8 (d) 3
(e) None of these

5. In a certain code, '467' means 'leaves are green'; '485' means 'green is good' and '639' means 'they are playing'. Which digit stands for 'leaves' in that code?
[NTSE 2003 - Haryana second stage paper]
(a) 4 (b) 6
(c) 7 (d) 3
(e) None of these

6. In a certain code language, '851' means 'good sweet fruit'; '783' means 'good red rose' and '341' means 'rose and fruit'. Which of the following digits stands for 'sweet' in that language?
[NTSE 2000 - Goa second stage paper]
(a) 8 (b) 5
(c) 1 (d) 3
(e) None of these

7. In a certain code language, '123' means 'hot filtered coffee' ; '356' means 'very hot day' and '589' means 'day and night'. Which digit stands for 'very'?
[NTSE 2001 - Punjab first stage paper]
(a) 2 (b) 4
(c) 5 (d) 9
(e) 6

8. In a certain code, '256' means 'red colour chalk'; '589' means 'green colour flower' and '245' means 'white colour chalk'. Which digit in that code means 'white'?
[NTSE 2000 – Himachal Pradesh first stage paper]
(a) 2 (b) 4
(c) 5 (d) Can't be determined
(e) None of these

9. In a certain code language, '526' means 'sky is blue' ; '24' means 'blue colour' and '436' means 'colour is fun'. Which digit in that language means 'fun'?
[NTSE 2012 - Assam first stage paper]
(a) 5 (b) 4
(c) 3 (d) 2
(e) None of these

10. In a certain code, '289' means 'read from paper'; '276' means 'tea from field' and '85' means 'wall paper'. Which of the following is the code for 'tea'?
[NTSE 2003 - Delhi first stage paper]
(a) 2 (b) 6
(c) Either 2 or 6 (d) Either 2 or 7
(e) Either 7 or 6

❑

Answer Key

1. (e)	2. (a)	3. (c)	4. (c)	5. (c)	6. (b)	7. (e)	8. (b)	9. (c)	10. (e)

Explanatory Notes

1. (e)
In the given statements, the common code digit is '3' and the common word is 'class'. So, '3' means 'class'. Thus, in the second statement, either 5 or 8 stands for 'caste'.

2. (a)
In the first and third statements, the common code digits are '4' and '3' and the common words are 'mangoes' and 'are'. So, '4' and '3' are the codes for 'mangoes' and 'are'. Thus, in the third statement, '9' means 'ripe'.

3. (c)
In the first and second statements, the common code digit is '2' and the common word is 'carpet'. So, '2' means 'carpet'.
In the second and third statements, the common code digit is '6' and the common word is 'one'. So, '6' means 'one'.
Therefore, in the second statement, '5' means 'dust'.

4. (c)
In the first and third statements, the common code digit is '5' and the common word is 'good'. So, '5' means 'good'.
In the second and third statements, the common code digit is '3' and the common word is 'bad'. So, '3' means 'bad'.
Thus, in third statement, '8' means 'and'.

5. (c)
In the first and second statements, the common code digit is '4' and the common word is 'green'. So, '4' means 'green'.
In the first and third statements, the common digit is '6' and the common word is 'are'. So, '6' means 'are'.
Thus, in the first statement, '7' means 'leaves'.

6. (b)
In the first and second statements, the common code digit is '8' and the common word is 'good'. So, '8' means 'good'.
In the first and third statements, the common code digit is '1' and the common word is 'fruit'. So, '1' means 'fruit'.
Thus, in the first statement, '5' means 'sweet'.

7. (e)
In the first and second statements, the common code digit is '3' and the common word is 'hot'. So, '3' means 'hot'.
In the second and third statements, the common code digit '5' and the common word is 'day'. So, '5' means 'day'.
Thus, in the second statement, '6' means 'very'.

8. (b)
In the second and third statements, the common code digit is '5' and the common word is 'colour'. So, '5' means 'colour'.
In the first and third statements, '5' means 'colour'. The other common code digit is '2' and the common word is 'chalk'. So, '2' means 'chalk'.
Thus, in the third statement, '4' means 'white'.

9. (c)
In the first and third statements, the common code digit is '6' and the common word is 'is'. So, '6' means 'is'.
In the second and third statements, the common code digit is '4' and the common word is 'colour'. So, '4' means 'colour'.
Thus, in the statement, '3' means 'fun'.

10. (e)
In the first and second statements, the common digit is '2' and the common word is 'from'. So, '2' is the code for 'from'.
In the first and third statements, the common code digit is '8' and the common word is 'paper'. So, '8' is the code for 'paper'.
Clearly, in the second statement, either '7' or '6' may be the code for 'tea'.

❐

UNIT 4

Direction Sense Test

There are four main directions : **East, West, North** and **South** as shown below :

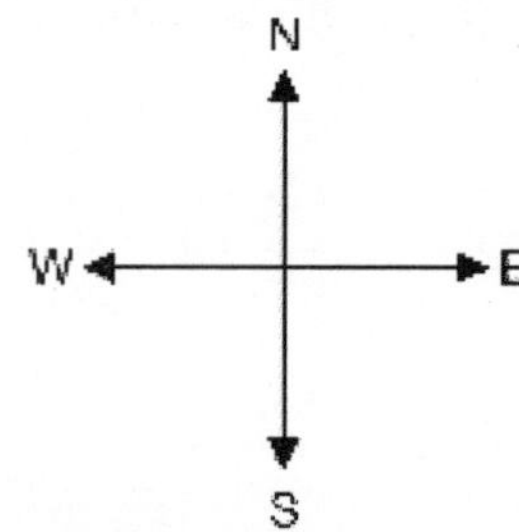

There are four cardinal directions - **North-East (N-E), North-West (N-W), South-East (S-E)**, and **South-West (S-W)** as shown below:

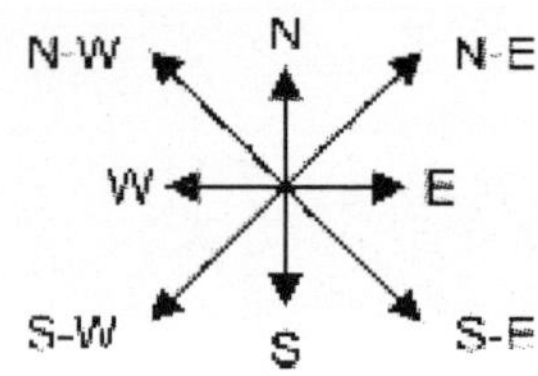

1. At the time of sunrise if a man stands facing the east, his shadow will be towards west.
2. At the time of sunset the shadow of an object is always in the east.
3. If a man stands facing the North, at the time of sunrise his shadow will be towards his left and at the time of sunset it will be towards his right.
4. At 12:00 noon, the rays of the sun are vertically downward; hence there will be no shadow.

Solved Examples

Example 1: Siva, starting from his house, goes 5 km in the East, and then he turns to his left and goes 4 km. Finally he turns to his left and goes 5 km. Now how far is he from his house and in what direction?

Solution: From third position, it is clear he is 4 km from his house and is in the North direction.

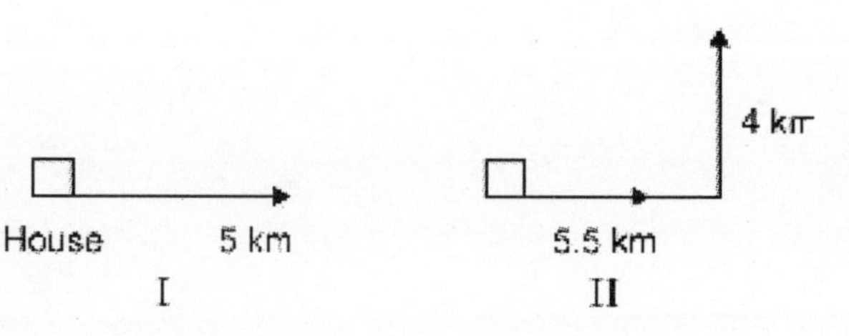

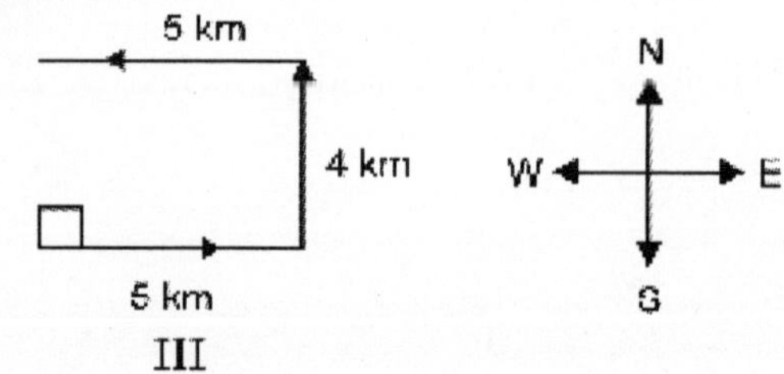

Example 2: Suresh, starting from his house, goes 4 km in the East, and then he turns to his right and goes 3 km. What minimum distance will be covered by him to come back to his house?

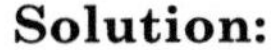

Solution:

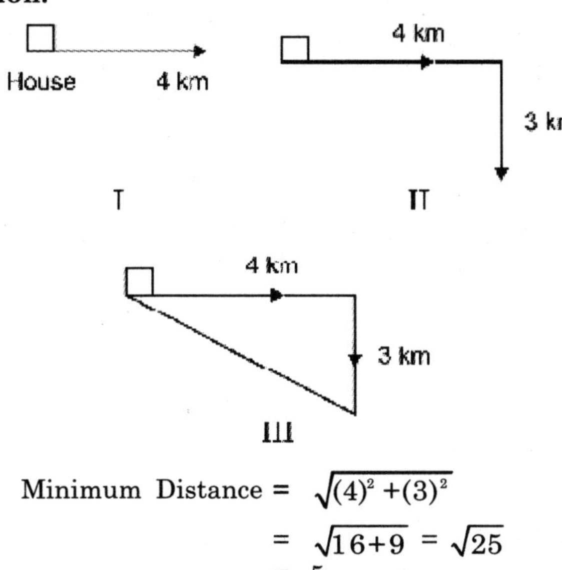

Minimum Distance $= \sqrt{(4)^2 + (3)^2}$

$= \sqrt{16+9} = \sqrt{25}$

$= 5$

Example 3: One morning after sunrise Juhi while going to school met Lalli at Boring road crossing. Lalli's shadow was exactly to the right of Juhi. If they were face to face, which direction was Juhi facing?

Solution: In the morning the sun rises in the east.
So, in morning the shadow falls towards the west.
Now Lalli's shadow falls to the right of the Juhi. Hence Juhi is facing the South.

Example 4: Hema, starting from her house, walked 5 km to reach the crossing of Palace. In which direction she was going, a road opposite to this direction goes to Hospital. The road to the right goes to station. If the road which goes to station is just opposite to the road which IT-Park, then in which direction to Hema is the road which goes to IT-Park?

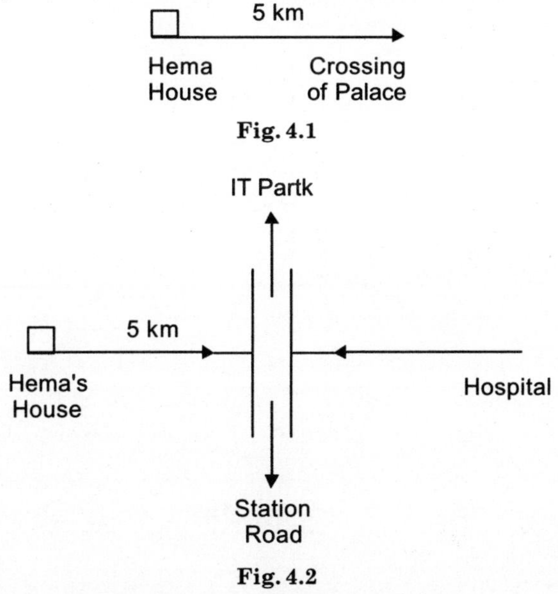

Fig. 4.1

Fig. 4.2

Solution: From II figure, it is clear that the road which goes to IT-Park is left to Hema.

Example 5: Dev, Kumar, Nilesh, Ankur and Pintu are standing facing the North in a playground such as given below:

(a) Kumar is at 40 m to the right of Ankur.
(b) Dev is at 60 m in the south of Kumar.
(c) Nilesh is at a distance of 25 m in the west of Ankur.
(d) Pintu is at a distance of 90 m in the North of Dev.

Which one is in the North-East of the person? Who is to the left of Kumar?

(a) Dev (b) Nilesh
(c) Ankur (d) Pintu

Solution: Option (d) is correct.

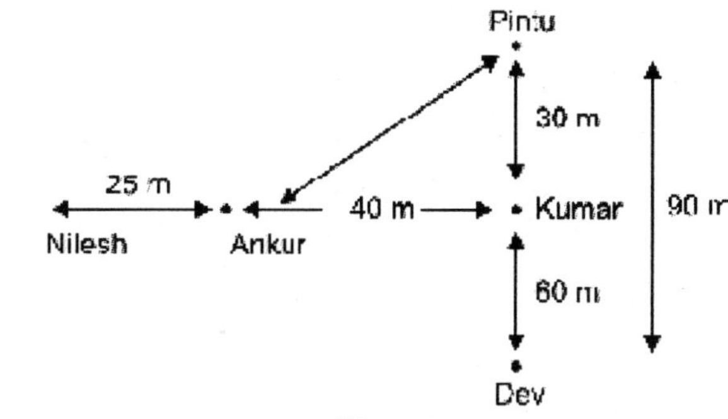

Fig. 4.3

Explanation: Ankur is in the left of Kumar. Hence Pintu is in North-East of Ankur.

Example 6: If a boy starting from Nilesh (Figure 4.3), met to Ankur and then to Kumar, and after this he met to Dev and then to Pintu and whole the time he walked in a straight line, then how much total distance did he cover?

(a) 215 m (b) 155 m
(c) 245 m (d) 185 m

Solution: Option (a) is correct.

Explanation:

Required distance = 25 m + 40 m + 60 m + 90 m
Required distance = 215 m

Example 7: A boy rode his bicycle Northward, then turned left and rode 1 km and again turned left and rode 2 km. He found himself 1 km west of his starting point. How far did he ride northward initially?

(a) 1 km (b) 2 km
(c) 3 km (d) 5 km

Solution: Option (b) is correct.

Explanation:

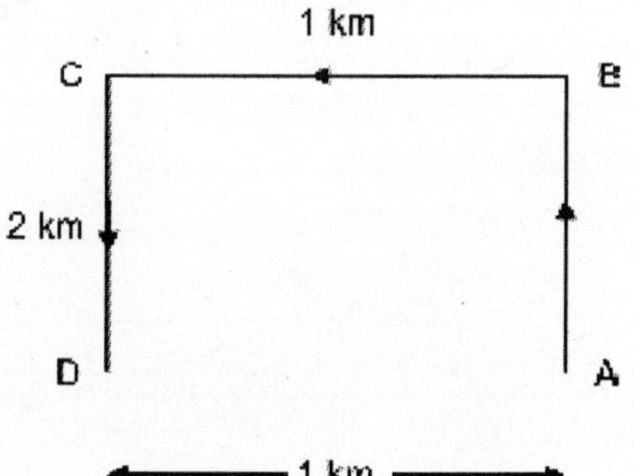

The boy rode 2 km. Northward.

Example 8: Rahul puts his timepiece on the table in such a way that at 6 P.M. the hour hand points to North. In which direction the minute hand will point at 9.15 P.M.?

(a) South-East (b) South
(c) North (d) West

Solution: Option d) is correct.

Explanation:

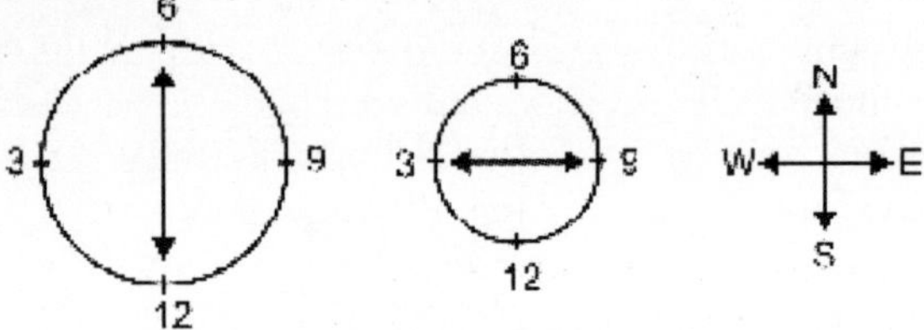

At 9.15 P.M., the minute hand will point towards west.

Example 9: A man walks 5 km toward south and then turns to the right. After walking 3 km he turns to the left and walks 5 km. Now in which direction is he from the starting place?

(a) West (b) South
(c) North-East (d) South-West

Solution: Option (d) is correct.

Explanation:

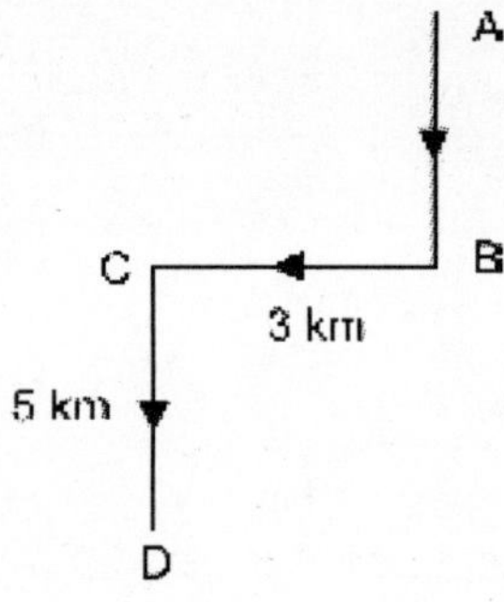

Hence the required direction is South-West.

Example 10: If South-East becomes North, North-East becomes West and so on. What will West become?

(a) North-East (b) North-West
(c) South-East (d) South-West

Solution: Option (c) is correct.

Explanation:

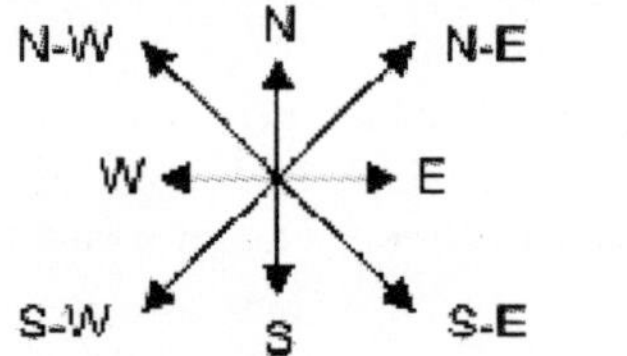

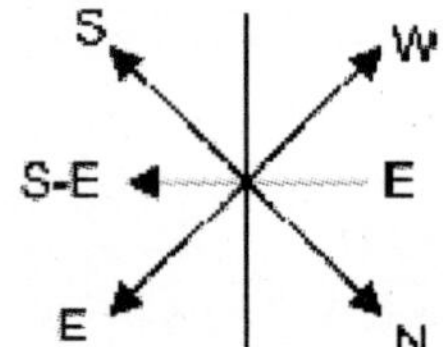

It is clear from the diagrams that new name of West will become South-East.

Multiple Choice Questions

1. Sachin walks 20 km towards North. He turns left and walks 40 km. He again turns left and walks 20 km. Finally he moves 20 km after turning to the left. How far is he from his starting position?
   (a) 20 km. (b) 30 km.
   (c) 50 km. (d) 60 km.
2. From his house, Lokesh went 15 km towards the North. Then he turned west and covered 10 km. Then he turned south and covered 5 km. Finally turning to the east, he covered 10 km. In which direction is he from his house?
   (a) East (b) West
   (c) North (d) South
3. Amit started walking positioning his back towards the sun. After some time, he turned left, then turned right and towards the left again. In which direction is he going now?
   (a) North or South
   (b) East or West
   (c) North or West
   (d) South or West
4. Rohit walked 25 m towards South. Then he turned to his left and walked 20 m. He then turned to his left and walked 25 m. He again turned to his right and walked 15 m. At what distance is he from the starting point and in which direction?
   (a) 35 m East (b) 35 m North
   (c) 30 m West (d) 45 m East
5. Village Q is to the North of the village P. The village R is in the East of Village Q. The village S is to the left of the village P. In which direction is the village S with respect to village R?
   (a) West (b) South-West
   (c) South (d) North-West
6. Radha moves towards South-East a distance of 7 km, then she moves towards West and travels a distance of 14 km. From here she moves towards North-West a distance of 7 km and finally she moves a distance of 4 km towards east. How far is she now from the starting point?
   (a) 3 km (b) 4 km
   (c) 10 km (d) 11 km
7. Sundar runs 20 m towards East and turns to right and runs 10 m. Then he turns to the right and runs 9 m. Again he turns to right and runs 5 m. After this he turns to left and runs 12 m and finally he turns to right and runs 6 m. Now to which direction is Sundar facing?
   (a) East (b) West
   (c) North (d) South
8. One morning after sunrise, Suresh was standing facing a pole. The shadow of the pole fell exactly to his right. To which direction was he facing?

(a) East (b) South
(c) West (d) Data is inadequate

9. A child went 90 m in the East to look for his father, then he turned right and went 20 m. After this he turned right and after going 30 m he reached to his uncle's house. His father was not there. From there he went 100 m to his North and met his father. How far did he meet his father from the starting point?
(a) 80 m (b) 100 m
(c) 140 m (d) 260 m

10. Four friends A, B, C and D live in a same locality. The house of B is in the east of A's house but in the north of C's house. The house of C is in the west of D's house. D's house is in which direction of A's house?
(a) South-East (b) North-East
(c) East (d) Data is inadequate

11. Umesh directly went from P to Q which is 9 feet distant. Then he turns to the right and walked 4 feet. After this he turned to the right and walked a distance which is equal from P to Q. Finally he turned to the right and walked 3 feet. How far is he from P now?
(a) 6 feet (b) 5 feet
(c) 1 feet (d) 0 feet

12. Shyam walks 5 km towards East and then turns left and walks 6 km. Again he turns right and walks 9 km. Finally he turns to his right and walks 6 km. How far is he from the starting point?
(a) 26 km (b) 21 km
(c) 14 km (d) 9 km

13. After walking 6 km, I turned to the right and then walked 2 km. After then I turned to the left and walked 10 km. In the end, I was moving towards the North. From which direction did I start my journey?
(a) North (b) South
(c) East (d) West

14. Ravi left home and cycled 10 km towards South, then he turned right and cycled 5 km and then again turned right and cycled 10 km. After this he turned left and cycled 10 km. How many kilometres would he have to cycle to reach his home straight?
(a) 10 km (b) 15 km
(c) 20 km (d) 25 km

15. Reena walked from A to B in the East 10 feet. Then she turned to the right and walked 3 feet. Again she turned to the right and walked 14 feet. How far is she from A?
(a) 4 feet (b) 5 feet
(c) 24 feet (d) 27 feet

16. One morning after sunrise Nivedita and Niharika were talking to each other face to face at the Dalphin crossing. If Niharika's shadow was exactly to the right of Nivedita, which direction Niharika was facing?
(a) North (b) South
(c) East (d) Data is inadequate

17. If A x B means A is to the south of B; A + B means A is to the north of B; A % B means A is to the east of B; A - B means A is to the west of B; then in P % Q + R - S, S is in which direction with respect to Q?
(a) South-West (b) South-East
(c) North-East (d) North-West

18. One morning after sunrise, Vimal started to walk. During this walking he met Stephen who was coming from opposite direction. Vimal watched that the shadow of Stephen was to the right of him (Vimal). To which direction Vimal was facing?
(a) East (b) West
(c) South (d) Data inadequate

19. Golu started from his house towards North. After covering a distance of 8 km. He turned towards left and covered a distance of 6 km. What is the shortest distance now from his house?
(a) 10 km (b) 16 km
(c) 14 km (d) 2 km

20. P started from his house towards west. After walking a distance of 25 m. He turned to the right and walked 10 m. Then he again turned to the right and walked 15 m. After this he is to turn right at 135° and to cover 30 m. In which direction should he go?
(a) West (b) South
(c) South-West (d) South-East

21. X started to walk straight towards South. After walking 5 m he turned to the left and walked 3 m. After this he turned to the right and walked 5 m. Now to which direction X is facing?
(a) North-East (b) South
(c) North (d) South-West

22. A man walks 2 km towards North. Then he turns to East and walks 10 km. After this he turns to North and walks 3 km. Again he turns towards East and walks 2 km. How far is he from the starting point?
(a) 10 km (b) 13 km
(c) 15 km (d) None of these

23. The length and breadth of a room are 8 m and 6 m respectively. A cat runs along all the four walls and finally along a diagonal order to catch a rat. How much total distance is covered by the cat?
(a) 10 m (b) 14 m
(c) 38 m (d) 48 m

24. One morning Sujata started to walk towards the Sun. After covering some distance she turned to right, then again to the right, and after covering some distance she again turns to the right. Now in which direction is she facing?
(a) North
(b) South
(c) North-East
(d) South-West

25. Some boys are sitting in three rows all facing North such that A is in the middle row. P is just to the right of A but in the same row. Q is just behind P while R is in the North of (A). In which direction of R is Q?
(a) South (b) South-West
(c) North-East (d) South-East

26. Rasik walked 20 m towards North. Then he turned right and walks 30 m. Then he turns right and walks 35 m. Then he turns left and walks 15 m. Finally he turns left and walks 15 m. In which direction and how many metres is he from the starting position?
(a) 15 m West (b) 30 m East
(c) 30 m West (d) 45 m East

27. Two cars start from the opposite places of a main road, 150 km apart. First car runs for 25 km and takes a right turn and then runs 15 km. It then turns left and then runs for another 25 km and then takes the direction back to reach the main road. In the mean time, due to minor break down the other car has run only 35 km along the main road. What would be the distance between two cars at this point?
(a) 65 km (b) 75 km
(c) 80 km (d) 85 km

28. Starting from the point X, Jayant walked 15 m towards West. He turned left and walked 20 m. He then turned left and walked 15 m. After this he turned to his right and walked 12 m. How far and in which direction is Jayant from X now ?
(a) 32 m, South (b) 47 m, East
(c) 42 m, North (d) 27 m, South

29. One evening before sunset Rekha and Hema were talking to each other face to face. If Hema's shadow was exactly to the right of Hema, which direction was Rekha facing?
(a) North (b) South
(c) East (d) Data is inadequate

30. A is 40 m south-west of B C is 40 m south-east of B. Then, C is in which direction of A?
(a) West (b) North-east
(c) South (d) East

❒

Answer Key

1. (a)	**2.** (c)	**3.** (a)	**4.** (a)	**5.** (b)	**6.** (c)	**7.** (c)	**8.** (b)
9. (b)	**10.** (a)	**11.** (c)	**12.** (c)	**13.** (b)	**14.** (b)	**15.** (b)	**16.** (a)
17. (b)	**18.** (c)	**19.** (a)	**20.** (c)	**21.** (b)	**22.** (b)	**23.** (c)	**24.** (a)
25. (d)	**26.** (d)	**27.** (a)	**28.** (a)	**29.** (b)	**30.** (d)		

Explanatory Notes

1. (a)

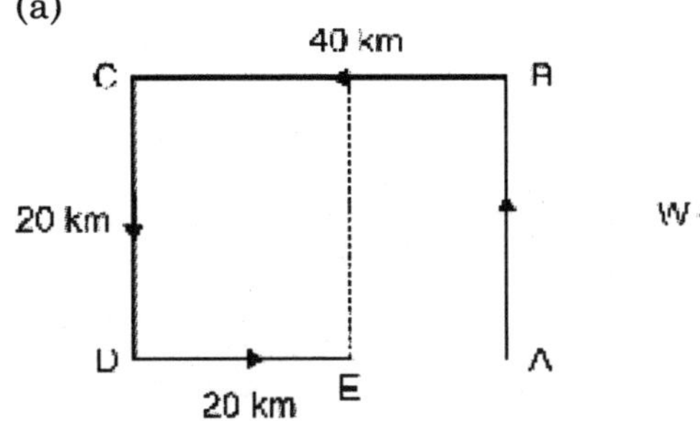

Required distance = 40 – 20 = 20 km.

2. (c)

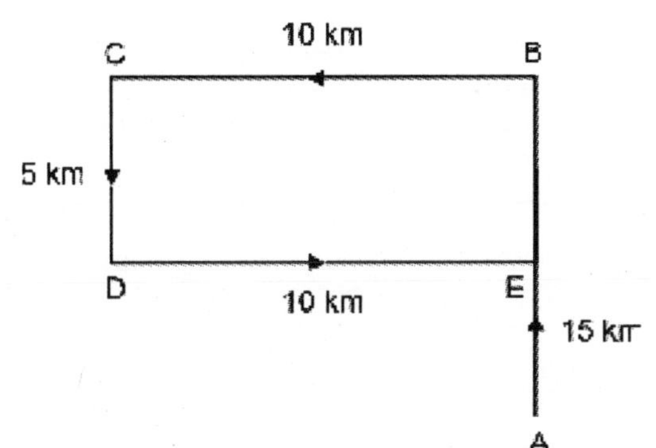

Therefore, it is clear that he is in the North from his house.

3. (a)

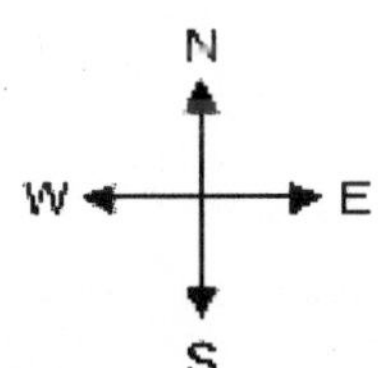

In the morning

B A C D E South

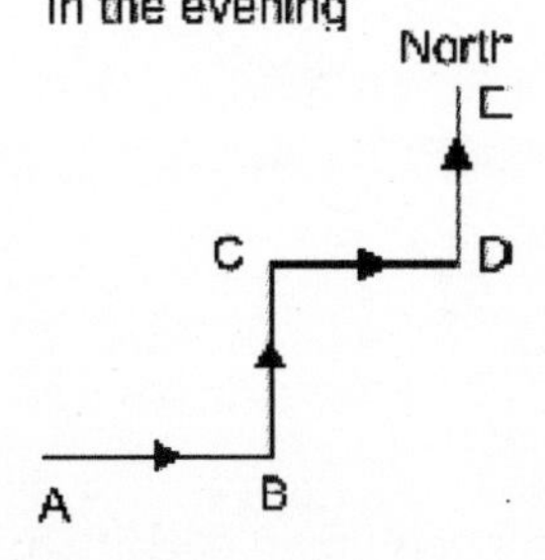

If he starts walking in the morning, then finally he will face towards South; and if he starts in the evening, then finally he will face towards North.

4. (a)

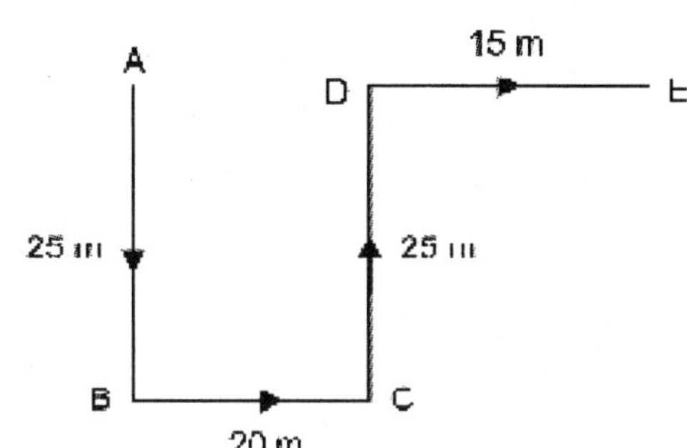

5. (b)

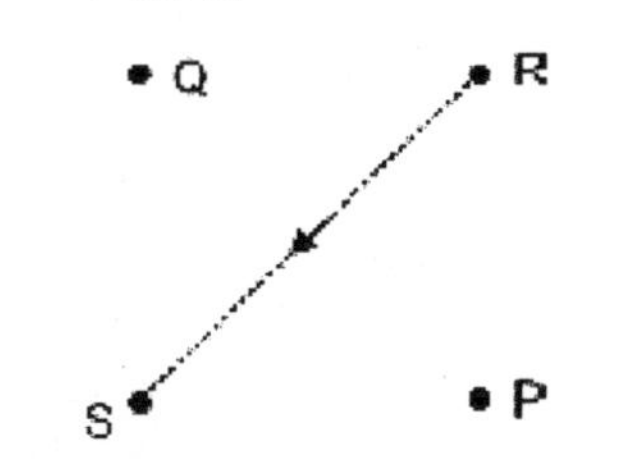

S is to the South-West of R.

6. (c)

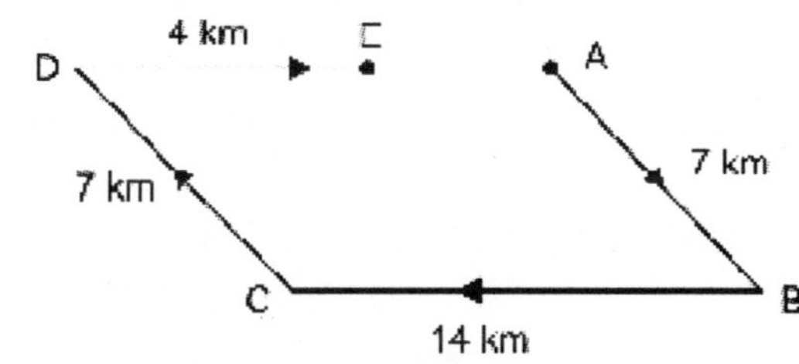

Required distance = AE
= 14 – 4
= 10 km.

7. (c)

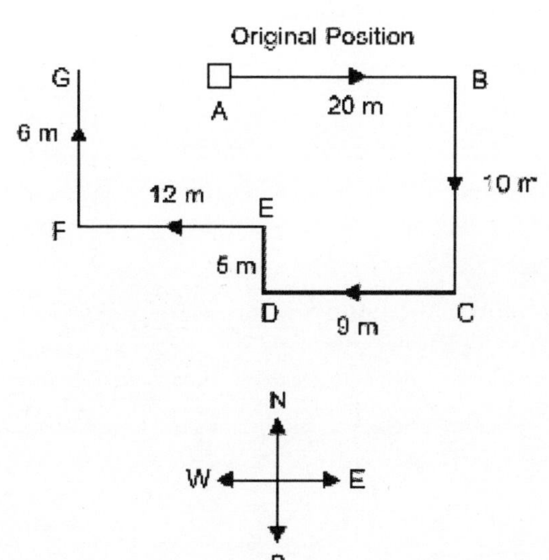

Therefore, it is clear that Sundar will face towards North.

8. (b)
The Sun rises in the east in the morning. Since the shadow of Suresh falls to his right. So he is facing south.

9. (b)

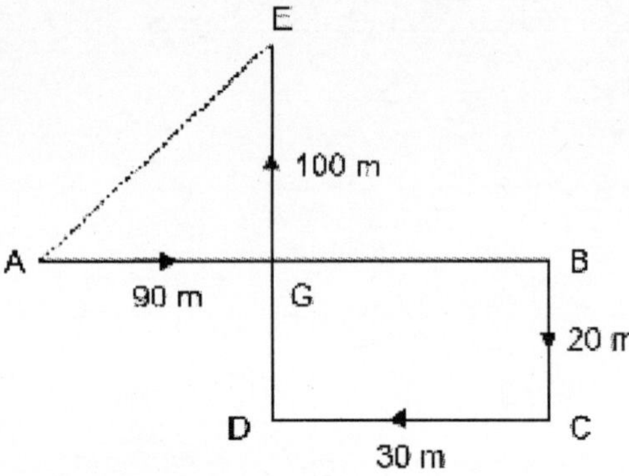

Required distance

$= AE$

$= \sqrt{AG^2 + EG^2}$

$= \sqrt{(90-30)^2 + (100+20)^2}$

$= \sqrt{(60)^2 + (80)^2}$

$= \sqrt{3600 + 6400}$

$= \sqrt{10000}$

$= 100$ m

10. (a)

C D

Therefore, D's house is in the South-East direction of (A)

11. (c)

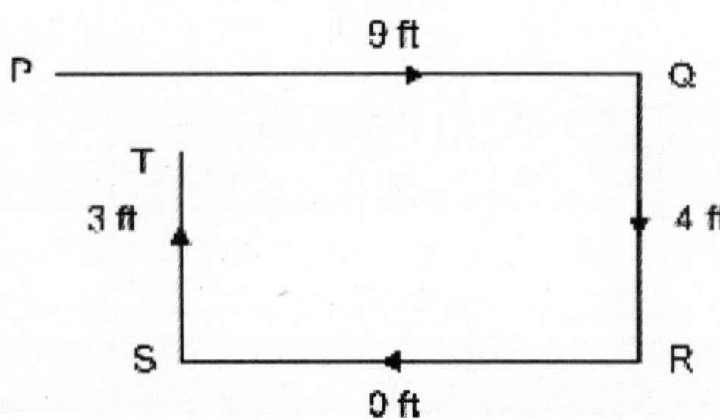

Required distance = PT = 4 – 3 = 1 ft.

12. (c)

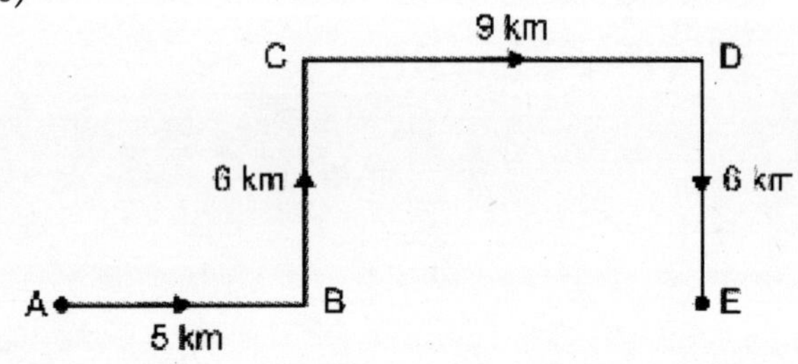

Required distance = AE
= 5 + 9
= 14 km.

13. (b)

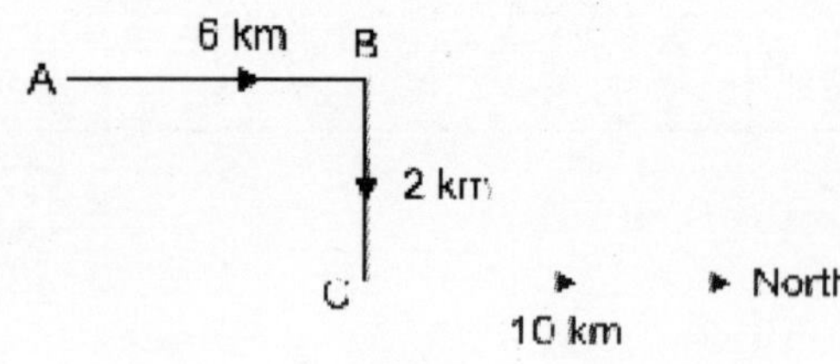

The journey was started from the South.

14. (b)

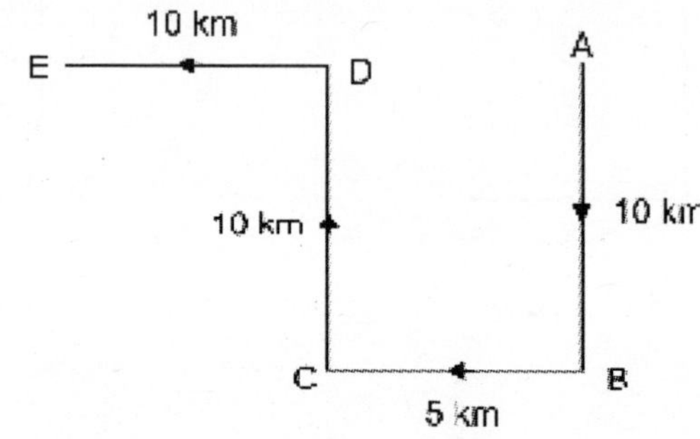

Required distance = AE
= 5 + 10
= 15 km.

15. (b)

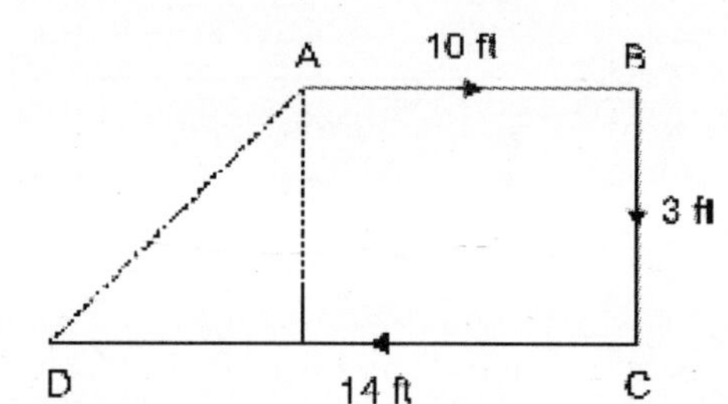

Required distance = AD

$= \sqrt{3^2 + (14-10)^2}$

$= \sqrt{9 + 16}$

= 5 ft.

16. (a)

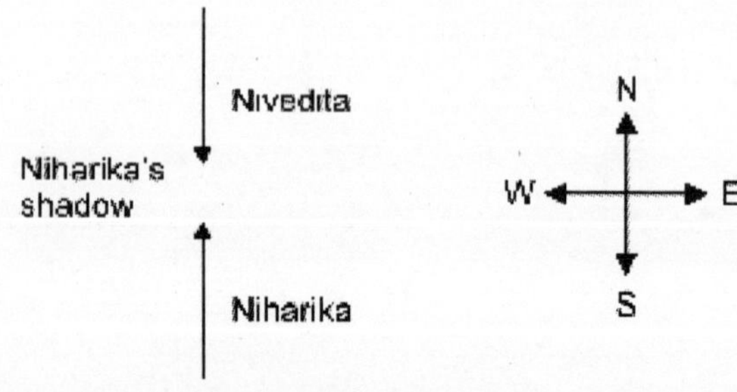

In the morning the sun rises in the East. Hence any shadow falls in the West. Since Niharika's shadow was exactly to the right of Nivedita. Hence, Niharika is facing towards North.

17. (b)
According to P % Q + R - S

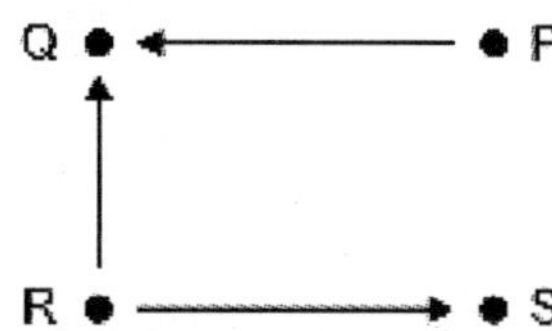

S is in the South-East of Q.

18. (c)
The Sun rises in the east. So the shadow of a man will always fall towards the west. Since the shadow of Stephen is to the right of Vimal. Hence Vimal is facing towards South.

19. (a)

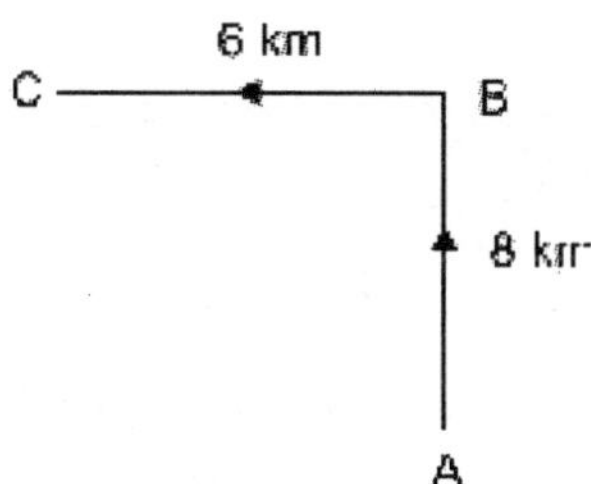

Required distance

$= AC$

$= \sqrt{8^2 + 6^2} = \sqrt{64 + 36}$

$= \sqrt{100} = 10$ km.

20. (c)

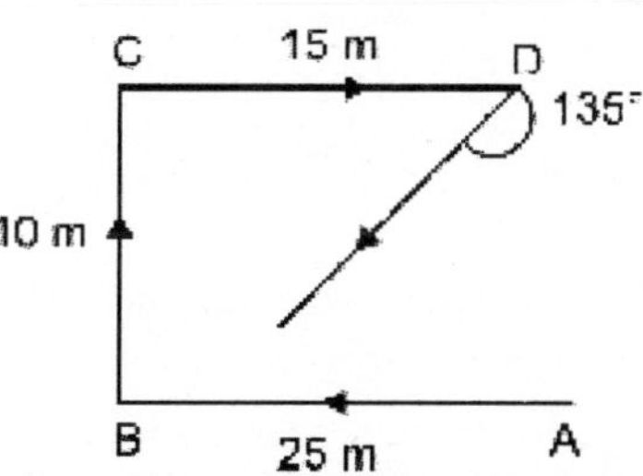

Hence, he should go in the South-West direction.

21. (b)

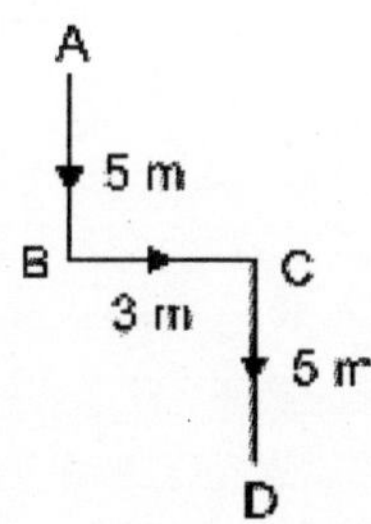

Hence, X will face in the end towards South.

22. (b)

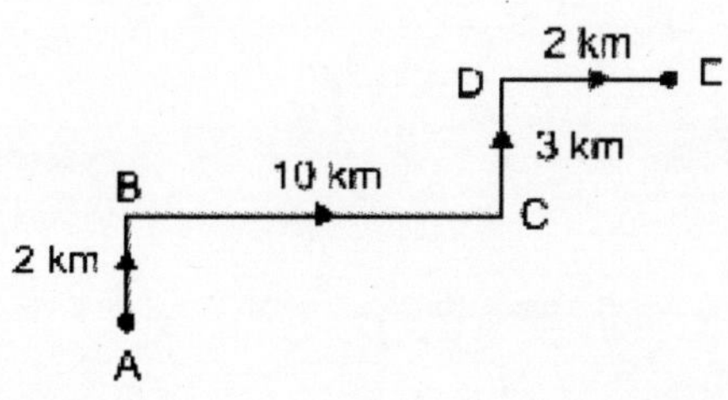

Required distance $= AE$

$= \sqrt{5^2 + 12^2}$

$= 13$ km.

23. (c)

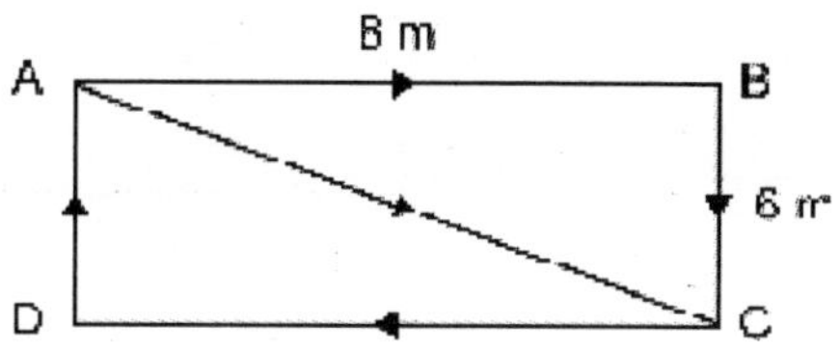

Required distance

$= 8 + 6 + 8 + 6 + \sqrt{8^2 + 6^2}$

$= 28 + \sqrt{100}$

$= 28 + 10$

$= 38$ m.

24. (a)

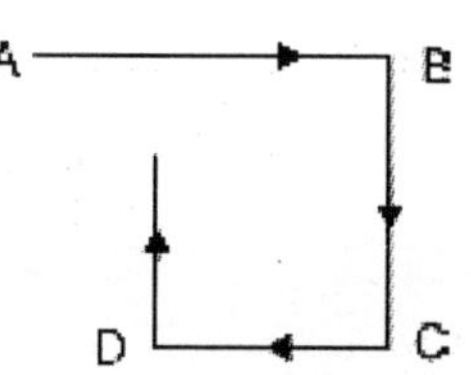

Hence, finally Sujata will face towards North.

25. (d)

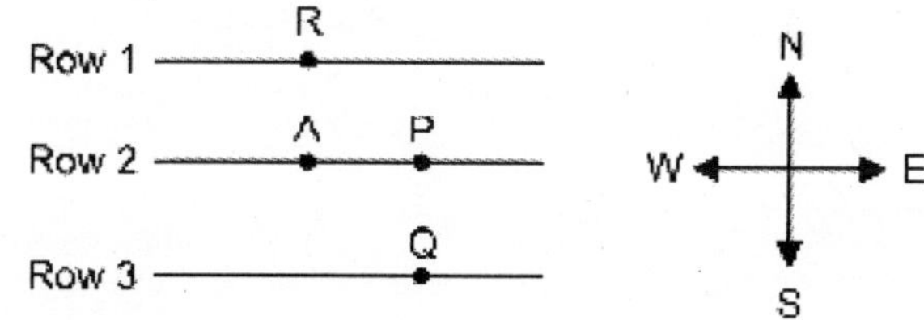

Q is in South-East of R.

26. (d)

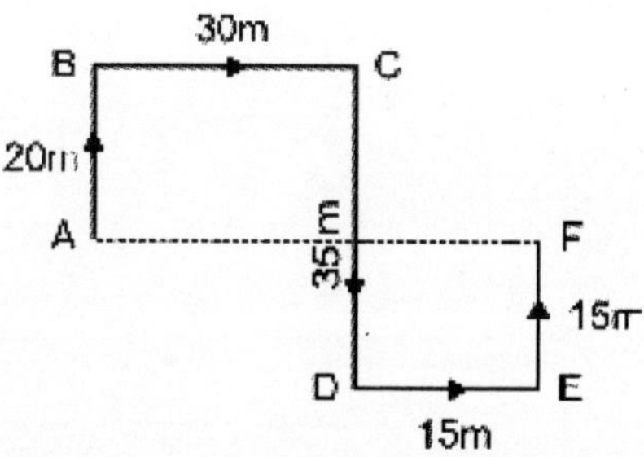

Required distance $= AF$

$= 30 + 15$

$= 45$ km.

From the above diagram, F is East direction from A. Hence the required answer is '45 m East'.

27. (a)

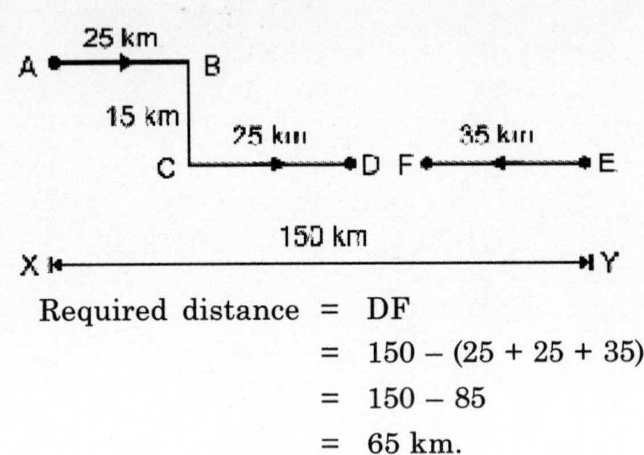

Required distance = DF

= 150 – (25 + 25 + 35)

= 150 – 85

= 65 km.

28. (a)

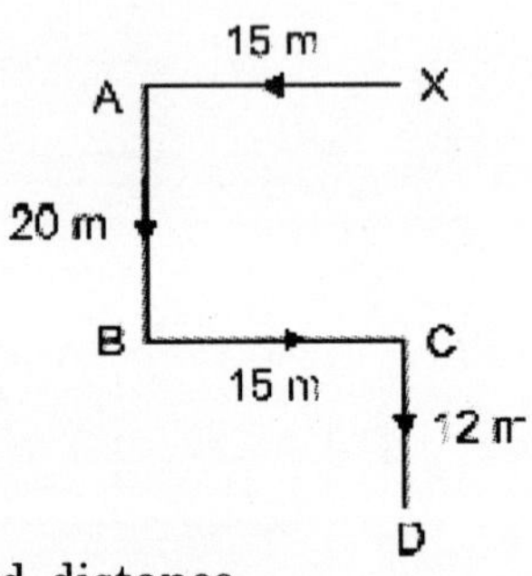

Required distance

= 20 + 12

= 32 m in south direction

29. (b)

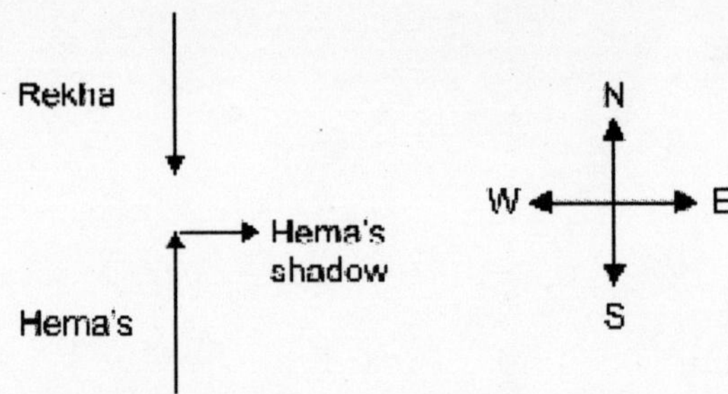

In the evening, the Sun sets in West. Hence, any shadow falls in the East. Since Hema's shadow was to the right of Hema. Hence, Rekha was facing towards South.

30. (d)

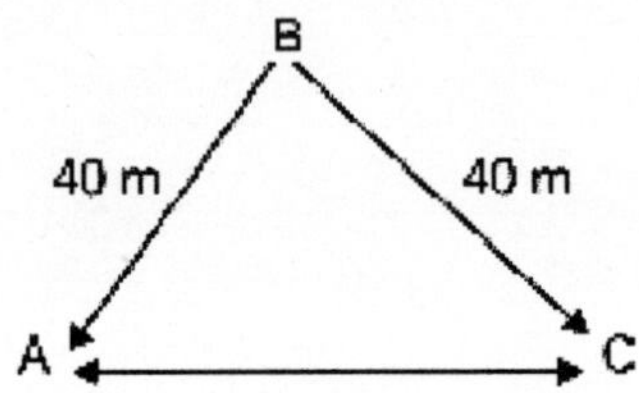

A is clear from the adjoining diagram; C lies to the east of A.

Previous Year Questions

☛ ***Direction to solve (1 to 4):*** *Each of the following questions is based on the following information:*

1. Six flats on a floor in two rows facing North and South are allotted to P, Q, R, S, T and U.
2. Q gets a North-facing flat and is not next to S.
3. S and U get diagonally opposite flats.
4. R next to U gets a South-facing flat and T gets North-facing flat.

[NTSE 2002 - Punjab second stage paper]

1. If the flats of P and T are interchanged, then whose flat will be next to that of U?
   (a) P (b) Q
   (c) R (d) T
2. Which of the following combination gets South-facing flats?
   (a) QTS (b) UPT
   (c) URP (d) Data is inadequate
3. The flats of which of the other pairs than SU are diagonally opposite to each other?
   (a) QP (b) QR
   (c) PT (d) TS
4. Whose flat is between Q and S?
   (a) T (b) U
   (c) R (d) P

☛ ***Direction to solve (5 to 7):*** *Each of the following questions is based on the following information:*

1. A # B means B is at 1 metre to the right of A.
2. A $ B means B is at 1 metre to the North of A.
3. A * B means B is at 1 metre to the left of A.
4. A @ B means B is at 1 metre to the south of A.
5. In each question the first person from the left is facing North.

[NTSE 2000 - Haryana first stage paper]

5. According to X @ B * P, P is in which direction with respect to X?
   (a) North (b) South
   (c) North-East (d) South-West
6. According to M # N $ T, T is in which direction with respect to M?
   (a) North-West (b) North-East
   (c) South-West (d) South-East
7. According to P # R $ A * U, in which direction is U with respect to P?
   (a) East (b) West
   (c) North (d) South

☛ ***Direction to solve (8 to 10):*** *Each of the following questions is based on the following information:*

1. 8-trees → mango, guava, papaya, pomeg-ranate, lemon, banana, raspberry and apple are in two rows, 4 in each facing North and South.
2. Lemon is between mango and apple but just opposite to guava.
3. Banana is at one end of a line and is just next in the right of guava or either banana tree is just after guava tree.
4. Raspberry tree which is at one end of a line, is just diagonally opposite to mango tree.

NTSE 2004 – Karnataka first stage paper]

8. Which of the following statements is definitely true?
   (a) Papaya tree is just near to apple tree.
   (b) Apple tree is just next to lemon tree.
   (c) Raspberry tree is either left to Pomegranate or after.
   (d) Pomegranate tree is diagonally opposite to banana tree.
9. Which tree is just opposite to Raspberry tree?
   (a) Papaya
   (b) Pomegranate
   (c) Papaya or Pomegranate
   (d) Data is inadequate
10. Which tree is just opposite to Banana tree?
    (a) Mango (b) Pomegranate
    (c) Papaya (d) Data is inadequate

❐

Answer Key

1. (c)	2. (c)	3. (a)	4. (a)	5. (d)	6. (b)	7. (c)	8. (b)	9. (c)	10. (a)

Explanatory Notes

1. (c)

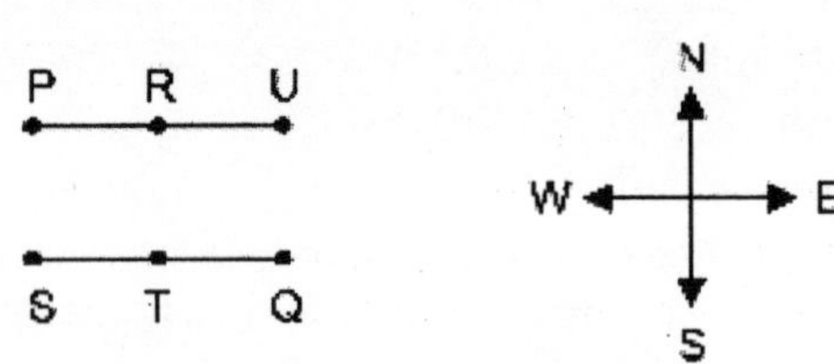

Interchanging the flats of P and T

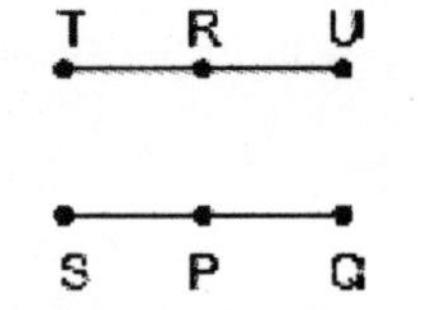

Hence, the flat of R will be next to that of U

2. (c)

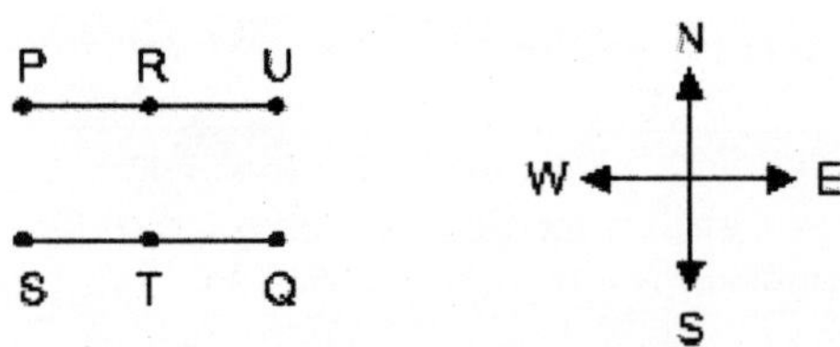

Hence, the flat combination of URP is South-facing.

3. (a)

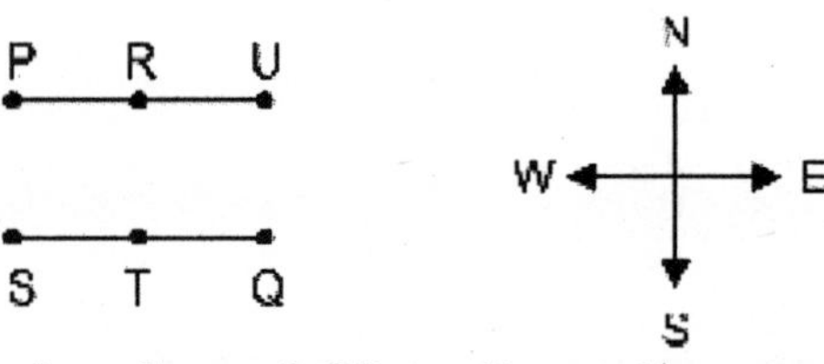

Hence that flats of QP is diagonally opposite to each other.

4. (a)

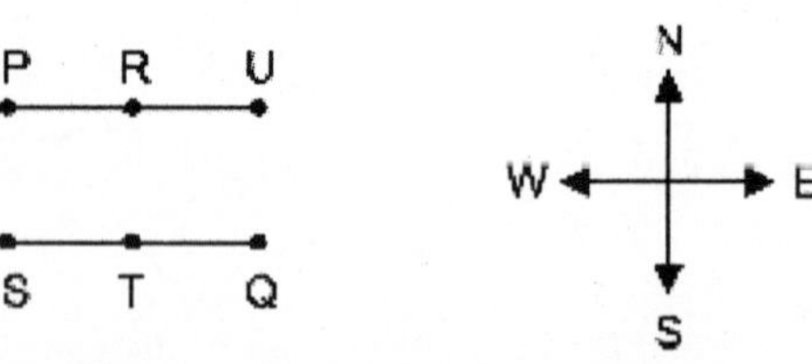

Hence the flat of T is between Q and S.

5. (d)
According to X @ B * Y

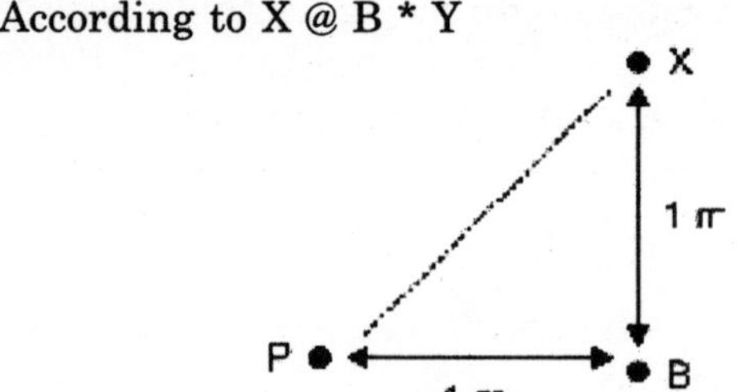

Hence, P is in South-West of X.

6. (b)
According to M # N $ T

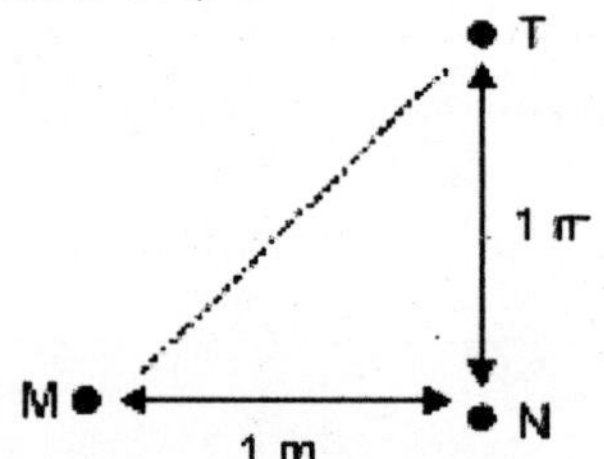

Hence T is in the North-East of M.

7. (c)
According to P # R $ A * U

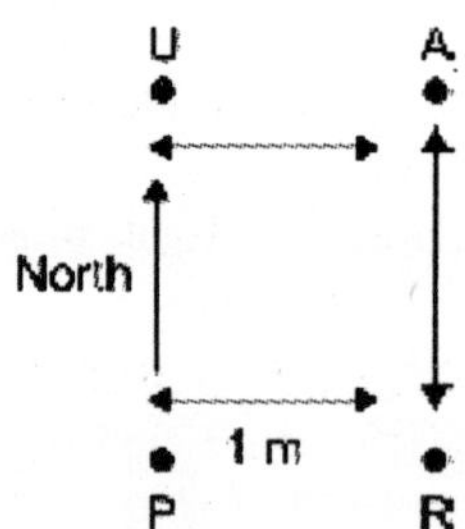

Hence, U is in North direction with respect to P.

8. (b)

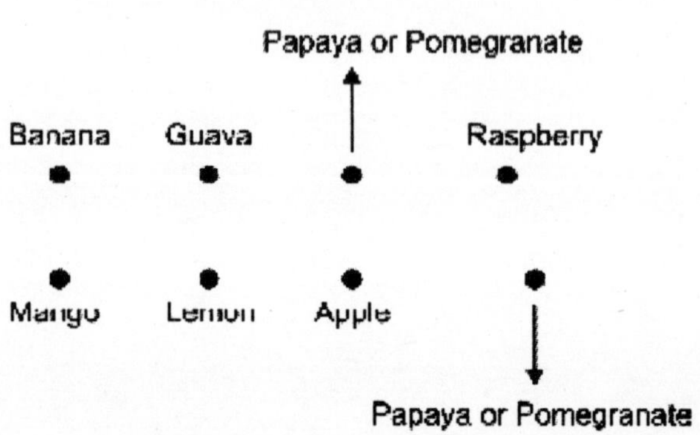

9. (c)

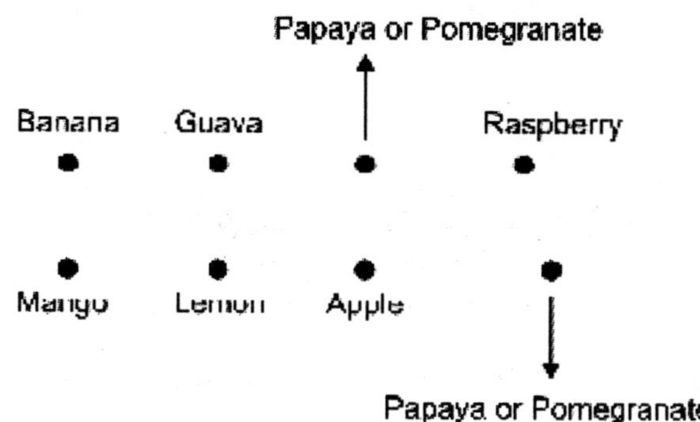
Papaya or Pomegranate
Banana
Guava
Raspberry
Mango
Lemon
Apple
Papaya or Pomegranate

10. (a)

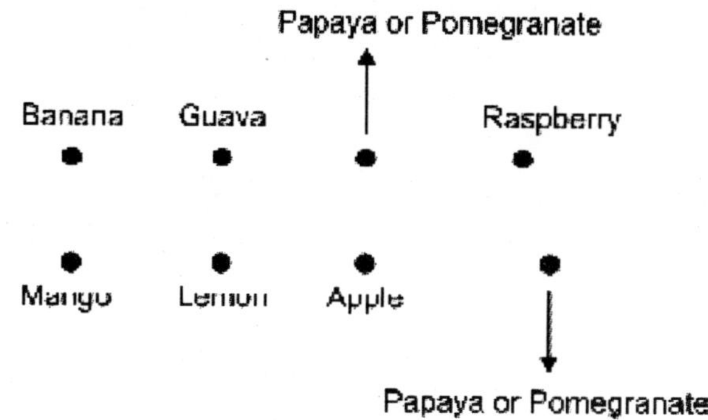
Papaya or Pomegranate
Banana
Guava
Raspberry
Mango
Lemon
Apple
Papaya or Pomegranate

UNIT 5

Series Completion Test

Number and letter series form an important part of the reasoning section in various competitive examinations. There are four board categories of questions that appear in various exams from this particular chapter.

Solved Examples

☛ ***Direction to solve (1-3):*** *Choose the correct alternative that will continue the same pattern and replace the question mark in the given series.*

1. 2, 3, 3, 5, 10, 13, ?, 43, 172, 177
   (a) 23 (b) 38
   (c) 39 (d) 40
   Solution: Option (c) is correct.
   Explanation: The pattern is + 1, x 1, + 2, x 2, + 3, x 3, + 4, x 4, + 5.
   So, the missing term = 13 × 3 = 39
2. Which of the following will not be a number of the series 1, 8, 27, 64, 125,.....?
   (a) 256 (b) 512
   (c) 729 (d) 1000
   Solution: Option (a) is correct.
   Explanation: The given series consists of cubes of natural numbers only. 256 is not the cube of any natural number.
3. 2, 1, 2, 4, 4, 5, 6, 7, 8, 8, 10, 11, ?
   (a) 9 (b) 10
   (c) 11 (d) 12
   Solution: Option (b) is correct.
   Explanation: The given sequence is a combination of three series:
   I. 1st, 4th, 7th, 10th, 13th terms i.e. 2, 4, 6, 8, ?
   II. 2nd, 5th, 8th, 11th terms i.e. 1, 4, 7, 10
   III. 3rd, 6th, 9th, 12th terms i.e. 2, 5, 8, 11
   Clearly, the I series consists of consecutive even numbers. So, the missing term is 10.

☛ ***Direction to solve (4-6):*** *In this type of questions, one term in the number series is wrong. Find out the wrong term.*

4. 4, 10, 22, 46, 96, 190, 382
   (a) 4 (b) 10
   (c) 96 (d) 382
   Solution: Option (c) is correct.
   Explanation: The correct pattern is + 6, + 12, + 24, + 48, + 96, + 192.
   So, 96 is wrong and must be replaced by (46 + 48) i.e. 94.
5. 105, 85, 60, 30, 0, - 45, - 90
   (a) 105 (b) 60
   (c) 0 (d) - 45
   Solution: Option (c) is correct.
   Explanation:
   The correct pattern is - 20, - 25, - 30,.....
   So, 0 is wrong and must be replaced by (30 - 35) i.e. - 5
6. 2, 5, 10, 17, 26, 37, 50, 64
   (a) 17 (b) 26
   (c) 37 (d) 64
   Solution: Option (d) is correct.
   Explanation:
   The terms of the series are $(1^2 + 1)$, $(2^2 + 1)$, $(3^2 + 1)$, $(4^2 + 1)$, $(5^2 + 1)$, $(6^2 + 1)$, (7^2+1),.....
   So, 64 is wrong and must be replaced by $(8^2 + 1)$ i.e. 65

☛ ***Direction to solve (7-11):*** *In each of the following questions, various terms of an alphabet series are given with one or more terms missing as shown by (?). Choose the missing terms out of the given alternatives.*

7. A, G, L, P, S, ?
   (a) U (b) W
   (c) X (d) Y
   Solution: Option (a) is correct.
   Explanation:
   A —+6→ G —+5→ L —+4→ P —+3→ S —+2→ (U)
8. ajs, gpy, ?, sbk, yhq
   (a) dmv (b) mve
   (c) oua (d) qzi
   Solution: Option (b) is correct.
   Explanation:
   1st letter :
   a —+6→ g —+6→ g (m) —+6→ s —+6→ y
   2nd letter :
   j —+6→ p —+6→ g (v) —+6→ b —+6→ h

3rd letter :

s $\xrightarrow{+6}$ y $\xrightarrow{+6}$ e $\xrightarrow{+6}$ k $\xrightarrow{+6}$ c

9. AB, DEF, HIJK, ?, STUVWX
   (a) LMNO (b) LMNOP
   (c) MNOPQ (d) QRSTU

   Solution: Option (c) is correct.

   Explanation: The number of letters in the terms of the given series increases by one at each step.
   The first letter of each term is two steps ahead of the last letter of the preceding term.
   However, each term consists of consecutive letters in order.

10. Y, B, T, G, O, ?
    (a) N (b) M
    (c) L (d) K

    Solution: Option (c) is correct.

    Explanation: The given sequence is a combination of two series:
    I Y,T, O and
    II B, G, ?
    I Series consist of 2nd, 7th and 12th letters from the end of the English alphabet, while
    II Series consists of 2nd, 7th and 12th letters from the beginning of the English alphabet.
    So, the missing letter in II is the 12th letter from the beginning of the English alphabet, which is L.

11. C, Z, F, X, I, V, L, T, O, ?, ?
    (a) O, P (b) P, Q
    (c) R, R (d) S, R

    Solution: Option (c) is correct.

    Explanation: The given sequence is a combination of two series:
    I. C, F, I, L, O, ?, and II. Z, X, V, T, ?

    The patter in I is

    C $\xrightarrow{+3}$ F $\xrightarrow{+3}$ I $\xrightarrow{+3}$ L $\xrightarrow{+3}$ O $\xrightarrow{+3}$ R

    The patter in II is

    Z $\xrightarrow{-2}$ X $\xrightarrow{-2}$ V $\xrightarrow{-2}$ T $\xrightarrow{-2}$ (R)

☛ ***Direction to solve (12-15):*** *In each of the following letter series, some of the letters are missing which are given in that order as one of the alternatives below it. Choose the correct alternative.*

12. _ tu _ rt _ s _ _ usrtu _
    (a) rtusru (b) rsutrr
    (c) rsurtr (d) rsurts

    Solution: Option (d) is correct.

    Explanation: The series rtus/rtus/rtus/rtus. Thus, the pattern 'rtus' is repeated.

13. _ a _ b _ abaa _ bab _ abb
    (a) aaabb (b) ababb
    (c) babab (d) babba

    Solution: Option (d) is correct.

    Explanation: The series is baa/bba/baa/bba/baa/bb. Thus, the pattern baa/bba is repeated.

14. abca _ bcaab _ ca _ bbc _ a
    (a) ccaa (b) bbaa
    (c) abac (d) abba

    Solution: Option (c) is correct.

    Explanation: The series is abc/aabc/aabbc/aabbcc/(a)

15. ac _ cab _ baca _ aba _ acac
    (a) aacb (b) aebe
    (c) babb (d) bcbb

    Solution: Option (a) is correct.

    Explanation: The series is acac/abab/acac/abab/acac. Thus, the pattern acac/abab is repeated.

Multiple Choice Questions

☛ ***Direction to solve (1 to 35):*** *Choose the correct alternative that will continue the same pattern and replace the question mark in the given series.*

1. 10, 100, 200, 310, ?
   (a) 400 (b) 410
   (c) 420 (d) 430
2. 11, 10, ?, 100, 1001, 1000, 10001
   (a) 101 (b) 110
   (c) 111 (d) None of these
3. 2, 7, 27, 107, 427, ?
   (a) 1262 (b) 1707
   (c) 4027 (d) 4207
4. 2, 3, 8, 27, 112,?
   (a) 226 (b) 339
   (c) 452 (d) 565
5. 6, 17, 39, 72, ?
   (a) 83 (b) 94
   (c) 116 (d) 127
6. 20, 20, 19, 16, 17, 13, 14, 11, ?, ?
   (a) 10, 10 (b) 10, 11
   (c) 13, 14 (d) 13, 16
7. 24, 60, 120, 210, ?
   (a) 300 (b) 336
   (c) 420 (d) 525
8. 625, 5, 125, 25, 25, ?, 5
   (a) 5 (b) 25
   (c) 125 (d) 625
9. 2, 2, 5, 13, 28, ?
   (a) 49 (b) 50
   (c) 51 (d) 52
10. 0, 2, 8, 14, ?, 34
    (a) 20 (b) 23
    (c) 24 (d) 25
11. 1, 5, 14, 30, 55, 91, ?
    (a) 130 (b) 140
    (c) 150 (d) 160

12. In the series 10, 17, 24, 31, 38,..... which of the following will be a number of the series ?
(a) 48 (b) 346
(c) 574 (d) 1003

13. 240, ?, 120, 40, 10, 2
(a) 180 (b) 240
(c) 420 (d) 480

14. 66, 36, 18, ?
(a) 3 (b) 6
(c) 8 (d) 9

15. In the series 3, 9, 15, ... what will be the 21st term?
(a) 117 (b) 121
(c) 123 (d) 129

16. 28, 33, 31, 36, ?, 39
(a) 32 (b) 34
(c) 38 (d) 40

17. 13, 32, 24, 43, 35, ?, 46, 65, 57, 76
(a) 45 (b) 52
(c) 54 (d) 55

18. 22, 24, 28, ?, 52, 84
(a) 36 (b) 38
(c) 42 (d) 46

19. 3, 15, ?, 63, 99, 143
(a) 27 (b) 35
(c) 45 (d) 56

20. 90, 180, 12, 50, 100, 200, ?, 3, 50, 4, 25, 2, 6, 30, 3
(a) 150 (b) 175
(c) 225 (d) 250

21. 120, 99, 80, 63, 48, ?
(a) 35 (b) 38
(c) 39 (d) 40

22. 589654237, 89654237, 8965423, 965423, ?
(a) 58965 (b) 65423
(c) 89654 (d) 96542

23. 3, 10, 101,?
(a) 10101 (b) 10201
(c) 10202 (d) 11012

24. In the series 2, 6, 18, 54, ... what will be the 8th term ?
(a) 4370 (b) 4374
(c) 7443 (d) 7434

25. 125, 80, 45, 20, ?
(a) 5 (b) 8
(c) 10 (d) 12

26. 1, 1, 4, 8, 9, 27, 16, ?
(a) 32 (b) 64
(c) 81 (d) 256

27. 1, 2, 3, 6, 9, 18, ?, 54
(a) 18 (b) 27
(c) 36 (d) 81

28. 6, 13, 25, 51, 101, ?
(a) 201 (b) 202
(c) 203 (d) 205

29. 5, 6, 9, 15, ?, 40
(a) 21 (b) 25
(c) 27 (d) 33

30. 1, 3, 4, 8, 15, 27, ?
(a) 37 (b) 44
(c) 50 (d) 55

31. 3, 4, 7, 7, 13, 13, 21, 22, 31, 34, ?
(a) 42 (b) 43
(c) 51 (d) 52

32. 198, 194, 185, 169, ?
(a) 92 (b) 112
(c) 136 (d) 144

33. 2, 3, 5, 7, 11 ,? , 17
(a) 12 (b) 13
(c) 14 (d) 15

34. 6, 12, 21, ?, 48
(a) 33 (b) 38
(c) 40 (d) 45

35. Which term of the series 5, 10, 20, 40, ... is 1280?
(a) 10th (b) 9th
(c) 8th (d) None of these

☛ ***Direction to solve (36 to 60)** : In this type of questions, one term in the number series is wrong. Find out the wrong term.*

36. 325, 259, 202, 160, 127, 105, 94
(a) 94 (b) 127
(c) 202 (d) 259

37. 1236, 2346, 3456, 4566, 5686
(a) 1236 (b) 3456
(c) 4566 (d) 5686

38. 93, 309, 434, 498, 521, 533
(a) 309 (b) 434
(c) 498 (d) 521

39. 24576, 6144, 1536, 386, 96, 24
(a) 96 (b) 386
(c) 1536 (d) 6144

40. 10, 14, 28, 32, 64, 68, 132
(a) 28 (b) 32
(c) 64 (d) 132

41. 46080, 3840, 384, 48, 24, 2, 1
(a) 384 (b) 48
(c) 24 (d) 2

42. 89, 78, 86, 80, 85, 82, 83
(a) 83 (b) 82
(c) 86 (d) 78

43. 0, 2, 3, 5, 8, 10, 15, 18, 24, 26, 35
(a) 18 (b) 24
(c) 26 (d) 10

44. 5, 27, 61, 122, 213, 340, 509
(a) 27 (b) 61
(c) 122 (d) 509

45. 3, 7, 15, 39, 63, 127, 255, 511
(a) 15 (b) 39
(c) 63 (d) 127

46. 380, 188, 92, 48, 20, 8, 2
(a) 8 (b) 20
(c) 48 (d) 188

47. 16, 22, 30, 45, 52, 66
(a) 30 (b) 45
(c) 52 (d) 66

48. 10, 26, 74, 218, 654, 1946, 5834
(a) 26 (b) 74
(c) 218 (d) 654

49. 25, 36, 49, 81, 121, 169, 225
(a) 36 (b) 49
(c) 169 (d) 225

50. 1, 3, 10, 21, 64, 129, 356, 777
(a) 21 (b) 129
(c) 10 (d) 356

51. 5, 10, 40, 80, 320, 550, 2560
(a) 80 (b) 320
(c) 550 (d) 2560

52. 2, 3, 4, 4, 6, 8, 9, 12, 16
(a) 3 (b) 6
(c) 9 (d) 12

53. 11, 5, 20, 12, 40, 26, 74, 54
(a) 5 (b) 20
(c) 40 (d) 26

54. 2, 6, 24, 96, 285, 568, 567
(a) 6 (b) 24
(c) 285 (d) 567

55. 3, 2, 8, 9, 13, 22, 18, 32, 23, 42
(a) 8 (b) 9
(c) 13 (d) 22

56. 196, 169, 144, 121, 101
(a) 101 (b) 121
(c) 169 (d) 196

57 56, 58, 62, 70, 84, 118, 182
(a) 58 (b) 62
(c) 84 (d) 118

58. 1, 5, 5, 9, 7, 11, 11, 15, 12, 17
(a) 11 (b) 12
(c) 17 (d) 15

59. 15, 16, 22, 29, 45, 70
(a) 16 (b) 22
(c) 45 (d) 70

60. 8, 14, 26, 48, 98, 194, 386
(a) 14 (b) 48
(c) 98 (d) 194

☛ ***Direction to solve (61 to 80) :*** *In each of the following questions, various terms of an alphabet series are given with one or more terms missing as shown by (?). Choose the missing term from the given alternatives.*

61. A, CD, GHI, ?, UVWXY
(a) LMNO (b) MNO
(c) MNOP (d) NOPQ

62. Z, Y, X, U, T, S, P, O, N, K, ?, ?
(a) H,G (b) H, I
(c) I, (d) J, I

63. U, B, I, P, W, ?
(a) D (b) F
(c) Q (d) Z

64. AI, BJ, CK, ?
(a) DL (b) DM
(c) GH (d) LM

65. Z, U, Q, ?, L
(a) I (b) K
(c) M (d) N

66. M, N, O, L, R, I, V, ?
(a) A (b) E
(c) F (d) H

67. B, D, F, I, L, P, ?
(a) R (b) S
(c) T (d) U

68. DHL, PTX, BFJ, ?
(a) CGK (b) KOS
(c) NRV (d) RVZ

69. A, D, H, M, ?, Z
(a) T (b) G
(c) N (d) S

70. Z, ?, T, ?, N, ?, H, ?, B
(a) W, Q, K, E (b) W, R, K, E
(c) X, Q, K, E (d) X, R, K, E

71. ejo tyd ins xch ?
(a) nrw (b) mrw
(c) msx (d) nsx

72. A, B, N, C, D, O, E, F, P, ?, ?, ?
(a) G, H, I (b) G, H, J
(c) G, H, Q (d) J, K, L

73. GH, JL, NQ, SW, YD, ?
(a) EJ (b) FJ
(c) EL (d) FL

74. R, U, X, A, D, ?
(a) F (b) G
(c) H (d) I

75. AYD, BVF, DRH, ?, KGL
(a) FMI (b) GMJ
(c) GLJ (d) HLK

76. AZ, CX, FU, ?
(a) IR (b) IV
(c) JQ (d) KP

77. A, B, B, D, C, F, D; H, E, ?, ?
(a) E, F (b) F, G
(c) F, I (d) J, F

78. Z, X, S, I, R, R, ?, ?
(a) G,I (b) J, I
(c) J,K (d) K,M

79. AYBZC, DWEXF, GUHVI, JSKTL, ?
   (a) MQORN (b) MQNRO
   (c) NQMOR (d) QMONR

80. T, R, P, N, L, ?, ?
   (a) J, G (b) J, H
   (c) K, H (d) K, I

☛ ***Direction to solve (81 to 90) :*** *In each of the following letter series, some of the letters are missing, which are given in the order as one of the alternatives below it. Choose the correct alternative.*

81. bca _ b _ aabc __ a __ caa
   (a) acab (b) bcbb
   (c) cbab (d) ccab

82. ab __ d __ aaba __ na _ badna _ b
   (a) andaa (b) babda
   (c) badna (d) dbanb

83. m _ nm _ n _ an _ a _ ma _
   (a) aamnan (b) ammanm
   (c) aammnn (d) amammn

84. _bcc _ ac _ aabb _ ab _ cc
   (a) aabca (b) abaca
   (c) bacab (d) bcaca

85. _ op _ mo _ n _ _ pnmop _.
   (a) mnpmon (b) mpnmop
   (c) mnompn (d) mnpomn

86. ab _ aa _ bbb _ aaa _ bbba
   (a) abba (b) baab
   (c) aaab (d) abab

87. _ nmmn _ mmnn _ mnnm _
   (a) nmmn (b) mnnm
   (c) nnmm (d) nmnm

88. a _ n _ b _ _ ncb _ _ ncb
   (a) abbbec (b) abebeb
   (c) bacbab (d) bcabab

89. a _ ba _ b _ b _ a _ b
   (a) abaab (b) abbab
   (c) aabba (d) bbabb

90. cccbb _ aa _ cc _ bbbaa _ c
   (a) aebe (b) baca
   (c) baba (d) acbaA

Answer Key

1. (d)	**16.** (b)	**31.** (b)	**46.** (c)	**61.** (c)	**76.** (c)
2. (a)	**17.** (c)	**32.** (d)	**47.** (b)	**62.** (d)	**77.** (d)
3. (b)	**18.** (a)	**33.** (b)	**48.** (d)	**63.** (a)	**78.** (a)
4. (d)	**19.** (b)	**34.** (a)	**49.** (a)	**64.** (a)	**79.** (b)
5. (c)	**20.** (a)	**35.** (b)	**50.** (d)	**65.** (d)	**80.** (b)
6. (a)	**21.** (a)	**36.** (c)	**51.** (c)	**66.** (b)	**81.** (a)
7. (b)	**22.** (d)	**37.** (d)	**52.** (c)	**67.** (c)	**82.** (a)
8. (c)	**23.** (c)	**38.** (d)	**53.** (c)	**68.** (c)	**83.** (c)
9. (d)	**24.** (b)	**39.** (b)	**54.** (b)	**69.** (d)	**84.** (c)
10. (c)	**25.** (a)	**40.** (d)	**55.** (b)	**70.** (a)	**85.** (a)
11. (b)	**26.** (b)	**41.** (c)	**56.** (a)	**71.** (b)	**86.** (b)
12. (b)	**27.** (b)	**42.** (c)	**57.** (c)	**72.** (c)	**87.** (c)
13. (b)	**28.** (c)	**43.** (a)	**58.** (b)	**73.** (d)	**88.** (d)
14. (c)	**29.** (b)	**44.** (a)	**59.** (b)	**74.** (b)	**89.** (d)
15. (c)	**30.** (c)	**45.** (b)	**60.** (b)	**75.** (b)	**90.** (b)

Explanatory Notes

1. (d)
The pattern is + 90 + 100, + 110,.....
So, the missing term = 310 + 120 = 430

2. (a)
The pattern is – 1, × 10 + 1, – 1, × 10 + 1, – 1, × 10 + 1, ...
So, the missing term = 10 × 10 + 1 = 101

3. (b)
The pattern is + 5, + 20, + 80, + 320, ... i.e. + (5×1^2), + (5×2^2), + (5×4^2), + (5×8^2),.....
So, the missing term = $427 + (5 \times 16^2)$
= 427 + 1280 = 1707

4. (d)
The pattern is × 1 + 1, × 2 + 2, × 3 + 3, × 4 + 4,.....
So, the missing term = 112 × 5 + 5 = 565

5. (c)
The pattern is + 11, + 22, + 33, ...
So, the missing term = 72 + 44 = 116

6. (a)
Let the missing terms of the series be x_1 and x_2.
Thus, the sequence 20, 20, 19, 16, 17, 13, 14, 11, x_1, x_2 is a combination of two series :
I Series 20, 19, 17, 14, x_1
II Series 20, 16, 13, 11, x_2
The pattern in I Series is – 1, – 2, – 3,......So, the missing term, x_1 = 14 – 4 = 10
The pattern in II Series is – 4, – 3, – 2,......So, the missing term, x_2 = 11 – 1 = 10

7. (b)
The pattern is + 36, + 60, + 90,.....i.e. + [6 × (6 + 0)], + [6 × (6 + 4)], + [6 × (6 + 9)],...
So, the missing term = 210 + [6 × (6 + 15)]
= 210 + 126 = 336

8. (c)
The given sequence is a combination of two series:
I. 625, 125, 25, 5
II. 5, 25, ?
The pattern in I series is ÷ 5, while that in II series is × 5. So, the missing term = 25 × 5 = 125

9. (d)
The pattern is + 0, + 3, + 8, + 15, ... i.e. + $(1^2 - 1)$, + $(2^2 - 1)$, + $(3^2 - 1)$, + $(4^2 - 1)$, ...
So, the missing term = $28 + (5^2 - 1)$ = 28 + 24
= 52

10. (c)
The pattern is + 2, + 6, + 6, + 10, + 10,.....
So, the missing term = 14 + 10 = 24

11. (b)
The pattern is + 4, + 9, + 16, + 25, + 36, ... i.e. + 2^2, + 3^2, + 4^2, + 5^2, + 6^2,.....
So, the missing term = $91 + 7^2$ = 91 + 49 = 140

12. (b)
The given series consists of numbers each of which, on dividing by 7, leaves a remainder 3. No other number except 346 satisfies the property.

13. (b)
The pattern is ÷ 1, ÷ 2, ÷ 3, ÷ 4, ÷ 5
So, the missing term = 240 ÷ 1 = 240

14. (c)
Each term in the series is the product of digits of the preceding term.
So, the missing term = 1 × 8 = 8

15. (c)
Clearly, 3 + 6 = 9, 9 + 6 = 15,.....
So, the series is an A.P. in which a = 3 and d = 6
Therefore 21st term $= a + (21 - 1)\,d$
$= a + 20d$
$= 3 + 20 \times 6 = 123$

16. (b)
The pattern is + 5, – 2, + 5, – 2, ...
So, the missing term = 36 – 2 = 34

17. (c)
The given sequence is a combination of two series:
I. 13, 24, 35, 46, 57
II. 32, 43, ?, 65, 76
The pattern in both I and II series is + 11. So, the missing term = 43 + 11 = 54

18. (a)
The pattern is + 2, + 4, + 8, + 16,.....
So, the missing term = 28 + 8 = 36

19. (b)
The terms of the given series are $(2^2 - 1)$, $(4^2 - 1)$,....., $(8^2 - 1)$, $(10^2 - 1)$, $(12^2 - 1)$
So, the missing term = $(6^2 - 1) - (36 - 1) = 35$

20. (a)
Clearly, 90 = 30 × 3, 180 = 6 × 30, 12 = 2 × 6
50 = 25 × 2, 100 = 4 × 25, 200 = 50 × 4
So, the missing term = 3 × 50 = 150.

21. (a)
The pattern is – 21, – 19, – 17, – 15,.....
So, the missing term = 48 – 13 = 35

22. (d)
The digits are removed one by one from the beginning and the end in order alternately so as to obtain the subsequent terms of the series.

23. (c)
Each term in the series is obtained by adding 1 to the square of the preceding term
So, the missing term = $(101)^2 + 1 = 10202$

24. (b)
Clearly, 2 × 3 = 6, 6 × 3 = 18, 18 × 3 = 54,.....
So, the series is a G.P. in which a = 2, r = 3.
Therefore 8th term $= ar^{8-1} = ar^7 = 2 \times 3^7$
$= (2 \times 2187) = 4374$

25. (a)
The pattern is – 45, – 35, – 25, ...
So, the missing term = 20 – 15 = 5

26. (b)
The series consists of squares and cubes of consecutive natural numbers i.e. $1^2, 1^3, 2^2, 2^3, 3^2, 3^3, 4^2$, ...
So, the missing term = $4^3 = 64$

27. (b)
The pattern is × 2, × 3/2, × 2, × 3/2, × 2,.....
So, the missing term = 18 × 3/2 = 27

28. (c)
The pattern is × 2 + 1, × 2 – 1, × 2 + 1, × 2 – 1,.....
So, the missing term = 101 × 2 + 1 = 203

29. (b)
The pattern is + 1, + 3, + 6,....., i.e. + 1, + (1, + 2), + (1 + 2 + 3),.....
So, the missing term = 15 + (1 + 2 + 3 + 4) = 25

30. (c)
The sum of any three consecutive terms of the series gives the next term.
So, the missing number = 8 + 15 + 27 = 50

31. (b)
The given sequence is a combination of two series:
I: 3, 7, 13, 21, 31, ? and II: 4, 7, 13, 22, 34
The pattern in I series is + 4, + 6, + 8, + 10,.....
The pattern in II series is + 3, + 6, + 9, + 12,.....
So, the missing term = 31 + 12 = 43

32. (d)
The pattern is – 4, – 9, – 16,.....i.e. $-2^2, -3^2, -4^2$,.....
So, the missing pattern $= 169 - 5^2 = 169 - 25$
$= 144$

33. (b)
Clearly, the given series consists of prime numbers starting from 2. So, the missing term is the prime number after 11, which is 13

34. (a)
The pattern is + 6, + 9, + 12, + 15, ...
So, the missing term = 21 + 12 = 33

35. (b)
Clearly, 5 × 2 = 10, 10 × 2 = 20, 20 × 2 = 40,.....
So, the series is a G.P. in which a = 5 and r = 2.
Let 1280 be the nth term of the series
Then, $5 \times 2^{n-1} = 1280 \iff 2^{n-1} = 256 = 2^8$
$\iff n - 1 = 8 \iff n = 9$

36. (c)
The correct pattern is – 66, – 55, – 44, – 33, – 22, – 11.
So, 202 is wrong and must be replaced by (259 – 55) i.e. 204.

37. (d)
The correct pattern in the series is + 1110.
So, 5686 is wrong and must be replaced by (4566 + 1110) i.e. 5676.

38. (d)
The correct pattern is + 6^3, + 5^3, + 4^3, + 3^3, ...
So, 521 is wrong and must be replaced by $(498 + 3^3)$ i.e. 525.

39. (b)
Each term of the series is obtained by dividing the preceding term by 4.
So, 386 is wrong and must be replaced by (1536 divided by 4) i.e. 384.

40. (d)
The correct pattern is + 4, × 2, + 4, × 2, ...
So, 132 is wrong and must be replaced by (68 × 2) i.e. 136.

41. (c)
The correct pattern is ÷ 12, ÷ 10, ÷ 8, ÷ 6,.....
So, 24 is wrong and must be replaced by (48 ÷ 6) i.e. 8.

42. (c)
The correct pattern is – 11, + 9, – 7, + 5, – 3, + 1.
So, 86 is wrong and must be replaced by (78 + 9) i.e. 87.

43. (a)
The given sequence is a combination of two series:
I. 0, 3, 8, 15, 24, 35
II. 2, 5, 10, 18, 26
The pattern in both I and II series is + 3, + 5, + 7, + 9,.....
So, in II series, 18 is wrong and must be replaced by (10 + 7) = 17

44. (a)
The terms of the series are $(2^3 - 3)$, $(3^3 - 3)$, $(4^3 - 3)$, $(5^3 - 3)$, $(6^3 - 3)$, $(7^3 - 3)$, $(8^3 - 3)$.
So, 27 is wrong and must be replaced by $(3^3 - 3) = 24$

45. (b)
The correct pattern is × 2 + 1
So, 39 is wrong and must be replaced by (15 – 2 + 1) = 31.

46. (c)
The correct pattern is – 192, – 96, – 48, – 24, – 12, – 6.
So, 48 is wrong and must be replaced by (92 – 48) = 44.

47. (b)
The correct pattern is + 6, + 8, + 10, + 12, + 14.
So, 45 is wrong and must be replaced by (30 + 10) = 40.

48. (d)
The correct pattern is × 3 – 4
So, 654 is wrong and must be replaced by (218 × 3 – 4) i.e. 650.

49. (a)
The correct sequence is 5^2, 7^2, 9^2, 11^2, 13^2, 15^2. So, 36 is wrong.

50. (d)
The correct pattern is × 2 + 1, × 3 + 1, × 2 + 1, × 3 + 1,.....
So, 356 is wrong and must be replaced by (129 × 3 + 1) = 388

51. (c)
The correct pattern is × 2, × 4, × 2, × 4, ...
So, 550 is wrong and must be replaced by (320 × 2) = 640

52. (c)
The given sequence is a combination of three series:
I. 1st, 4th, 7th terms i.e. 2, 4, 9,.....
II. 2nd, 5th, 8th terms i.e. 3, 6, 12,.....
III. 3rd, 6th, 9th terms i.e. 4, 8, 16,.....
In each one of I, II and III, each term is twice the preceding term. So, 9 is wrong and must be replaced by (4 × 2) i.e. 8.

53. (c)
The given sequence is a combination of two series :
I. 11, 20, 40, 74 and II. 5, 12, 26, 54
The correct pattern in I is + 9, + 18, + 36,.....
So, 40 is wrong and must be replaced by (20 + 18) i.e. 38.

54. (b)
The correct pattern is × 6 – 6, × 5 – 5, × 4 – 4,.....
So, 24 is wrong and must be replaced by (6 x 5 - 5) i.e. 25.

55. (b)
The given sequence is a combination of two series:
I. 3, 8, 13, 18, 23 and II. 2, 9, 22, 32, 42
The pattern in I series is + 5, and the pattern in II series is + 10. So, in II, 9 is wrong and must be replaced by (2 + 10) i.e. 12.

56. (a)
The sequence is $(14)^2$, $(13)^2$, $(12)^2$, $(11)^2$, $(10)^2$.
So, 101 is wrong and must be replaced by $(10)^2$ i.e. 100.

57. (c)
The correct pattern is + 2, + 4, + 8, + 16, + 32, + 64 i.e. + 2, + 2^2, + 2^3, + 2^4, + 2^5, + 2^6.
So, 84 is wrong and must be replaced by (70 + 16) i.e. 86.

58. (b)
The given sequence is a combination of two series:
I. 1, 5, 7, 11, 12
II. 5, 9, 11, 15, 17
The pattern in both I series and II series is + 4, + 2, + 4, + 2. So, 12 is wrong and must be replaced by (11 + 2) i.e. 13.

59. (b)
The correct pattern is + 1, + 4, + 9, + 16, + 25 i.e. + 1^2, + 2^2, + 3^2, + 4^2, + 5^2
So, 22 is wrong and must be replaced by (16 + 4) i.e. 20

60. (b)
The correct pattern is × 2 – 2.
So, 48 is wrong and must be replaced by (26 × 2 – 2) i.e. 50.

61. (c)
Each term consists of consecutive letters in order. The number of letters in the terms goes on increasing by one at each step.
Also, there is a gap of one letter between the last letter of the first term and the first letter of the second term; a gap of two letters between the last letter of the second term and the first letter of the third term; and so on.
So, there should be a gap of three letters between the last letter of the third term and the first letter of the desired term.

62. (d)

(Z → Y → X) $\xrightarrow{-3}$ (U → T → S) $\xrightarrow{-3}$ (P → O → N) $\xrightarrow{-3}$ (K → (J) → (I))

63. (a)

U $\xrightarrow{+7}$ B $\xrightarrow{+7}$ I $\xrightarrow{+7}$ P $\xrightarrow{+7}$ W $\xrightarrow{+7}$ (D)

64. (a)
1st Letter :

A $\xrightarrow{+1}$ B $\xrightarrow{+1}$ C $\xrightarrow{+1}$ (D)

2nd Letter :

$$I \xrightarrow{+1} J \xrightarrow{+1} K \xrightarrow{+1} \text{(L)}$$

65. (d)

$$Z \xrightarrow{-5} U \xrightarrow{-4} Q \xrightarrow{-3} \text{(N)} \xrightarrow{-2} L$$

66. (b)
The given sequence is a combination of two series:
I. M, O, R, V and II. N, L, I, ?
The pattern in I is :

$$M \xrightarrow{+2} O \xrightarrow{+3} R \xrightarrow{-4} V$$

The pattern in II is :

$$N \xrightarrow{-2} L \xrightarrow{-3} I \xrightarrow{-4} \text{(E)}$$

67. (c)

$$B \xrightarrow{12} D \xrightarrow{12} F \xrightarrow{13} I \xrightarrow{13} L \xrightarrow{14} P \xrightarrow{14} \text{(T)}$$

68. (c)
1st Letter :

$$D \xrightarrow{+12} P \xrightarrow{+12} B \xrightarrow{+12} \text{(N)}$$

2nd Letter :

$$H \xrightarrow{+12} T \xrightarrow{+12} F \xrightarrow{+12} \text{(R)}$$

3rd Letter :

$$L \xrightarrow{+12} X \xrightarrow{+12} J \xrightarrow{+12} \text{(V)}$$

69. (d)

$$A \xrightarrow{+3} D \xrightarrow{+4} H \xrightarrow{+5} M \xrightarrow{+6} \text{(S)} \xrightarrow{+7} Z$$

70. (a)

$$Z \xrightarrow{-6} T \xrightarrow{-6} N \xrightarrow{-6} H \xrightarrow{-6} B$$

$$Z \xrightarrow{-3} \text{(W)} \xrightarrow{-3} T \xrightarrow{-3} \text{(O)} \xrightarrow{-3} N \xrightarrow{-3} \text{(K)} \xrightarrow{-3} H \xrightarrow{-3} \text{(E)} \rightarrow B$$

71. (b)
There is a gap of four letters between the first and second, the second and third letters of each term, and also between the last letter of a term and the first letter of the next term.

72. (c)
The given series may be divided into 2 groups :
I. A, B, C, D, E, F, ?, ? and II. N, O, P, ?
Clearly, the given series consists of two terms of I followed by one term of II.
The missing terms in I are G and H while the missing term in II is Q.

73. (d)
1st letter :

$$G \xrightarrow{+3} J \xrightarrow{+4} N \xrightarrow{+5} S \xrightarrow{+6} Y \xrightarrow{+7} \text{(F)}$$

2nd letter :

$$H \xrightarrow{+4} L \xrightarrow{+5} Q \xrightarrow{+6} W \xrightarrow{+7} D \xrightarrow{+8} \text{(L)}$$

74. (b)

$$R \xrightarrow{+3} U \xrightarrow{+3} X \xrightarrow{+3} A \xrightarrow{+3} D \xrightarrow{+3} G$$

75. (b)
1st letter :

$$A \xrightarrow{+1} B \xrightarrow{+2} D \xrightarrow{+3} G \xrightarrow{+4} \text{(K)}$$

2nd letter :

$$Y \xrightarrow{-3} V \xrightarrow{-4} R \xrightarrow{-5} M \xrightarrow{+4} \text{(G)}$$

3rd letter :

$$D \xrightarrow{+2} F \xrightarrow{+2} H \xrightarrow{+2} J \xrightarrow{+2} \text{(L)}$$

76. (c)
1st letter :

$$A \xrightarrow{+2} C \xrightarrow{-3} F \xrightarrow{+4} \text{(J)}$$

2nd letter :

$$Z \xrightarrow{-2} X \xrightarrow{-3} U \xrightarrow{-4} \text{(Q)}$$

77. (d)
The given sequence is a combination of two series :
I. 1st, 3rd, 5th, 7th, 9th, 11th terms i.e. A, B, C, D, E, ?
II. 2nd, 4th, 6th, 8th, 10th terms i.e. B, D, F, H, ?
Clearly, I consists of consecutive letters while II consists of alternate letters. So, the missing letter in I is F, while that in II is J. So, the missing terms i.e. 10th and 11th terms are J and F respectively.

78. (a)

$$Z \xrightarrow{-2} X \xrightarrow{-5} S \xrightarrow{-10} I \xrightarrow{-17} R \xrightarrow{-26} R \xrightarrow{-37} \text{(G)} \xrightarrow{-50} \text{(I)}$$

Note that the numbers representing the difference between the consecutive terms of the series again from a series - 2, 5, 10, 17, 26, 37, 50 - in which the pattern is +3, +5, +7, +9, +11, +13.

79. (b)
1st letter :

$$A \xrightarrow{+3} D \xrightarrow{+3} G \xrightarrow{+3} J \xrightarrow{+3} \text{(M)}$$

2nd letter :

$$Y \xrightarrow{-2} W \xrightarrow{-2} U \xrightarrow{-2} S \xrightarrow{-2} \text{(Q)}$$

3rd letter :

$$B \xrightarrow{+3} E \xrightarrow{+3} H \xrightarrow{+3} K \xrightarrow{+3} \text{(N)}$$

80. (b)

$$T \xrightarrow{-2} R \xrightarrow{-2} P \xrightarrow{-2} N \xrightarrow{-2} L \xrightarrow{-2} \text{(J)} \xrightarrow{-2} \text{(H)}$$

81. (a)
The series is bca<u>a</u>/b<u>c</u>aa/bc<u>a</u>a/<u>b</u>caa. Thus, the pattern 'bcaa' is repeated.

82. (a)
The series is ab<u>a</u>d<u>n</u>a/aba<u>d</u>na/<u>a</u>badna/<u>a</u>b. Thus, the pattern 'abadna' is repeated.

83. (c)
The series is man/man/man/man/man. Thus, the pattern 'man' is repeated.

84. (c)
The series is bbccaa/ccaabb/aabbcc. Thus, the letter pairs move in a cyclic order.

85. (a)
The series is mopn/mopn/mopn/mopn. Thus, the pattern 'mopn' is repeated.

86. (b)
The series is abb/aaabbb/aaaabbbb/a. Thus the letters are repeated twice, then thrice, then four times and so on.

87. (c)
The series is nnmm/nnmn/nnmm/nnmm. Thus, the pattern 'nnmm' is repeated.

88. (d)
The series is abncb/abncb/abncb. Thus, the pattern 'abncb' is repeated.

89. (d)
The series is abb/abb/abb/abb. Thus, the pattern 'abb' is repeated.

90. (b)
The series is ccc bbb aaa/ccc bbb aaa/c. Thus, the pattern ccc bbb aaa is repeated.

❐

Previous Year Questions

☛ ***Direction to solve (1 to 4) :*** *Choose the correct alternative that will continue the same pattern and replace the question mark in the given series.*

1. 2, 5, 9, ?, 20, 27
[NTSE 2005 - UP first stage paper]
(a) 14 (b) 16
(c) 18 (d) 24

2. 2, 3, 3, 5, 10, 13, ?, 43, 172, 177
[NTSE 2003 – Delhi first stage paper]
(a) 23 (b) 38
(c) 39 (d) 40

3. 9, 27, 31, 155, 161, 1127, ?
[NTSE 2005 - Assam first stage paper]
(a) 316 (b) 1135
(c) 1288 (d) 2254

4. 13, 32, 24, 43, 35, ?, 46, 65, 57, 76
[NTSE 2012 - UP first stage paper]
(a) 45 (b) 52
(c) 54 (d) 55

☛ ***Direction to solve: (5 to 6)*** *: In this type of questions, one term in the number series is wrong. Find out the wrong term.*

5. 3, 10, 27, 4, 16, 64, 5, 25, 125
[NTSE 2005 - Delhi first stage paper]
(a) 3 (b) 4
(c) 10 (d) 27

6. 1, 5, 9, 15, 25, 37, 49
[NTSE 2004 - Bihar first stage paper]
(a) 9 (b) 15
(c) 25 (d) 37

7. Choose the missing terms out of the given alternatives.
PMT, OOS, NQR, MSQ, ?
[NTSE 2000 - Goa first stage paper]
(a) LUP (b) LVP
(c) LVR (d) LWP

☛ ***Direction to solve (8 to 15) :*** *In each of the following letter series, some of the letters are missing, which are given in that order as one of the alternatives below it. Choose the correct alternative.*

8. _ aa _ ba _ bb _ ab _ aab
[NTSE 2005 – Tamilnadu first stage paper]
(a) aaabb (b) babab
(c) bbaab (d) bbbaa

9. c _ bba _ cab _ ac _ ab _ ac
[NTSE 2002 - UP first stage paper]
(a) abebe (b) acbcb
(c) babec (d) bcacb

10. ba _ cb _ b _ bab _
[NTSE 1999 - Meghalaya first stage paper]
(a) acbb (b) bacc
(c) bcaa (d) cabb

11. _ bc _ ca _ aba _ c _ ca
[NTSE 2001 - Punjab first stage paper]
(a) abcbb (b) bbbec
(c) bacba (d) abbec

12. ab _ _ baa _ _ ab _
[NTSE 2003 - Orissa first stage paper]
(a) aaaaa (b) aabaa
(c) aabab (d) baabb

13. _ _aba _ _ ba _ ab
[NTSE 2012 –Himachal Pradesh first stage Paper]
(a) abbba (b) abbab
(c) baabb (d) bbaba

14. c _ bbb _ _ abbbb _ abbb _
[NTSE 2002 – Jammu second stage paper]
(a) aabcb (b) abccb
(c) abacb (d) baebb

15. _ bbca _ bcca _ ac _ a _ cb
NTSE 2000 - WB first stage paper]
(a) abeba (b) acbab
(c) bacab (d) bcaajb

❐

Answer Key

1. (a)	2. (c)	3. (b)	4. (c)	5. (c)	6. (b)	7. (a)	8. (c)	9. (b)	10. (b)	11. (a)
12. (b)	13. (b)	14. (b)	15. (b)							

Explanatory Notes

1. (a)
The pattern is + 3, + 4, + 5, + 6,.....
So, missing term = 9 + 5 = 14

2. (c)
The pattern is + 1, × 1, + 2, × 2, + 3, × 3, + 4, × 4, + 5
So, missing term = 13 × 3 = 39

3. (b)
The pattern is × 3, + 4, × 5, + 6, × 7,.....
So, missing term = 1127 + 8 = 1135

4. (c)
The given sequence is a combination of two series:
I : 13, 24, 35, 46, 57
II : 32, 43, ?, 65, 76
The pattern in both I and II is + 11. So, missing term = 43 + 11 = 54

5. (c)
The correct sequence is 3, 3^2, 3^3, 4, 4^2, 4^3, 5, 5^2, 5^3.
So, 10 is wrong and must be replaced by 3^2 i.e. 9.

6. (b)
The terms of the given series are 1^2, $(2^2 + 1)$, 3^2, $(4^2..+ 1)$, 5^2, $(6^2 + 1)$, 7^2.
So, 15 is wrong and must be replaced by $(4^2 + 1)$ i.e. 17.

7. (a)
1st letter :
P $\xrightarrow{-1}$ O $\xrightarrow{-1}$ N $\xrightarrow{-1}$ M $\xrightarrow{-1}$ (L)
2ns letter :
M $\xrightarrow{+2}$ O $\xrightarrow{+2}$ Q $\xrightarrow{+2}$ S $\xrightarrow{+2}$ (U)
3rd letter :
T $\xrightarrow{-1}$ S $\xrightarrow{-1}$ R $\xrightarrow{-1}$ Q $\xrightarrow{-1}$ (P)

8. (c)
The series is baab/baab/baab/baab. Thus, the pattern 'baab' is repeated.

9. (b)
The series is cabbac/cabbac/cabbac. Thus, the pattern 'cabbac' is repeated.

10. (b)
The series is babc/babc/babc. Thus, the pattern 'babc' is repeated.

11. (a)
The series is abc/bca/cab/abc/bca, Thus, the letters change places in a cyclic order.

12. (b)
The series is aba/aba/aba/aba Thus, the pattern 'aba' is repeated.

13. (b)
The series is ab/ab/ab/ab/ab/ab. Thus, the pattern 'ab' is repeated.

14. (b)
The series is cabbbb/cabbbb/cabbbb. Thus, the pattern 'cabbbb' is repeated.

15. (b)
The series is abbc/ac/bcca/ba/caab/cb.

❒

UNIT 6

Arithmetical Reasoning Test

Arithmetic Reasoning tests the ability to solve basic arithmetic problems encountered in everyday life. These problems require basic mathematical skills like addition, subtraction, multiplication, division etc. The tests include operations with whole numbers, rational numbers, ratio and proportion, interest and percentage, and measurement. Arithmetic reasoning is one factor that helps characterize mathematics comprehension, and it also assesses logical thinking.

Solved Examples

1. If a clock takes seven seconds to strike seven, how long will it take to strike ten?
   (a) 7 seconds (b) 9 seconds
   (c) 10 seconds (d) None of these
   Solution: Option (d) is correct.
   Explanation: Clearly, seven strikes of a clock have 6 intervals while 10 strikes have 9 intervals
   $\therefore$ Required time $=\left(\frac{7}{6}\times 9\right)=10.5$ seconds

2. If every 2 out of 3 readymade shirts need alterations in the sleeves, and every 4 out of 5 need it in the body, how many alterations will be required for 60 shirts ?
   (a) 88 (b) 123
   (c) 133 (d) 143
   Solution: Option (c) is correct.
   Explanation: Number of alterations required in 1 shirt
   $$=\left(\frac{2}{3}+\frac{3}{4}+\frac{4}{5}\right)=\frac{133}{60}$$
   $\therefore$ Number of alterations required in 60 shirts
   $$=\left(\frac{133}{60}\times 60\right)=133$$

3. At the end of a business conference the ten people present all shake hands with each other once. How many handshakes will there be altogether?
   (a) 20 (b) 45
   (c) 55 (d) 90
   Solution: Option (b) is correct.
   Explanation: Clearly, total number of handshakes $= (9 + 8 + 7 + 6 + 5 + 4 + 3 + 2 + 1)$
   $= 45$.

4. Nitin's age was equal to square of some number last year and the following year it would be cube of a number. If again Nitin's age has to be equal to the cube of some number, then for how long he will have to wait?
   (a) 10 years (b) 38 years
   (c) 39 years (d) 64 years
   Solution: Option (b) is correct.
   Explanation: Clearly, we have to first find two numbers whose difference is 2 and of which the smaller one is a perfect square and the bigger one a perfect cube.
   Such numbers are 25 and 27.
   Thus, Nitin is now 26 years old. Since the next perfect cube after 27 is 64
   So required time period = (64 – 26) years = 38 years.

5. An enterprising businessman earns an income of Re. 1 on the first day of his business. On every subsequent day, he earns an income which is just double of that made on the previous day. On the 10th day of business, his income is
   (a) Rs. 2^9 (b) Rs. 2^{10}
   (c) Rs. 2^{10} (d) Rs. 10^2
   Solution: Option (a) is correct.
   Explanation: Income on the first day = Re. 1
   Income on the 2nd day = Rs. (1×2) = Rs. 2^1
   Income on the 3rd day = Rs. $(2^1 \times 2)$
   = Rs. 2^2 and so on
   Thus, Income on the rth day = Rs. 2^{n-1}
   Therefore Income on the 10th day = Rs. 2^9

6. A number consists of two digits whose sum is 11. If 27 is added to the number, then the digits change their places. What is the number?
   (a) 47 (b) 65
   (c) 83 (d) 92
   Solution: Option (a) is correct.
   Explanation: Let the ten's digit be x. Then, unit's digit $= (11 - x)$.
   So, number $= 10x + (11 - x) = 9x + 11$
   Therefore $(9x + 11) + 27 = 10(11 - x) + x$
   $\Leftrightarrow 9x + 38 = 110 - 9x$ $18x = 72, x = 4$
   Thus, ten's digit = 4 and unit's digit = 7
   Hence, required number = 47

7. A monkey climbs 30 feet at the beginning of each hour and rests for a while when he slips back 20 feet before he again starts climbing in the beginning of the next hour. If he begins his ascent at 8.00 a.m., at what time will he first touch a flag at 120 feet from the ground?
(a) 4 p.m. (b) 5 p.m.
(c) 6 p.m. (d) None of these
Solution: Option (c) is correct.
Explanation: Net ascent of the monkey in 1 hour
= (30 – 20) feet = 10 feet
So, the monkey ascends 90 feet in 9 hours i.e. till 5 p.m. Clearly, in the next 1 hour i.e. till 6 p.m. the monkey ascends remaining 30 feet to touch the flag.

8. In a caravan, in addition to 50 hens, there are 45 goats and 8 camels with some keepers. If the total number of feet be 224 more than the number of heads in the caravan, the number of keepers is
(a) 5 (b) 8
(c) 10 (d) 15
Solution: Option (d) is correct.
Explanation: Let the number of keepers be x. Then,
Total number of feet
$= 2 \times 50 + 4 \times 45 + 4 \times 8 + 2x = 2x + 312$
Total number of heads $= 50 + 45 + 8 + x = 103 + x$
Therefore $(2x + 312) = (103 + x) + 224$ or $x = 15$

9. A group of 1200 persons consisting of captains and soldiers is travelling in a train. For every 15 soldiers there is one captain. The number of captains in the group is:
(a) 85 (b) 80
(c) 75 (d) 70
Solution: Option (c) is correct.
Explanation: Clearly, out of every 16 persons, there is one captain. So, the number of captains (1200/16) = 75

10. A player holds 13 cards of four suits, of which seven are black and six are red. There are twice as many diamonds as spades and twice as many hearts as diamonds. How many clubs does he hold?
(a) 4 (b) 5
(c) 6 (d) 7
Solution: Option (c) is correct.
Explanation: Clearly, the black cards are either clubs or spades while the red cards are either diamonds or hearts.
Let the number of spades be x. Then, the number of clubs $= (7 - x)$
Number of diamonds $= 2x$ number of spades $= 2x$
Number of hearts $= 2x$ number of diamonds $= 4x$
Total number of cards $= x + 2x + 4x + 7 - x - 6x + 7$
Therefore $6x + 7 = 13 \Leftrightarrow 6x = 6 \Leftrightarrow x - 1$
Hence, number of clubs $= (7 - x) = 6$

Multiple Choice Questions

1. Ayush was born two years after his father's marriage. His mother is five years younger than his father but 20 years older than Ayush who is 10 years old. At what age did the father get married?
(a) 23 years (b) 25 years
(c) 33 years (d) 35 years

2. At a dinner party every two guests used a bowl of rice between them, every three guests used a bowl of dal between them and every four used a bowl of mutton between them. There were altogether 65 dishes. How many guests were present at the party?
(a) 60 (b) 65
(c) 90 (d) None of these

3. In a family, each daughter has the same number of brothers as she has sisters and each son has twice as many sisters as he has brothers. How many sons are there in the family?
(a) 2 (b) 3
(c) 4 (d) 5

4. The total number of digits used in numbering the pages of a book having 366 pages is
(a) 732 (b) 990
(c) 1098 (d) 1305

5. In a cricket match, five batsmen A, B, C, D and E scored an average of 36 runs. D Scored 5 more than E; E scored 8 fewer than A; B scored as many as D and E combined; and B and C scored 107 between them. How many runs did E score?
(a) 62 (b) 45
(c) 28 (d) 20

6. In three coloured boxes - Red, Green and Blue, 108 balls are placed. There are twice as many balls in the green and red boxes combined as there are in the blue box and twice as many in the blue box as there are in the red box. How many balls are there in the green box?
(a) 18 (b) 36
(c) 45 (d) None of these

7. In a family, the father took 1/4 of the cake and he had 3 times as much as each of the other members had. The total number of family members is
(a) 3 (b) 7
(c) 10 (d) 12

8. A shepherd had 17 sheep. All but nine died. How many was he left with?
(a) Nil (b) 8
(c) 9 (d) 17

9. The number of boys in a class is three times the number of girls. Which one of the following numbers cannot represent the total number of children in the class?
(a) 48 (b) 44
(c) 42 (d) 40

10. Ravi's brother is 3 years senior to him. His father was 28 years of age when his sister was born while his mother was 26 years of age when he was born. If his sister was 4 years of age when his brother was born, what were the ages of Ravi's father and mother respectively when his brother was born?
(a) 32 years, 23 years (b) 32 years, 29 years
(c) 35 years, 29 years (d) 35 years, 33 years

11. A certain number of horses and an equal number of men are going somewhere. Half of the owners are on their horses' back while the remaining ones are walking along leading their horses. If the number of legs walking on the ground is 70, how many horses are there?
(a) 10 (b) 12
(c) 14 (d) 16

12. When Rahul was born, his father was 32 years older than his brother and his mother was 25 years older than his sister. If Rahul's brother is 6 years older than him and his mother is 3 years younger than his father, how old was Rahul's sister when he was born?
(a) 7 years (b) 10 years
(c) 14 years (d) 19 years

13. In a class, 20% of the members own only two cars each, 40% of the remaining own three cars each and the remaining members own only one car each. Which of the following statements is definitely true from the given statements?
(a) Only 20% of the total members own three cars each.
(b) 48% of the total members own only one car each.
(c) 60% of the total members own at least two cars each.
(d) 80% of the total members own at least one car.

14. Three friends had dinner at a restaurant. When the bill was received, Amita paid 2/3 as much as Veena paid and Veena paid 1/2 as much as Tanya paid. What fraction of the bill did Veena pay?
(a) 1/3 (b) 3/11
(c) 12/13 (d) 5/8

15. What is the smallest number of ducks that could swim in this formation - two ducks in front of a duck, two ducks behind a duck and a duck between two ducks?
(a) 3 (b) 5
(c) 7 (d) 9

16. Mr. Johnson was to earn £ 300 and a free holiday for seven weeks' work. He worked for only 4 weeks and earned £ 30 and a free holiday. What was the value of the holiday?
(a) £ 300 (b) £ 330
(c) £ 360 (d) £ 420

17. A bird shooter was asked how many birds he had in the bag. He replied that there were all sparrows but six, all pigeons but six, and all ducks but six. How many birds he had in the bag in all?
(a) 9 (b) 18
(c) 27 (d) 36

18. Today is Varun's birthday. One year, from today he will be twice as old as he was 12 years ago. How old is Varun today?
(a) 20 years (b) 22 years
(c) 25 years (d) 27 years

19. A is three times as old as B. C was twice as old as A four years ago. In four years' time, A will be 31. What are the present ages of B and C?
(a) 9, 46 (b) 9, 50
(c) 10, 46 (d) 10, 50

20. In a city, 40% of the adults are illiterate while 85% of the children are literate. If the ratio of the adults to that of the children is 2 : 3, then what percent of the population is literate?
(a) 20% (b) 25%
(c) 50% (d) 75%

21. A farmer built a fence around his square plot. He used 27 fence poles on each side of the square. How many poles did he need altogether?
(a) 100 (b) 104
(c) 108 (d) None of these

22. A, B, C, D and E play a game of cards. A says to B, "If you give me 3 cards, you will have as many as I have at this moment while if D takes 5 cards from you, he will have as many as E has." A and C together have twice as many cards as E has. B and D together also have the same number of cards as A and C taken together. If together they have 150 cards, how many cards has C got?
(a) 28 (b) 29
(c) 31 (d) 35

23. A bus starts from city X. The number of women in the bus is half of the number of men. In city Y, 10 men leave the bus and five women enter. Now, the number of men and women is equal. In the beginning, how many passengers entered the bus?
(a) 15 (b) 30
(c) 36 (d) 45

24. Five bells begin to toll together and toll respectively at intervals of 6, 5, 7, 10 and 12 seconds. How many times will they toll together in one hour excluding the one at the start?
(a) 7 times (b) 8 times
(c) 9 times (d) 11 times

25. If 100 cats kill 100 mice in 100 days, then 4 cats would kill 4 mice in how many days?
(a) 1 day (b) 4 days
(c) 40 days (d) 100 days

26. If you write down all the numbers from 1 to 100, then how many times do you write 3?
(a) 11 (b) 18
(c) 20 (d) 21

27. A waiter's salary consists of his salary and tips. During one week his tips were 5/4 of his salary. What fraction of his income came from tips?
(a) 4/9 (b) 5/4
(c) 5/8 (d) 5/9

28. A father is now three times as old as his son. Five years back, he was four times as old as his son. The age of the son (in years) is
(a) 12 (b) 15
(c) 18 (d) 20

29. In a class, there are 18 boys who are over 160 cm tall. If these constitute three-fourths of the boys and the total number of boys is two-thirds of the total number of students in the class, what is the number of girls in the class?
(a) 6 (b) 12
(c) 18 (d) 24

30. Mac has £ 3 more than Ken, but then Ken wins on the horses and trebles his money, so that he now has £ 2 more than the original amount of money that the two boys had between them. How much money did Mac and Ken have between them before Ken's win?
(a) £ 9 (b) £ 11
(c) £ 13 (d) £ 15

31. A motorist knows four different routes from Bristol to Birmingham. From Birmingham to Sheffield he knows three different routes and from Sheffield to Carlisle he knows two different routes. How many routes does he know from Bristol to Carlisle?
(a) 4 (b) 8
(c) 12 (d) 24

32. A man wears socks of two colours - black and brown. He has altogether 20 black socks and 20 brown socks in a drawer. Supposing he has to take out the socks in the dark, how many must he take out to be sure that he has a matching pair?
(a) 3 (b) 20
(c) 39 (d) None of these

33. There are deer and peacocks in a zoo. By counting heads they are 80. The number of their legs is 200. How many peacocks are there?
(a) 20 (b) 30
(c) 50 (d) 60

34. In a class of 60 students, the number of boys and girls participating in the annual sports is in the ratio 3 : 2 respectively. The number of girls not participating in the sports is 5 more than the number of boys not participating in the sports. If the number of boys participating in the sports is 15, then how many girls are there in the class?
(a) 20 (b) 25
(c) 30 (d) Data inadequate

35. A tailor had a number of shirt pieces to cut from a roll of fabric. He cut each roll of equal length into 10 pieces. He cut at the rate of 45 cuts a minute. How many rolls would be cut in 24 minutes?
(a) 32 rolls (b) 54 rolls
(c) 108 rolls (d) 120 rolls

36. 12 year old Manick is three times as old as his brother Rahul. How old will Manick be when he is twice as old as Rahul?
(a) 14 years (b) 16 years
(c) 18 years (d) 20 years

37. In a garden, there are 10 rows and 12 columns of mango trees. The distance between the two trees is 2 metres and a distance of one metre is left from all sides of the boundary of the garden. The length of the garden is
(a) 20 m (b) 22 m
(c) 24 m (d) 26 m

38. The 30 members of a club decided to play a badminton singles tournament. Every time a member loses a game he is out of the tournament. There are no ties. What is the minimum number of matches that must be played to determine the winner?
(a) 15 (b) 29
(c) 61 (d) None of these

39. A is 3 years older to B and 3 years younger to C, while B and D are twins. How many years older is C to D?
(a) 2 (b) 3
(c) 6 (d) 12

40. What is the product of all the numbers in the dial of a telephone?
(a) 1, 58,480 (b) 1, 59,450
(c) 1, 59,480 (d) None of these

Answer Key

1. (a)	**2.** (a)	**3.** (b)	**4.** (b)	**5.** (d)	**6.** (d)	**7.** (c)	**8.** (c)
9. (c)	**10.** (a)	**11.** (c)	**12.** (b)	**13.** (b)	**14.** (b)	**15.** (a)	**16.** (b)
17. (a)	**18.** (c)	**19.** (b)	**20.** (d)	**21.** (b)	**22.** (a)	**23.** (d)	**24.** (b)
25. (d)	**26.** (c)	**27.** (d)	**28.** (b)	**29.** (b)	**30.** (c)	**31.** (d)	**32.** (a)
33. (d)	**34.** (c)	**35.** (d)	**36.** (b)	**37.** (c)	**38.** (b)	**39.** (c)	**40.** (d)

Explanatory Notes

1. (a)
Ayush's present age = 10 years
His mother's present age = (10 + 20) years = 30 years
Ayush's father's present age = (30 + 5) years = 35 years
Ayush's father's age at the time of Ayush's birth = (35 – 10) years = 25 years
Therefore Ayush's father's age at the time of marriage = (25 – 2) years = 23 years

2. (a)
Let the number of guests be x. Then,
Number of bowls of rice = $x/2$; number of bowls of dal = $x/3$;
Number of bowls of mutton = $x/4$
Therefore,
$x/2 + x/3 + x/4 = 65$
$x = (65 \text{ x} 12)/13 = 60$

3. (b)
Let d and s represent the number of daughters and sons respectively.
Then, we have :
$d - 1 = s$ and $2(s - 1) = (d)$
Solving these two equations, we get:
$$d = 4, s = 3.$$

4. (b)
Total number of digits = No. of digits in 1-digit page numbers + No. of digits in 2-digit page numbers + No. of digits in 3 - digit page numbers
= $(1 \times 9 + 2 \times 90 + 3 \times 267) = (9 + 180 + 801) = 990$

5. (d)
Total runs scored = $(36 \times 5) = 180$
Let the runs scored by E be x
Then, runs scored by D = $x + 5$; runs scored by A = $x + 8$; runs scored by B = $x + x + 5 = 2x + 5$;
Runs scored by C = $(107 - \text{B}) = 107 - (2x + 5) = 102 - 2x$
So, total runs = $(x + 8) + (2x + 5) + (102 - 2x) + (x + 5) + x = 3x + 120$
Therefore $3x + 120 = 180 \Leftrightarrow 3x = 60 \Leftrightarrow x = 20$

6. (d)
Let R, G and B represent the number of balls in re green and blue boxes respectively.
Then, .
$$\text{R} + \text{G} + \text{B} = 108 \quad ...(i)$$
$$\text{G} + \text{R} = 2\text{B} \quad ...(ii)$$
$$\text{B} = 2\text{R} \quad ...(iii)$$
From (*ii*) and (*iii*), we have G + R = $2x$ 2R = 4R or G = 3R.
Putting G = 3R and B = 2R in (i), we get:
R + 3R + 2R = 108 $\Leftrightarrow$ 6R = 108 $\Leftrightarrow$ R = 18
Therefore Number of balls in green box = G = 3R = $(3 \times 18) = 54$

7. (c)
Let there be $(x + 1)$ members. Then,
Father's share = 1/4, share of each other member = $3/4x$.
Therefore $3(3/4\text{x}) = 1/4; x = 9$
Hence, total number of family members =10

8. (c)
'All but nine died' means 'All except nine died' i.e. 9 shee remained alive.

9. (c)
Let number of girls = x and number of boys = $3x$.
Then, $3x + x = 4x$ = total number of students.
Thus, to find exact value of x, the total number students must be divisible by 4.

10. (a)
When Ravi's brother was born, let Ravi's father's ag = x years and mother's age = y years.
Then, sister's age = $(x - 28)$ years. So, $x - 28 = 4$ or $x = 3$
Ravi's age = $(y - 26)$ years. Age of Ravi's brother = $(y - 26 + 3)$ years = $(y - 23)$ years.
Now, when Ravi's brother was born, his age = 0 i.e. $y - 23 = 0$ or $y = 23$.

11. (c)
Let number of horses = number of men = x
Then, number of legs = $4x + 2\,x\,(x/2) = 5x$
So, $5x = 70$ or $x = 14$

12. (b)
When Rahul was born, his brother's age = 6 years; his father's age = (6 + 32) years = 38 years, his mother's age = (38 – 3) years = 35 years; his sister's age = (35 – 25) years = 10 years

13. (b)
Let total number of members be 100,
Then, number of members owning only 2 cars = 20
Number of members owning 3 cars = 40% of 80 = 32
Number of members owning only 1 car
= 100 – (20 + 32) = 48
Thus, 48% of the total members own one car each.

14. (b)
Let Tanya's share = Rs. x. Then, Veena's share
= Rs. $(x/2)$
Total bill = Rs. $(x + x/2 + x/3)$ = Rs. $(11x/6)$
Amita's share = Rs. $(2/3 \times x/2)$ = Rs. $(x/3)$
Therefore,
Required fraction = $(x/2) \times (6/11x) = 3/11$

15. (a)
Clearly, the smallest such number is 3.

```
D┐
┌D┘
└D
```

Three ducks can be arranged as shown above to satisfy all the three given conditions.

16. (b)
Let the value of the holiday be x.
Then, pay for the seven weeks' work = £ 300 + x
So, $[(£\ 300 + x)/7] \times 4 = £\ 30 + x$
$£\ 1200 + 4x = £\ 210 + 7x$
$3x = £\ 990$
$x = £\ 990/3 = £\ 330$

17. (a)
There were all sparrows but six' means that six birds were not sparrows but only pigeons and ducks.
Similarly, number of sparrows + number of ducks = 6 and number of sparrows + number of pigeons = 6.

18. (c)
Let Varun's age today = x years.
Then, Varun's age after 1 year = $(x + 1)$ years
Therefore $x + 1 = 2(x - 12) \Leftrightarrow x + 1 = 2x - 24 \Leftrightarrow x = 25$

19. (b)
We have : A = 3B ...(i) and
C – 4 = 2 (A – 4) ...(ii)
Also, A + 4 = 31 or A = 31– 4 = 27
Putting A = 27 in (i), we get: B = 9
Putting A = 27 in (ii), we get C = 50

20. (d)
Let the number of adults and children be $2x$ and $3x$ respectively.
Then, literate population
= (100 – 40) % of $2x$ + 85% of $3x$
= $(60/100) \times 2x + (85/100) \times 3x$
= $6x/5 + 51x/20 = 75x/20$
Therefore,
Required percentage = $(75x/20) \times (1/5x) \times 100\% = 75\%$

21. (b)
Since each pole at the corner of the plot is common to its two sides, so we have :
Total number of poles needed = 27 x 4 – 4 = 108 – 4 = 104.

22. (a)
Clearly, we have :

$$A = B - 3 \quad ...(i)$$
$$D + 5 = E \quad ...(ii)$$
$$A + C = 2E \quad ...(iii)$$
$$B + D = A + C = 2E \quad ...(iv)$$
$$A + B + C + D + E = 150 \quad ...(v)$$

From (iii), (iv) and (v), we get:
5E = 150 or E = 30
Putting E = 30 in (ii), we get: D = 25
Putting E = 30 and D = 25 in (iv), we get: B = 35
Putting B = 35 in (i), we get: A = 32
Putting A = 32 and E = 30 in (iii), we get: C = 28

23. (d)
Originally, let number of women = x. Then, number of men = $2x$
So, in city Y, we have :
$(2x - 10) = (x + 5)$ or $x - 15$
Therefore, total number of passengers in the beginning = $(x + 2x) = 3x = 45$

24. (b)
L.C.M. of 6, 5, 7, 10 and 12 is 420
So, the bells will toll together after every 420 seconds i.e. 7 minutes
Now, 7 × 8 = 56 and 7 × 9 = 63
Thus, in 1-hour (or 60 minutes), the bells will toll together 8 times, excluding the one at the start.

25. (d)
Less cats, More days (Indirect Proportion)
Less Mice, Less days (Direct Proportion)
Let the required number of days be x.
Then, according to question,
$100 \times 4 \times x = 4 \times 100 \times 100$
$x = (4 \times 100 \times 100) / (100 \times 4) = 100$

26. (c)
Clearly, from 1 to 100, there are ten numbers with 3 as the unit's digit - 3, 13, 23, 33, 43, 53, 63, 73, 83, 93; and ten numbers with 3 as the ten's digit - 30, 31, 32, 33, 34, 35, 36, 37, 38, 39
So, required number = 10 + 10 = 20

27. (d)
Let salary = Rs. x. Then tips = Rs. $(5x/4)$
Total income = Rs. $(x + 5x/4)$ = Rs. $(9x/4)$
Therefore fraction = $(5x/4) \times (4/9x) = 5/9$

28. (b)
Let son's age be x years. Then, father's age = $(3x)$ years
Five years ago, father's age = $(3x - 5)$ years and son's age = $(x - 5)$ years
So, $3x - 5 = 4(x - 5) \Leftrightarrow 3x - 5 = 4x - 20 \Leftrightarrow x = 15$

29. (b)
Let the number of boys be x. Then, $(3/4)x = 18$
or $x = 18 \times (4/3) = 24$
If total number of students is y, then $(2/3)\ y = 24$
or $y = 24 \times (3/2) = 36$
Therefore, the number of girls in the class
$= (36 - 24) = 12$

30. (c)
Let money with Ken $= x$. Then, money with Mac
$= x + £\ 3$
Now, $3x = (x + x + £\ 3) + £\ 2 \Leftrightarrow x = £\ 5$
Therefore total money with Mac and Ken
$= 2x + £\ 3 = £\ 13$

31. (d)
Total number of routes from Bristol to Carlisle
$= (4 \times 3 \times 2) = 24$

32. (a)
Since there are socks of only two colours, so two out of any three socks must always be of the same colour

33. (d)
Let x and y be the number of deer and peacocks in the zoo respectively. Then,
$x + x = 80$ ...(i) and
$4x + 2y = 200$
or $2x + y = 100$ ...(ii)
Solving (i) and (ii), we get) $x = 20$, $y = 60$

34. (c)
Let the number of boys and girls participating in sports be $3x$ and $2x$ respectively.
Then, $3x = 15$ or $x = 5$
So, the number of girls participating in sports
$= 2x = 10$
Number of students not participating in sports
$= 60 - (15 + 10) = 35$
Let number of boys not participating in sports be y
Then, number of girls not participating in sports
$= (35 - y)$
Therefore $(35 - y) = y + 5$ $2y$ 30 $y = 15$
So, number of girls not participating in sports
$= (35 - 15) = 20$
Hence, total number of girls in the class
$= (10 + 20) = 30$

35. (d)
Number of cuts made to cut a roll into 10 pieces = 9
Therefore, required number of rolls = $(45 \times 24)/9 = 120$

36. (b)
Manick's present age = 12 years, Rahul's present age
= 4 years
Let Manick be twice as old as Rahul after x years from now
Then, $12 + x = 2\ (4 + x)$
$12 + x = 8 + 2x$
$x = 4$
Hence, Manick's required age $= 12 + x = 16$ years

37. (c)
Each row contains 12 plants
There are 11 gapes between the two corner trees (11×2) metres and 1 metre on each side is left.
Therefore, length = (22 + 2) m = 24 m

38. (b)
Clearly, every member except one (i.e. the winner) must lose one game to decide the winner. Thus, minimum number of matches to be played = 30 – 1 = 29

39. (c)
Since B and D are twins, so B = D
Now, A = B + 3 and A = C - 3.
Thus, B + 3 = C – 3; D + 3 = C – 3 C – D = 6

40. (d)
Since one of the numbers on the dial of a telephone is zero, so the product of all the numbers on it is 0.

Previous Year Questions

1. A man has Rs. 480 in the denominations of one-rupee notes, five-rupee notes and ten-rupee notes. The number of notes of each denomination is equal. What is the total number of notes that he has?
[NTSE 2003 - Punjab first stage paper]
(a) 45 (b) 60
(c) 75 (d) 90

2. A girl counted in the following way on the fingers of her left hand. She started by calling the thumb 1, the index finger 2, middle finger 3, ring finger 4, little finger 5 and then reversed direction calling the ring finger 6, middle finger 7 and so on. She counted up to 1994. She ended counting on which finger?
[NTSE 2002 - Delhi second stage paper]
(a) Thumb (b) Index finger
(c) Middle finger (d) Ring finger

3. A woman says, "If you reverse my own age, the figures represent my husband's age. He is, of course, senior to me and the difference between our ages is one-eleventh of their sum." The woman's age is
[NTSE 2000 – UP first stage paper]
(a) 23 years (b) 34 years
(c) 45 years (d) None of these

4. A pineapple costs Rs. 7 each. A watermelon costs Rs. 5 each. X spends Rs. 38 on these fruits. The number of pineapples purchased is
[NTSE 2004 - Tripura first stage paper]
(a) 2 (b) 3
(c) 4 (d) Data inadequate

5. A, B, C, D and E play a game of cards. A says to B, "If you give me three cards, you will have as many as E has and if I give you three cards, you will have as many as D has." A and B together have 10 cards more than what D and E together have. If B has two cards more than what C has and the total number of cards be 133, how many cards does B have?
[NTSE 2001 - Haryana second stage paper]
(a) 22 (b) 23
(c) 25 (d) 35

6. A number of friends decided to go on a picnic and planned to spend Rs. 96 on eatables. Four of them, however, did not turn up. As a consequence, the remaining ones had to contribute Rs. 4 each extra. The number of those who attended the picnic was
[NTSE 2001 - Delhi first stage paper]
(a) 8 (b) 12
(c) 16 (d) 24

7. Two bus tickets from city A to B and three tickets from city A to C cost Rs. 77 but three tickets from city A to B and two tickets from city A to C cost Rs. 73. What are the fares for cities B and C from A?
[NTSE 2003 - MP first stage paper]
(a) Rs. 4, Rs. 23 (b) Rs. 13, Rs. 17
(c) Rs. 15, Rs. 14 (d) Rs. 17, Rs. 13

8. The total of the ages of Amar, Akbar and Anthony is 80 years. What was the total of their ages three years ago?
[NTSE 2012 - Chandigarh first stage paper]
(a) 71 years (b) 72 years
(c) 74 years (d) 77 years

9. I have a few sweets to be distributed. If I keep 2, 3 or 4 in a pack, I am left with one sweet. If I keep 5 in a pack, I am left with none. What is the minimum number of sweets I have to pack and distribute?
[NTSE 2004 - WB second stage paper]
(a) 25 (b) 37
(c) 54 (d) 65

10. A printer numbers the pages of a book starting with 1 and uses 3189 digits in all. How many pages does the book have?
[NTSE 2012 - Rajasthan first stage paper]
(a) 1000 (b) 1074
(c) 1075 (d) 1080

❑

Answer Key

1. (d)	2. (b)	3. (c)	4. (c)	5. (c)	6. (a)	7. (b)	8. (a)	9. (a)	10. (b)

Explanatory Notes

1. (d)
Let number of notes of each denomination be x.
Then, $x + 5x + 10x = 480$ $16x = 480$ $x = 30$.
Hence, total number of notes $= 3x = 90$.

2. (b)
Clearly, while counting, the numbers associated to the thumb will be : 1, 9,17, 25,.....
i.e. numbers of the form $(8n + 1)$.
Since $1994 = 249 \times 8 + 2$, so 1993 shall correspond to the thumb and 1994 to the index finger.

3. (c)
Let x and y be the ten's and unit's digits respectively of the numeral denoting the woman's age.
Then, woman's age $= (10x + y)$ years; husband's age $= (10y + x)$ years.
Therefore $(10y + x) - (10x + y) = (1/11)$
$(10y + x - 10x - y)$
$(9y - 9x) = (1/11)$
$(11y + 11x) = (x + y)$
$10x = 8y$ $x = (4/5)y$
Clearly, y should be a single-digit multiple of 5, which is 5.
So, $x = 4$, $y = 5$.
Hence, woman's age $= 10x + y = 45$ years.

4. (c)
Let the number of pineapples and watermelons be x and y respectively.
Then, $7x + 5y = 38$
Or $y = (38 - 7x)/5$
Clearly, y is a whole number, only when $(38 - 7x)$ is divisible by 5.
This happens when $x = 4$

5. (c)
Clearly, we have:
$$B-3 = E \quad ...(i)$$
$$B + 3 = D \quad ...(ii)$$
$$A + B = D + E + 10 \quad ...(iii)$$
$$B = C + 2 \quad ...(iv)$$
$$A + B + C + D + E= 133 \quad ...(v)$$
From (i) and (ii), we have : $2B = D + E$ ...(vi)
From (iii) and (vi), we have : $A = B + 10$ ...(vii)
Using (iv), (vi) and (vii) in (v), we get:
$(B + 10) + B + (B - 2) + 2B = 133$
$5B = 125$ $B = 25$

6. (a)
Let the number of persons be x. Then,
$$96/(x - 4) - 96/x = 4$$
$$1/(x - 4) - 1/x = 4/96$$
$$[x - (x - 4)]/x (x - 4) = 1/24$$
$$x^2 - 4x - 96 = 0$$
$$(x - 12)(x + 8) = 0$$
$$x = 12$$
So, required number $= x - 4 = 8$

7. (b)
Let Rs. x be the fare of city B from city A and Rs. y be the fare of city C from city A.
Then, $2x + 3y = 77$ ...(i) and
$3x + 2y = 73$ ...(ii)
Multiplying (i) by 3 and (ii) by 2 and subtracting, we get: $5y = 85$ or $y = 17$
Putting $y = 17$ in (i), we get: $x = 13$

8. (a)
Required sum
$= (80 - 3 \times 3)$ years $= (80 - 9)$ years $= 71$ years

9. (a)
Clearly, the required number would be such that it leaves a remainder of 1 when divided by 2, 3 or 4 and no remainder when divided by 5. Such a number is 25.

10. (b)
No. of digits in 1-digit page numbers $= 1 \times 9 = 9$
No. of digits in 2-digit page numbers $= 2 \times 90 = 180$
No. of digits in 3-digit page numbers $= 3 \times 900 = 2700$
No. of digits in 4-digit page numbers
$= 3189 - (9 + 180 + 2700) = 3189 - 2889 = 300$
Therefore no. of pages with 4-digit page numbers $= (300/4) = 75$
Hence, total number of pages $= (999 + 75) = 1074$

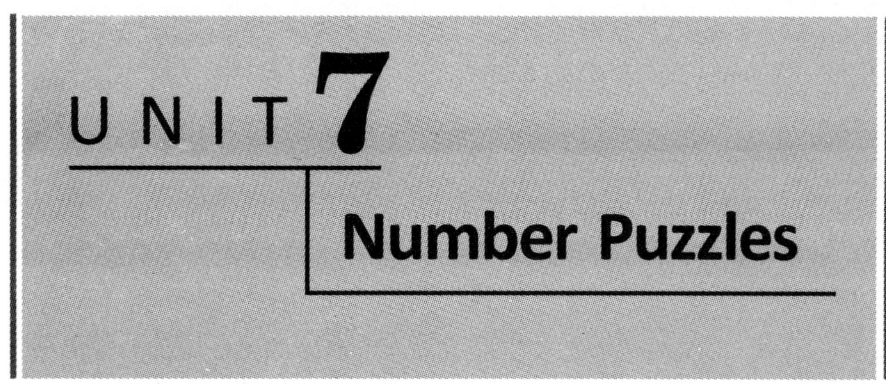

In the questions based on 'Mathematical Operations', a figure or a matrix is given in which some numbers are filled according to a rule. A place is left blank. The candidates have to find out a character (a number or a letter) from the given possible answers to fill in the blank space.

Solved Examples

1. Which one will replace the question mark?

5			
32	?	44	7
6			

(a) 33 (b) 38
(c) 32 (d) 37

Solution: Option (d) is correct.

Explanation:

$(5 \times 6) + 2 = 32$
$(7 \times 6) + 2 = 44$
$(7 \times 5) + 2 = 37$

2. Which one will replace the question mark?

3	6	8
5	8	4
4	7	?

(a) 6 (b) 7
(c) 8 (d) 9

Solution: Option (a) is correct.

Explanation:

$(5 + 3)/2 = 4$
and $(6 + 8)/2 = 7$
Therefore $(8 + 4)/2 = 6$

3. Which one will replace the question mark?

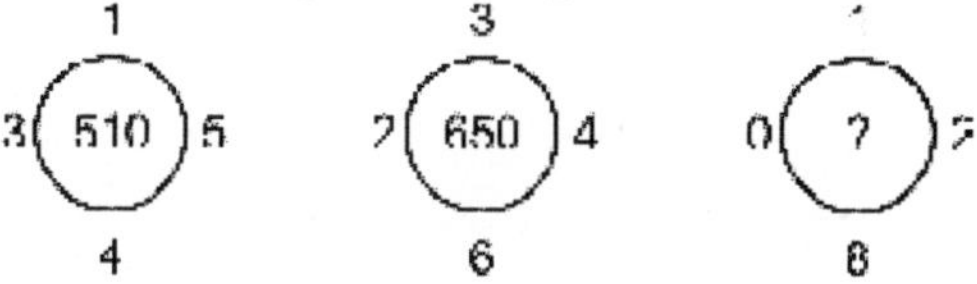

(a) 660 (b) 670
(c) 610 (d) 690

Solution: Option (d) is correct.

Explanation:

$(1)^2 + (5)^2 + (4)^2 + (3)^2 = 51 \times 10 = 510$
and $(3)^2 + (4)^2 + (6)^2 + (2)^2 = 65 \times 10 = 650$
Similarly $(0)^2 + (1)^2 + (2)^2 + (8)^2 = 69 \times 10 = 690$

4. Which one will replace the question mark?

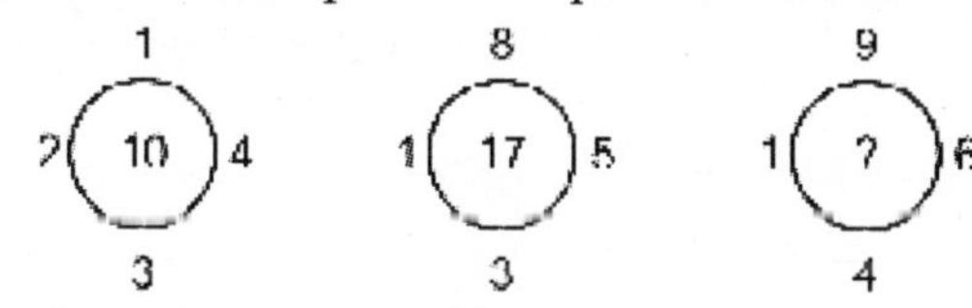

(a) 18 (b) 20
(c) 21 (d) 19

Solution: Option (b) is correct.

Explanation:

$1 + 2 + 3 + 4 = 10$
and $1 + 3 + 5 + 8 = 17$
Similarly, $1 + 4 + 6 + 9 = 20$

5. Which one will replace the question mark?

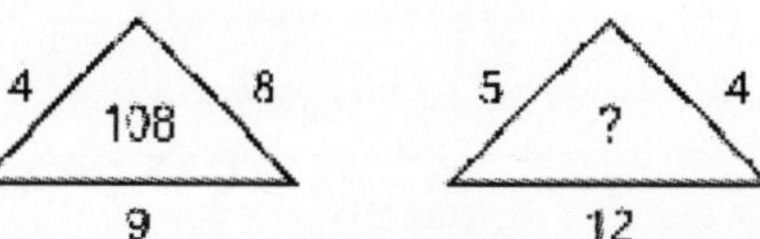

(a) 80 (b) 114
(c) 108 (d) None of these

Solution: Option (c) is correct.

Explanation:

$(4 + 8) \times 9 = 108$
$(5 + 4) \times 12 = 108$

6. Which one will replace the question mark?

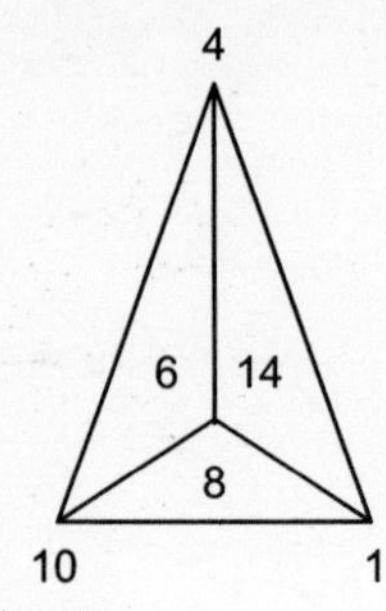

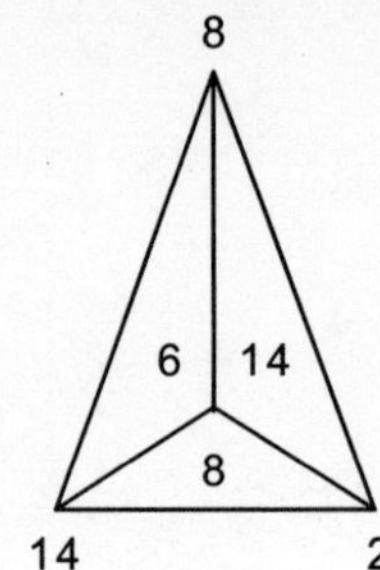

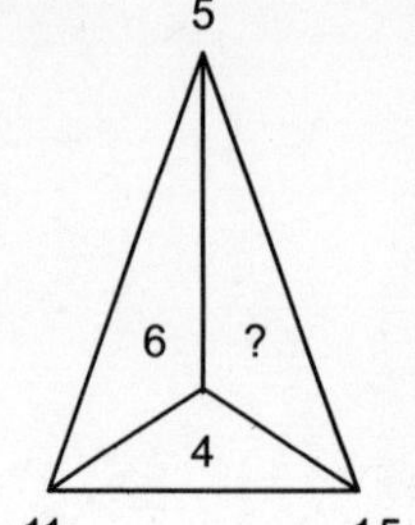

(a) 8 (b) 14
(c) 10 (d) 6

Solution: Option (c) is correct.

Explanation: For first triangle,

10 – 4 = 6
18 – 10 = 8
18 – 4 = 14

For second triangle,

14 – 8 = 6
22 – 14 = 8
22 – 8 = 14

For third triangle,

11 – 5 = 6
15 – 11 = 4
15 – 5 = 10

7. Which one will replace the question mark?

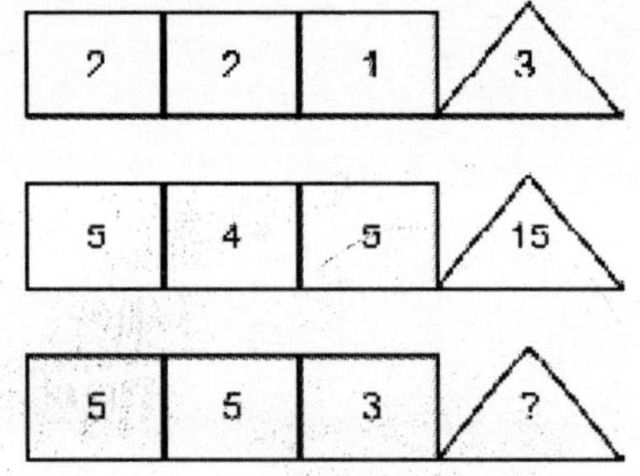

(a) 11 (b) 19
(c) 15 (d) 22

Solution: Option (d) is correct.

Explanation:

(2 × 2 – 1) = 3
and (5 × 4 – 5) = 15
(5 × 5 – 3) = 22

8. Which one will replace the question mark?

A_2	C_4	E_6
G_3	I_5	?
M_5	O_8	Q_{14}

(a) L_{10} (b) K_{15}
(c) I_{15} (d) K_8

Solution: Option (d) is correct.

Explanation:

$A_2 \xrightarrow{+2} C_4 \xrightarrow{+2} E_6$

$M_5 \xrightarrow{+2} O_9 \xrightarrow{+2} Q_{14}$

$G_3 \xrightarrow{+2} I_5 \xrightarrow{+2} K_8$

How is the number obtained?

(a) 2 + 4 = 6 (b) 5 + 9 = 14
(c) Similarly (d) 3 + 5 = 8
(e) Therefore, the answer is K_8

9. Which one will replace the question mark?

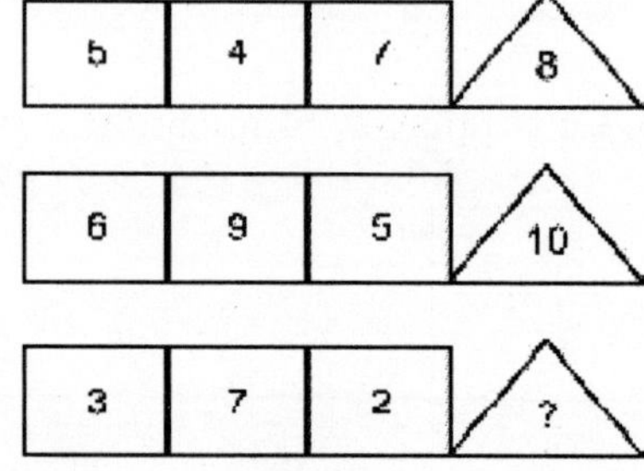

(a) 1 (b) 4
(c) 3 (d) 6

Solution: Option (d) is correct.

Explanation:

(5 + 4 + 7)/2 = 8
(6 + 9 + 5)/2 = 10
(3 + 7 + 2)/2 = 6

10. Which one will replace the question mark?

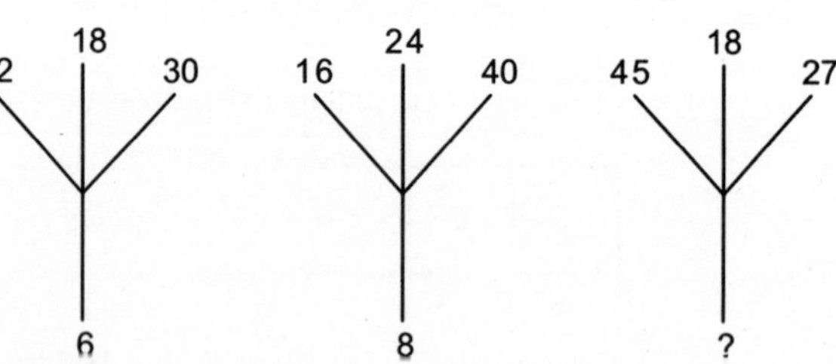

(a) 18 (b) 12
(c) 9 (d) 6

Solution: Option (c) is correct.

Explanation:

(12 + 18 + 30)/10 = 6
(16 + 24 + 40)/10 = 8
Similarly, (45 + 18 + 27)/10 = 9

Multiple Choice Questions

1. Which one will replace the question mark?

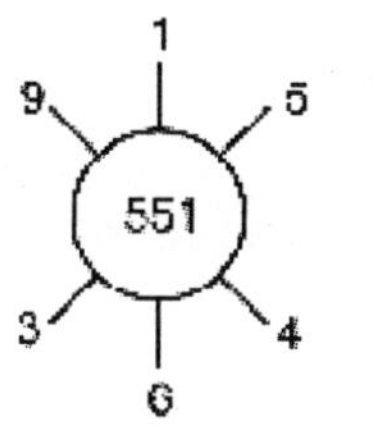

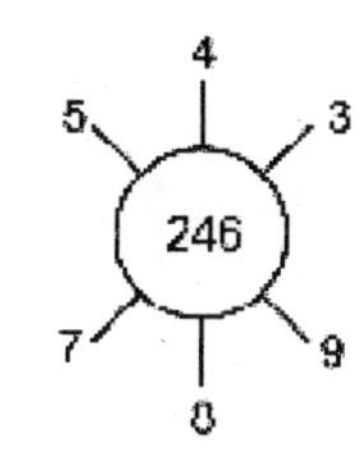

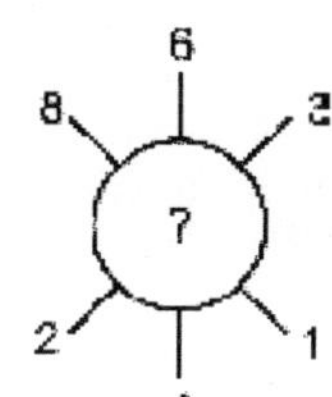

(a) 262 (b) 622
(c) 631 (d) 824

2. Which one will replace the question mark?

4	7	5
33	78	46
8	?	9

(a) 12 (b) 13
(c) 11 (d) 10

3. Which one will replace the question mark?

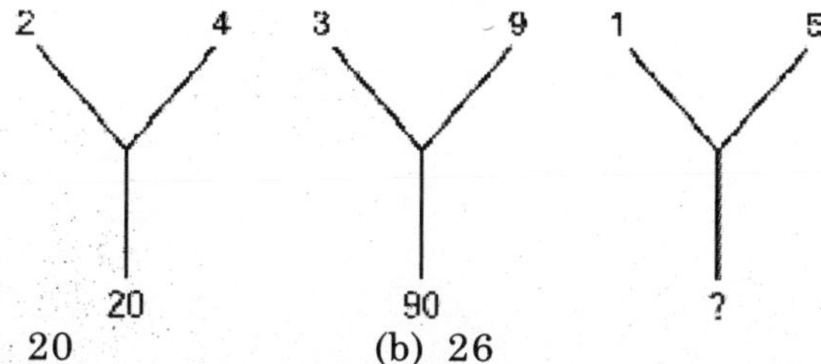

(a) 20 (b) 26
(c) 25 (d) 75

4. Which one will replace the question mark?

3	?	5
5	4	7
4	4	4
60	96	140

(a) 4 (b) 6
(c) 9 (d) 8

5. Which one will replace the question mark?

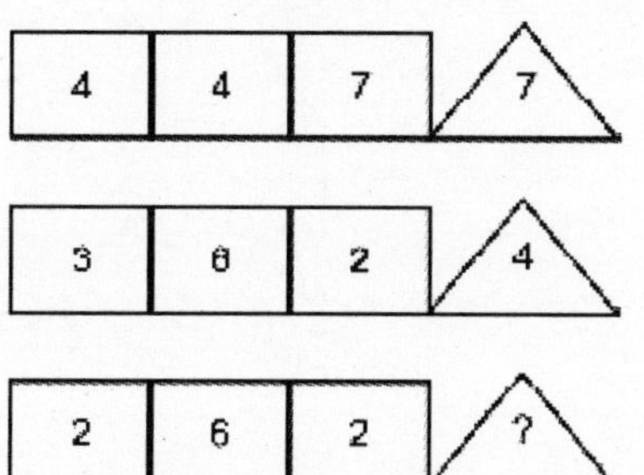

(a) 2 (b) 4
(c) 6 (d) 8

6. Which one will replace the question mark?

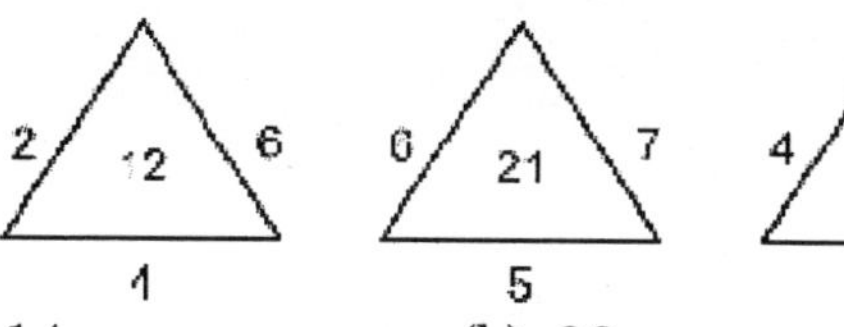

(a) 14 (b) 22
(c) 32 (d) 320

7. Which one will replace the question mark?

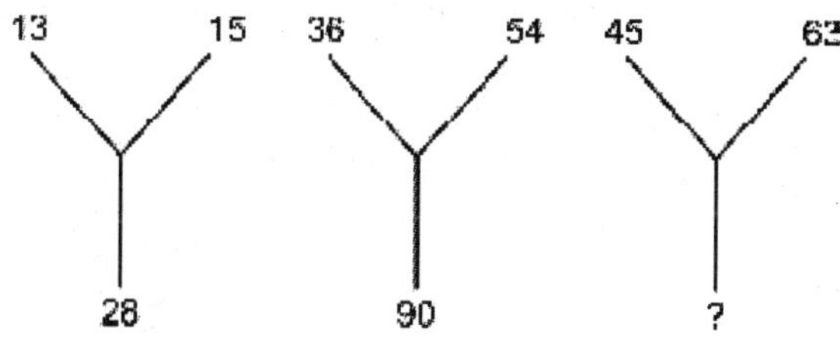

(a) 18 (b) 90
(c) 108 (d) 28

8. Which one will replace the question mark?

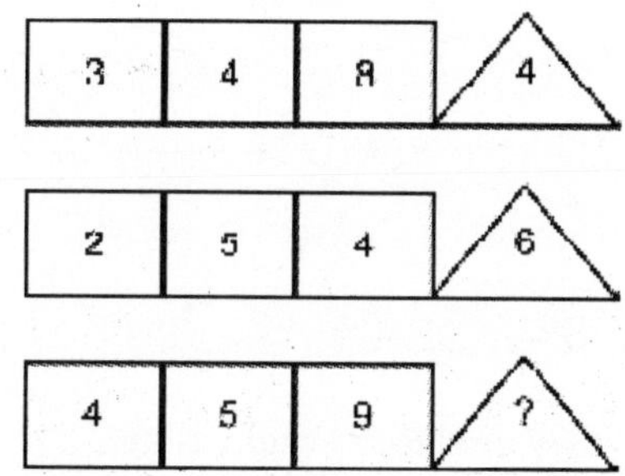

(a) 8 (b) 9
(c) 10 (d) 11

9. Which one will replace the question mark?

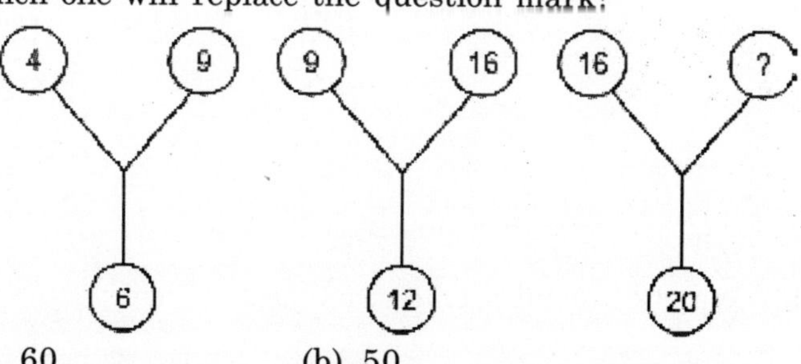

(a) 60 (b) 50
(c) 25 (d) 21

10. Which one will replace the question mark?

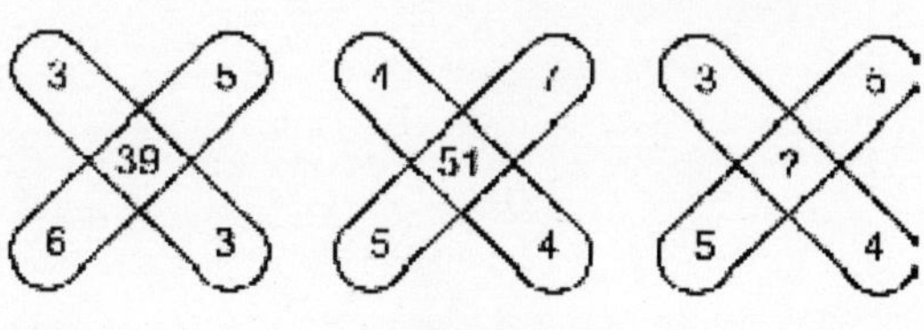

(a) 47 (b) 45
(c) 37 (d) 35

11. Which one will replace the question mark?

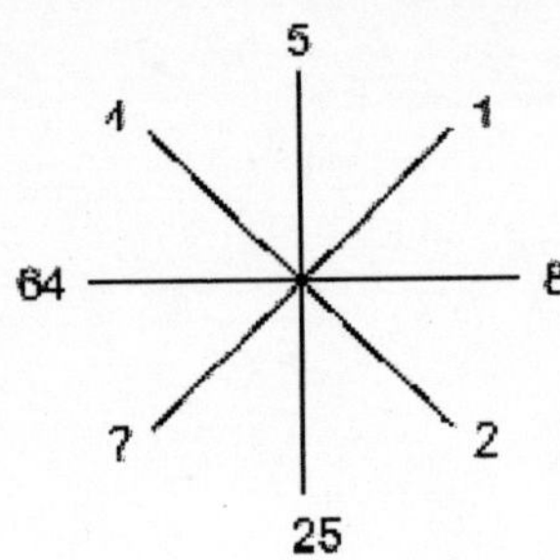

(a) 1 (b) 2
(c) 3 (d) 4

12. Which one will replace the question mark?

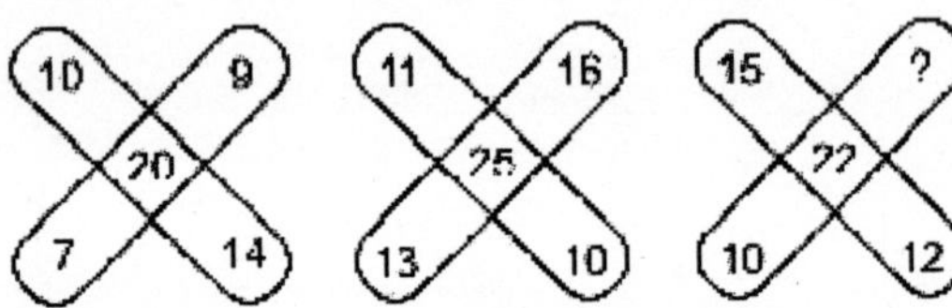

(a) 6 (b) 7
(c) 8 (d) 9

13. Which one will replace the question mark?

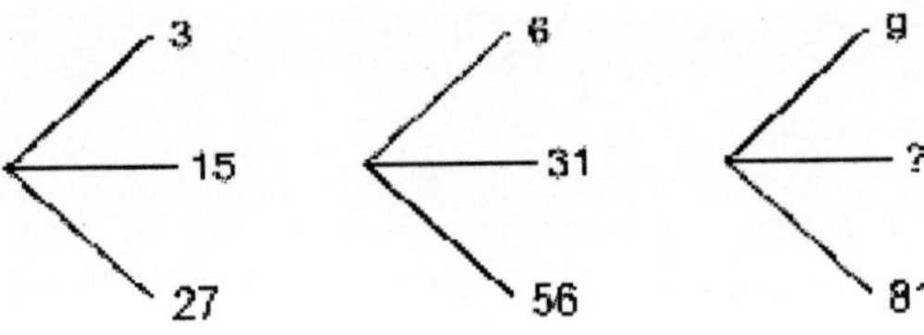

(a) 45 (b) 41
(c) 32 (d) 40

14. Which one will replace the question mark?

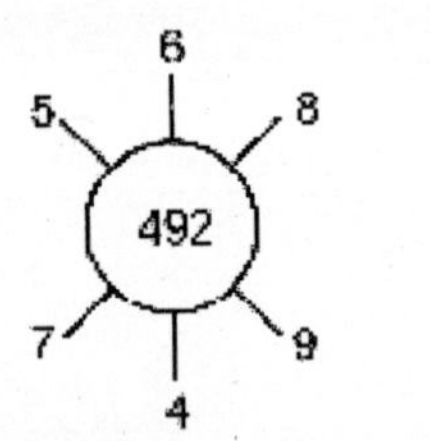

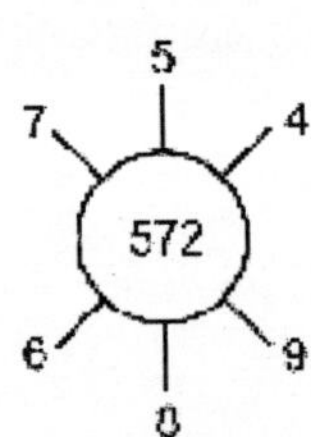

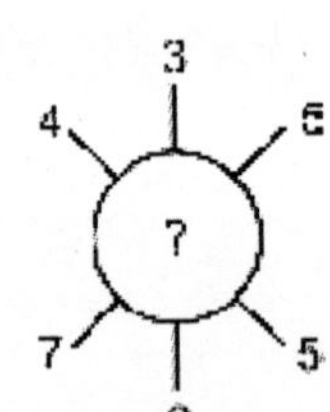

(a) 115 (b) 130
(c) 135 (d) 140

15. Which one will replace the question mark?

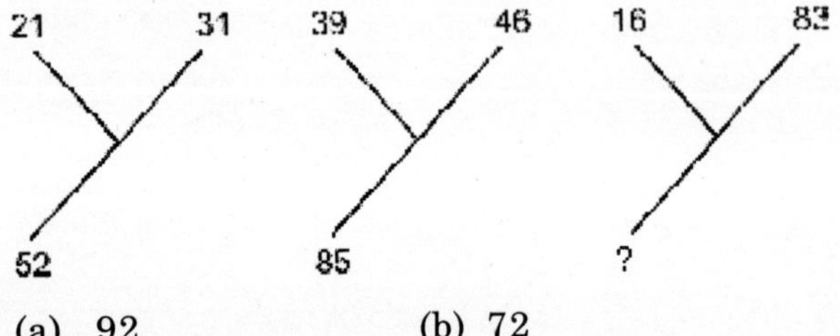

(a) 92 (b) 72
(c) 62 (d) 99

16. Which one will replace the question mark?

18	24	32
12	14	16
3	?	4
72	112	128

(a) 2 (b) 3
(c) 4 (d) 5

17. Which one will replace the question mark?

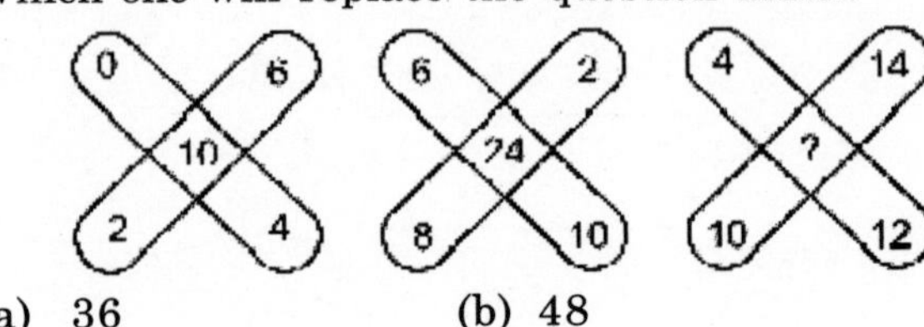

(a) 36 (b) 48
(c) 38 (d) 30

18. Which one will replace the question mark?

(a) 41
(b) 64
(c) 35
(d) 61

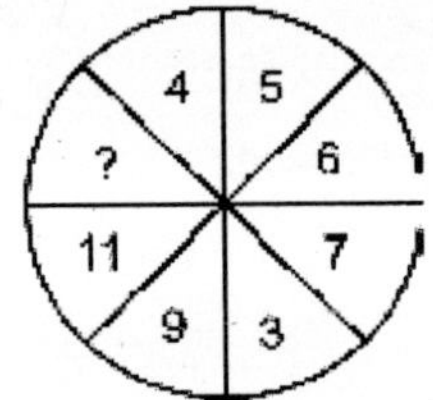

19. Which one will replace the question mark?

(a) 13 (b) 14
(c) 12 (d) 15

20. Which number will replace the question mark?

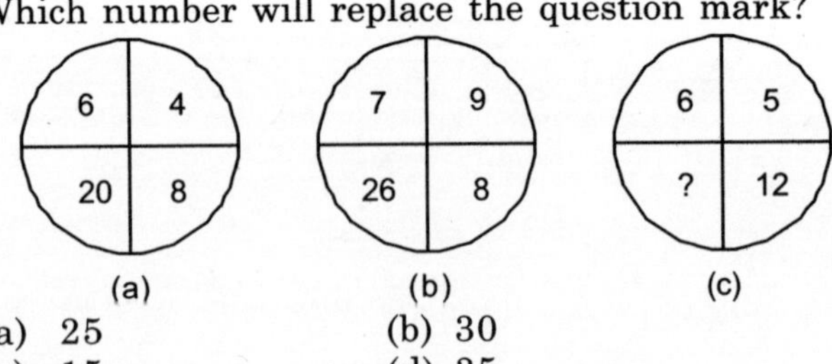

(a) 25 (b) 30
(c) 15 (d) 35

21. Which number will replace the question mark?

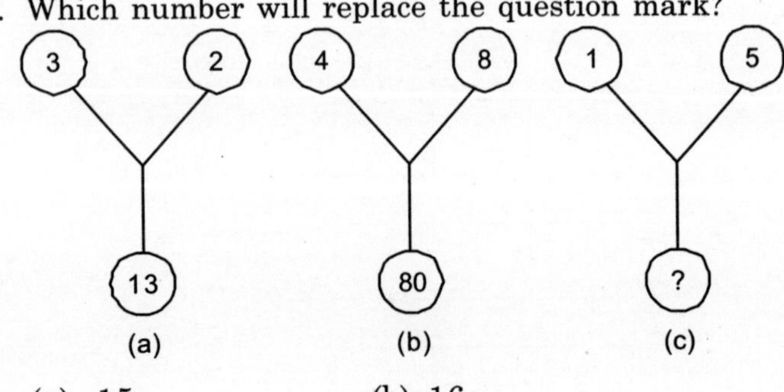

(a) 15 (b) 16
(c) 26 (d) 36

22. Which number will replace the question mark?

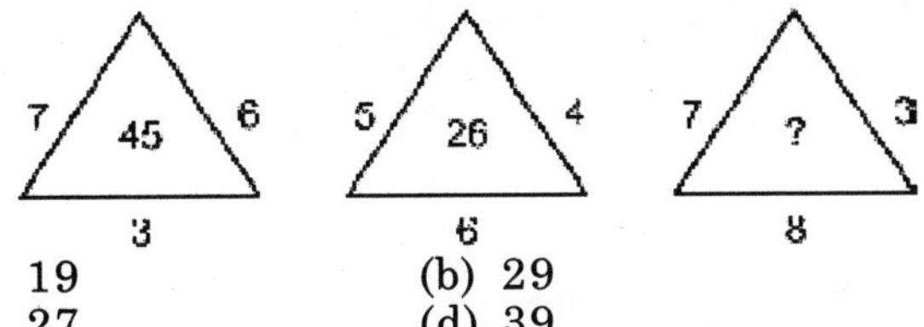

(a) 19 (b) 29
(c) 27 (d) 39

23. Which number will replace the question mark?

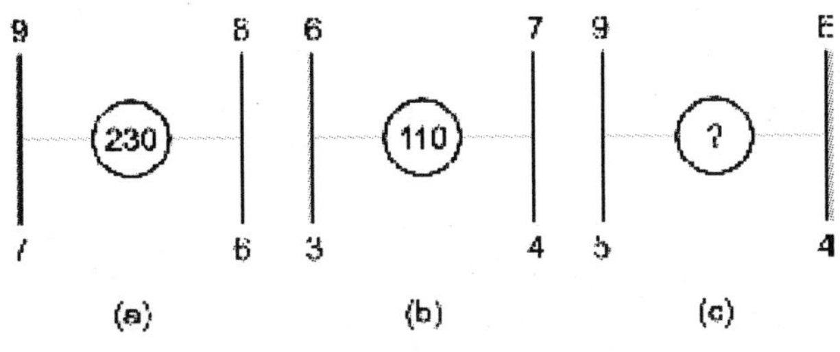

(a) 145 (b) 155
(c) 158 (d) 162

24. Which number will replace the question mark?

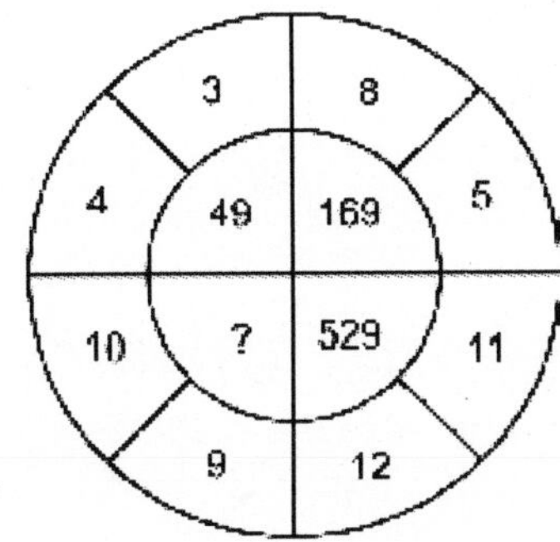

(a) 156 (b) 264
(c) 361 (d) 551

25. Which number will replace the question mark?

9	17	16
5	4	8
5	4	?
9	17	8

(a) 2 (b) 4
(c) 6 (d) 8

26. Which number will replace the question mark?

(a)

	5	
8	28	4
	3	

(b)

	7	
12	12	8
	9	

(c)

	3	
5	21	6
	?	

(a) -1 (b) 1
(c) 2 (d) -4

27. Which number will replace the question mark?

4A	6C	24B
5A	?	45C
9B	4C	36A

(a) 9B (b) 9A
(c) 45C (d) 4A

28. Which number will replace the question mark?

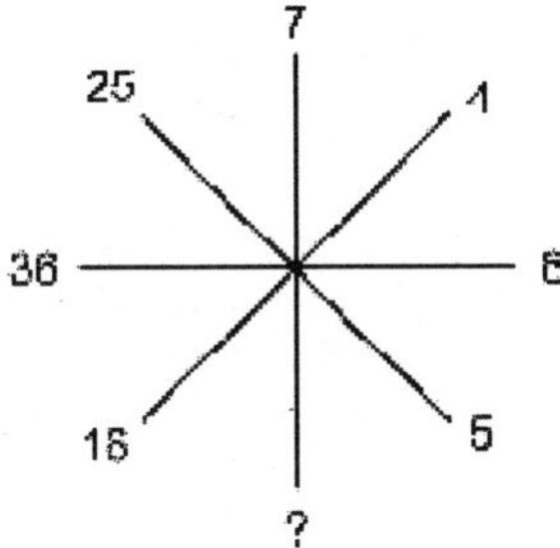

(a) 45 (b) 49
(c) 55 (d) 88

29. Which one will replace the question mark?

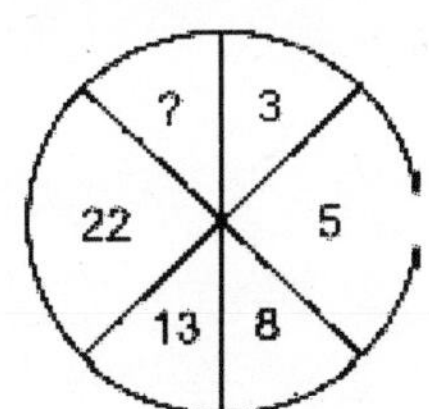

(a) 45 (b) 29
(c) 39 (d) 37

30. Which one will replace the question mark?

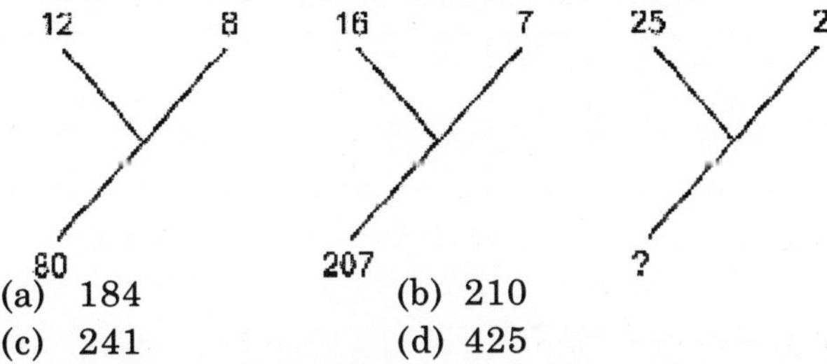

(a) 184 (b) 210
(c) 241 (d) 425

31. Which one will replace the question mark?

2	4	0
1	2	4
3	1	3
36	?	91

(a) 25 (b) 59
(c) 48 (d) 73

32. Which one will replace the question mark?

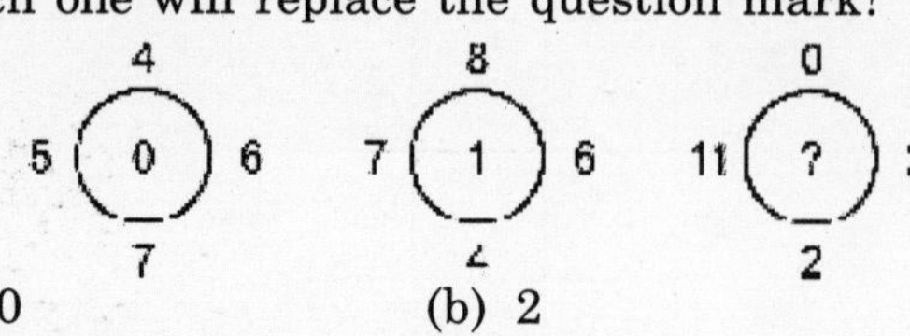

(a) 0 (b) 2
(c) 11 (d) 12

33. Which one will replace the question mark?

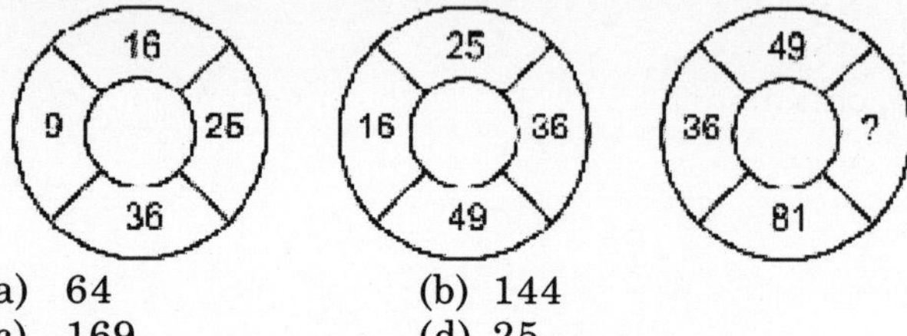

(a) 64 (b) 144
(c) 169 (d) 25

34. Which one will replace the question mark?

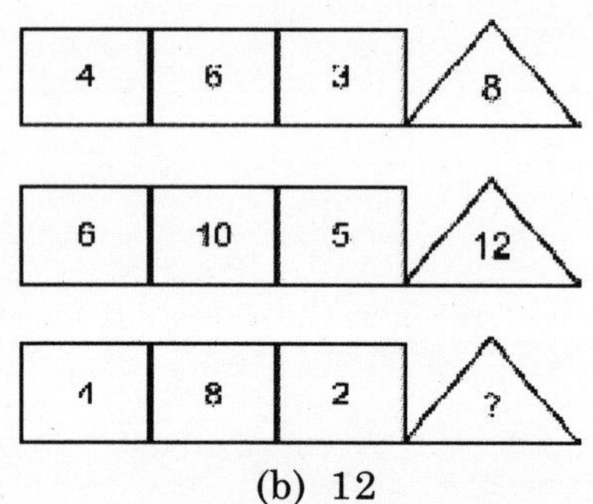

(a) 8 (b) 12
(c) 16 (d) 20

35. Which one will replace the question mark?

7	4	5
8	7	6
3	3	?
29	19	31

(a) 3 (b) 5
(c) 4 (d) 6

36. Which one will replace the question mark?

4	5	6
2	3	7
1	8	3
21	98	?

(a) 94 (b) 76
(c) 16 (d) 73

37. Which one will replace the question mark?

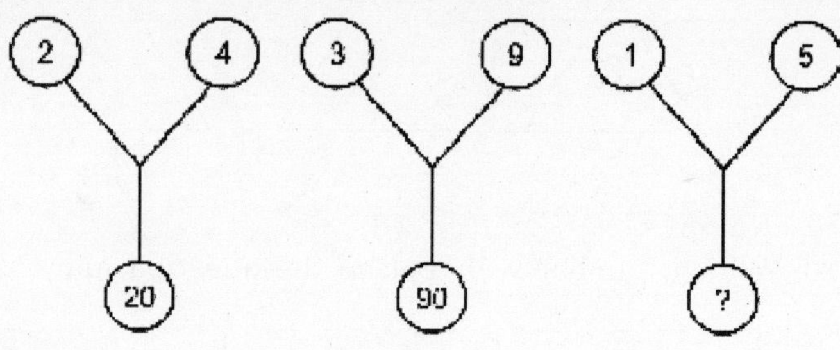

(a) 75 (b) 26
(c) 25 (d) 20

38. Which one will replace the question mark?

7	9	21	27
4	2	36	18
9	4	54	?

(a) 18 (b) 24
(c) 36 (d) 58

39. Which one will replace the question mark?

16	28	29
13	12	16
14	10	15
15	30	?

(a) 60 (b) 30
(c) 20 (d) 45

40. Which one will replace the question mark?

3	15	4
7	38	5
3	?	5

(a) 15 (b) 19
(c) 20 (d) 18

❒

Answer Key

1. (b)	**2.** (c)	**3.** (b)	**4.** (b)	**5.** (c)	**6.** (c)	**7.** (c)	**8.** (d)	**9.** (c)	**10.** (c)	**11.** (a)
12. (b)	**13.** (a)	**14.** (b)	**15.** (d)	**16.** (b)	**17.** (c)	**18.** (b)	**19.** (d)	**20.** (a)	**21.** (c)	**22.** (b)
23. (c)	**24.** (c)	**25.** (b)	**26.** (a)	**27.** (a)	**28.** (b)	**29.** (c)	**30.** (a)	**31.** (d)	**32.** (c)	**33.** (a)
34. (c)	**35.** (b)	**36.** (a)	**37.** (b)	**38.** (b)	**39.** (b)	**40.** (d)				

Explanatory Notes

1. (b)
$(915 - 364) = 551$
$(789 - 543) = 246$
$(863 - 241) = 622$

2. (c)
$(4 \times 8) + 1 = 33$
$(5 \times 9) + 1 = 46$
Similarly, $(7 \times 11) + 1 = 78$

3. (b)
$(2)^2 + (4)^2 = 20$
$(3)^2 + (9)^2 = 90$
Therefore, $(1)^2 + (5)^2 = 26$

4. (b)
$3 \times 5 \times 4 = 60$
$5 \times 7 \times 4 = 140$
Therefore, $4 \times 4 \times ? = 96$
$? = (96/16) = 6$

5. (c)
$(4 \times 7)\ \%\ 4 = 7$
$(6 \times 2)\ \%\ 3 = 4$
Therefore, $(6 \times 2)\ \%\ 2 = 6$

6. (c)
$(5 \times 6 \times 4)/10 = 12$
$(6 \times 7 \times 5)/10 = 21$
Therefore $(4 \times 8 \times 10)/10 = 32$

7. (c)
$13 + 15 = 28$
$36 + 54 = 90$
Therefore, $45 + 63 = 108$

8. (d)
$(3 \times 4 - 8) = 4$
$(2 \times 5 - 4) = 6$
$(4 \times 5 - 9) = 11$

9. (c)
$\sqrt{4 \times 9} = 6$
$\sqrt{9 \times 16} = 12$
Therefore $\sqrt{16 \times ?} = 20$
$? = 25$

10. (c)
$(3 \times 3) + (5 \times 6) = 39$
$(4 \times 4) + (5 \times 7) = 51$
Therefore, $(3 \times 4) + (5 \times 5) = 37$

11. (a)
$(2)^2 = 4$
$(8)^2 = 64$
$(5)^2 = 25$
$(1)^2 = 1$

12. (b)
$(10 + 9 + 14 + 7)/2 = 20$
$(11 + 16 + 10 + 13)/2 = 25$
Therefore, $(15 + ? + 12 + 10)/2 = 22$
Hence $37 + ? = 44$
$? = 44 - 37$
$? = 7$

13. (a)
$(15 \times 2 - 3) = 27$
$(31 \times 2 - 6) = 56$
$(45 \times 2 - 9) = 81$

14. (b)
$(5 \times 6 \times 8) + (7 \times 4 \times 9) = 492$
$(7 \times 5 \times 4) + (6 \times 8 \times 9) = 572$
Therefore $(4 \times 3 \times 5) + (7 \times 2 \times 5) = 130$

15. (d)
$21 + 31 = 52$
$39 + 46 = 85$
Therefore, $16 + 83 = 99$

16. (b)
$(18 \times 12)/3 = 72$
$(32 \times 16)/4 = 128$
Therefore, $(24 \times 14)/? = 112$
$(336/?) = 112$
$? = (336/112)$
$? = 3$

17. (c)
$(0 + 2 + 6 + 4) - 2 = 10$
$(6 + 2 + 10 + 8) - 2 = 24$
Therefore, $(4 + 14 + 12 + 10) - 2 = 38$

18. (b)
$(1)^3 = 1,\ (2)^3 = 8,\ (3)^3 = 27$
Therefore, $(4)^3 = 64$

19. (d)
Sum of numbers in lower half of the circle
$= 11 + 9 + 3 + 7 = 30$
Sum of numbers in upper half of the circle
$= ? + 4 + 5 + 6 = ? + 15$

Upper half = Lower half

30 = ? + 15

? = 30 – 15

? = 15

Therefore, 15 is the answer

20. (a)

From fig. a: 6 + 4 + 8 = 18

18 + 2 = 20

From fig. b: 7 + 9 + 8 = 24

24 + 2 = 26

From fig. c: 6 + 5 + 12 = 23

23 + 2 = **25**

Hence, the number 25 will replace the question mark.

21. (c)

From fig. a: $(3)^2 + (2)^2 = 13$

From fig. b: $(4)^2 + (8)^2 = 80$

From fig. c: $? = (1)^2 + (5)^2$

? = 1 + 25

? = **26**

Hence, the number 26 will replace the question mark.

22. (b)

From fig. a: 7 × 6 + 3 = 45

From fig. b: 5 × 4 + 6 = 26

From fig. c: 7 × 3 + 8 = **29**

Hence, the number 29 will replace the question mark.

23. (c)

From fig. a:

$9^2 + 8^2 + 7^2 + 6^2 = 81 + 64 + 49 + 36 = 230$

From fig.

b: $6^2 + 7^2 + 3^2 + 4^2 = 36 + 49 + 9 + 16 = 110$

From fig. c:

$9^2 + 6^2 + 5^2 + 4^2 = 81 + 36 + 25 + 16 =$ **158**

Hence, the number 158 will replace the question mark.

24. (c)

$(4 + 3)^2 = (7)^2 = 49$

$(8 + 5)^2 = (13)^2 = 169$

$(11 + 12)^2 = (23)^2 = 529$

$(10 + 9)^2 = (19)^2 =$ **361**

Hence, the number 361 will replace the question mark.

25. (b)

From column I : (9 × 5) % 5 = 9

From column II : (17 × 4) % 4 = 17

From column III : (16 × ?) % 8 = 8

16 × ? = 64

? = **4**

Hence, the number 4 will replace the question mark.

26. (a)

From fig. a : (8 × 5) – (4 × 3) = 28

From fig. b : (12 × 7) – (8 × 9) = 12

From fig. c : (5 × 3) – (6 × ?) = 21

15 – 6 × ? = 21

6 × ? = – 6

? = – **1**

Hence, the number – 1 will replace the question mark.

27. (a)

In each row there are 'A', 'B' and 'C'

In second row 'A' and 'C' are already there

Hence in place of ?, there will be 'B'.

From first row : 4A × 6C = 24B

From third row : 9B × 4C = 36A

From second row : 5A × ? = 45C

? = (45C/5A)

? = 9B

Hence, the number 9B will replace the question mark.

28. (b)

$(5)^2 = 25$

$(6)^2 = 36$

$(4)^2 = 16$

$(7)^2 = 49$

Hence, the number 49 will replace the question mark.

29. (c)

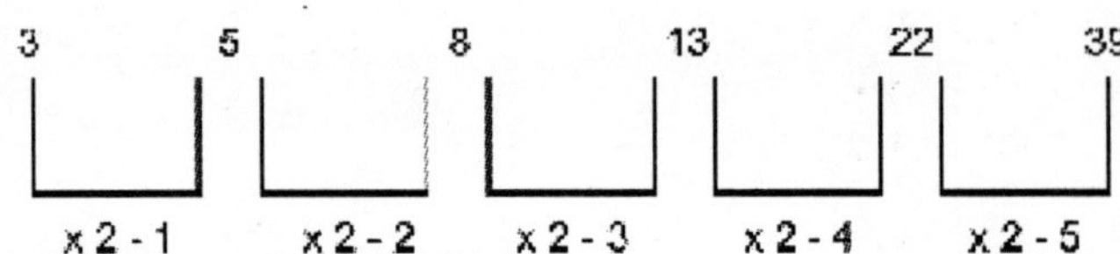

30. (a)

$(12)^2 - (8)^2 = 8$

and $(16)^2 - (7)^2 = 207$

Therefore $(25)^2 - (21)^2 = 184$.

31. (d)

$(2)^3 + (1)^3 + (3)^3 = 36$

and $(0)^3 + (4)^3 + (3)^3 = 91$

Therefore, $(4)^3 + (2)^3 + (1)^3 = 73$

32. (c)

(6 + 5) – (7 + 4) = 0

and (7 + 6) – (8 + 4) = 1

Therefore (11 + 2) – (2 + 0) = 11

33. (a)

The numbers are squared in ascending order

In first circle,

$(3)^2 = 9$

$(4)^2 = 16$

$(5)^2 = 25$

$(6)^2 = 36$

In second circle,

$(4)^2 = 16$

$(5)^2 = 25$

$(6)^2 = 36$

$(7)^2 = 49$

In third circle,

$(6)^2 = 36$

$(7)^2 = 49$

$(8)^2 = 64$

$(9)^2 = 81$

34. (c)

(4 × 6) % 3 = 8

(6 × 10) % 5 = 12

(4 × 8) % 2 = 16

35. (b)
$(7 \times 3) + 8 = 29$
$(4 \times 3) + 7 = 19$
$(5 \times ?) + 6 = 31$
$? = 5$

36. (a)
$(4)^2 + (2)^2 + (1)^2 = 21$
$(5)^2 + (3)^2 + (8)^2 = 98$
Therefore $(6)^2 + (7)^2 + (3)^2 = 94$

37. (b)
$(2)^2 + (4)^2 = 20$
$(3)^2 + (9)^2 = 90$
Therefore $(1)^2 + (5)^2 = 26$

38. (b)
$(7 \times 3) = 21$ $(9 \times 3) = 27$
$(4 \times 9) = 36$ $(2 \times 9) = 18$
Therefore $(9 \times 6) = 54$ $(4 \times 6) = 24$

39. (b)
$(16 + 13) = (14 + 15)$
$(28 + 12) = (10 + 30)$
Therefore $(29 + 16) = (15 + 30)$

40. (d)
$(3 \times 4) + 3 = 15$
$(7 \times 5) + 3 = 38$
Therefore $(3 \times 5) + 3 = 18$

❐

Previous Year Questions

1. Which one will replace the question mark?
[NTSE 2002 - Maharashtra second stage paper]

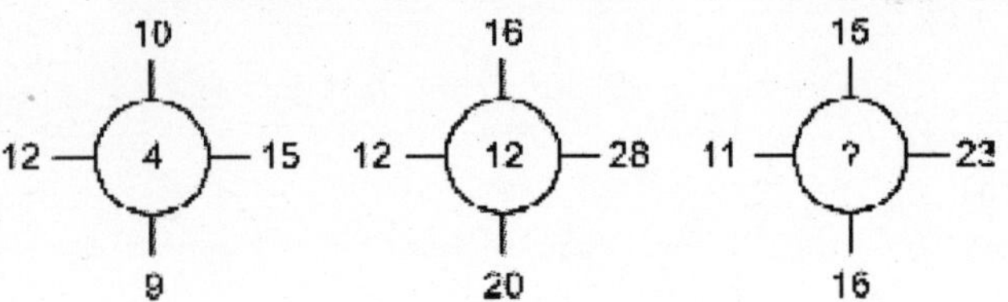

(a) 11 (b) 14
(c) 10 (d) 12

2. Which one will replace the question mark?
[NTSE 2000 - Delhi first stage paper]

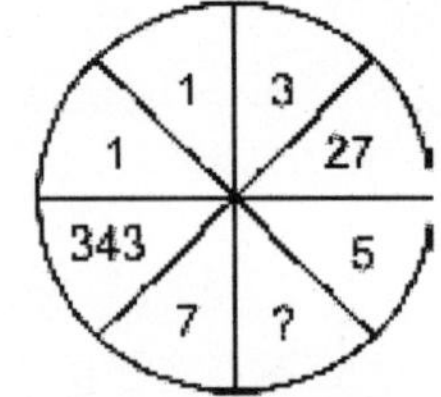

(a) 25 (b) 625
(c) 125 (d) 50

3. Which one will replace the question mark?
[NTSE 2003 - MP second stage paper]

4	9	2
3	5	7
8	1	?

(a) 9 (b) 6
(c) 15 (d) 14

4. Which one will replace the question mark?
[NTSE 2004 – Jammu second stage paper]

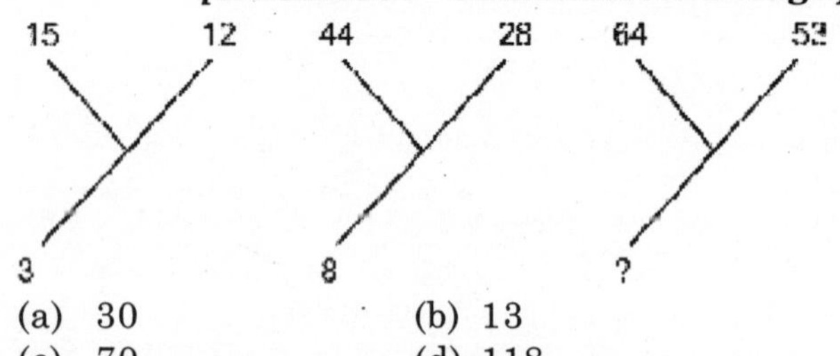

(a) 30 (b) 13
(c) 70 (d) 118

5. Which one will replace the question mark?
[NTSE 2012 - UP first stage paper]

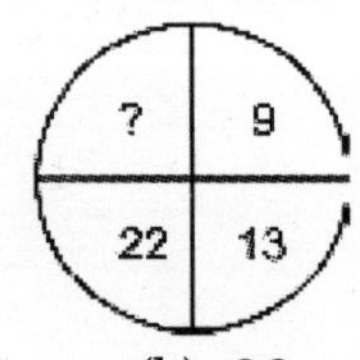

(a) 40 (b) 38
(c) 44 (d) 39

6. Which one will replace the question mark?
[NTSE 2000 - Punjab second stage paper]

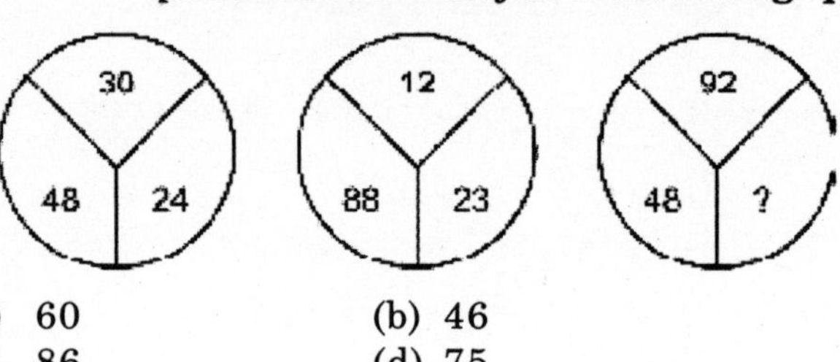

(a) 60 (b) 46
(c) 86 (d) 75

7. Which one will replace the question mark?
[NTSE 2005 - Delhi second stage paper]

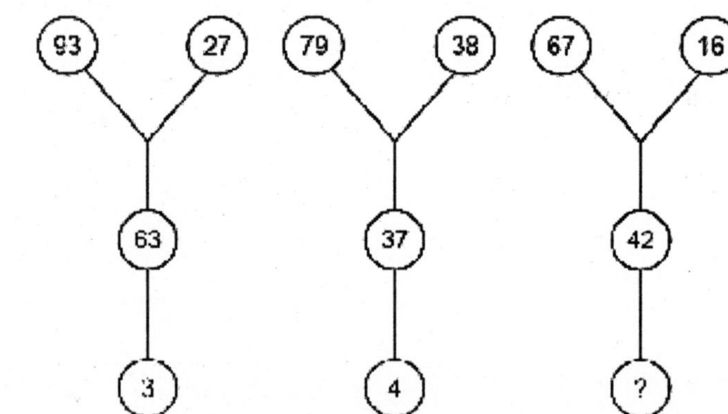

(a) 5 (b) 6
(c) 8 (d) 9

8. Which one will replace the question mark?
[NTSE 2002 - Bihar first stage paper]

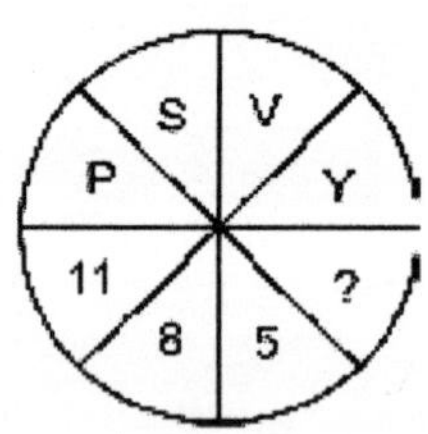

(a) 3 (b) 2
(c) 7 (d) 6

9. Which one will replace the question mark?
[NTSE 2001 - Punjab second stage paper]

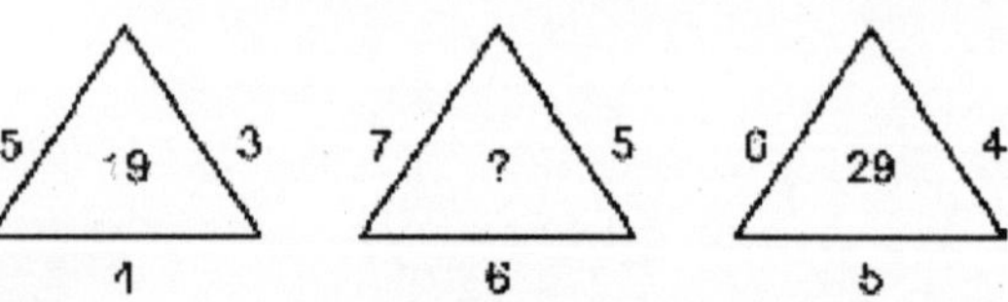

(a) 25 (b) 37
(c) 41 (d) 47

Answer Key

1. (a)	2. (c)	3. (b)	4. (b)	5. (b)	6. (c)	7. (d)	8. (b)	9. (c)

Explanatory Notes

1. (a)
(15 – 12) + (10 – 9) = 4
(28 – 12) + (16 – 20) = 12
Similarly, (23 – 11) + (15 – 16) = 11

2. (c)
All numbers are cubed,
$(7)^3 = 343$
$(1)^3 = 1$
$(3)^3 = 27$
Similarly, $(5)^3 = 125$

3. (b)
(4 + 9 + 2) = (3 + 5 + 7) = (8 + 1 + 6)
The sum of numbers in each row = 15

4. (b)
(15 + 12)/9 = 3
(44 + 28)/9 = 8
Therefore, (64 + 53)/9 = 13

5. (b)
$9 + (2)^2 = 13$
$13 + (3)^2 = 22$
$22 + (4)^2 = 38$

6. (c)
(30 – 24) × 8 = 48
and (23 – 12) × 8 = 88
Therefore, (92 – 86) × 8 = 48

7. (d)
93 – (27 + 3) = 63
79 – (38 + 4) = 37
Therefore, 67 – (16 + X) = 42
X = 9

8. (b)
Putting the position of the letters in reverse order
P = 11, S = 8, V = 5 and Y = 2

9. (c)
(5 × 3) + 4 = 19
(6 × 4) + 5 = 29
Therefore, (7 × 5) + 6 = 41

❐

UNIT 8

Logical Venn Diagrams

Venn diagrams are illustrations used in the branch of mathematics known as set theory. They are used to show the mathematical or logical relationship between different groups of things (sets). A Venn diagram shows all the logical relations between the sets.

The questions on diagrams test the ability of candidates to understand the relations among some items of a group. So you have to comprehend all the the relations expressed by digrams to solve such questions.

Illustrations

1. If all the words are of different groups, then they will be shown by the diagram as given below.

Dog, Cow, Horse

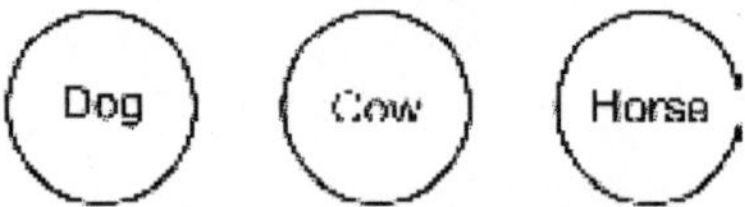

All these three are animals but of different groups, there is no relation between them. Hence they will be represented by three different circles.

2. If the first word is related to second word and second word is related to third word. Then they will be shown by diagram as given below.

Unit, Tens, Hundreds

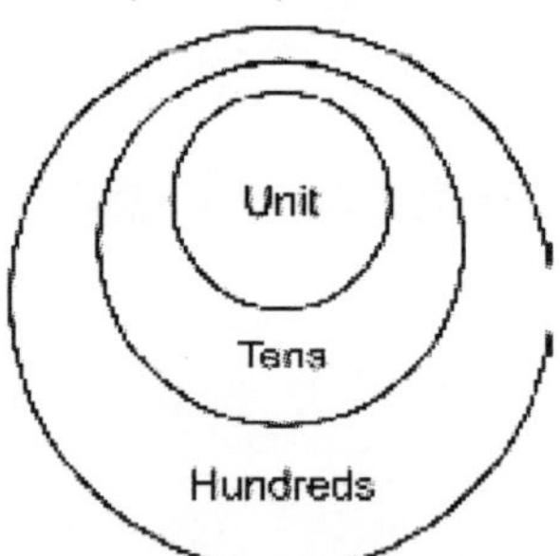

Ten units together make one Tens or in one tens, whole unit is available and ten tens together make one hundreds.

3. If two different items are completely related to third item, they will be shown as below.

Pen, Pencil, Stationery

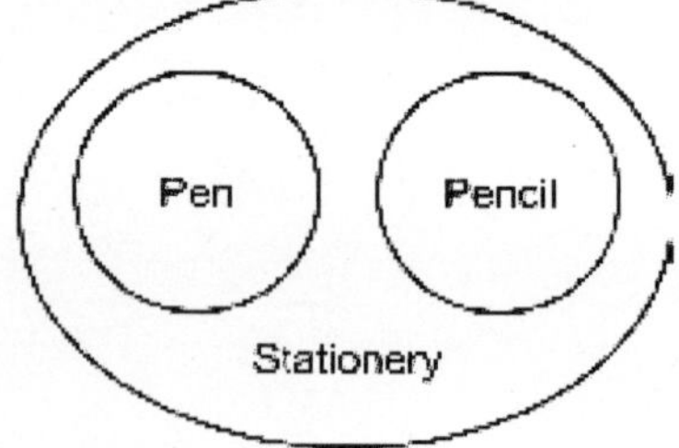

4. If there is some relation between two items and these two items are completely related to a third item they will be shown as given below.

Women, Sisters, Mothers

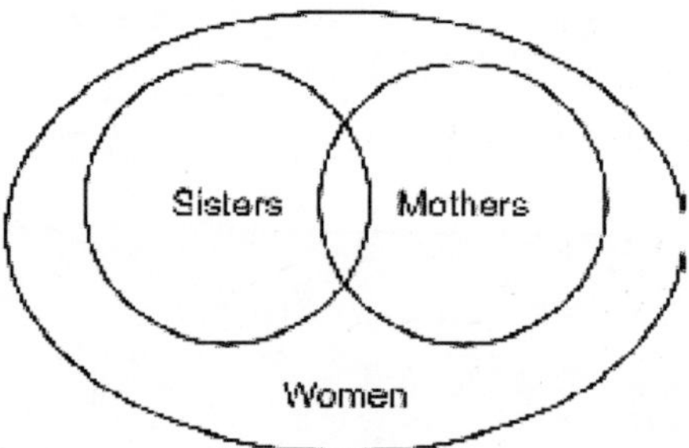

Some sisters may be mothers and vice-versa. Similarly some mothers may not be sisters and vice-versa. But all the sisters and all the mothers belong to women group.

5. Two items are related to a third item to some extent but not completely and first two items totally different.

Students, Boys, Girls

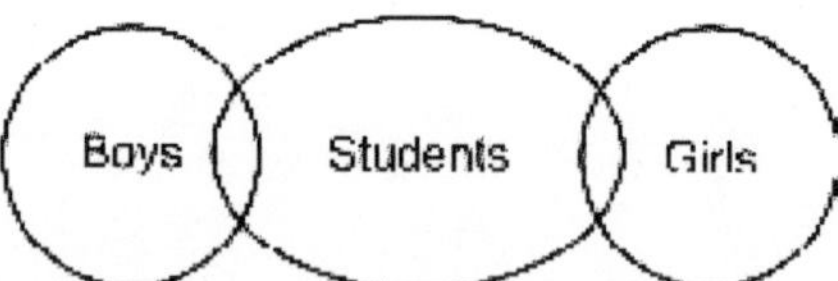

The boys and girls are different items while some boys may be students. Similarly among girls some may be students.

6. All the three items are related to one another but to some extent not completely.

Boys, Students, Athletes

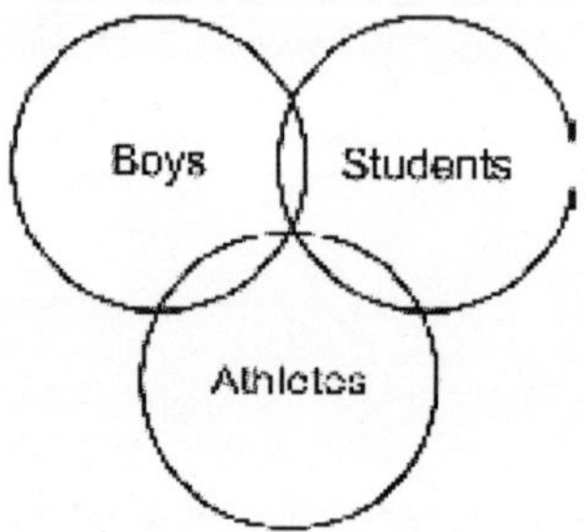

Some boys may be students and vice-versa. Similarly some boys may be athletes and vice-versa. Some students may be athletes and vice-versa.

7. Two items are related to each other completely and third item is entirely different from first two.

Lions, Carnivorous, Cows

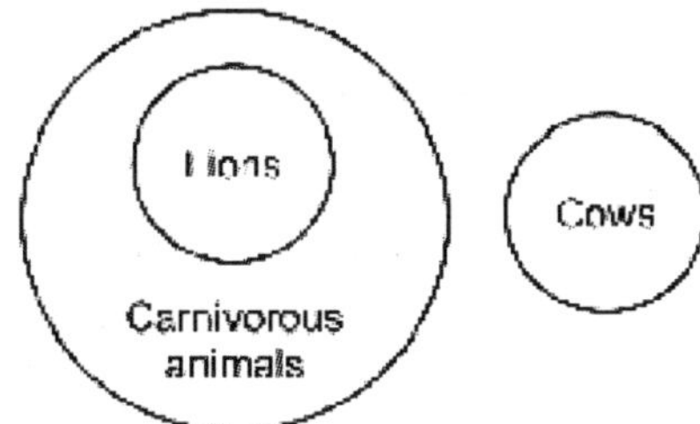

All the lions are carnivorous but no cow is lion or carnivorous.

8. First item is completely related to second and third item is partially related to first and second item.

Dogs, Animals, Flesh-eaters

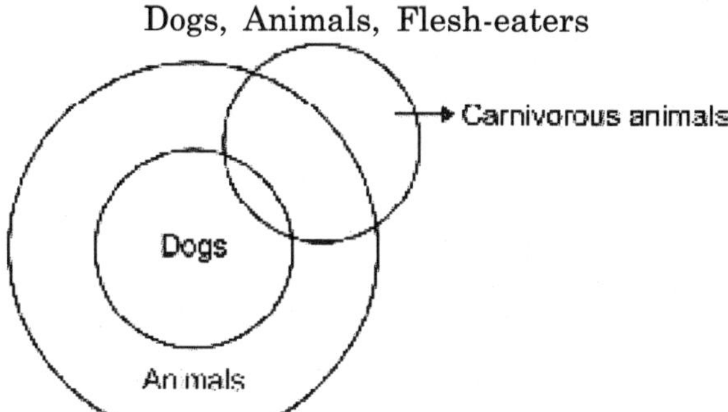

All the dogs belong to animals but some dogs are flesh eaters but not all.

9. First item is partially related to second but third is entirely different from the first two.

Dogs, Flesh-eaters, Cows

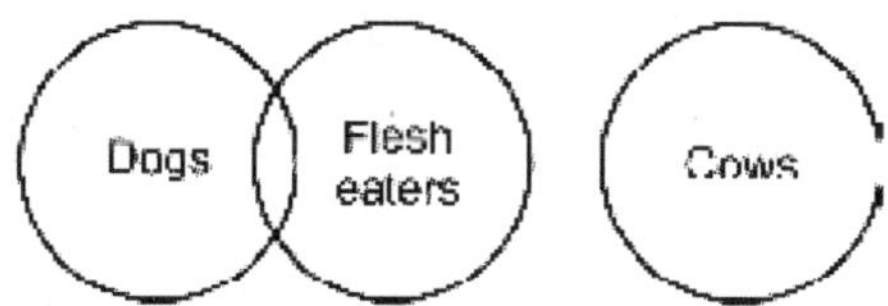

Some dogs are flesh-eaters but not all while any dog or any flesh-eater cannot be cow.

Solved Examples

Direction to solve (1 to 6): *Each of the questions given below contains three elements. These elements may or may not have some inter linkage. Each group of elements may fit into one of these diagrams at (A), (B), (C), (D) and/or (E). You have to indicate the group of elements which correctly fits into the diagrams.*

1. Which of the following diagrams indicates the best relation between Paper, Stationery and Ink?

A. 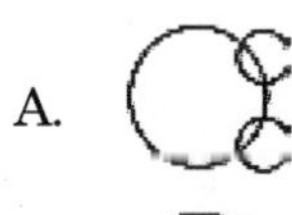 B. 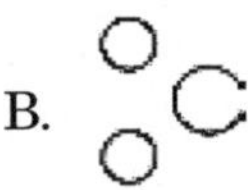

C.  D. 

Solution: Option (a) is correct.

Explanation: Paper and Ink are different from each other but both belong to stationery.

2. Which of the following diagrams indicates the best relation between Oil, Wick and Lamp?

A. 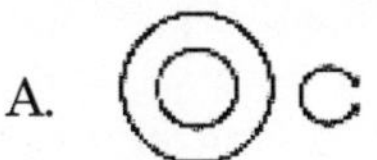 B. 

C.  D. 

Solution: Option (d) is correct.

Explanation: Oil and Wick are different from each other but they both are used in lamp.

3. Which of the following diagrams indicates the best relation between Football, Player and Field?

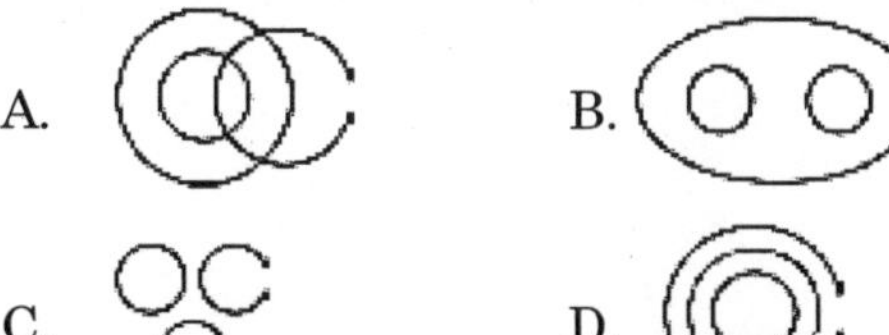

Solution: Option (c) is correct.

Explanation: Football, Players and Field all are different.

4. Which of the following diagrams indicates the best relation between Sweets, Rasagulla and Apple?

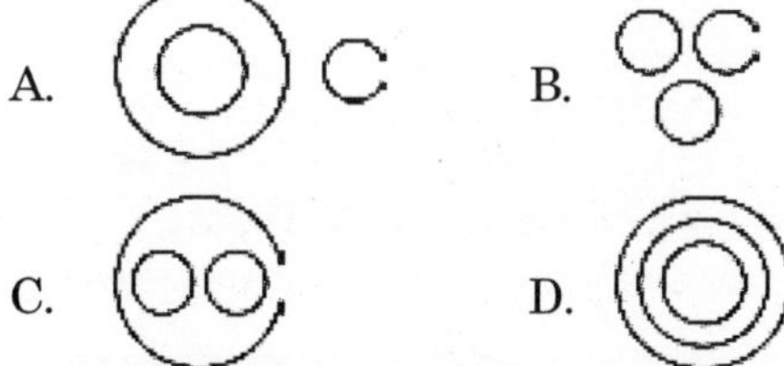

Solution: Option (a) is correct.

Explanation: Rasagulla is one of the sweets while apple is different from these.

5. Which of the following diagrams indicates the best relation between Mammal, Cow and Bat?

A. 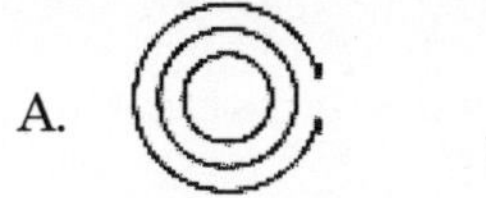 B. 

Solution: Option (b) is correct.

Explanation: Cow and Bat are different from each other but both are mammal.

6. Which of the following diagrams indicates the best relation between Tall man, Black haired people and Indians?

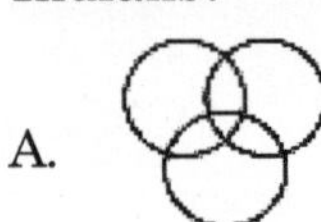

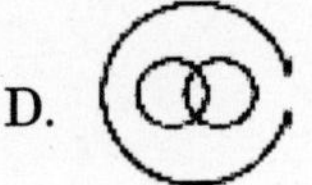

Solution: Option (a) is correct.

Explanation:

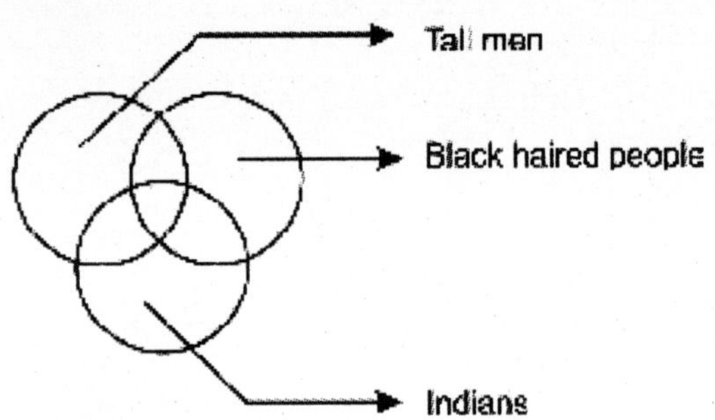

Multiple Choice Questions

Each of these questions given below contains three elements. These elements may or may not have some inter linkage. Each group of elements may fit into one of these diagrams at (A), (B), (C), (D). You have to indicate the group of elements which correctly fits into the diagrams.

1. Which of the following diagrams indicates the best relation between Sailor, Ship and Ocean?

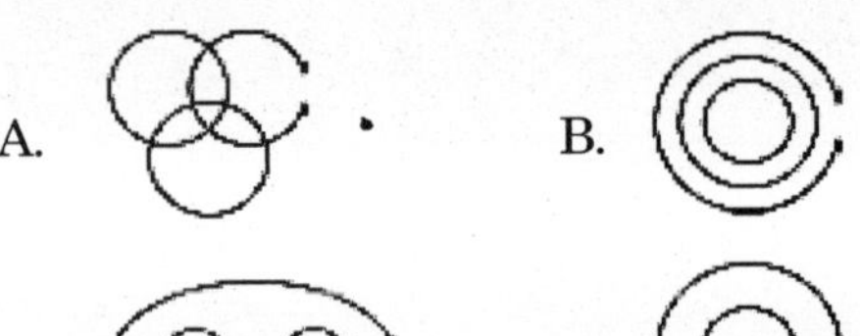

2. Which of the following diagrams indicates the best relation between Gold, Metal and Zinc?

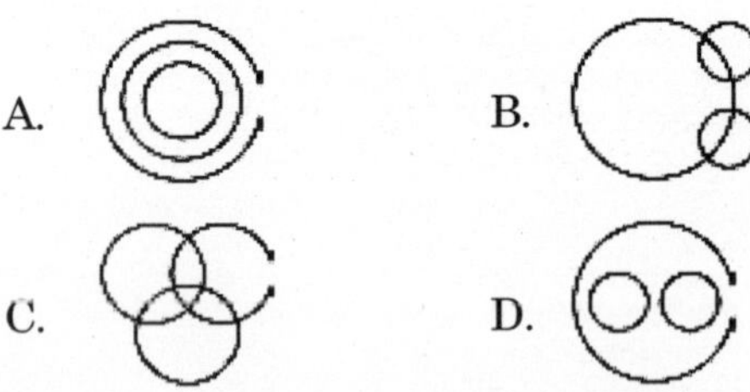

3. Which of the following diagrams indicates the best relation between Professors, Doctors and Men?

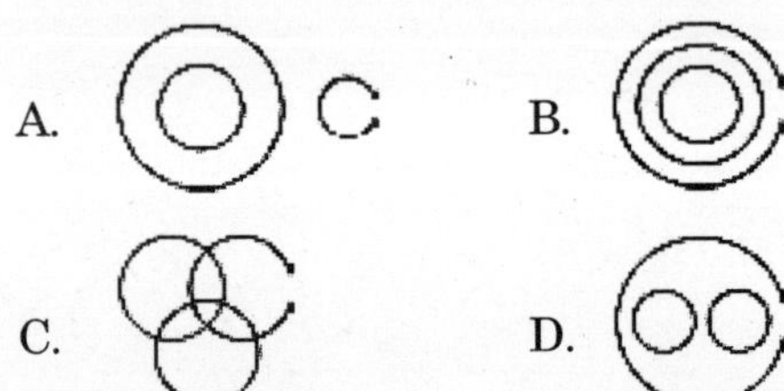

4. Which of the following diagrams indicates the best relation between Ass, Pet and Horse?

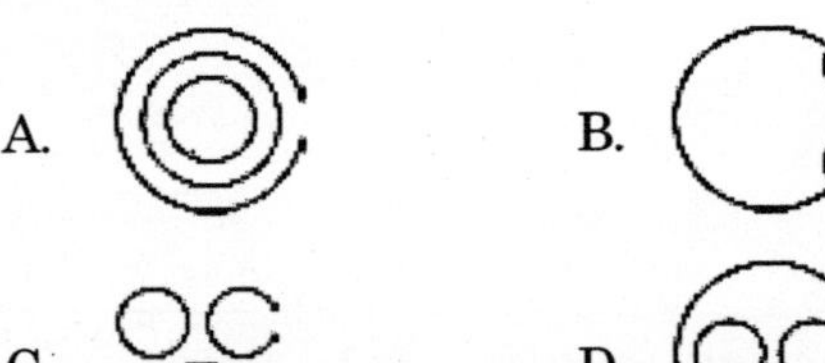

5. Which of the following diagrams indicates the best relation between Page, Chapter and Book?

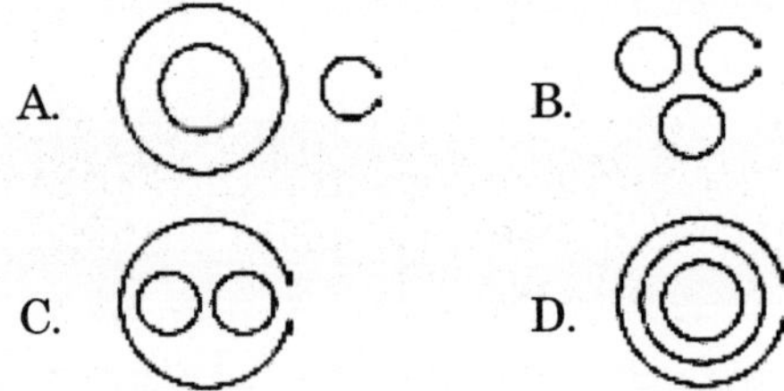

6. Which of the following diagrams indicates the best relation between Parents, Mother and Father?

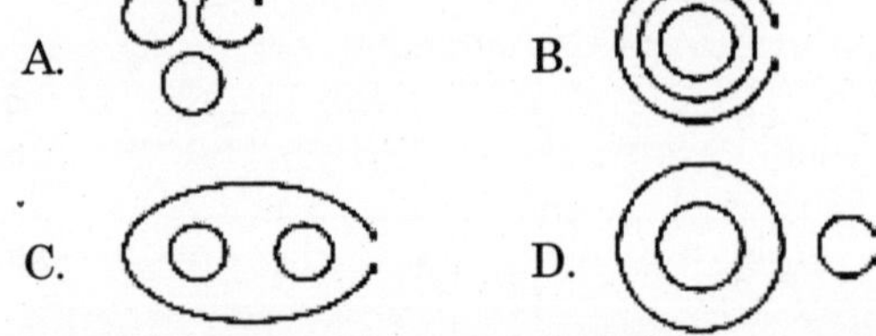

7. Which of the following diagrams indicates the best relation between Men, Rodents and Living beings?

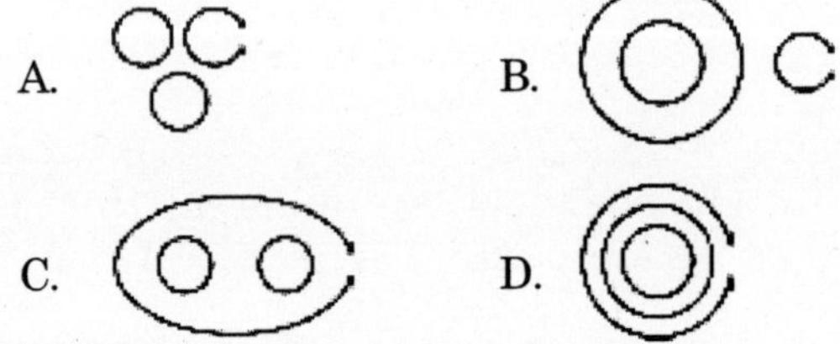

8. Which of the following diagrams indicates the best relation between Elephants, Wolves and Animals?

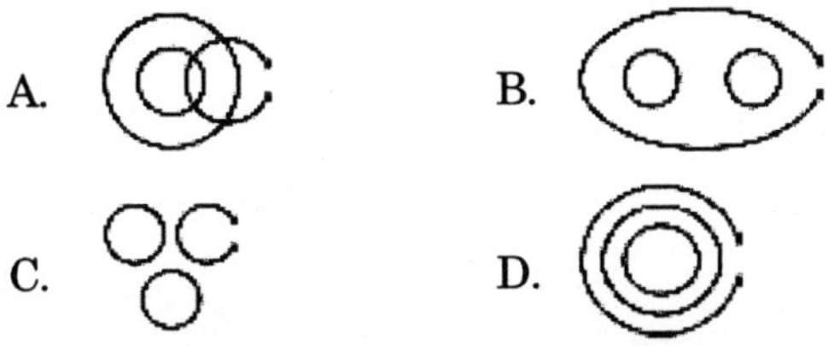

A. B.

C. D.

9. Which of the following diagrams indicates the best relation between Furniture, Chairs and Tables?

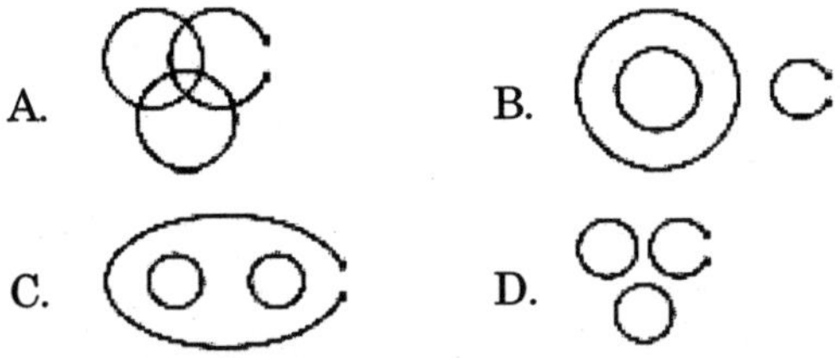

A. B.

C. D.

10. Which of the following diagrams indicates the best relation between Elephant, Carnivorous and Tiger?

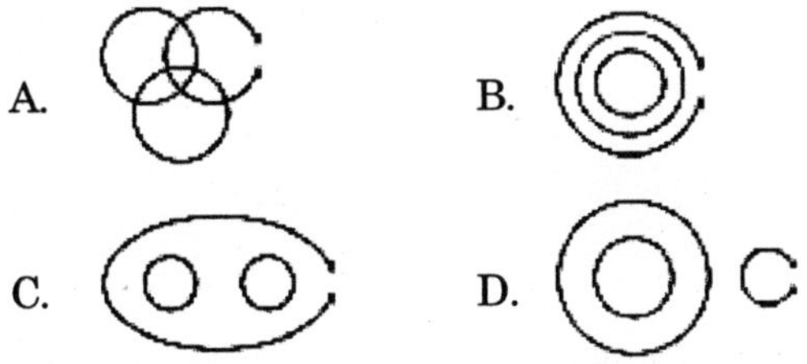

A. B.

C. D.

11. Which of the following diagrams indicates the best relation between Class, Blackboard and School?

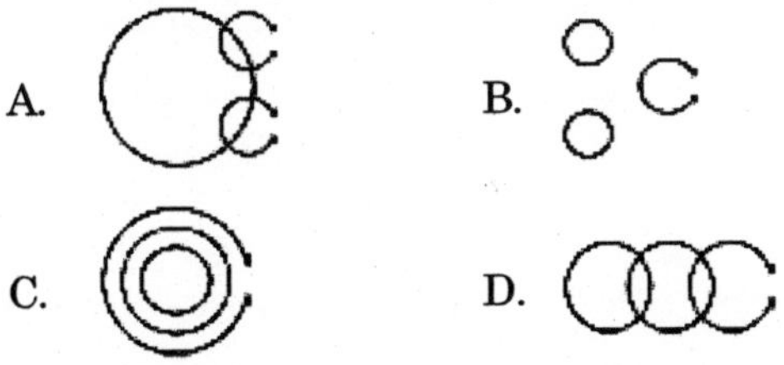

A. B.

C. D.

12. Which of the following diagrams indicates the best relation between Rabi-Crop, Paddy and Wheat?

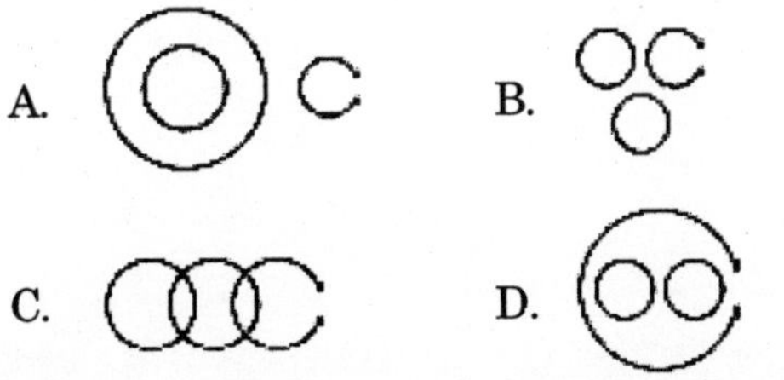

A. B.

C. D.

13. Which of the following diagrams indicates the best relation between Hospital, Nurse and Patient?

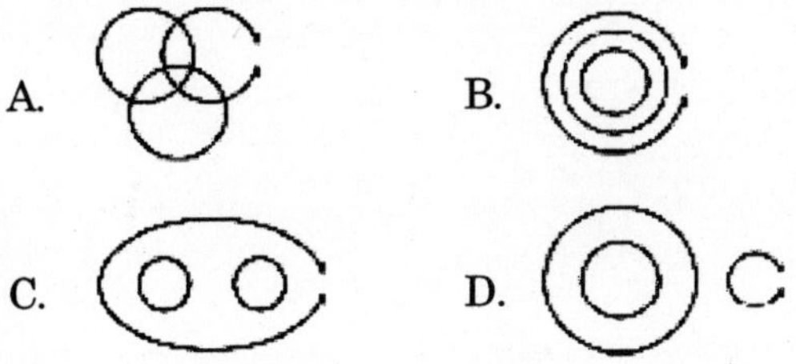

A. B.

C. D.

14. Which of the following diagrams indicates the best relation between Mercury, Zinc and Metal?

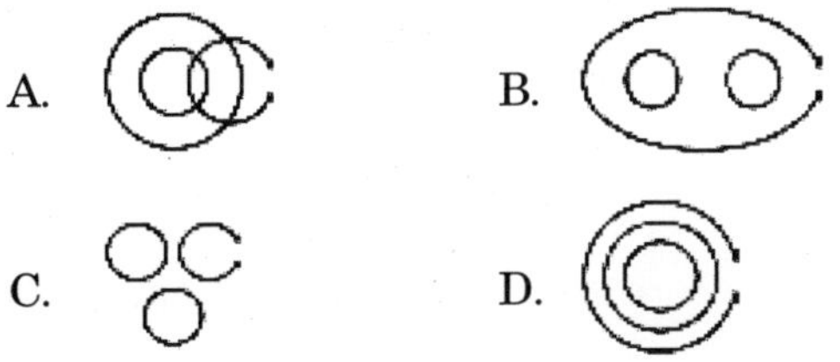

A. B.

C. D.

15. Which of the following diagrams indicates the best relation between Teacher, Writer and Musician?

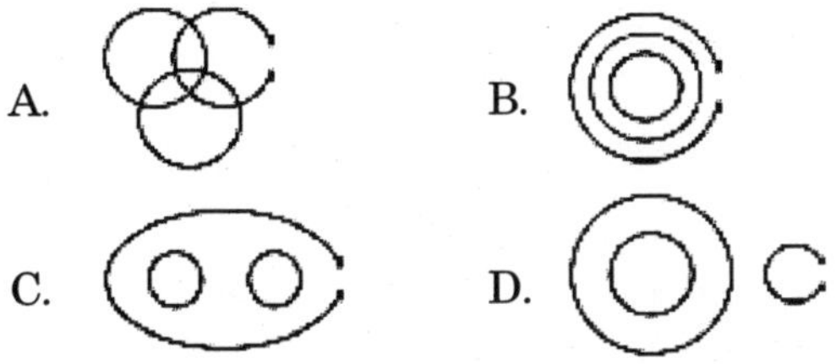

A. B.

C. D.

16. Which of the following diagrams indicates the best relation between Iron, Lead and Nitrogen?

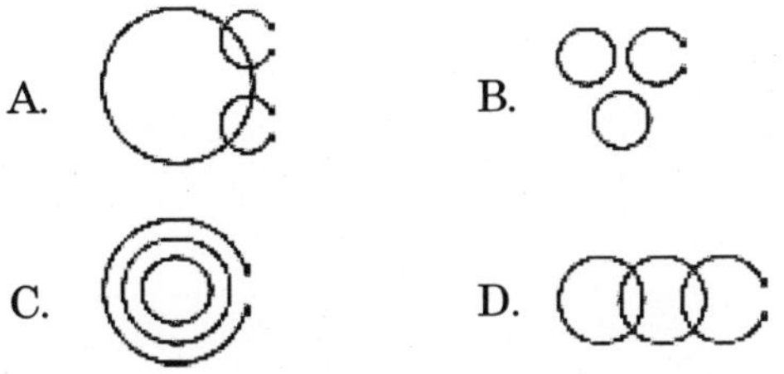

A. B.

C. D.

17. Which of the following diagrams indicates the best relation between Examination, Questions and Practice?

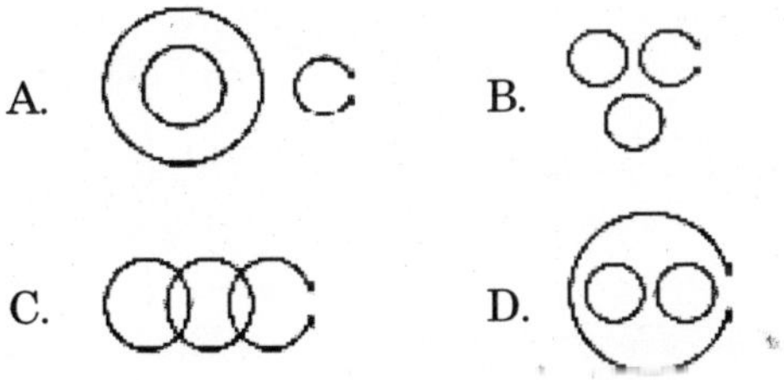

A. B.

C. D.

18. Which of the following diagrams indicates the best relation between Bulb, Lamp and Light?

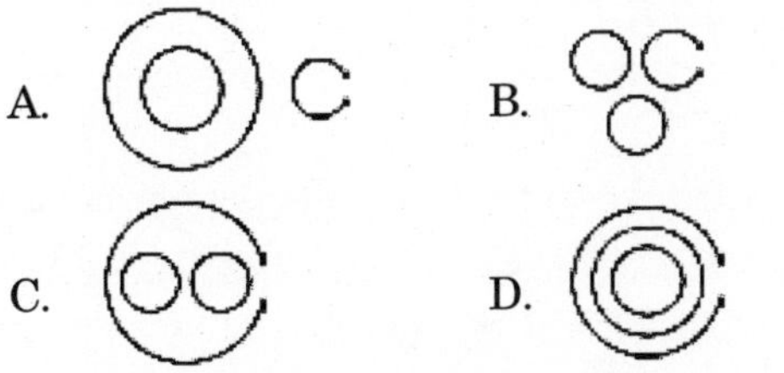

A. B.

C. D.

19. Which of the following diagrams indicates the best relation between Lion, Dog and Snake?

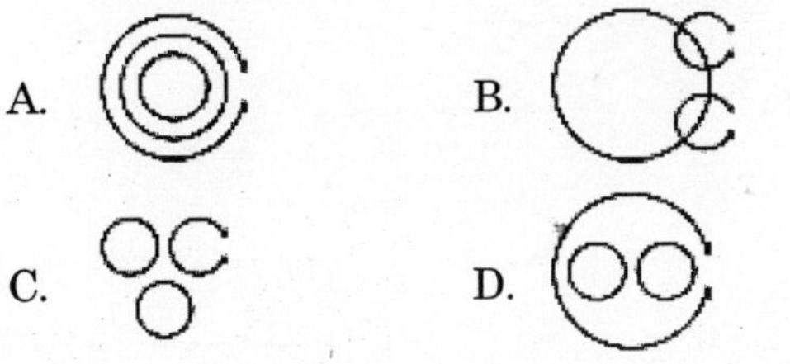

A. B.

C. D.

20. Which of the following diagrams indicates the best relation between Moon, Sun and Earth?

A. 

B. 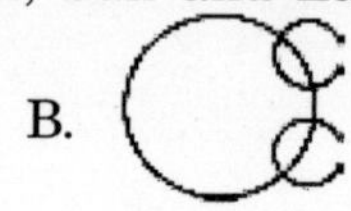

C.

D.

☛ ***Direction to solve (21 to 24) :** Study the following figure and answer the questions given below.*

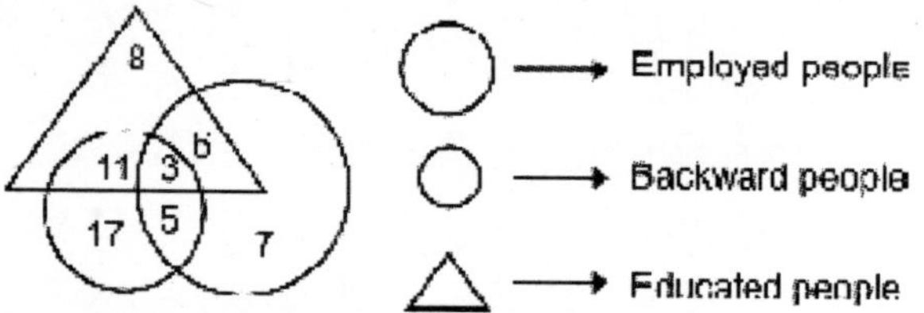

21. How many educated people are employed?
a. 9 b. 18
c. 20 d. 15

22. How many backward people are educated?
a. 9 b. 28
c. 14 d. 6

23. How many backward uneducated people are employed?
a. 14 b. 5
c. 7 d. 11

24. How many backward people are not educated?
a. 3 b. 14
c. 22 d. 25

☛ ***Direction to solve (25 to 29) :** In the following figure Small Square represents the persons who know English, triangle to those who know Marathi, big square to those who know Telugu and circle to those who know Hindi. In the different regions of the figures from 1 to 12 are given.*

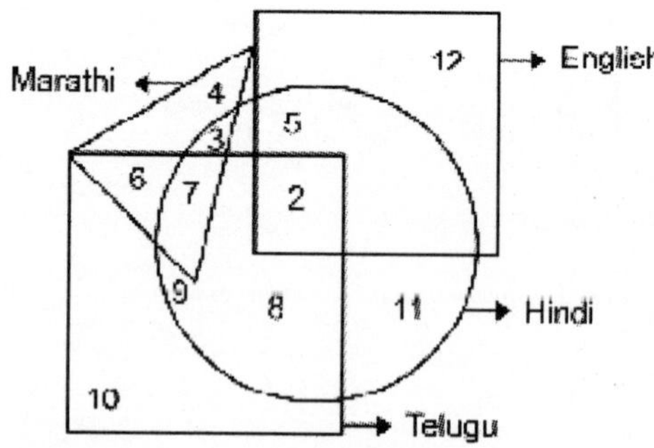

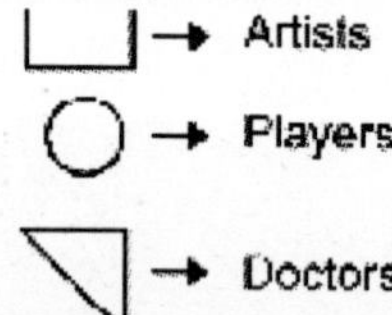

25. How many persons can speak English and Hindi both the languages only?
a. 5 b. 8
c. 7 d. 18

26. How many persons can speak Marathi and Telugu both?
a. 10 b. 11
c. 13 d. None of these

27. How many persons can speak only English?
a. 9 b. 12
c. 7 d. 19

28. How many persons can speak English, Hindi and Telugu?
a. 8 b. 2
c. 7 d. None of these

29. How many persons can speak all the languages?
a. 1 b. 8
c. 2 d. None

☛ ***Direction to solve (30 to 34) :** Study the diagram given below and answer each of the following questions.*

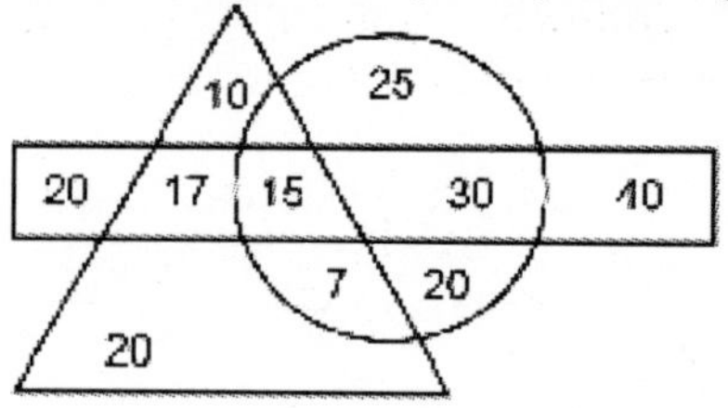

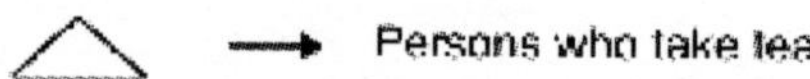

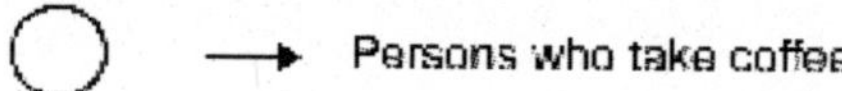

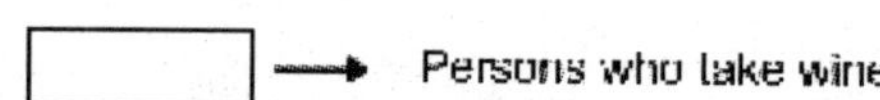

30. How many persons take tea and wine but not coffee?
a. 20 b. 17
c. 25 d. 15

31. How many persons take both tea and coffee but not wine?
a. 22 b. 17
c. 7 d. 20

32. How many persons take wine?
a. 100 b. 82
c. 92 d. 122

33. How many persons take only coffee?
a. 90 b. 45
c. 25 d. 20

34. How many persons take all the three?
a. 20 b. 17
c. 25 d. 15

35. Study the diagram and identify the people who can speak only one language.

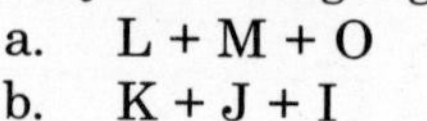

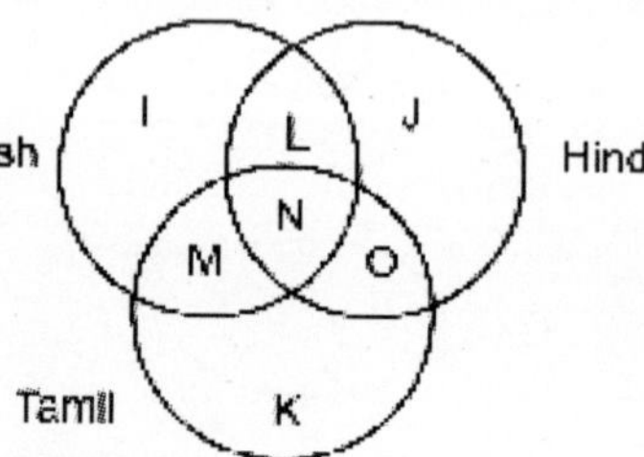

a. L + M + O
b. K + J + I
c. K
d. I

Answer Key

1. (b)	**2.** (d)	**3.** (c)	**4.** (d)	**5.** (d)	**6.** (c)	**7.** (c)	**8.** (b)	**9.** (c)	**10.** (d)	**11.** (c)
12. (a)	**13.** (c)	**14.** (b)	**15.** (a)	**16.** (b)	**17.** (c)	**18.** (c)	**19.** (c)	**20.** (c)	**21.** (a)	**22.** (c)
23. (b)	**24.** (c)	**25.** (a)	**26.** (c)	**27.** (b)	**28.** (b)	**29.** (d)	**30.** (b)	**31.** (c)	**32.** (d)	**33.** (b)
34. (d)	**35.** (b)									

Explanatory Notes

1. (b)
As ship is in the ocean, in the same way sailor is in the ship.

2. (d)
Gold and Zinc are different from each other but both are metal.

3. (c)
Some doctors may be professors and vice-versa.
Some professors may be men and vice-versa.
Some doctors may be men and vice-versa.
Some doctors may be men and professors as well.

4. (d)
Ass and Horse are different from each other but both are pet.

5. (d)
Page is in Chapter and Chapter is in book.

6. (c)
Father and mother are parents but father and mother are two opposite sexes.

7. (c)
Men and Rodents are different from each other but both these belong to living beings.

8. (b)
Elephant and Wolves bear no relationship to each other while both are animals.

9. (c)
Both chairs and tables are furniture but no chair is table.

10. (d)
Tiger is carnivorous but Elephant is different from these two.

11. (c)
Blackboard is in class and class is in the school.

12. (a)
Wheat and Paddy are different from each other but Wheat is the Rabi-Crop.

13. (c)
Hospital consists of nurse and patient but nurse and patient are of two different nature.

14. (b)
Mercury and Zinc both are different from each other but belong to metal.

15. (a)
A teacher may or may not be a writer and musician. Similarly a musician may or may not be a teacher and writer and so a writer may or may not be a teacher and musician.

16. (b)
All the three elements are different from each other.

17. (c)
Some questions are asked in examination and some in practice but examination and practice are different from each other.

18. (c)
Bulb and Lamp are different from each other but light is obtained from both.

19. (c)
All the three are different from each other.

20. (c)
All the three are different from each other.

21. (a)
Number of educated people who are employed
$= 3 + 6 = 9$

22. (c)
Number of backward people who are educated
$= 11 + 3 = 14$

23. (b)
Number of backward and uneducated people who are employed is 5

24. (c)
Number of backward people who are not educated
$= 17 + 5 = 22$

25. (a)
Number of persons who can speak English and Hindi both only is 5

26. (c)
$6 + 7 = 13$

27. (b)
Number of persons who can speak English is 12

28. (b)
Number of persons who can speak English, Hindi and Telugu is 2

29. (d)
There is no such person who can speak all the languages

30. (b)
17 persons take tea and wine but not coffee.

31. (c)
Number of persons who can take both tea and coffee but not wine is 7.

32. (d)
122 persons take wine.

33. (b)
$25 + 20 = 45$

34. (d)
15 persons take all the three.

35. (b)
The regions represented by the letters K, J and I denote such people who can speak only one language. ❐

Previous Year Questions

Direction to solve (1 to 5): *Study the following figure and answer the questions given below.*

[NTSE 2002 – Tamilnadu second stage paper]

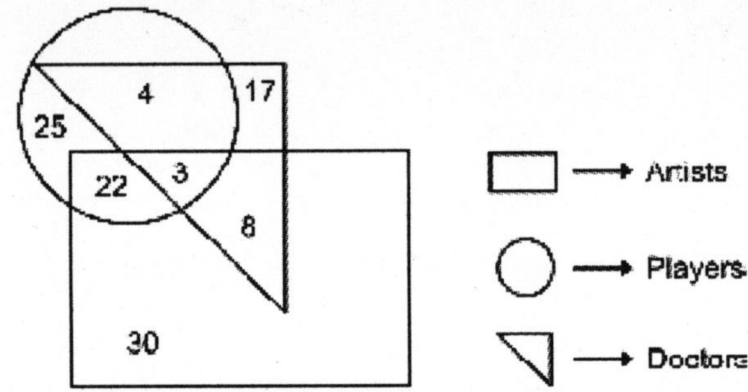

1. How many doctors are neither artists nor players?
   a. 17 b. 5
   c. 10 d. 30
2. How many doctors are both players and artists?
   a. 22 b. 8
   c. 3 d. 30
3. How many artists are players?
   a. 5 b. 8
   c. 25 d. 16
4. How many players are neither artists nor doctors?
   a. 25 b. 17
   c. 5 d. 10
5. How many artists are neither players nor doctors?
   a. 10 b. 17
   c. 30 d. 15
6. In the following diagram Rectangle represents men, Triangle represents educated, Circle represents urban and Square represents government employees.

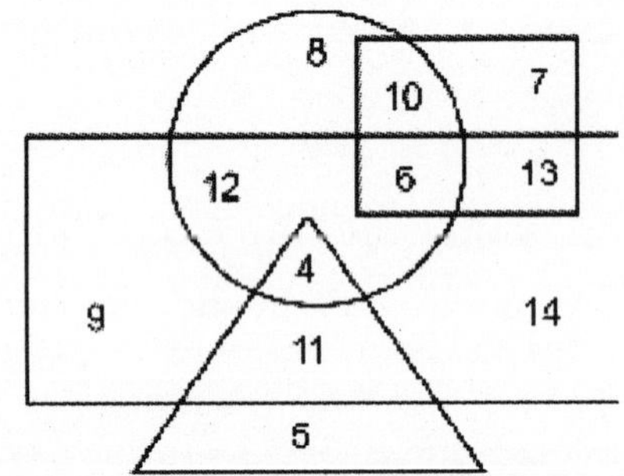

Which one of the following represents a woman who is urban as well as government employee?

[NTSE 2012 – Delhi second stage paper]

   a. 7 b. 13
   c. 10 d. 6
7. In the following diagram the boys who are athletic and are disciplined are indicated by which number?

[NTSE 2001– Tripura first stage paper]

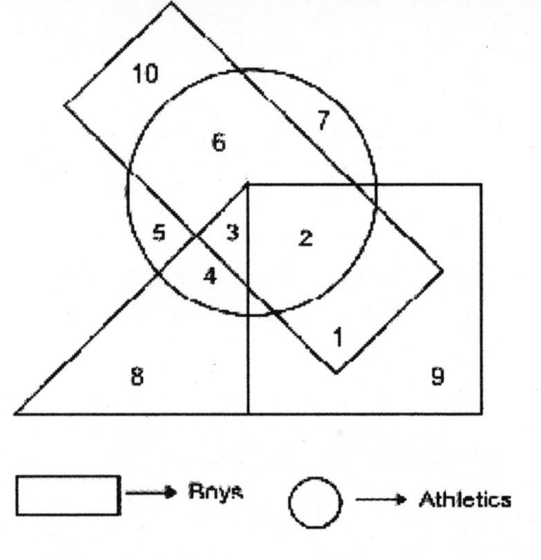

Girls Disciplined

   a. 1 b. 2
   c. 10 d. 6
8. In an organization of pollution control board, engineers are represented by a circle, legal experts by a square and environmentalist by a triangle. Who is most represented in the board as shown in the following figure?

[NTSE 2012 – Maharashtra first stage paper]

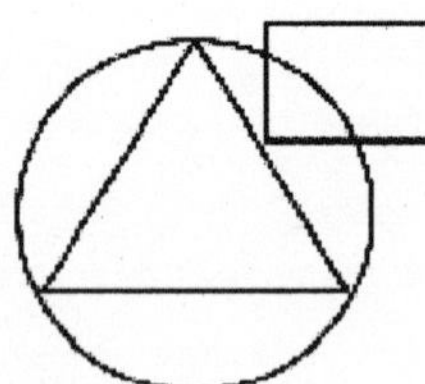

   a. Environmentalists
   b. Legal Experts
   c. Engineers with legal background
   d. Environmentalists with Engineering background
9. In the following figure triangle represents 'girls', square 'players' and 'circle' coach. Which part of the diagram represents the girls who are player but not coach?

[NTSE 2000 – Delhi second stage paper]

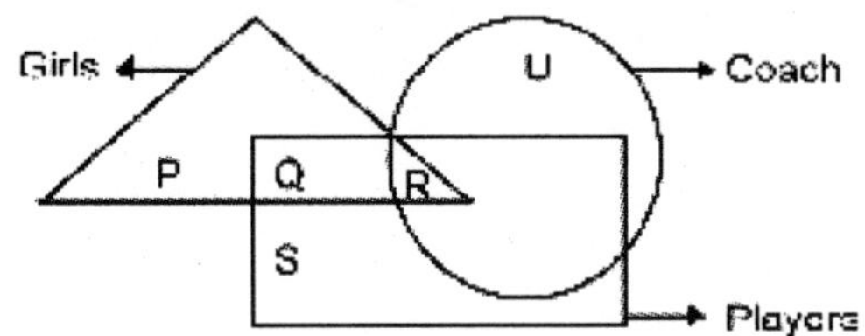

a. P b. Q
c. R d. S

10. The diagram given below represents those students who play Cricket, Football and Kabaddi.

Study the diagram and identify the students who play all the three games.

[NTSE 2003 – Chandigarh first stage paper]

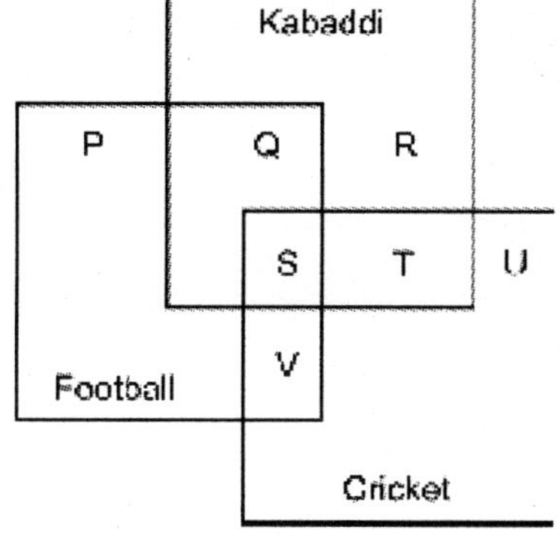

a. P + Q + R b. V + T
c. S + T + V d. S

Answer Key

1. (a)	2. (c)	3. (c)	4. (a)	5. (c)	6. (c)	7. (b)	8. (d)	9. (b)	10. (d)

Explanatory Notes

1. (a)
The number of doctors who are neither artists nor players is 17.

2. (c)
The number of doctors who are both players and artists is 3.

3. (c)
The number of artists who are players is 22 + 3 = 25.

4. (a)
The number of players who are neither artists nor doctors is 25.

5. (c)
The number of artists who are neither players nor doctors is 30.

6. (c)
Rectangle represents men; therefore the area outside the rectangle should represent women.
Ans. = [Woman, Urban and Government Employee]
Conditions: Outside the rectangle(women), Circle (urban) and Square (Govt. employee)
From the given diagram we can find that the value 10 satisfies the above conditions.
Therefore the answer is 10.

7. (b)
The required number is 2.

8. (d)
Environmentalists with Engineering background are most represented in the board.

9. (b)
The Q part of the figure represents those girls who are players but not coach.

10. (d)
S indicates those students who play all three games.

❐

UNIT 9

Blood Relations

What is Blood Relation?

Blood relation logical problems mainly deal with the hierarchical structure of a family i.e. grandparents, parents and children etc. Different relationships between the family members of different generations is given. To solve the questions related to blood relations, the entire family tree has to be drawn by putting down the various relationships.

In such problems, the aptitude of candidates is shown by the knowledge of various blood relations. The typical relationships that are commonly used in blood relation problems are summarized as follows :

Types of Relations

Relations of Paternal side

- Father's father → Grandfather
- Father's brother → Uncle
- Children of uncle → Cousin
- Children of aunt → Cousin
- Father's mother → Grandmother
- Father's sister → Aunt
- Wife of uncle → Aunt
- Husband of aunt → Uncle

Relations of Maternal side

- Mother's father → Maternal grandfather
- Mother's brother → Maternal uncle
- Children of maternal uncle → Cousin
- Mother's mother → Maternal grandmother
- Mother's sister → Aunt
- Wife of maternal uncle → Maternal aunt

Relations from one generation to next

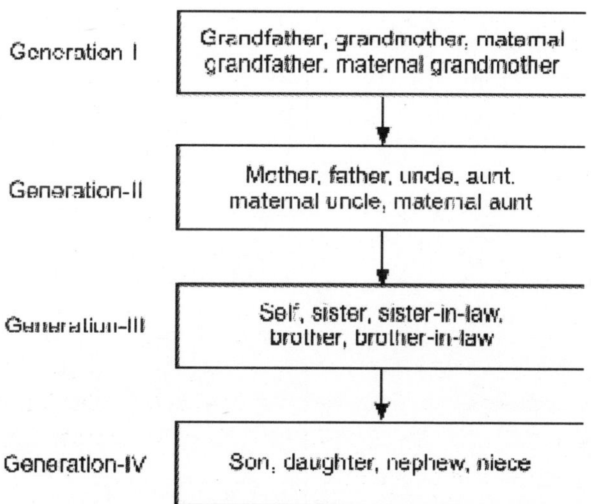

Some more tips:

- Grand Father's daughter – in – law = Mother
- Father's Son = Brother
- Father's Daughter = Sister
- Grand Father's son = Father/Uncle
- Grand Father's only son (Same in the case of Grand Mother) = Father

Approach to draw the family relations diagram

- Identify the persons who are in the given information.
- Identify who are male and who are female.
- Determine the generations of family.
- Identify the positions and generation of the family members and draw the diagram with relationships among family members using notations.
- Once the diagram is filled, you can find the solution to the given question.

Solved Examples

1. If A + B means A is the mother of B; A - B means A is the brother B; A % B means A is the father of B and A x B means A is the sister of B, which of the following shows that P is the maternal uncle of Q?
   a. $Q - N + M \times P$ b. $P + S \times N - Q$
   c. $P - M + N \times Q$ d. $Q - S \% P$
   Solution: Option (c) is correct.
   Explanation:
   $P - M \rightarrow$ P is the brother of M
   $M + N \rightarrow$ M is the mother of N
   $N \times Q \rightarrow$ N is the sister of Q
   Therefore, P is the maternal uncle of Q.
2. If A is the brother of B; B is the sister of C; and C is the father of D, how D is related to A?
   a. Brother b. Sister
   c. Nephew d. Cannot be determined
   Solution: Option (d) is correct.
   Explanation:
   If D is Male, the answer is Nephew.
   If D is Female, the answer is Niece.
   As the sex of D is not known, hence, the relation between D and A cannot be determined.

> ***Note :*** Niece - A daughter of one's brother or sister, or of one's brother-in-law or sister-in-law.
> Nephew - A son of one's brother or sister, or of one's brother-in-law or sister-in-law.

3. Pointing to a photograph of a boy Suresh said, "He is the son of the only son of my mother." How is Suresh related to that boy?
   a. Brother b. Uncle
   c. Cousin d. Father
   Solution: Option (d) is correct.
   Explanation: The boy in the photograph is the only son of the son of Suresh's mother i.e., the son of Suresh. Hence, Suresh is the father of boy.
4. Pointing to a man on the stage, Ritu said, "He is the brother of the daughter of the wife of my husband." How is the man on the stage related to Ritu?
   a. Husband b. Cousin
   c. Nephew d. Son
   Solution: Option (d) is correct.
   Explanation: Because, Wife of Husband - Herself; Brother of daughter - Son. So, the man is Ritu's Son.
5. A party consists of grandmother, father, mother, four sons and their wives and one son and two daughters to each of the sons. How many females are there is all?
   a. 14 b. 19
   c. 12 d. 25
   Solution: Option (a) is correct.
   Explanation: Grandmother is one female, mother is another, wives of four sons are the four females and two daughters of all four sons are eight females.
   So, in all there are 1 + 1 + 4 + 8 = 14 females.
6. Lata and Mona are Ravi's wives. Shalu is Mona's Step-daughter. How is Lata related to Shalu?
   a. Sister b. Mother-in-Law
   c. Mother d. Step-mother
   Solution: Option (c) is correct.
   Explanation: Shalu is Mona's step-daughter means Shalu is the daughter of the other wife of Ravi. So, Shalu is the daughter of Leena or Leena is the mother of Shalu.
7. Deepak has a brother Amit. Deepak is the son of Chaya. Binod is Chaya's father. In terms of relationship, what is Amit of Binod?
   a. Son b. Grandson
   c. Brother d. Grandfather
   Solution: Option (b) is correct.
   Explanation: Amit is the brother of Deepak and Deepak is the son of Chaya.So, Amit is the son of Chaya. Now, Binod is the father of Chaya.So, Amit is the grandson of Binod.
8. Disha's mother is the only daughter of Mona's father. How is Mona's husband related to Disha?
   a. Uncle b. Father
   c. Grandfather d. Brother
   Solution: Option (b) is correct.
   Explanation: Clearly, the only daughter of Mona's father is Mona herself. So, Disha's mother is Mona. Thus, Mona's husband is the father of Disha.
9. If (i) M is brother of N
   (ii) B is brother of N
   (iii) M is brother of D
   then which of the following statements is definitely true?
   a. N is brother of B b. N is brother of D
   c. M is brother of B d. D is brother of M
   Solution: Option (c) is correct.

Explanation: M is the brother of N and B is the brother of N. So, M is the brother of B.

10. Daya is brother of Raj. Rita is sister of Amit. Raj is son of Rita. How is Daya related to Rita?
    a. Son b. Brother
    c. Nephew d. Father
    Solution: Option (a) is correct.
    Explanation: Daya is the son of Raj, who is the son of Rita. Thus, Daya is the son of Rita.
11. A is B's sister. C is B's mother. D is C's father. E is D's mother .Then, how is A related to D?
    a. Grandmother
    b. Grandfather
    c. Daughter
    d. Grand daughter
    Solution: Option (d) is correct.
    Explanation: A is the sister of B and B is the daughter of C. So, A is the daughter of C. Also, D is the father of C. So, A is the granddaughter of D.
12. Given that:
    i. A is brother of B.
    ii. C is father of A
    iii. D is brother of E
    iv. E is daughter of B
    The uncle of D is:
    a. A b. B
    c. C d. E
    Solution: Option (a) is correct.
    Explanation: Clearly, D is the brother of E and E is the daughter of B. So, D is the son of B. Also, A is the brother of B. So, A is the uncle of D.
13. Pointing to Lalit in the photograph, Rajan said, "His mother has only one grandchild whose mother is my sister."How is Rajan related to Lalit?
    a. Brother
    b. Brother-in-law
    c. Father-in-law
    d. Data inadequate
    Solution: Option (b) is correct.
    Explanation:

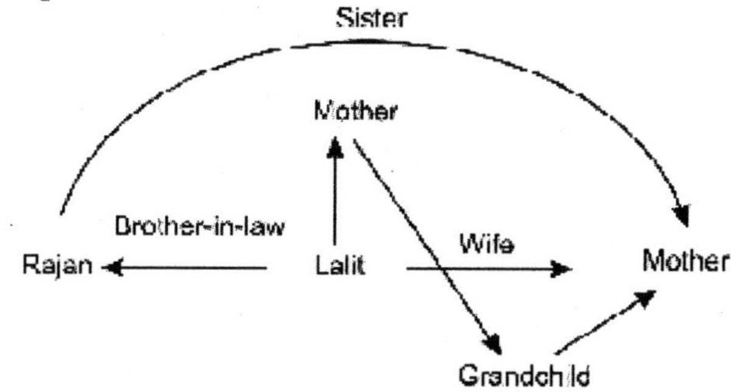

Multiple Choice Questions

1. If X + Y means X is the daughter of Y; X - Y means X is the brother of Y; X % Y means X is the father of Y and X x Y means X is the sister of Y. Which of the following means I is the niece of J?
   (a) J – N % C × I (b) I × C – N % J
   (c) J + M × C % I (d) I × C + N – J
2. M is the father of N who is the son of V. In order to know the relation of M to P, which of the statement/ statements is/are necessary?
   1. P is the brother of V.
   2. The daughter of N is the granddaughter of V.
   (a) Only (1) (b) Only (2)
   (c) Either (1) or (2) (d) (1) and (2) both
3. A is the son of C; C and Q are sisters; Z is the mother of Q and P is the son of Z. Which of the following statements is true?
   (a) P and A are cousins
   (b) P is the maternal uncle of A
   (c) Q is the maternal grandfather of A
   (d) C and P are sisters
4. If M x N means M is the daughter of N; M + N means M is the father of N; M % N means M is the mother of N and M – N means M is the brother of N, then P % Q + R – T x K indicates which relation of P to K?
   (a) Daughter-in-law
   (b) Sister-in-law
   (c) Aunt
   (d) None of these
5. If P + Q means P is the brother of Q; P x Q means P is the father of Q and P - Q means P is the sister of Q, which of the following relations shows that I is the niece of K?
   (a) K + Y + Z – I (b) K + Y x I – Z
   (c) Z – I x Y + K (d) K x Y + I – Z
6. Pointing towards a girl, Abhisek says, "This girl is the daughter of only a child of my father." What is the relation of Abhisek's wife to that girl?
   (a) Daughter (b) Mother
   (c) Aunt (d) Sister
7. A $ B means A is the father of B; A # B means A is the sister of B; A * B means A is the daughter of B and A @ B means A is the brother of (B) Which of the following indicates that M is the wife of Q?
   (a) Q $ R # T @ M (b) Q $ R @ T # M
   (c) Q $ R * T # M (d) Q $ R @ T * M
8. If A $ B means A is the brother of B; B * C means B is the son of C; C @ D means C is the wife of D and A # D means A is the son of D, how C is related to A?

(a) Maternal grandmother
(b) Maternal aunt
(c) Aunt
(d) Mother

9. Pointing to a girl Sandeep said, "She is the daughter of the only sister of my father." How is Sandeep related to the girl?
(a) Uncle (b) Cousin
(c) Father (d) Grandfather

10. Pointing to a boy in the photograph Reena said, "He is the only son of the only child of my grandfather." How Reena is related to that boy?
(a) Mother (b) Sister
(c) Aunt (d) Cannot be determined

11. Introducing a man, a woman said, "He is the only son of the mother of my mother." How is the woman related to the man?
(a) Mother (b) Sister
(c) Niece (d) Maternal aunt

12. Pointing to Gopi, Nalni says, "I am the daughter of the only son of his grandfather." How is Nalni related to Gopi?
(a) Niece (b) Daughter
(c) Sister (d) Cannot be determined

13. A's son B is married with C whose sister D is married to E the brother of (B) How D is related to A?
(a) Sister (b) Daughter's-in-law
(c) Sister-in-law (d) Cousin

14. Pointing to a lady a person said, "The son of her only brother is the brother of my wife." How is the lady related to the person?
(a) Maternal aunt
(b) Grandmother
(c) Sister of father-in-law
(d) None of these

15. Read the following statements:
1. B5D means B is the father of (D)
2. B9D means B is the sister of (D)
3. B4D means B is the brother of (D)
4. B3D means B is the wife of (D)
Which of the following means F is the mother of K?
(a) F3M5K (b) F5M3K
(c) F9M4N3K (d) F3M5N3K

16. Pointing to a photograph Anjali said, "He is the son of the only son of my grandfather." How is the man in the photograph related to Anjali?
(a) Brother (b) Uncle
(c) Son (d) Data is inadequate

17. Pointing to a person, Deepak said, "His only brother is the father of my daughter's father". How is the person related to Deepak?
(a) Father (b) Grandfather
(c) Uncle (d) Brother-in-law

18. P is the mother of K; K is the sister of D; D is the father of J. How is P related to J?
(a) Mother (b) Grandmother
(c) Aunt (d) Data inadequate

19. If P $ Q means P is the father of Q; P # Q means P is the mother of Q and P * Q means P is the sister of Q, then N # L $ P * Q shows which relation of Q to N?
(a) Grandson (b) Granddaughter
(c) Nephew (d) Data is inadequate

20. If A $ B means A is the brother of B; A @ B means A is the wife of B; A # B means A is the daughter of B; and A * B means A is the father of B, which of the following indicates that U is the father-in-law of P?
(a) P @ Q $ T # U * W
(b) P @ W $ Q * T # U
(c) P @ Q $ W * T # U
(d) P @ Q $ T # W * U

21. If A + B means A is the brother of B; A % B means A is the father of B and A x B means A is the sister of (B) Which of the following means M is the uncle of P?
(a) M % N x P (b) N x P % M
(c) M + S % R % P (d) M + K % T x P

22. Pointing to Varman, Madhav said, "I am the only son of one of the sons of his father." How is Varman related to Madhav?
(a) Nephew (b) Uncle
(c) Father or Uncle (d) Father

23. Introducing a woman, Shashank said, "She is the mother of the only daughter of my son." How that woman is related to Shashank?
(a) Daughter (b) Sister-in-law
(c) Wife (d) Daughter-in-law

24. If A + B means B is the brother of A; A x B means B is the husband of A; A - B means A is the mother of B and A % B means A is the father of B, which of the following relations shows that Q is the grandmother of T?
(a) Q - P + R % T (b) P x Q % R - T
(c) P x Q % R + T (d) P + Q % R – T

25. Read the following statements:
1. A3P means A is the mother of P
2. A4P means A is the brother of P
3. A9P means A is the husband of P
4. A5P means A is the daughter of P
Which of the following means that K is the mother-in-law of M?
(a) M9N3K4J (b) M9N5K3J
(c) K5J9M3N (d) K3J9N4M

26. Amit said - "This girl is the wife of the grandson of my mother". How is Amit related to the girl?
(a) Brother (b) Grandfather
(c) Husband (d) Father-in-law

27. A and B are children of (D) Who is the father of A? To answer this question which of the statements (1) and (2) is necessary?
1. C is the brother of A and the son of E.
2. F is the mother (B)

(a) Only (1)
(b) Only (2)
(c) Either (1) or (2)
(d) (1) and (2) both

28. Pointing towards a man, a woman said, "His mother is the only daughter of my mother." How is the woman related to the man?
(a) Mother (b) Grandmother
(c) Sister (d) Daughter

29. Introducing Salman, Aamir says, "She is the wife of only nephew of only brother of my mother." How Salman is related to Aamir?
(a) Wife (b) Sister
(c) Sister-in-law (d) Data is inadequate

30. Deepak said to Nitin, "That boy playing with the football is the younger of the two brothers of the daughter of my father's wife." How is the boy playing football related to Deepak?
(a) Son (b) Brother
(c) Cousin (d) Brother-in-law

31. Veena who is the sister-in-law of Ashok, is the daughter-in-law of Kalyani. Dheeraj is the father of Sudeep who is the only brother of Ashok. How Kalyani is related to Ashok?
(a) Mother-in-law (b) Aunt
(c) Wife (d) None of these

32. If A + B means A is the sister of B; A x B means A is the wife of B, A % B means A is the father of B and A - B means A is the brother of (B) Which of the following means T is the daughter of P?
(a) P x Q % R + S – T (b) P x Q % R – T + S
(c) P x Q % R + T – S (d) P x Q % R + S + T

33. Pointing to a woman, Abhijit said, "Her granddaughter is the only daughter of my brother." How is the woman related to Abhijit?
(a) Sister (b) Grandmother
(c) Mother-in-law (d) Mother

34. Pointing to a photograph Lata says, "He is the son of the only son of my grandfather." How is the man in the photograph related to Lata?
(a) Brother (b) Uncle
(c) Cousin (d) Data is inadequate

35. If A + B means A is the brother of B; A x B means A is the son of B; and A % B means B is the daughter of A then which of the following means M is the maternal uncle of N?
(a) M + O x N (b) M % O x N + P
(c) M + O % N (d) None of these

36. If D is the brother of B, how B is related to C? To answer this question which of the statements is/are necessary?
1. The son of D is the grandson of (C)
2. B is the sister of (D)
(a) Only 1
(b) Only 2
(c) Either 1 or 2
(d) 1 and 2 both are required

37. If A + B means A is the father of B; A - B means A is the brother B; A % B means A is the wife of B and A x B means A is the mother of B, which of the following shows that M is the maternal grandmother of T?
(a) M x N % S + T (b) M x N - S % T
(c) M x S - N % T (d) M x N x S % T

38. Pointing to a photograph. Bajpai said, "He is the son of the only daughter of the father of my brother." How Bajpai is related to the man in the photograph?
(a) Nephew (b) Brother
(c) Father (d) Maternal Uncle

39. Introducing a boy, a girl said, "He is the son of the daughter of the father of my uncle." How is the boy related to the girl?
(a) Brother (b) Nephew
(c) Uncle (d) Son-in-law

40. Read the following statements:
1. A + B means A is the mother of (B)
2. A - B means A is the sister of (B)
3. A * B means A is the father of (B)
4. A β B means A is the brother of (B)

Which of the following means that N is the maternal uncle of M?
(a) N β P - L + E – M
(b) N - Y + A β M
(c) M - Y * P – N
(d) N β C + F * M

41. Pointing to a girl Sandeep said, "She is the daughter of the only sister of my father." How is Sandeep related to the girl?
(a) Uncle (b) Cousin
(c) Father (d) Grandfather

42. Pointing to a boy in the photograph Reena said, "He is the only son of the only child of my grandfather." How is Reena related to that boy?
(a) Mother (b) Sister
(c) Aunt (d) Cannot be determined

43. A is the son of C; C and Q are sisters; Z is the mother of Q and P is the son of Z. Which of the following statements is true?
(a) P and A are cousins
(b) P is the maternal uncle of A
(c) Q is the maternal grandfather of A
(d) C and P are sisters

44. If P + Q means P is the brother of Q; P x Q means P is the wife of Q and P % Q means P is the daughter of Q, then which of the following means D is the uncle of A?
(a) A % B x C + D (b) A x B + C % D
(c) A + C % B x D (d) None of these

45. P is the mother of K; K is the sister of D; D is the father of J. How is P related to J?
    (a) Mother (b) Grandmother
    (c) Aunt (d) Data is inadequate
46. Sanjay introduces Ravi as the son of the only brother of his father's wife. How is Ravi related to Sanjay?
    (a) Cousin (b) Son
    (c) Son-in-law (d) Uncle
47. Praveen said to Nilesh, "That boy playing with the football is the younger of the brothers of the daughter of my father's wife". How is the boy playing football related to Praveen?
    (a) Son (b) Brother
    (c) Cousin (d) Nephew
48. Raj told Anil, "Yesterday I defeated the only brother of the daughter of my grandmother". Who did Raj defeat?
    (a) Nephew (b) Uncle
    (c) Son (d) Father
49. Ankit is the son of Zubin. Manju is the daughter of Anil. Sheela is the mother of Manju. Mohan is the brother of Manju. How is Mohan related to Sheela?
    (a) Brother (b) Father
    (c) Son (d) None of these
50. Prakash is the son of Pramo(d) Neha is the daughter of Abhishek. Ruchi is the mother of Neh(a) Awadhesh is the brother of Neh(a) How is Awadhesh related to Ruchi?
    (a) Brother (b) Father
    (c) Son (d) Cannot be determined

Answer Key

1. (d)	**2.** (a)	**3.** (b)	**4.** (d)	**5.** (b)	**6.** (b)	**7.** (d)	**8.** (d)	**9.** (b)
10. (b)	**11.** (c)	**12.** (c)	**13.** (b)	**14.** (c)	**15.** (a)	**16.** (a)	**17.** (c)	**18.** (b)
19. (d)	**20.** (a)	**21.** (d)	**22.** (c)	**23.** (d)	**24.** (a)	**25.** (b)	**26.** (d)	**27.** (b)
28. (a)	**29.** (a)	**30.** (b)	**31.** (d)	**32.** (b)	**33.** (d)	**34.** (a)	**35.** (d)	**36.** (d)
37. (a)	**38.** (d)	**39.** (a)	**40.** (a)	**41.** (b)	**42.** (b)	**43.** (b)	**44.** (d)	**45.** (b)
46. (a)	**47.** (b)	**48.** (d)	**49.** (c)	**50.** (c)				

Explanatory Notes

1. (d)
   $I \times C \rightarrow$ I is the sister of C
   $C + N \rightarrow$ C is the daughter of N
   and $N - J \rightarrow$ N is the brother of I.
   Hence, I is niece of J.

2. (a)
   M is the father of N and N is the son of V.
   Hence, V is the mother of N.
   From (1), P is the brother of V
   Therefore, M is the brother-in-law of P because V is the wife of M.
   From (2), the daughter of N is the granddaughter of V.
   From this we do not get any relation of M to P.

3. (b)
   C and Q are sisters and A is the son of C. Hence, C is the mother of A or Z is the mother Q.
   Hence, Z is the maternal grandmother of A. P is the son of Z. Hence, P is the maternal uncle of A.

4. (d)
   P % Q $\rightarrow$ P is the mother of Q
   $Q + R \rightarrow$ Q is the father of R
   $R - T \rightarrow$ R is the brother of T
   Hence Q is the father of T
   $T \times K \rightarrow$ T is the daughter of K
   Hence Q is the husband of K
   Therefore, P is the mother-in-law of K

5. (b)
   $K + Y \rightarrow$ K is the brother of Y
   $Y \times I \rightarrow$ Y is the father of I
   Hence, $\rightarrow$ K is the uncle of I
   and $I - Z \rightarrow$ I is the sister of Z
   Hence I is the niece of K

6. (b)
   The only child of my father means 'Abhisek' himself. This means the girl is the daughter of Abhisek. Hence, Abhisek's wife is the mother of the girl.

7. (d)
   Q $ R $\rightarrow$ Q is the father of R
   R @ T $\rightarrow$ R is the brother of T
   Hence Q is the father of T
   T * M $\rightarrow$ T is the daughter of M
   Hence M is the mother of T
   Hence, M is the wife of Q.

8. (d)
   A $ B$\rightarrow$ A is the brother of B
   B * C $\rightarrow$ B is the son of C
   Hence A is the son of C
   C @ D $\rightarrow$ C is the wife of D
   Hence C is the mother of A.

9. (b)
   The girl is the daughter of the sister of Sandeep's father. Hence, the girl is the cousin or Sandeep is the cousin of the girl.

10. (b)
    The boy in the photograph is the only son of Reena's grandfather's only son; i.e., the boy is the only son of Reena's father.
    Hence, the boy is the brother of Reena or Reena is the sister of the boy.

11. (c)
    The man is the only son of the mother of the woman. Hence, the man is the maternal uncle of the woman. So, the woman is the niece of the man.

12. (c)
    Nalni is the daughter of the only son of Gopi's grandfather. Hence, it's clear that Nalni is the sister of Gopi.

13. (b)
    Since E is the brother of B
    Therefore, A is the father of E
    but D is the wife of E
    Hence, D is the daughter-in-law of A

14. (c)
    Brother of person's wife $\rightarrow$ brother-in-law of the person.
    Hence, the son of lady's brother is brother-in-law of the person.
    Therefore, the brother of the lady is the father-in-law of the person. Hence, the lady is the sister of the person's father-in-law.

15. (a)
    F3M $\rightarrow$ F is the wife of M
    M5K $\rightarrow$ M is the father of K
    Therefore, F is the mother of K

16. (a)
    The man in the photograph is son of Anjali's grandfather's son i.e., the son of Anjali's father. Hence, the boy is the brother of Anjali.

17. (c)
Father of Deepak's daughter's father → Deepak's father
Hence, the person is the brother of Deepak's father
Therefore, the person is the uncle of Deepak.

18. (b)
P is the mother of K
K is the sister of D
D is the father of J.
Therefore, J is the nephew or niece of K and P is the grandmother of J.

19. (d)
As the sex of Q is not known, hence, data is inadequate.

20. (a)
P @ Q → P is the wife of Q ...(1)
Q $ T → Q is the brother of T ...(2)
T # U → T is the daughter of U
Hence Q is the son of U ...(3)
U * W → U is the father of W.
From (1) and (3), U is the father-in-law of P.

21. (d)
M + K → M is the brother of K
K % T → K is the father of T
T x P → T is the sister of P
Therefore, K is the father of P and M is the uncle of P.

22. (c)
Madhav is the only son of one of the sons of Varman's father → Either Varman is the father or uncle of Madhav.

23. (d)
The woman is the mother of Shashank's granddaughter.
Hence, the woman is the daughter-in-law of Shashank.

24. (a)
Q – P → Q is the mother of P
P + R → R is the brother of P
Hence q is the mother of R
R % T → R is the father of T
Hence, Q is the grandmother of T

25. (b)
M9N → M is the husband of N
N5K → N is the daughter of K
Hence M is the son-in-law of K
K3J → K is the mother of J
Hence K is a lady
Hence K is the mother-in-law of M.

26. (d)
The girl is the wife of grandson of Amit's mother i.e., the girl is the wife of son of Amit. Hence, Amit is the father-in-law of the girl.

27. (b)
A and B are children of D.
From (1), C is the brother B and son of E.
Since, the sex of D and E are not known. Hence (1) is not sufficient to answer the question.
From (2), F is the mother of B. Hence, F is also the mother of A. Hence D is the father of A.
Thus, (2) is sufficient to answer the question.

28. (a)
Only daughter of my mother → myself
Hence, the woman is the mother of the man.

29. (a)
Brother of mother means maternal uncle. Hence only nephew of Aamir's maternal uncle means Aamir himself. Therefore, Salman is the wife of Aamir.

30. (b)
Father's wife → mother
Hence, the daughter of the mother means sister and sister's younger brother means brother. Therefore, the boy is the brother of Deepak.

31. (d)
Ashok is the only brother of Sudeep and Veena is the sister-in-law of Ashok. Hence Veena is the wife of Sudeep. Kalyani is the mother-in-law of Veena. Kalyani is the mother of Ashok.

32. (b)
P × Q → P is the wife of Q
Q % R → Q is the father of R
R – T → R is the brother of T
T + S → T is the sister of S
Therefore, T is the daughter of P

33. (d)
Daughter of Abhijit's brother → niece of Abhijit
Thus, the granddaughter of the woman is Abhijit's niece.
Hence, the woman is the mother of Abhijit.

34. (a)
The man in the photograph is the son of the only son of Lata's grandfather i.e., the man is the son of Lata's father. Hence, the man is the brother of Lata.

35. (d)
Because the sex of O is not known

36. (d)
Given: D is the brother of B.
From statement 1, we can detect that D is son of C (son of D is the grandson of C).
From statement 2, we can detect that B is 'Female' (sister of D).
Therefore, B is daughter of C.

37. (a)
M × N → M is the mother of N
N % S → N is the wife of S
and S + T → is the father of T
Hence, M is the maternal grandmother of T

38. (d)
The man in the photo is the son of the sister of Bajpai. Hence, Bajpai is the maternal uncle of the man in the photograph.

39. (a)
The father of the boy's uncle → the grandfather of the boy and daughter of the grandfather → sister of father

40. (a)
N β P → N is the brother of P
P – L → P is the sister of L

L + E → L is the mother of E
E – M → E is the sister of M.
Hence, L is the mother of M, P is the maternal aunt of M and N is the maternal uncle of M.

41. (b)
The girl is the daughter of the sister of Sandeep's father. Hence, the girl is the cousin or Sandeep is the cousin of the girl.

42. (b)
The boy in the photograph is the son of the only child of Reena's grandfather i.e. the boy is the son of Reena's father. Hence Reena is the sister of that boy.

43. (b)
C and Q are sisters and A is the son of C. Hence, C is the mother of A or Z is the mother Q.
Hence, Z is the maternal grandmother of A. P is the son of Z. Hence, P is the maternal uncle of A.

44. (d)

45. (b)
P is the mother of K
K is the sister of D
D is the father of J.
Therefore, J is the nephew or niece of K and P is the grandmother of J.

46. (a)
Only brother of his father's wife - Sanjay's maternal uncle and Ravi is the son of Sanjay's maternal uncle. Hence, Ravi is the cousin of Sanjay.

47. (b)
Brothers of the daughter of my (Praveen) father's wife". - Praveen's Brother and sister.
Hence, the boy playing the football is the younger brother of Praveen.

48. (d)
Daughter of grandmother - Aunt; Aunt's only brother — Father.

49. (c)
Mohan is the brother of Manju and Sheela is the mother of the Manju. Hence, Mohan is the Son of Sheela.

50. (c)
Awadesh is brother of Neha and Neha is daughter of Ruchi. Hence, Awadesh is the Son of Ruchi.

❐

Previous Year Questions

1. Deepak said to Nitin, "The boy playing with the football is the younger of the two brothers of the daughter of my father's wife." How is the boy playing football related to Deepak? ***[NTSE 2003 – Punjab first stage paper]***
   (a) Cousin (b) Brother
   (c) Son (d) Brother-in-law

2. B is the brother of A, S is the sister of B, E is the brother of D, D is the daughter of A, and F is the father of S. Then, the uncle of E is: ***[NTSE 2004 - Jammu second stage paper]***
   (a) A (b) B
   (c) F (d) D

3. Introducing a boy, a girl said, "He is the only son of my mother's mother". How is the girl related to that boy? ***[NTSE 2000 - UP first stage paper]***
   (a) Aunt (b) Niece
   (c) Sister (d) Mother

4. If Y says that his mother is the only daughter of X's mother, How is X' related to Y? ***[NTSE 2004 - Delhi first stage paper]***
   (a) Uncle (b) Brother
   (c) Cousin (d) Maternal uncle

5. Pointing to Sagar in a photograph, Manjula said, "His brother's father is the only son of my grandfather. "How is Manjula related to Sagar? ***[NTSE 2012 - Delhi first stage paper]***
   (a) Aunt (b) Sister
   (c) Mother (d) None of these

6. Sia introduced Raghav as the son of the only daughter of the father of her uncle. How is Raghav related to Sia? ***[NTSE 2000 - Jharkhand first stage paper]***
   (a) Brother (b) Cousin
   (c) Nephew (d) Can't be determined

7. Anirban said, "The girl is the wife of the grandson of my mother" .Who is Anirban to the girl? ***[NTSE 2001 - UP first stage paper]***
   (a) Father (b) Grandfather
   (c) Husband (d) Father-in-law

8. Introducing a woman, Nisha said, "She is the daughter-in-law of the grandmother of my father's only son." How is the woman related to Nisha? ***[NTSE 2000 – Assam first stage paper]***
   (a) Grandmother (b) Sister-in-law
   (c) Sister (d) Mother

9. If A is the mother of D, B is not the son of C, C is the father of D, D is the sister of B, then how is A related to B ? ***[NTSE 1999- Chandigarh first stage paper]***
   (a) Mother (b) Brother
   (c) Step son (d) Sister

10. Showing the lady in the park, Adarsh said, "She is the daughter of my grand-father's only son." How is Adarsh related to that lady? ***[NTSE 2006 - Goa second stage paper]***
    (a) Brother (b) Father-in-law
    (c) Maternal uncle (d) Husband

Answer Key

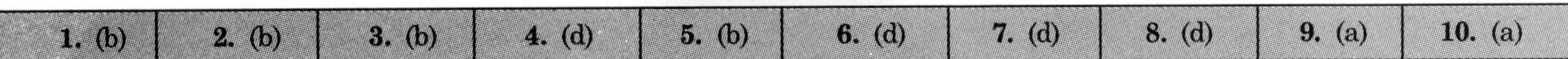

1. (b)	2. (b)	3. (b)	4. (d)	5. (b)	6. (d)	7. (d)	8. (d)	9. (a)	10. (a)

Explanatory Notes

1. (b)

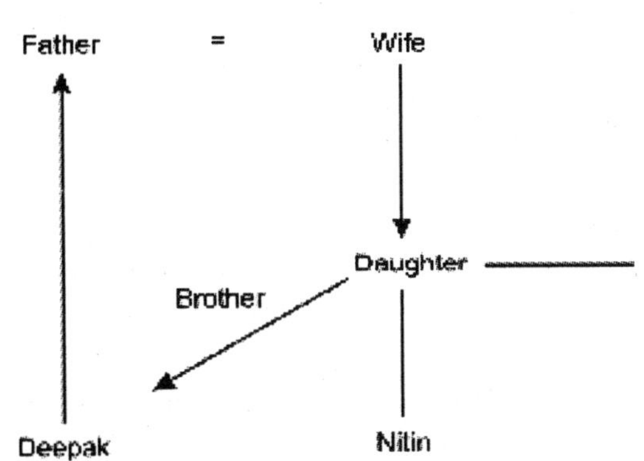

2. (b)

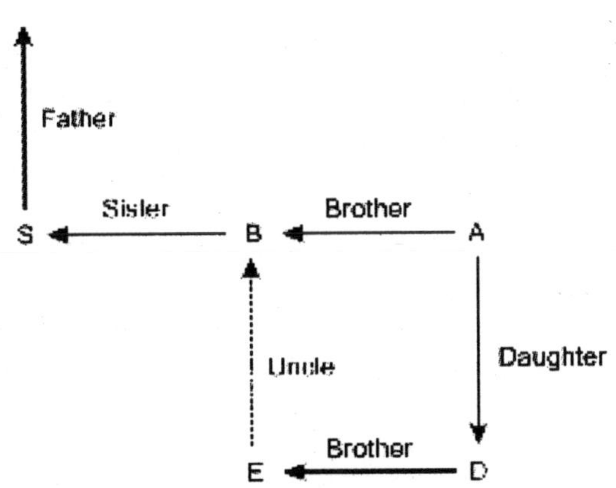

E and D are children of A and B is the brother of A. So, B is the Uncle of E.

3. (b)

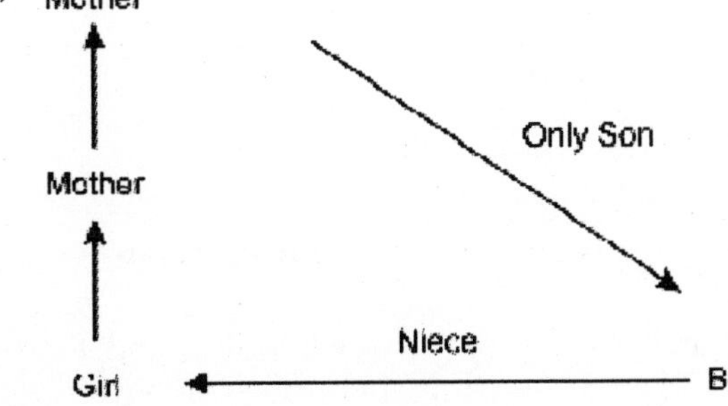

4. (d)
Assume Y's mother be S, and X's mother be T, As S is the only daughter of T. So, X is the son of T. The family tree can be draw as follows.

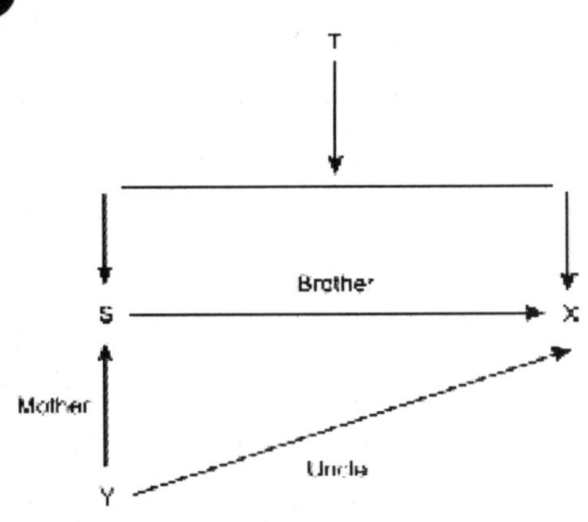

So, X is maternal uncle of Y.

5. (b)
Only son of Manjula's grandfather—Manjula's father and Sagar's brother's father—Sagar's father. So, Manjula is Sagar's sister.

6. (d)
Only daughter of uncle's father—uncle's sister. But it is not clear that uncle's sister is Sia's mother.

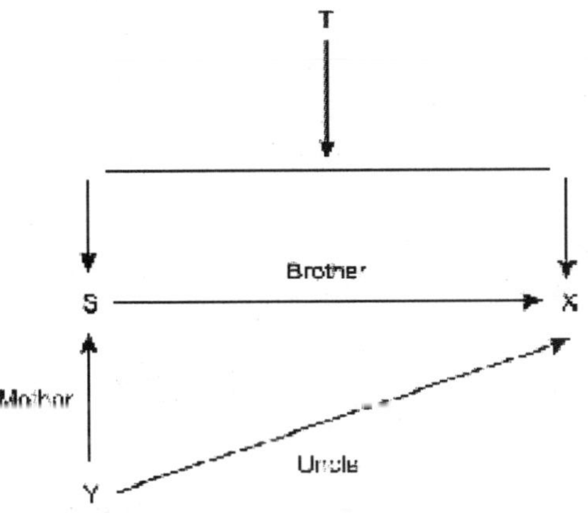

Hence, the answer is (d) cannot be determined.

7. (d)
The girl is the wife of grandson of Amit's mother i.e., the girl is the wife of son of Amit. Hence, Amit is the father-in-law of the girl.

8. (d)
My father's only son – My brother; grandmother of my brother – My grandmother; Daughter – in – law of my grandmother – My mother. So the lady is girl's mother.

9. (a)
B is not son of C means B is the daughter of C. Hence, A is the mother of B since D and B are sisters only.

10. (a)
My (Adarsh) grandfather only son's – Adarsh's father. Hence, Adarsh is the brother of that lady.

❐

UNIT 10

Sitting Arrangements

In this type of questions, some clues regarding seating or placing (linear/ circular) of some persons or items is given. The candidate is required to form the paper sequence using these clues and answer the questions accordingly.

Candidates are required to arrange the objects either in a row or in a circle on the basis of such conditions. Information given in the question is presented in distorted form to create confusion and to test candidate's ability to analyse the information step by step in order to answer the question correctly.

Seating Arrangement questions involve arrangement of persons in a circular table, rectangular table or linear arrangement with some given conditions. In order to solve these types of questions, best strategy is to develop a rough pictorial diagram. Once diagram is complete, questions that follow can be answered in no time.

Solved Examples

Example-1

1. 6 Boys are sitting in a circle and facing towards the centre of the circle.
2. Rajeev is sitting to the right of Mohan but he is not just at the left of Vijay.
3. Suresh is between Babu and Vijay.
4. Ajay is sitting to the left of Vijay.

Who is sitting to the left of Mohan?

Solution:

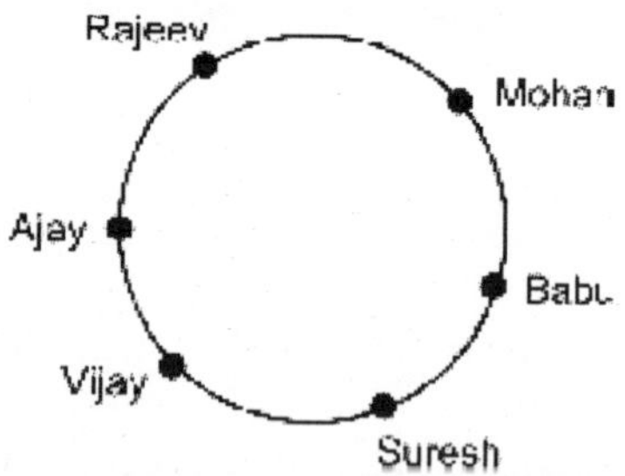

Hence, Babu is sitting to the left of Mohan.

Example-2

1. Eleven students A, B, C, D, E, F, G, H, I, J and K are sitting in first line facing to the teacher.
2. D who is just to the left of F, is to the right of C at second place.
3. A is second to the right of E who is at one end.
4. J is the nearest neighbour of A and B and is to the left of G at third place.
5. H is next to D to the right and is at the third place to the right of I.

Who is just in the middle?

Solution:

Teacher

•

•	•	•	•	•	•	•	•	•	•	•
E	K	A	J	B	I	G	C	H	D	F

Hence, I is just in the middle.

Example 3:

Siva, Sathish, Amar and Praveen are playing cards. Amar is to the right of Sathish, who is to the right of Siva.

Who is to the right of Amar?

Solution:

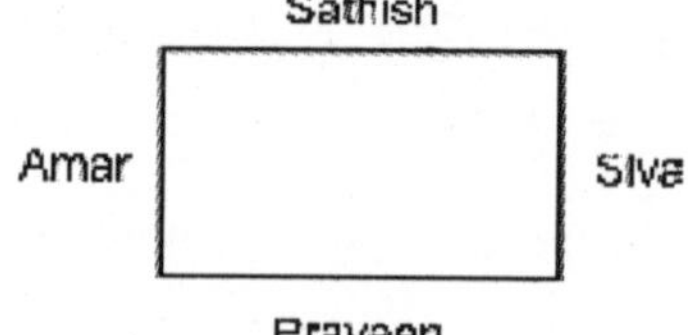

Hence, Praveen is to the right of Amar.

Example 4:

1. A, B and C are three boys while R, S and T are three girls. They are sitting such that the boys are facing the girls.
2. A and R are diagonally opposite to each other.
3. C is not sitting at any of the ends.
4. T is left to R but opposite to (C)

(A) Who is sitting opposite to B?

(B) Who is sitting diagonally opposite to B?

Solution:

Ist Position :

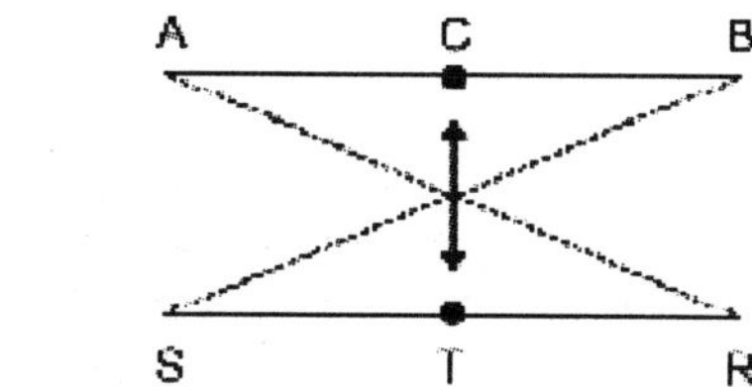

IInd Position :

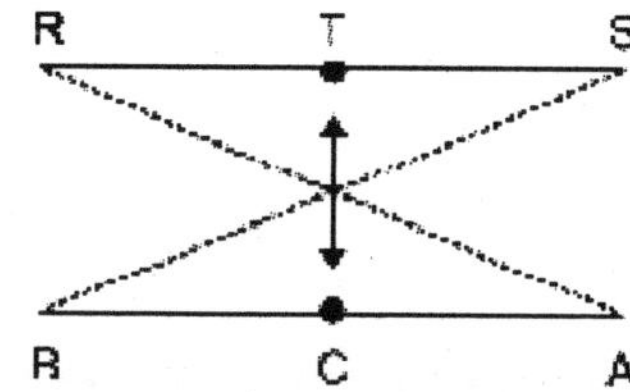

(A) Hence, R is sitting opposite to (B)
(B) Hence, S is sitting diagonally opposite to (B)

Example 5:

A, B, C, D and E are sitting on a bench. A is sitting next to B, C is sitting next to D, D is not sitting with E who is on the left end of the bench. C is on the second position from the right. A is to the right of B and E. A and C are sitting together. In which position A is sitting?

Solution: As per question, we have to draw a figure given below.

Therefore, A is sitting in between B and (C)

Multiple Choice Questions

☛ ***Direction to solve (1 to 5) :*** *Each of these quest-ions are based on the information given below:*

1. 8 persons E, F, G, H, I, J, K and L are seated around a square table - two on each side.
2. There are 3 ladies who are not seated next to each other.
3. J is between L and F.
4. G is between I and F.
5. H, a lady member is second to the left of J.
6. F, a male member is seated opposite to E, a lady member.
7. There is a lady member between F and I.

1. Who among the following is to the immediate left of F?
   (a) G (b) I
   (c) J (d) H
2. What is true about J and K?
   (a) J is male, K is female
   (b) J is female, K is male
   (c) Both are female
   (d) Both are male
3. How many persons are seated between K and F?
   (a) 1 (b) 2
   (c) 3 (d) 4
4. Who among the following are three lady members?
   (a) E, H and J (b) E, F and G
   (c) E, H and G (d) C, H and J
5. Who among the following is seated between E and H?
   (a) F (b) I
   (c) K (d) Cannot be determined

☛ ***Direction to solve (6 to 9) :*** *In a class there are seven students (including boys and girls) A, B, C, D, E, F and G. They sit on three benches I, II and III such that at least two students on each bench and at least one girl on each bench. C who is a girl student, does not sit with A, E and D. F the boy student sits with only B. A sits on the bench I with his best friends. G sits on the bench III. E is the brother of C.*

6. How many girls are there out of these 7 students?
   (a) 3 (b) 3 or 4
   (c) 4 (d) Data inadequate
7. Which of the following is the group of girls?
   (a) BAC (b) BFC
   (c) BCD (d) CDF
8. Who sits with C?
   (a) B (b) D
   (c) G (d) E
9. On which bench are there three students?
   (a) Bench I (b) Bench II
   (c) Bench III (d) Bench I or II

☛ ***Direction to solve (10 to 13) :*** *Six girls are sitting in a circle facing to the centre of the circle. They are P, Q, R, S, T and V. T is not between Q and S but some other one. P is next to the left of V. R is 4th to the right of P.*

10. Which of the following statements is not true?
    (a) S is just next to the right to R
    (b) T is just next to the right of V
    (c) R is second to the left of T
    (d) P is second to the right of R

11. If P and R interchange their positions then which of the following pairs will sit together?
(a) RT (b) PV
(c) VT (d) QV
12. What is the position of T?
(a) Just next to the right of Q
(b) Second to the left of P
(c) Between Q and R
(d) To the immediate right of V
13. Which one is sitting just right to the V?
(a) P (b) T
(c) R (d) S/Q

☛ ***Direction to solve (14 to 17) :*** *A, B, C, D, E, F and G are sitting in a row facing North:*
1. F is to the immediate right of E.
2. E is 4th to the right of G.
3. C is the neighbour of B and D.
4. Person who is third to the left of D is at one of ends.

14. Who are to the left of C?
(a) Only B (b) G, B and D
(c) G and B (d) D, E, F and A
15. Which of the following statements is not true?
(a) E is to the immediate left of D
(b) A is at one of the ends
(c) G is to the immediate left of B
(d) F is second to the right of D
16. Who are the neighbours of B?
(a) C and D (b) C and G
(c) G and F (d) C and E
17. What is the position of A?
(a) Between E and D
(b) Extreme left
(c) Centre
(d) Extreme right

☛ ***Direction to solve (18 to 22) :*** *Each of these questions is based on the information given below:*
1. A ,B, C, D and E are five men sitting in a line facing to south - while M, N, O, P and Q are five ladies sitting in a second line parallel to the first line and are facing to North.
2. B who is just next to the left of D, is opposite to Q.
3. C and N are diagonally opposite to each other.
4. E is opposite to O who is just next right of M.
5. P who is just to the left of Q, is opposite to D.
6. M is at one end of the line.

18. Who is sitting third to the right of O?
(a) Q (b) N
(c) M (d) Data inadequate
19. If B shifts to the place of E, E shifts to the place of Q, and Q shifts to the place of B, then who will be the second to the left of the person opposite to O ?
(a) Q (b) P
(c) E (d) D
20. Which of the following pair is diagonally opposite to each other?
(a) EQ (b) BO
(c) AN (d) AM
21. If O and P, A and E and B and Q interchange their positions, then who will be the second person to the right of the person who is opposite to the person second of the right of P?
(a) D (b) A
(c) E (d) O
22. In the original arrangement who is sitting just opposite to N?
(a) B (b) A
(c) C (d) D

☛ ***Direction to solve (23 to 26) :*** *Six friends P, Q, R, S, T and U are sitting around the hexagonal table each at one corner and are facing the centre of the hexagonal. P is second to the left of U. Q is neighbour of R and S. T is second to the left of S.*

23. Which one is sitting opposite to P?
(a) R (b) Q
(c) T (d) S
24. Who is the fourth person to the left of Q?
(a) P (b) U
(c) R (d) Data inadequate
25. Which of the following are the neighbours of P?
(a) U and P (b) T and R
(c) U and R (d) Data inadequate
26. Which one is sitting opposite to T?
(a) R
(b) Q
(c) Cannot be determined
(d) S

☛ ***Direction to solve (27 to 31) :*** *In an Exhibition seven cars of different companies - Cadillac, Ambassador, Fiat, Maruti, Mercedes, Bedford and Fargo are standing facing to east in the following order:*
1. Cadillac is next to right of Fargo.
2. Fargo is fourth to the right of Fiat.
3. Maruti car is between Ambassador and Bedford.
4. Fiat which is third to the left of Ambassador is at one end.

27. Which of the cars are on both the sides of Cadillac car?
(a) Ambassador and Maruti
(b) Maruti and Fiat
(c) Fargo and Mercedes
(d) Ambassador and Fargo
28. Which of the following statements is correct?
(a) Maruti is next to the left of Ambassador.
(b) Bedford is next to the left of Fiat.
(c) Bedford is at one end.
(d) Fiat is next second to the right of Maruti.

29. Which one of the following statements is correct?
    (a) Fargo car is in between Ambassador and Fiat.
    (b) Cadillac is next left to Mercedes car.
    (c) Fargo is next right of Cadillac.
    (d) Maruti is fourth right of Mercedes.
30. Which of the following groups of cars is to the right of Ambassador?
    (a) Cadillac, Fargo and Maruti
    (b) Mercedes, Cadillac and Fargo
    (c) Maruti, Bedford and Fiat
    (d) Bedford, Cadillac and Fargo
31. Which one of the following is the correct position of Mercedes?
    (a) Next to the left of Cadillac
    (b) Next to the left of Bedford
    (c) Between Bedford and Fargo
    (d) Fourth to the right of Maruti

☛ ***Direction to solve (32 to 35) :*** *Six friends are sitting in a circle and are facing the centre of the circle. Deepa is between Prakash and Pankaj. Priti is between Mukesh and Lalit. Prakash and Mukesh are opposite to each other.*

32. Who is sitting opposite to Prakash?
    (a) Mukesh (b) Deepa
    (c) Pankaj (d) Lalit
33. Who is just right to Pankaj?
    (a) Deepa (b) Lalit
    (c) Prakash (d) Priti
34. Who are the neighbours of Mukesh?
    (a) Prakash and Deepa
    (b) Deepa and Priti
    (c) Priti and Pankaj
    (d) Lalit and Priti
35. Who is sitting opposite to Priti?
    (a) Prakash (b) Deepa
    (c) Pankaj (d) Lalit

❐

Answer Key

1. (c)	**2.** (d)	**3.** (c)	**4.** (c)	**5.** (c)	**6.** (b)	**7.** (c)	**8.** (c)	**9.** (a)	**10.** (c)
11. (c)	**12.** (d)	**13.** (b)	**14.** (c)	**15.** (a)	**16.** (b)	**17.** (d)	**18.** (b)	**19.** (a)	**20.** (d)
21. (b)	**22.** (b)	**23.** (d)	**24.** (a)	**25.** (b)	**26.** (b)	**27.** (c)	**28.** (a)	**29.** (b)	**30.** (b)
31. (d)	**32.** (a)	**33.** (a)	**34.** (c)	**35.** (b)					

Explanatory Notes

1. (c)

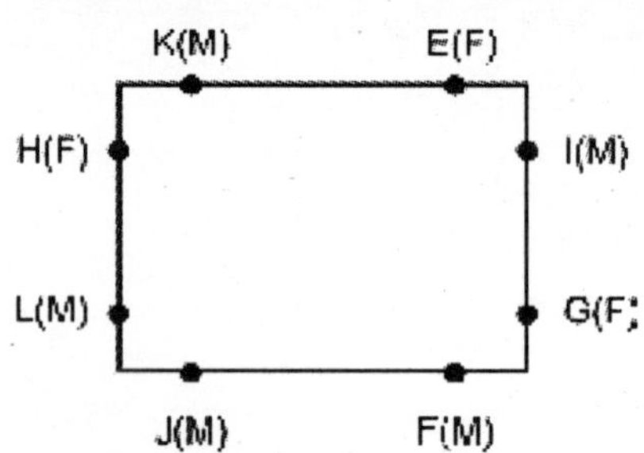

Here M = male
F = female

J is to the immediate left of F

2. (d)

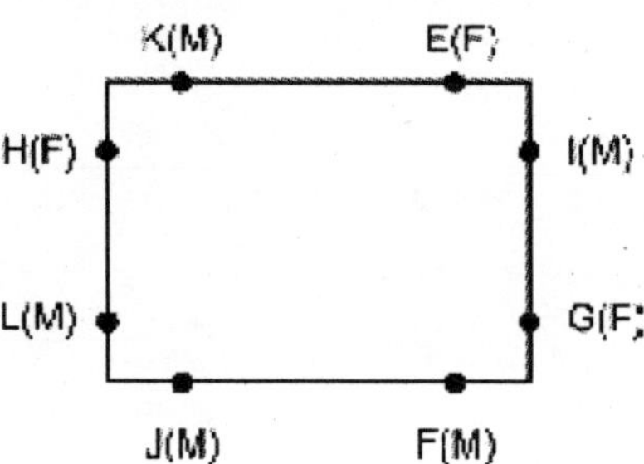

Here M = male
F = female

Both are male

3. (c)

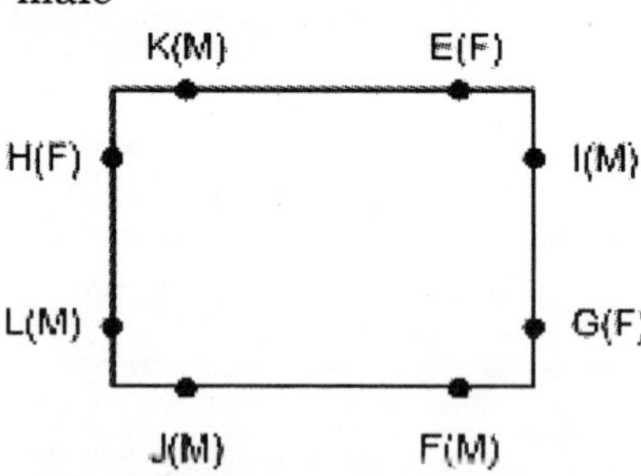

Here M = male
F = female

Three persons are seated between K and F(H, L and J) or E, I and G

4. (c)

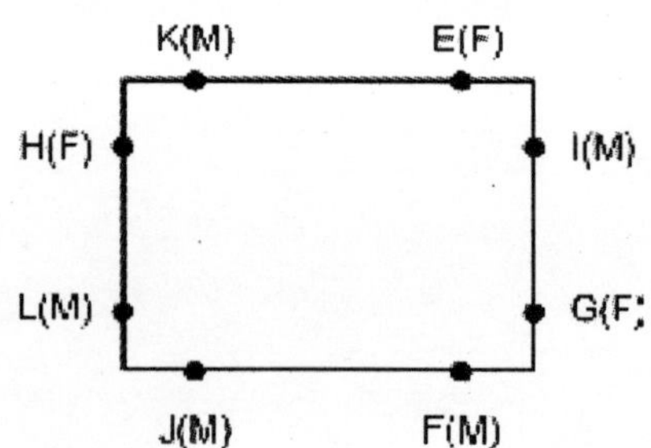

Here M = male
F = female

The three lady members are E, H and G

5. (c)

K(M) E(F)
H(F) I(M)
L(M) G(F)
J(M) F(M)

Here M = male
F = female

K is seated between E and H

6. (b)

Bench-I A E D
Bench-II F B
Bench-III G C
Boy
Girl

The number of girls is either 3 or 4.

7. (c)

Bench-I A E D
Bench-II F B
Bench-III G C
Boy
Girl

BCD is the group of girls.

8. (c)

Bench-I A E D
Bench-II F B
Bench-III G C
Boy
Girl

G sits with C.

9. (a)

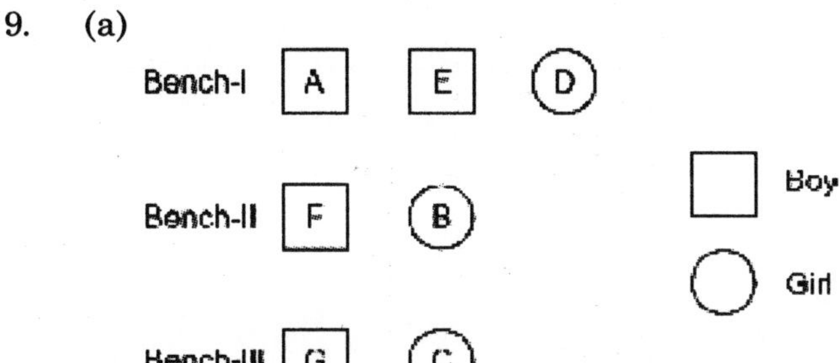

There are three students on Bench I.

10. (c)

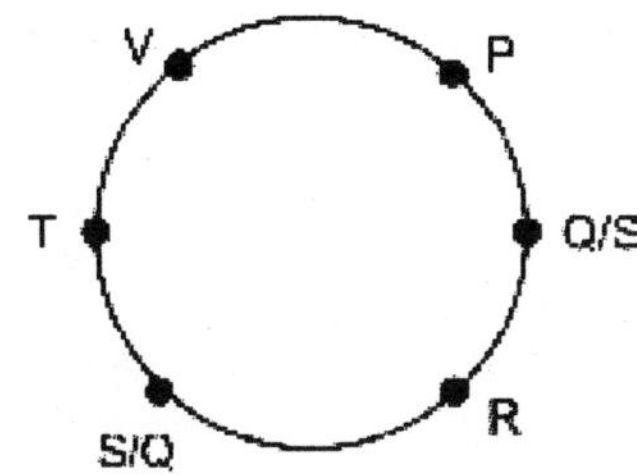

11. (c)

After changing the position of P and Rs

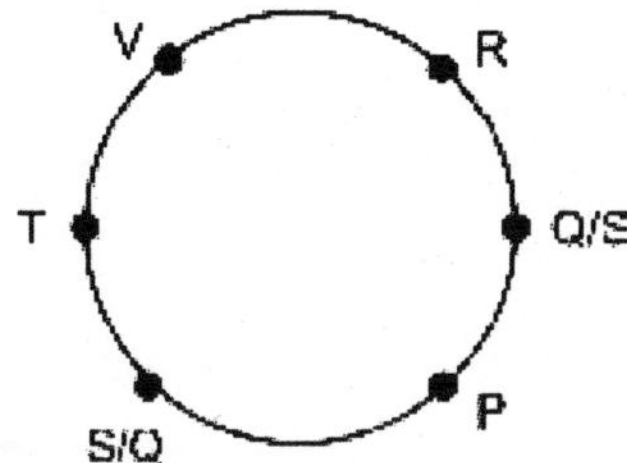

V and T are sitting together.

12. (d)

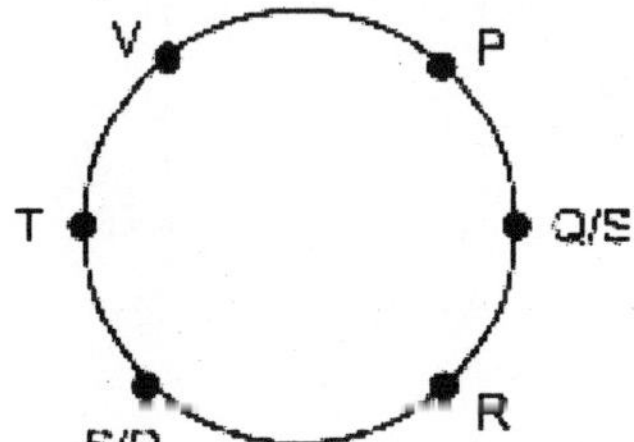

13. (b)

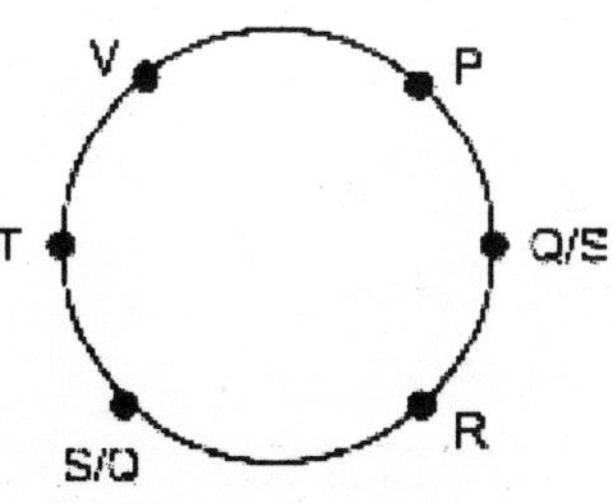

T is sitting just right to the V.

14. (c)

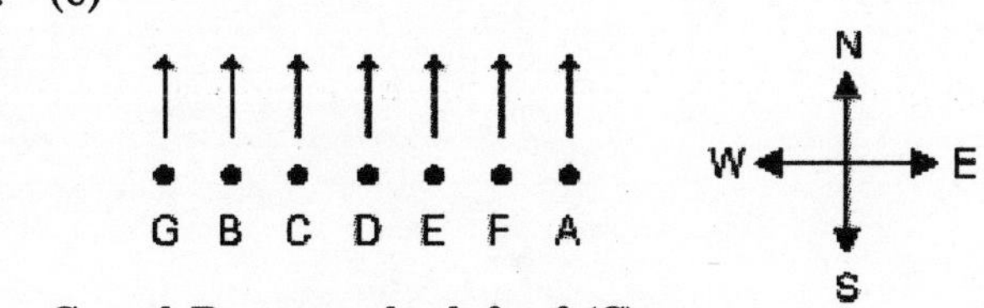

G and B are to the left of (C)

15. (a)

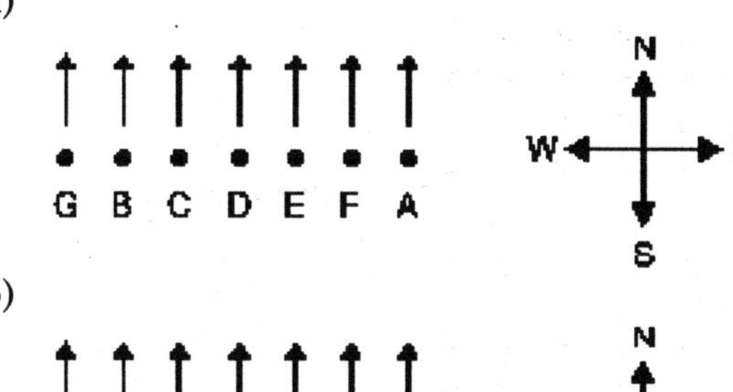

16. (b)

C and G are the neighbours of B.

17. (d)

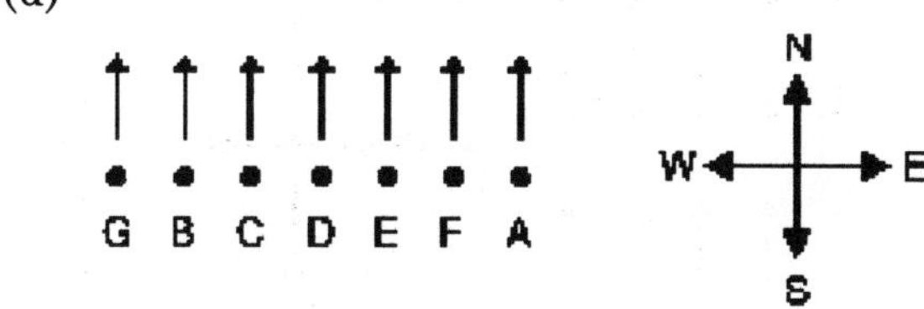

A is in extreme right.

18. (b)

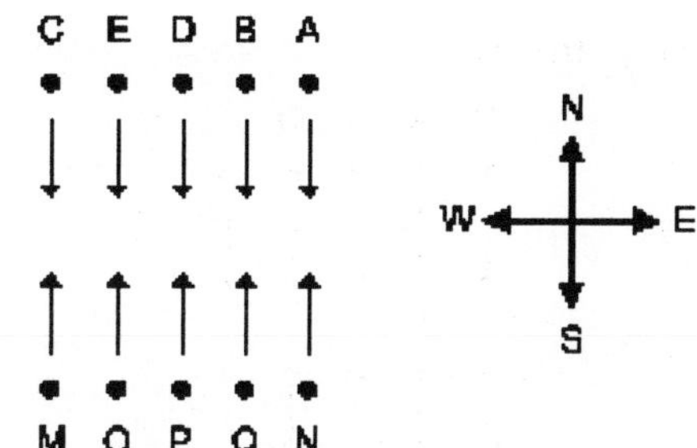

19. (a)

Initial arrangement:

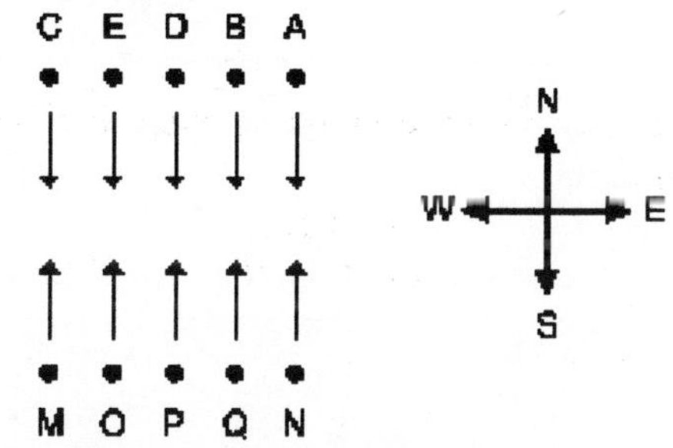

New arrangement after shifting:

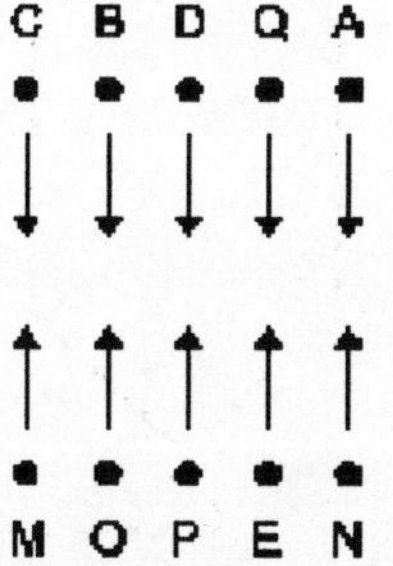

B is opposite to O and second person left to Bis Q.

20. (d)

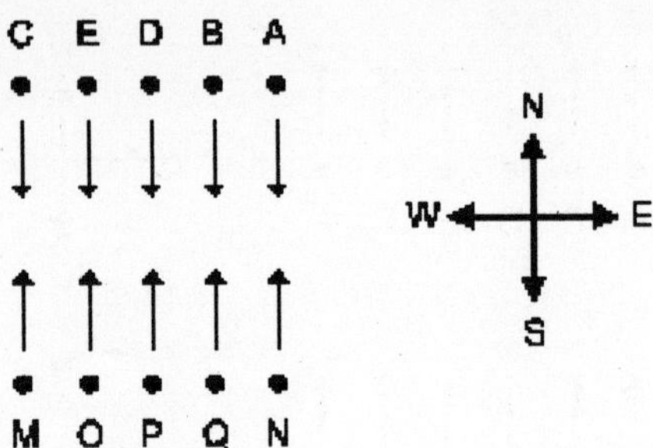

21. (b)

Old arrangement:

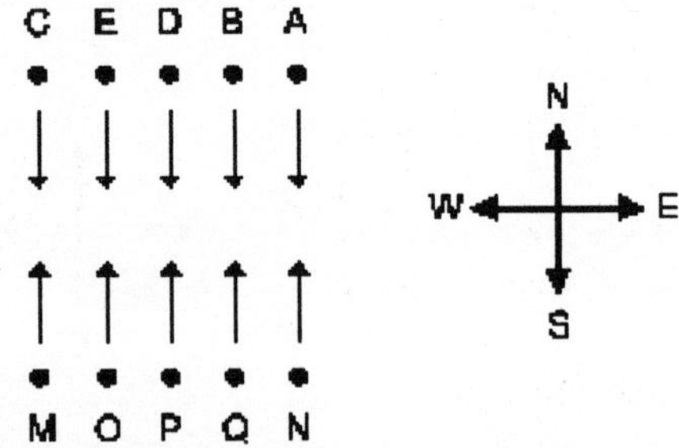

New arrangement:

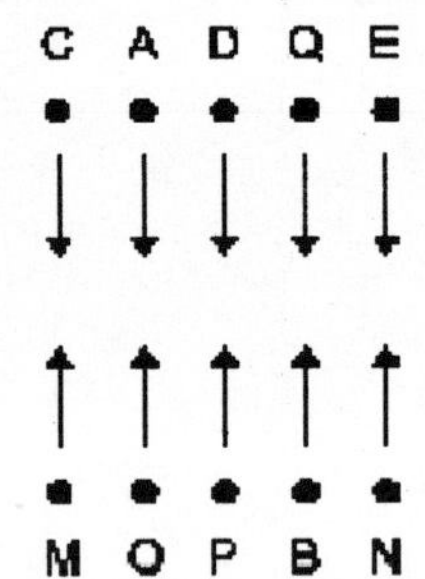

22. (b)

It could easily be understood by each line. The following arrangement is

C E D B A
M O P Q N

23. (d)

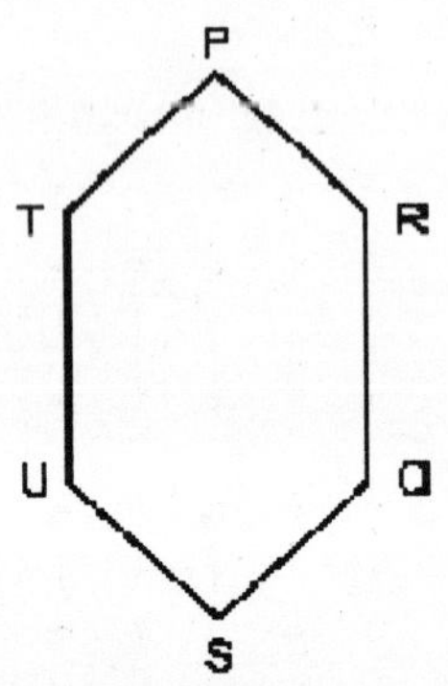

S is sitting opposite to P.

24. (a)

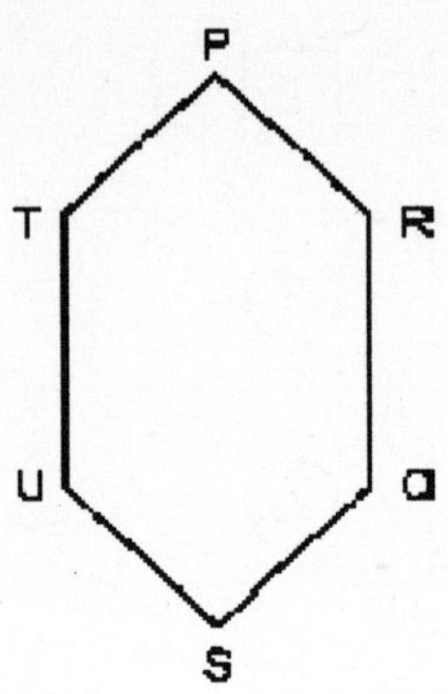

P is the fourth person to the left of Q.

25. (b)

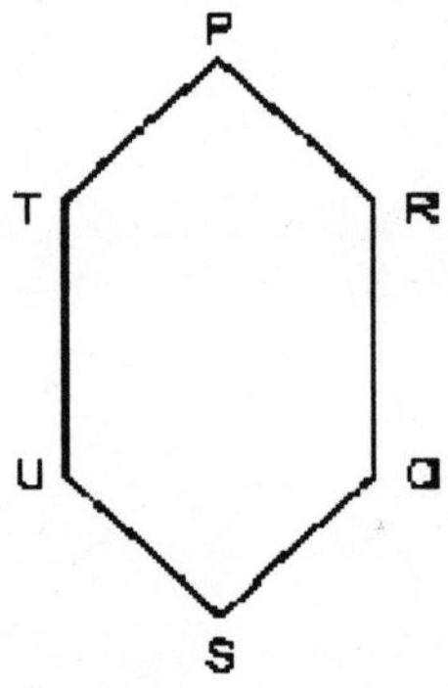

T and R are the neighbours of P.

26. (b)

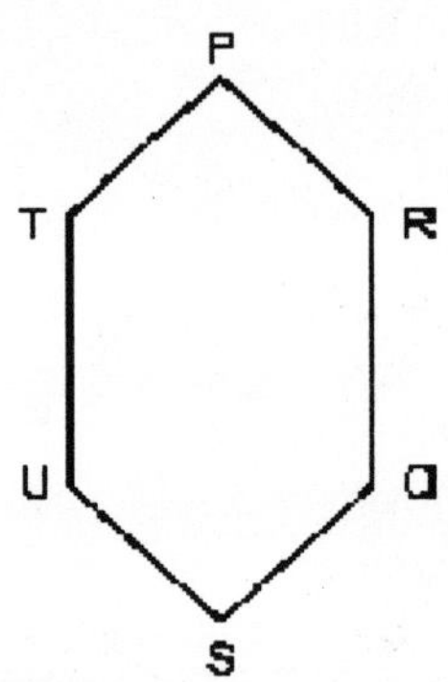

Q is sitting opposite to T.

27. (c)

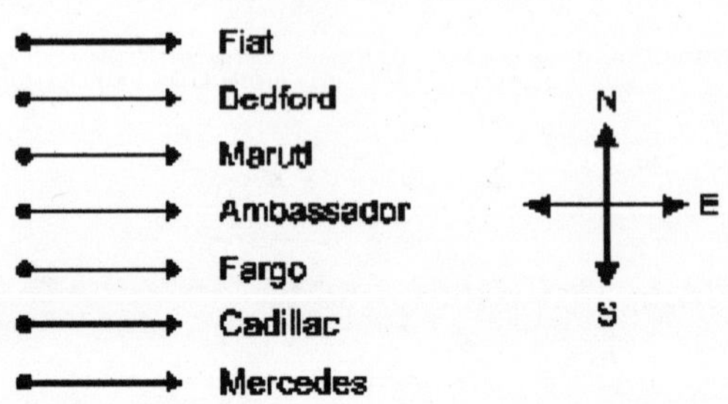

Fargo and Mercedes are on both the sides of cadillac car.

28. (a)

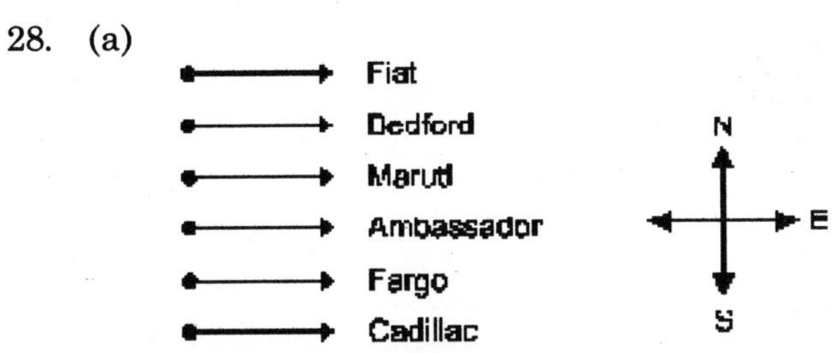

Therefore, Maruti is next to the left of Ambassador.

29. (b)

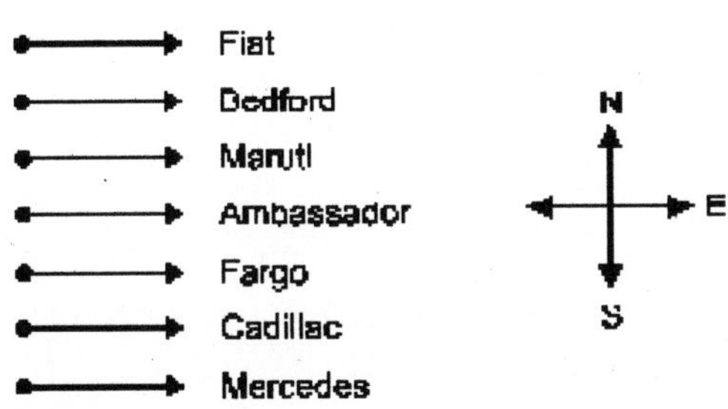

Therefore, Cadillac is next left to Mercedes car.

30. (b)

Mercedes, Cadillac and Fargo cars are to the right of Ambassador.

31. (d)

The correct position of Mercedes is fourth to the right of Maruti.

32. (a)

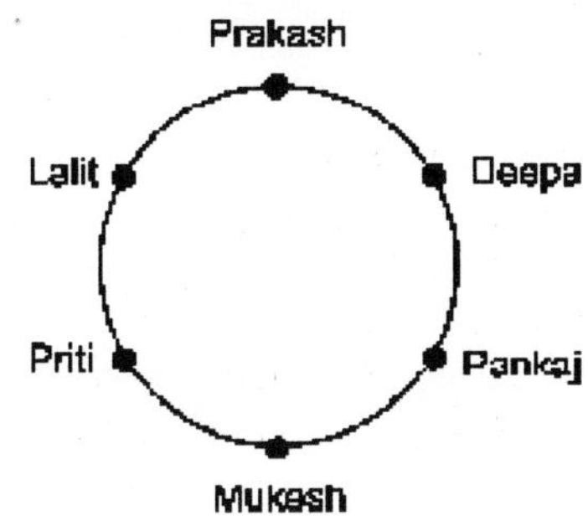

Hence, Mukesh is sitting opposite to Prakash.

33. (a)

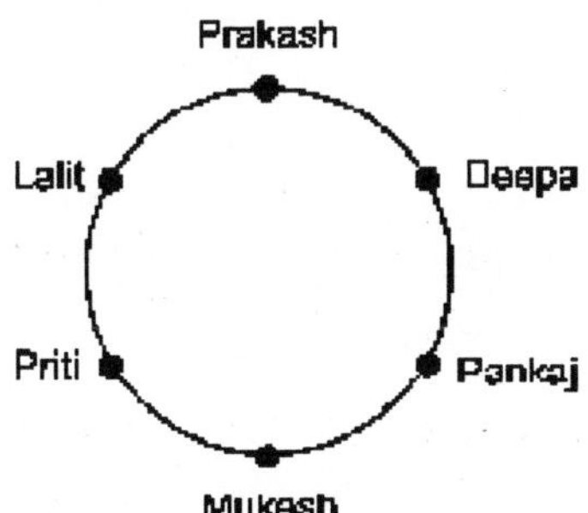

Hence, Deepa is sitting just right to Pankaj.

34. (c)

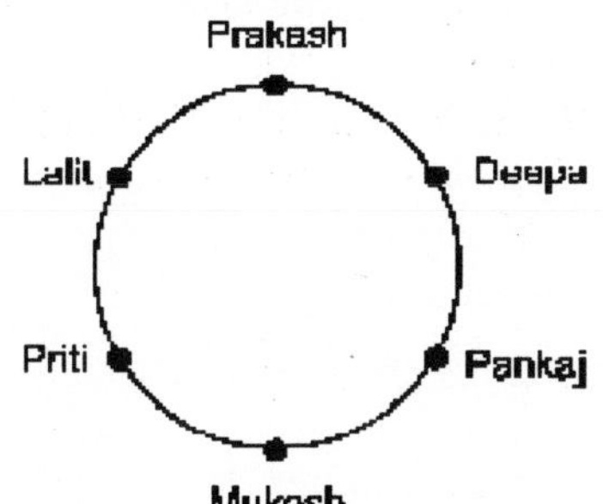

Hence, Priti and Pankaj are the neighbours of Mukesh.

35. (b)

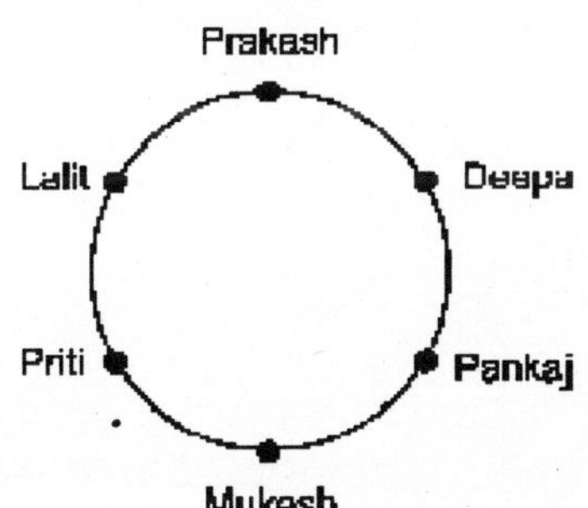

Hence, Deepa is sitting opposite to Priti.

❒

Previous Year Questions

☛ ***Direction to solve (1 to 4) :*** *Five girls are sitting on a bench to be photographed. Seema is to the left of Rani and to the right of Bindu. Mary is to the right of Rani. Reeta is between Rani and Mary.*

[NTSE 2012 – Tamilnadu second stage paper]

1. Who is sitting immediate right to Reeta?
   (a) Bindu (b) Rani
   (c) Mary (d) Seema
2. Who is in the middle of the photograph?
   (a) Bindu (b) Rani
   (c) Reeta (d) Seema
3. Who is second from the right?
   (a) Mary (b) Rani
   (c) Reeta (d) Bindu
4. Who is second from the left in photograph?
   (a) Reeta (b) Mary
   (c) Bindu (d) Seema

☛ ***Direction to solve (5 to 8):*** *P, Q, R, S, T, U, V and W are sitting round the circle and are facing the centre:*

1. P is second to the right of T who is the neighbour of R and V.
2. S is not the neighbour of P.
3. V is the neighbour of U.
4. Q is not between S and W. W is not between U and S.

[NTSE 2004 - Rajasthan First stage Paper]

5. Which two of the following are not neighbours?
   (a) RV (b) UV
   (c) RP (d) QW
6. Which one is immediate right to the V?
   (a) P (b) U
   (c) R (d) T
7. Which of the following is correct?
   (a) P is to the immediate right of Q
   (b) R is between U and V
   (c) Q is to the immediate left of W
   (d) U is between W and S
8. What is the position of S?
   (a) Between U and V
   (b) Second to the right of P
   (c) To the immediate right of W
   (d) Data inadequate.
9. A, P, R, X, S and Z are sitting in a row. S and Z are in the centre. A and P are at the ends. R is sitting to the left of A. Who is to the right of P?

   [NTSE 2005 - Maharashtra second stage paper]

   (a) A (b) X
   (c) S (d) Z

❒

Answer Key

1. (c)	**2.** (b)	**3.** (c)	**4.** (d)	**5.** (a)	**6.** (d)	**7.** (c)	**8.** (c)	**9.** (b)

Explanatory Notes

1. (c)

Bindu Seema Rani Reeta Mary

Mary is sitting immediate right to Reeta.

2. (b)

Bindu Seema Rani Reeta Mary

Rani is in the middle of the photograph.

3. (c)

Bindu Seema Rani Reeta Mary

Reeta is sitting second from the right.

4. (d)

Bindu Seema Rani Reeta Mary

Seema is sitting second from the left in photograph.

5. (a)

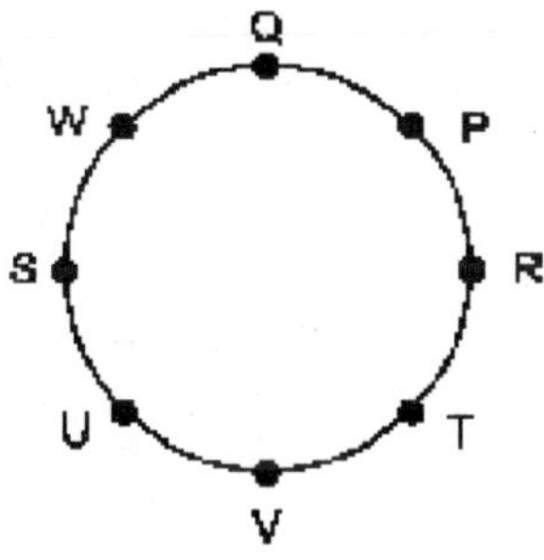

6. (d)

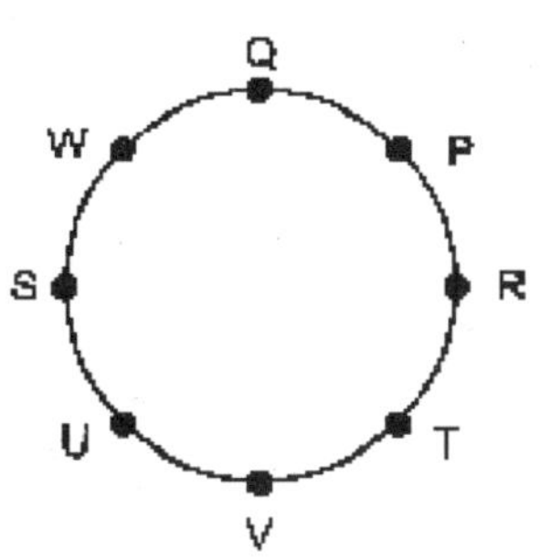

T is immediate right to the V.

7. (c)

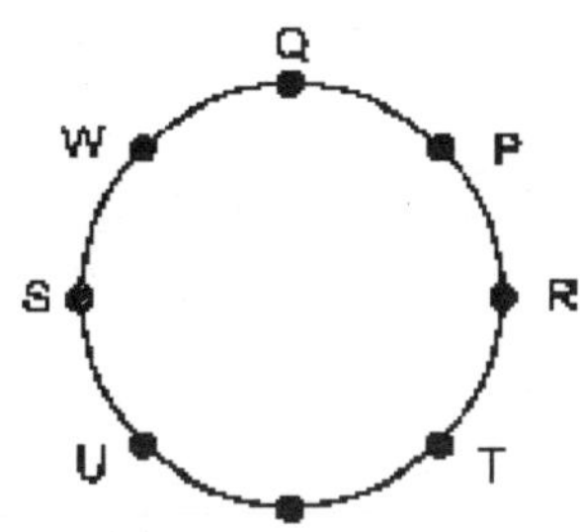

8. (c)

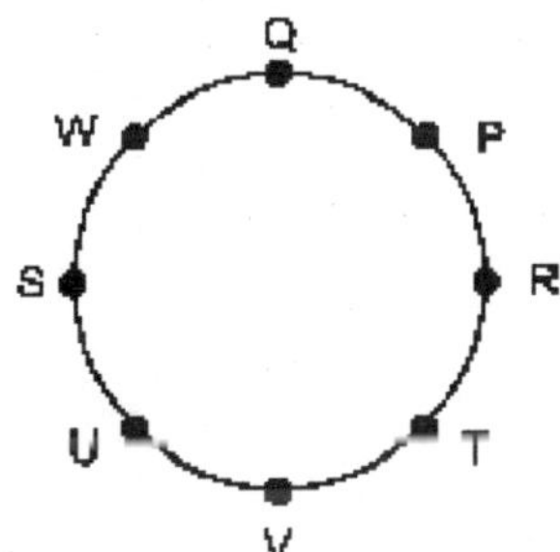

9. (b)

The seating arrangement is as follows:

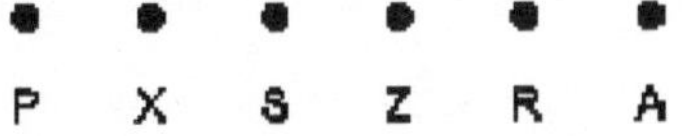

Therefore, right of P is X.

❐

UNIT 11

Logical Sequence of Words

In these types of questions, certain interrelated words are given and numbered, followed by various sequences of numbers denoting them, as alternatives. The candidate is required to arrange these words in a logical sequence based on a common property and then choose the correctly graded sequence from the given alternatives.

Solved Examples

☛ ***Direction to Solve (1 to 5):*** *In each of the following questions, arrange the given words in a meaningful sequence and thus find the correct answer from alternatives.*

1. Arrange the words given below in a meaningful sequence.
   1. Post-box 2. Letter 3. Envelope 4. Delivery
   5. Clearance
   (a) 2, 3, 1, 4, 5 (b) 3, 2, 1, 4, 5
   (c) 3, 2, 1, 5, 4 (d) 3, 2, 4, 5, 1
   Solution: Option (c) is correct.
2. Arrange the words given below in a meaningful sequence.
   1. Mother 2. Child 3. Milk 4. Cry 5. Smile
   (a) 1, 5, 2, 4, 3 (b) 2, 4, 1, 3, 5
   (c) 2, 4, 3, 1, 5 (d) 3, 2, 1, 5, 4
   Solution: Option (b) is correct.
3. Arrange the words given below in a meaningful sequence.
   1. Puberty 2. Adulthood 3. Childhood 4. Infancy
   5. Senescence 6. Adolescence
   (a) 2, 4, 6, 3, 1, 5 (b) 4, 3, 1, 6, 2, 5
   (c) 4, 3, 6, 2, 1, 5 (d) 5, 6, 2, 3, 4, 1
   Solution: Option (b) is correct.
4. Arrange the words given below in a meaningful sequence.
   1. Atomic Age 2. Metallic Age
   3. Stone Age 4. Alloy Age
   (a) 1, 3, 4, 2 (b) 2, 3, 1, 4
   (c) 3, 2, 4, 1 (d) 4, 3, 2, 1
   Solution: Option (c) is correct.
5. Arrange the words given below in a meaningful sequence.
   1. Book 2. Pulp 3. Timber 4. Jungle 5. Paper
   (a) 2, 5, 1, 4, 3 (b) 3, 2, 5, 1, 4
   (c) 4, 3, 2, 5, 1 (d) 5, 4, 3, 1, 2
   Solution: Option (c) is correct.

Multiple Choice Questions

☛ ***Direction to Solve (1 to 35):*** In each of the following questions, arrange the given words in a meaningful sequence and thus find the correct answer from alternatives.

1. Arrange the words given below in a meaningful sequence.
   1. Sentence 2. Chapter 3. Letter 4. Book
   5. Word 6. Paragraph
   (a) 4, 2, 1, 6, 5, 3 (b) 4, 2, 6, 1, 5, 3
   (c) 4, 6, 1, 2, 3, 5 (d) 4, 6, 2, 5, 1, 3
2. Arrange the words given below in a meaningful sequence.
   1. Leaf 2. Fruit 3. Stem 4. Root 5. Flower
   (a) 3, 4, 5, 1, 2 (b) 4, 1, 3, 5, 2
   (c) 4, 3, 1, 2, 5 (d) 4, 3, 1, 5, 2
3. Arrange the words given below in a meaningful sequence.
   1. College 2. Child 3. Salary 4. School
   5. Employment
   (a) 1, 2, 4, 3, 5 (b) 2, 4, 1, 5, 3
   (c) 4, 1, 3, 5, 2 (d) 5, 3, 2, 1, 4
4. Arrange the words given below in a meaningful sequence.
   1. Never 2. Sometimes 3. Generally 4. Seldom
   5. Always
   (a) 5, 2, 1, 3, 4 (b) 5, 2, 4, 3, 1
   (c) 5, 3, 2, 1, 4 (d) 5, 3, 2, 4, 1
5. Arrange the words given below in a meaningful sequence.
   1. Index 2. Contents 3. Title 4. Chapters
   5. Introduction
   (a) 2, 3, 4, 5, 1 (b) 3, 2, 5, 1, 4
   (c) 3, 2, 5, 4, 1 (d) 5, 1, 4, 2, 3

6. Arrange the words given below in a meaningful sequence.
1. Shooting 2. Dubbing 3.Story 4. Releasing 5. Editing 6. Casting
(a) 1, 2, 5, 3, 4, 6 (b) 3, 6, 1, 2, 5, 4
(c) 3, 1, 5, 2, 6, 4 (d) 3, 5, 1, 2, 4, 6

7. Arrange the words given below in a meaningful sequence.
1. Table 2. Tree 3. Wood 4. Seed 5. Plant
(a) 1, 2, 3, 4, 5 (b) 1, 3, 2, 4, 5
(c) 4, 5, 2, 3, 1 (d) 4, 5, 3, 2, 1

8. Arrange the words given below in a meaningful sequence.
1. Windows 2. Walls 3. Floor 4. Foundation 5. Roof 6. Room
(a) 4, 1, 5, 6, 2, 3 (b) 4, 2, 1, 5, 3, 6
(c) 4, 3, 5, 6, 2, 1 (d) 4, 5, 3, 2, 1, 6

9. Arrange the words given below in a meaningful sequence.
1. Presentation 2. Recommendation 3. Arrival 4. Discussion 5. Introduction
(a) 3, 5, 1, 4, 2 (b) 3, 5, 4, 2, 1
(c) 5, 3, 1, 2, 4 (d) 5, 3, 4, 1, 2

10. Arrange the words given below in a meaningful sequence.
1. Butterfly 2. Cocoon 3. Egg 4. Worm
(a) 1, 3, 4, 2 (b) 1, 4, 3, 2
(c) 2, 4, 1, 3 (d) 3, 4, 2, 1

11. Arrange the words given below in a meaningful sequence.
1. Rain 2. Monsoon 3. Rescue 4. Flood 5. Shelter 6. Relief
(a) 1, 2, 3, 4, 5, 6 (b) 1, 2, 4, 5, 3, 6
(c) 2, 1, 4, 3, 5, 6 (d) 4, 1, 2, 3, 5, 6

12. Arrange the words given below in a meaningful sequence.
1. Milky way 2. Sun 3. Moon 4. Earth 5. Stars
(a) 1, 4, 3, 2, 5 (b) 2, 3, 4, 5, 1
(c) 3, 4, 2, 5, 1 (d) 4, 3, 2, 5, 1

13. Arrange the words given below in a meaningful sequence.
1. Foetus 2. Child 3. Baby 4. Adult 5. Youth
(a) 1, 2, 4, 3, 5 (b) 1, 3, 2, 5, 4
(c) 2, 3, 5, 4, 1 (d) 5, 4, 2, 3, 1

14. Arrange the words given below in a meaningful sequence.
1. Sea 2. Rivulet 3. Ocean 4. River 5. Glacier
(a) 5, 2, 1, 3, 4 (b) 5, 2, 4, 1, 3
(c) 5, 4, 2, 3, 1 (d) 5, 4, 3, 2, 1

15. Arrange the words given below in a meaningful sequence.
1. Doctor 2. Fever 3. Prescribe 4. Diagnose 5. Medicine
(a) 1, 4, 3, 2, 5 (b) 2, 1, 3, 4, 5
(c) 2, 1, 4, 3, 5 (d) 2, 4, 3, 5, 1

16. Arrange the words given below in a meaningful sequence.
1. Reading 2. Composing 3. Writing 4. Printing
(a) 1, 3, 2, 4 (b) 2, 3, 4, 1
(c) 3, 1, 2, 4 (d) 3, 2, 4, 1

17. Arrange the words given below in a meaningful sequence.
1. Hecto 2. Centi 3. Deca 4. Kilo 5. Deci
(a) 1, 3, 4, 5, 2 (b) 1, 5, 3, 4, 2
(c) 2, 5, 3, 1, 4 (d) 5, 2, 1, 4, 3

18. Arrange the words given below in a meaningful sequence.
1. Honey 2. Flower 3. Bee 4. Wax
(a) 1, 3, 4, 2 (b) 2, 1, 4, 3
(c) 2, 3, 1, 4 (d) 4, 3, 2, 1

19. Arrange the words given below in a meaningful sequence.
1. District 2. Village 3. State 4. Town 5. City
(a) 2, 4, 1, 5, 3 (b) 2, 1, 4, 5, 3
(c) 5, 3, 2, 1, 4 (d) 2, 5, 3, 4, 1

20. Arrange the words given below in a meaningful sequence.
1. Rainbow 2. Rain 3. Sun 4. Happy 5. Child
(a) 2, 1, 4, 3, 5 (b) 2, 3, 1, 5, 4
(c) 4, 2, 3, 5, 1 (d) 4, 5, 1, 2, 3

21. Arrange the words given below in a meaningful sequence.
1. Cutting 2. Dish 3. Vegetable 4. Market 5. Cooking
(a) 1, 2, 4, 5, 3 (b) 3, 2, 5, 1, 4
(c) 4, 3, 1, 5, 2 (d) 5, 3, 2, 1, 4

22. Arrange the words given below in a meaningful sequence.
1. Cut 2. Put on 3. Mark 4. Measure 5. Tailor
(a) 1, 3, 2, 4, 5 (b) 2, 4, 3, 1, 5
(c) 3, 1, 5, 4, 2 (d) 4, 3, 1, 5, 2

23. Arrange the words given below in a meaningful sequence.
1. Patient 2. Diagnosis 3. Bill 4. Doctor 5. Treatment
(a) 1, 4, 2, 3, 5 (b) 1, 4, 3, 2, 5
(c) 1, 4, 2, 5, 3 (d) 4, 1, 2, 3, 5

24. Arrange the words given below in a meaningful sequence.
1. Study 2. Job 3. Examination 4. Earn 5. Apply
(a) 1, 3, 2, 5, 4 (b) 1, 2, 3, 4, 5
(c) 1, 3, 5, 2, 4 (d) 1, 3, 5, 4, 2

25. Arrange the words given below in a meaningful sequence.
1. Rock 2. Hill 3. Mountain 4. Range 5. Stone
(a) 1, 3, 4, 2, 5 (b) 5, 1, 2, 3, 4
(c) 2, 3, 1, 5, 4 (d) 4, 5, 1, 2, 3

26. Arrange the words given below in a meaningful sequence.
    1. Income 2. Status 3. Education 4. Well-being 5. Job
    (a) 3, 1, 5, 2, 4 (b) 1, 3, 2, 5, 4
    (c) 1, 2, 5, 3, 4 (d) 3, 5, 1, 2, 4
27. Arrange the words given below in a meaningful sequence.
    1. Leaves 2. Branch 3. Flower 4. Tree 5. Fruit
    (a) 4, 3, 1, 2, 5 (b) 4, 2, 5, 1, 3
    (c) 4, 3, 2, 1, 5 (d) 4, 2, 1, 3, 5
28. Arrange the words given below in a meaningful sequence.
    1. Tree 2. Seed 3. Flowers 4. Fruit 5. Plant
    (a) 5, 2, 1, 3, 4 (b) 2, 5, 1, 4, 3
    (c) 2, 5, 1, 3, 4 (d) 2, 5, 3, 1, 4
29. Arrange the words given below in a meaningful sequence.
    1. Protect 2. Pressure 3. Relief 4. Rain 5. Flood
    (a) 2, 4, 3, 1, 5 (b) 2, 4, 5, 1, 3
    (c) 2, 5, 4, 1, 3 (d) 3, 2, 4, 5, 1
30. Arrange the words given below in a meaningful sequence.
    1. Dinner 2. Lunch 3. Breakfast 4. Bed Tea 5. Afternoon Tea
    (a) 3, 5, 2, 1, 4 (b) 4, 1, 5, 2, 3
    (c) 4, 3, 2, 5, 1 (d) 1, 3, 5, 2, 4
31. Arrange the words given below in a meaningful sequence.
    1. Probation 2. Interview 3. Selection 4. Appointment 5. Advertisement 6. Application
    (a) 5, 6, 3, 2, 4, 1 (b) 5, 6, 4, 2, 3, 1
    (c) 5, 6, 2, 3, 4, 1 (d) 6, 5, 4, 2, 3, 1
32. Arrange the words given below in a meaningful sequence.
    1. Gold 2. Iron 3. Sand 4. Platinum 5. Diamond
    (a) 5, 4, 3, 2, 1 (b) 4, 5, 1, 3, 2
    (c) 3, 2, 1, 5, 4 (d) 2, 4, 3, 5, 1
33. Arrange the words given below in a meaningful sequence.
    1. Nation 2. Village 3. City 4. District 5. State
    (a) 2, 3, 4, 5, 1 (b) 2, 3, 4, 1, 5
    (c) 1, 3, 5, 4, 2 (d) 1, 2, 3, 4, 5
34. Arrange the words given below in a meaningful sequence.
    1. Caste 2. Family 3. Newly married Couple 4. Clan 5. Species
    (a) 2, 3, 1, 4, 5 (b) 3, 4, 5, 1, 2
    (c) 3, 2, 1, 4, 5 (d) 4, 5, 3, 2, 1
35. Arrange the words given below in a meaningful sequence.
    1. Pulp 2. Print 3. Paper 4. Purchase 5. Publish
    (a) 1, 3, 2, 5, 4 (b) 1, 2, 3, 4, 5
    (c) 2, 1, 5, 4, 3 (d) 5, 4, 1, 3, 4

Answer Key

1. (b)	**2.** (d)	**3.** (b)	**4.** (d)	**5.** (c)	**6.** (b)	**7.** (c)	**8.** (b)
9. (a)	**10.** (d)	**11.** (c)	**12.** (c)	**13.** (b)	**14.** (b)	**15.** (c)	**16.** (d)
17. (c)	**18.** (c)	**19.** (a)	**20.** (b)	**21.** (c)	**22.** (d)	**23.** (c)	**24.** (c)
25. (b)	**26.** (d)	**27.** (d)	**28.** (c)	**29.** (b)	**30.** (c)	**31.** (c)	**32.** (c)
33. (a)	**34.** (c)	**35.** (a)					

❑

Previous Year Questions

☛ ***Direction to Solve (1 to 10):*** *In each of the following questions, arrange the given words in a meaningful sequence and thus find the correct answer from alternatives.*

1. Arrange the following words in a meaningful order.
[NTSE 2003 - Punjab first stage paper]
1. Death 2. Marriage 3. Education 4. Birt 5. Funeral
(a) 5, 1, 2, 3, 4 (b) 4, 2, 3, 1, 5
(c) 4, 3, 2, 5, 1 (d) 4, 3, 2, 1, 5

2. Arrange the words given below in a meaningful sequence.
[NTSE 2012 – Tamilnadu second stage paper]
1. Country 2. Furniture 3. Forest 4. Wood 5. Trees
(a) 1, 3, 5, 4, 2 (b) 1, 4, 3, 2, 5
(c) 2, 4, 3, 1, 5 (d) 5, 2, 3, 1, 4

3. Arrange the words given below in a meaningful sequence.
[NTSE 2004 - Rajasthan first stage paper]
1. Site 2. Plan 3. Rent 4. Money 5. Building 6. Construction
(a) 1, 2, 3, 6, 5, 4 (b) 2, 3, 6, 5, 1, 4
(c) 3, 4, 2, 6, 5, 1 (d) 4, 1, 2, 6, 5, 3

4. Arrange the words given below in a meaningful sequence.
[NTSE 2005 - Maharashtra second stage paper]
1. Key 2. Door 3. Lock 4. Room 5. Switch on
(a) 1, 2, 3, 5, 4 (b) 1, 3, 2, 4, 5
(c) 4, 2, 1, 5, 3 (d) 5, 1, 2, 4, 3

5. Arrange the words given below in a meaningful sequence. ***[NTSE 2012 - Delhi first stage paper]***
1. Heel 2. Shoulder 3. Skull 4. Neck 5. Knee 6. Chest 7. Thigh 8. Stomach 9. Face 10. Hand
(a) 2, 4, 7, 10, 1, 5, 8, 9, 6, 3
(b) 3, 4, 7, 9, 2, 5, 8, 10, 6, 1
(c) 4, 7, 10, 1, 9, 6, 3, 2, 5, 8,
(d) 3, 9, 4, 2, 10, 6, 8, 7, 5, 1

6. Arrange the words given below in a meaningful sequence.
[NTSE 2006 – Uttar Pradesh second stage paper]
1. Elephant 2. Cat 3. Mosquito 4. Tiger 5. Whale
(a) 1, 3, 5, 4, 2 (b) 2, 5, 1, 4, 3
(c) 3, 2, 4, 1, 5 (d) 5, 3, 1, 2, 4

7. Arrange the words given below in a meaningful sequence. ***[NTSE 2007 - MP first stage paper]***
1. Yarn 2. Plant 3. Saree 4. Cotton 5. Cloth
(a) 2, 4, 1, 5, 3 (b) 2, 4, 3, 5, 1
(c) 2, 4, 5, 1, 3 (d) 2, 4, 5, 3, 1

8. Arrange the words given below in a meaningful sequence. ***[NTSE 2007 - Bihar first stage paper]***
1. Police 2. Punishment 3. Crime 4. Justice5 . Judgement
(a) 1, 2, 3, 4, 5 (b) 3, 1, 2, 4, 5
(c) 3, 1, 4, 5, 2 (d) 5, 4, 3, 2, 1

9. Arrange the words given below in a meaningful sequence.
[NTSE 2004 - Karnataka first stage paper]
1. Andhra Pradesh 2. Universe 3. Tirupati 4. World 5. India
(a) 1, 5, 3, 2, 4 (b) 2, 1, 3, 5, 4
(c) 3, 1, 5, 4, 2 (d) 5, 4, 2, 1, 3

10. Arrange the following words in a logical sequence.
[NTSE 2007 - Delhi second stage paper]
1. Grass 2. Curd 3. Milk 4. Cow 5. Butter
(a) 1, 2, 3, 4, 5 (b) 2, 3, 4, 5, 1
(c) 4, 1, 3, 2, 5 (d) 5, 4, 3, 2, 1

Answer Key

1. (d)	2. (a)	3. (d)	4. (b)	5. (d)	6. (c)	7. (a)	8. (c)	9. (c)	10. (c)

❑

UNIT 12

Verification of Truth of Statement

The candidate here is required to stress only on the truth of the facts that always hold in the context of a particular thing or factor that is always characterized by a specific part.

Solved Examples

☛ ***Directions:*** *Find the absolute truth out of the given alternatives.*

1. If we are going early in the morning towards the south, the sun will be visible at our left:
   (a) Always (b) Never
   (c) Often (d) Sometimes
   Solution: Option (a) is correct.
   Explanation: Early in the morning the sun is in the direction of east. If we are going towards the south, our face will be in the direction of South and our left hand will be in the direction of east.
   Hence if we go early in the morning towards the south the sun will always be visible at our left.
2. A boy is sitting at the back seat of a car. When the driver suddenly starts moving the car (in forward direction), the boy experiences a backward force?
   (a) Always (b) Never
   (c) Often (d) Sometimes
   Solution: Option (a) is correct.
   Explanation: When a car suddenly starts, the lower part of the boy's body will be in the motion while his upper will be at rest.
   Hence, he will always experience backward force.
3. Yesterday I saw an ice cube which had already melted due to heat of a nearby furnace.
   (a) Always (b) Never
   (c) Often (d) Sometimes
   Solution: Option (b) is correct.
   Explanation: Since the ice cube had already melted due to the heat of a nearby furnace, so the ice cannot remain as ice cube.

Multiple Choice Questions

☛ ***Direction to solve (1 to 20):*** *Find the absolute truth from the given alternatives.*

1. Which one of the following is always in 'Sentiment'?
   (a) Cruelty (b) Insight
   (c) Neutrality (d) Emotion
2. Controversy always involves:
   (a) Dislike (b) Injustice
   (c) Disagreement (d) Passion
3. What is found necessarily in newspaper?
   (a) Date (b) Advertisement
   (c) News (d) Editor
4. A camera always has:
   (a) Reels (b) Flash
   (c) Stand (d) Lens
5. What is found necessarily in a race?
   (a) Judge (b) Spectators
   (c) Competitor (d) Prize
6. What is found necessarily in game?
   (a) Players (b) Spectators
   (c) Referee (d) Victory
7. Which one of the following is always found in factories?
   (a) Chimney (b) Workers
   (c) Electricity (d) Sellers
8. A hill always has:
   (a) Trees (b) Height
   (c) Animals (d) Water
9. My ten years old niece is taller than my twelve years old son:
   (a) Always (b) Never
   (c) Often (d) Sometimes
10. What is always in worry?
    (a) Difficulty (b) Unrest
    (c) Non-Cooperation (d) Poignancy

11. Which one of the following is always associated with 'tree'?
    (a) Flowers (b) Leaves
    (c) Fruits (d) Roots
12. Which one of the following is always associated with 'justice'?
    (a) Hypocrisy (b) Legitimate
    (c) Magnanimity (d) Diminutiveness
13. A car always has:
    (a) Driver (b) Wheels
    (c) Bonnet (d) Bumper
14. Danger always involves:
    (a) Enemy (b) Attack
    (c) Fear (d) Help
15. A disease always has:
    (a) Cure (b) Germs
    (c) Cause (d) Patient
16. Management always involves:
    (a) Regulation (b) Counsel
    (c) Exhortation (d) Coercion
17. Which one of the following is always found in 'Phrase'?
    (a) Nomenclature (b) Manifestation
    (c) Pictorial effect (d) Glossary
18. A bulb always has:
    (a) Glass (b) Current
    (c) Filament (d) Light
19. A mirror always:
    (a) Retracts (b) Distorts
    (c) Refracts (d) Reflects
20. A lotus flower always has:
    (a) Mud (b) Petals
    (c) Root (d) Water

Answer Key

1. (d)	**2.** (c)	**3.** (c)	**4.** (d)	**5.** (c)	**6.** (a)	**7.** (b)	**8.** (b)	**9.** (d)
10. (b)	**11.** (d)	**12.** (b)	**13.** (b)	**14.** (c)	**15.** (c)	**16.** (a)	**17.** (d)	**18.** (c)
19. (d)	**20.** (b)							

❒

Previous Year Questions

☛ ***Direction to solve (1 to 10):*** *Find the absolute truth out of the given alternatives.*

1. In India a widow can marry her brother-in-law although a man cannot marry the sister of his dead wife?
   [NTSE 2007 - UP first stage paper]
   (a) Always (b) Never
   (c) Often (d) Sometimes
2. Which one of the following is always found in 'Remedy of fault'?
   [NTSE 2001 - Karnataka first stage paper]
   (a) Punishment (b) Remedy
   (c) Fault (d) Scolding
3. Which one of the following is always with 'Bargain'?
   [NTSE 2007 - Punjab first stage paper]
   (a) Exchange (b) Sumptuousness
   (c) Triviality (d) Eloquence
4. Which one of the following a 'Drama' must have?
   [NTSE 2004 - Delhi first stage paper]
   (a) Actors (b) Story
   (c) Sets (d) Director
5. Which one of the following is always found in 'Wonder'?
   [NTSE 2012 - UP first stage paper]
   (a) Crowd (b) Lumber
   (c) Astonishment (d) Rustic
6. Disclosure always involves:
   [NTSE 2003 - Karnataka first stage paper]
   (a) Agents (b) Display
   (c) Exposition (d) Secrets
7. A train always has:
   [NTSE 2000 - Assam first stage paper]
   (a) Rails (b) Driver
   (c) Guard (d) Engine
8. Which one of the following is always found in 'Bravery'?
   [NTSE 2002 - UP first stage paper
   (a) Experience (b) Power
   (c) Courage (d) Knowledge
9. A song always has
   [NTSE 2007 - Gujarat first stage paper
   (a) Word (b) Chorus
   (c) Musician (d) Instruments
10. What is found necessarily in milk?
   [NTSE 20012 - Delhi first stage paper
   (a) Cream (b) Curd
   (c) Water (d) Whiteness

Answer Key

1. (d)	2. (c)	3. (a)	4. (b)	5. (c)	6. (d)	7. (d)	8. (c)	9. (a)	10. (d)

❐

UNIT 13

Analytical Reasoning

Analytical Reasoning involves problems related to the counting of geometrical plane figures in a complex figure. The systemic method for finding the number of any particular type of elements like straight lines, triangles, squares, rectangles etc. is to start searching from smaller components to bigger components in the complex figure.

Solved Examples

1. Find the number of triangles in the given figure.

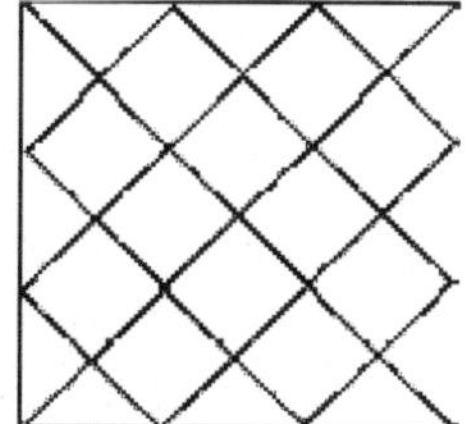

(a) 28 (b) 32
(c) 36 (d) 40

Solution: Option (c) is correct.

Explanation: The figure may be labelled as shown.

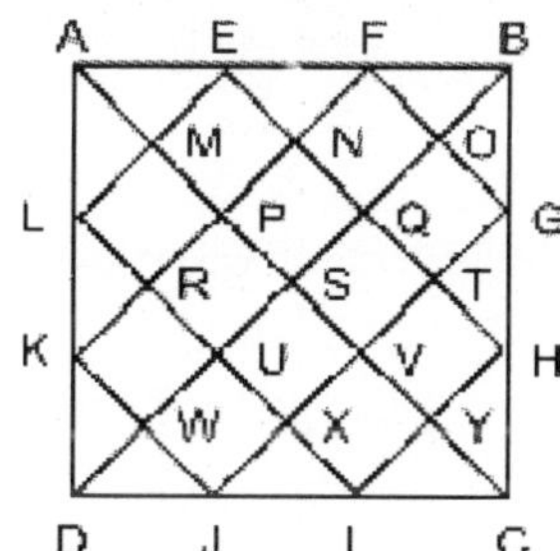

The simplest triangles are AML, LRK, KWD, DWJ, JXI, IYC, CYH, HTG, GOB, BOF, FNE and EMA i.e. 12 in number.

The triangles composed of two components each are AEL, KDJ, HIC and FBG i.e. 4 in number.

The triangles composed of three components each are APF, EQB, BQH, GVC, CVJ, IUD, DUL and KPA i.e. 8 in number.

The triangles composed of six components each are ASB, BSG, CSD, DSA, AKF, EBH, GGJ and IDL i.e. 8 in number.

The triangles composed of twelve components each are ADB, ABC, BCD and CDA i.e. 4 in number.

Total number of triangles in the figure = 12 + 4 + 8 + 8 + 4 = 36.

2. What is the number of triangles that can be formed whose vertices are the vertices of an octagon but have only one side common with that of octagon?

(a) 64 (b) 32
(c) 24 (d) 16

Solution: Option (b) is correct.

Explanation:

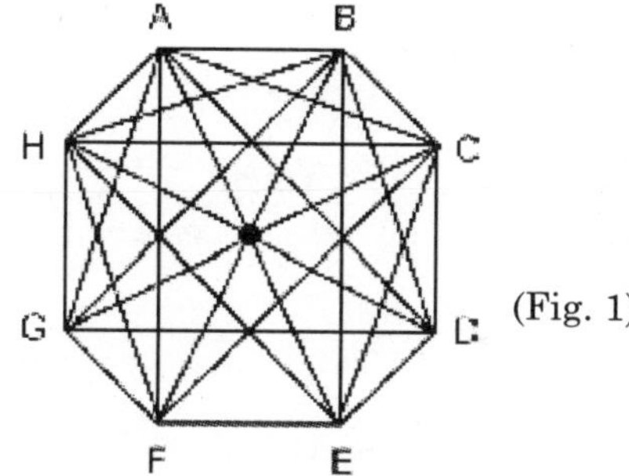

(Fig. 1)

When the triangles are drawn in an octagon with vertices same as those of the octagon and have one side common to that of the octagon, the figure will appear as shown in (Fig. 1).

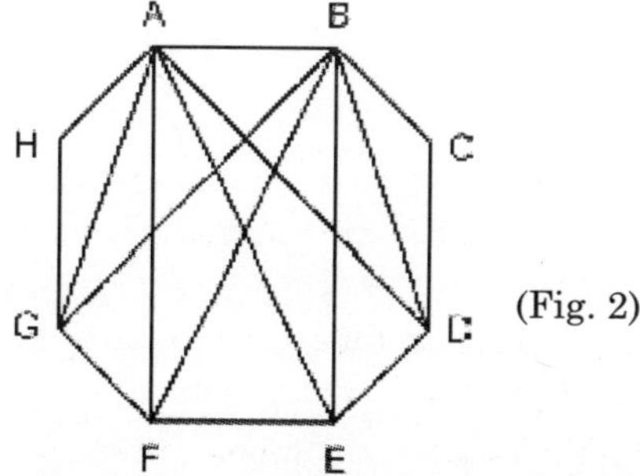

(Fig. 2)

Now, we shall first consider the triangles having only one side AB common with octagon ABCDEFGH and having vertices common with the octagon (See Fig. 2). Such triangles are ABD, ABE, ABF and ABG i.e. 4 in number.

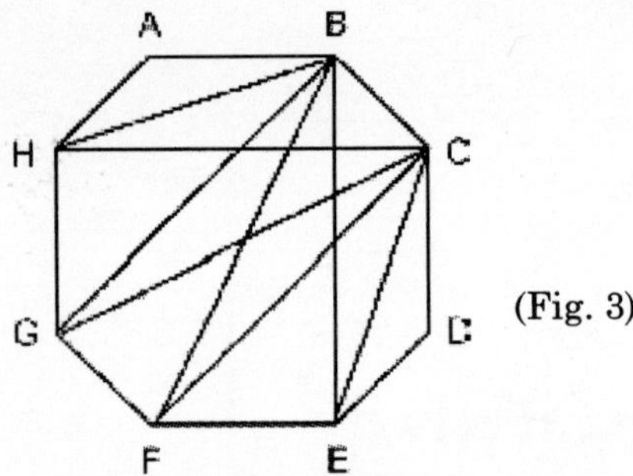

(Fig. 3)

Similarly, the triangles having only one side BC common with the octagon and also having vertices common with the octagon are BCE, BCF, BCG and BCH (as shown in Fig. 3). i.e. There are 4 such triangles.

This way, we have 4 triangles for each side of the octagon. Thus, there are 8 × 4 = 32 such triangles.

3. Find the number of triangles in the given figure.

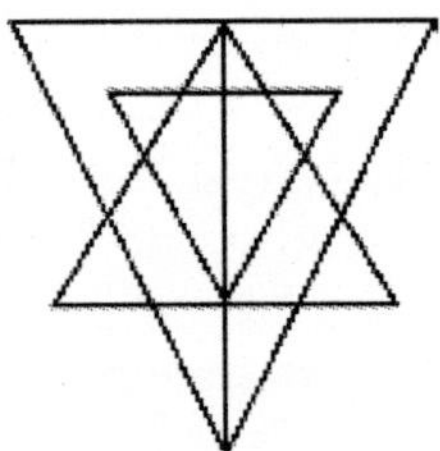

(a) 27 (b) 25
(c) 23 (d) 21

Solution: Option (a) is correct.

Explanation: The figure may be labelled as shown.

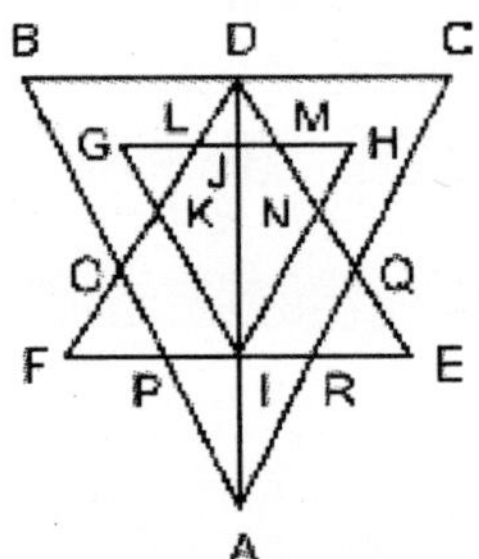

The simplest triangles are GLK, DLJ, DJM, HMN, QRE, IRA, IPA and FPO i.e. 8 in number.

The triangles having two components each are BDO, CDQ, DLM, PRA, KFI, NEI, HJI, GJI, DKI and DNI i.e. 10 in number.

The triangles having four components each are DIE, DFI, DOA, DQA and GHI i.e. 5 in number.

The triangles having six components each are DCA and DBA i.e. 2 in number.

DEF is the only triangle having eight components.

ABC is the only triangle having twelve components.

Thus, there are 8 + 10 + 5 + 2 + 1 + 1 = 27 triangles in the figure.

4. Count the number of parallelogram in the given figure.

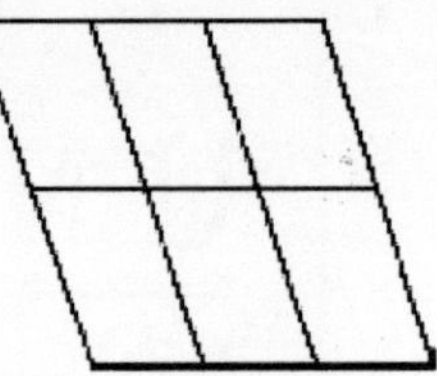

(a) 20 (b) 18
(v) 16 (d) 12

Solution: Option (b) is correct.

Explanation: The figure may be labelled as shown.

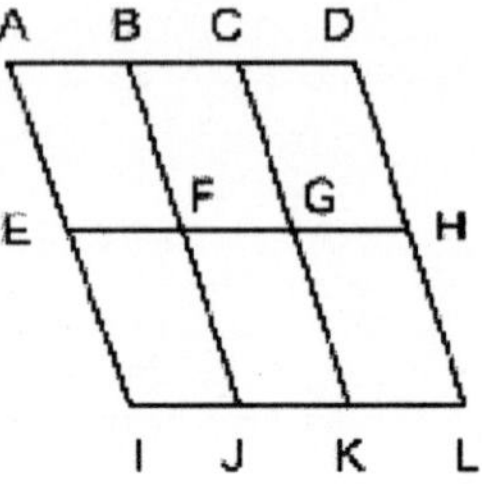

The simplest Parallelograms are ABFE, BCGF, CDHG, EFJI, FGKJ and GHLK. These are 6 in number.

The parallelograms composed of two components each are ACGE, BDHF, EGKI, FHLJ, ABJI, BCKJ and CDLK. Thus, there are 7 such parallelograms.

The parallelograms composed of three components each are ADHE and EHLI i.e. 2 in number.

The parallelograms composed of four components each are ACKI and BDLJ i.e. 2 in number

There is only one parallelogram composed of six components, namely ADLI.

Thus, there are 6 + 7 + 2 + 2 + 1 = 18 parallelograms in the figure.

5. How many triangles and parallelograms are there in the following figure?

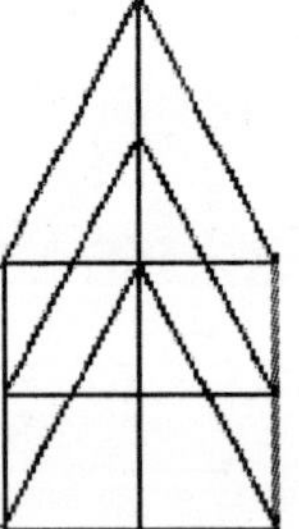

(a) 21, 17 (b) 19, 13
(c) 21, 15 (d) 19, 17

Solution: Option (a) is correct.

Explanation: The figure may be labelled as shown.

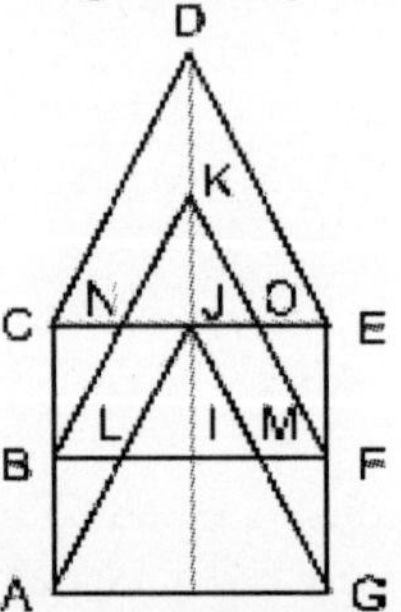

Triangles: The simplest triangles are KJN, KJO, CNB, OEF, JIL, JIM, BLA and MFG i.e. 8 in number.

The triangles composed of two components each are CDJ, EDJ, NKO, JLM, JAH and JGH i.e. 6 in number.

The triangles composed of three components each are BKI, FKI, CJA and EJG i.e. 4 in number.

The triangles composed of four components each are CDE and AJG i.e. 2 in number.

The only triangle composed of six components is BKF.

Thus, there are 8 + 6 + 4 + 2 + 1 = 21 triangles in the given figure.

Parallelograms: The simplest parallelograms are NJLB and JOFM i.e. 2 in number.

The parallelograms composed of two components each are CDKB, DEFK, BIHA and IFGH i.e. 4 in number.

The parallelograms composed of three components each are BKJA, KFGJ, CJIB and JEFI i.e.4 in number.

There is only one parallelogram i.e. BFGA composed of four components.

The parallelograms composed of five components each are CDJA, DEGJ, CJHA and JEGH i.e. 4 in number.

The only parallelogram composed of six components is CEFB.

The only parallelogram composed of ten components is CEGA.

Thus, there are 2 + 4 + 4 + 1 + 4 + 1 + 1 = 17 parallelograms in the given figure.

(Note that the squares and rectangles are also counted amongst the parallelograms).

6. Count the number of parallelograms in the given figure.

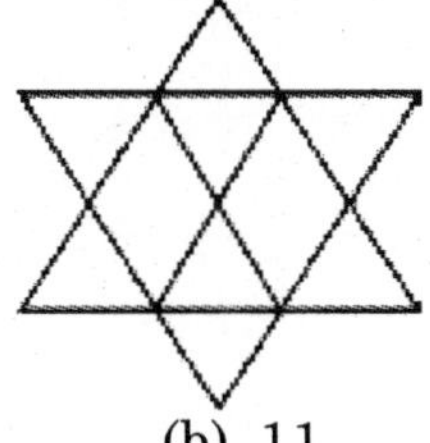

(a) 8 (b) 11
(c) 12 (d) 15

Solution: Option (d) is correct.

Explanation: The figure may be labelled as shown.

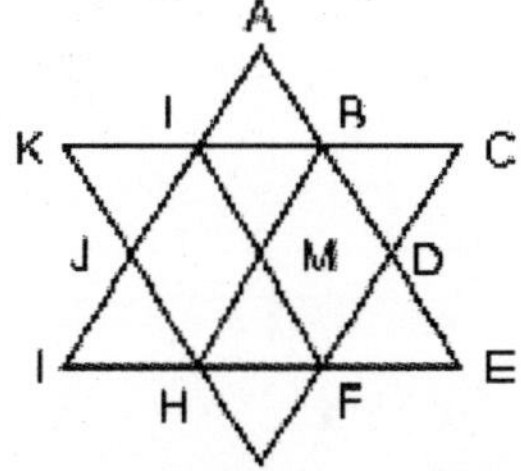

The simplest parallelograms are LMHJ and BDFM i.e. 2 in number. The parallelograms composed of two components each are ABML and MFGH i.e. 2 in number.

The parallelograms composed of three components each are LBHI, LBEF, BDGH, DFLA, BCFH, KLFH, A6HJ and LFGJ i.e. 8 in number.

The parallelograms composed of six components each are LCFI, KBEH and ADGJ i.e. 3 in number.

Total number of parallelograms in the figure = 2 + 2 + 8 + 3 = 15

7. Count the number of pentagons in the adjoining figure.

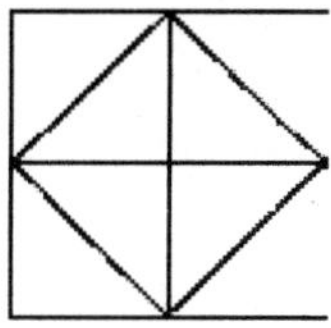

(a) 16 (b) 12
(c) 8 (d) 4

Solution: Option (b) is correct.

Explanation: The figure may be labelled as shown.

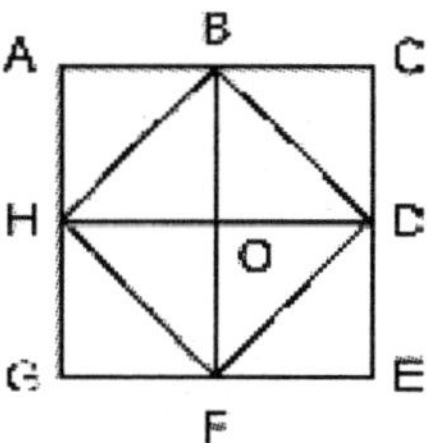

The pentagons in the figure are ABDFH, CDFHB, EFHBD, GHBDF, ACDFG, CEFHA, EGHBC, GABDE, BDEGH, DFGAB, FHACD and HBCEF. Thus, these are 12 in number.

8. Find the number of triangles in the given figure.

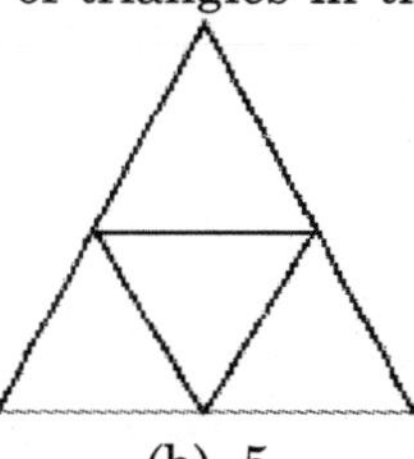

(a) 4 (b) 5
(c) 6 (d) 7

Solution: Option (b) is correct.

Explanation: The figure may be labelled as shown.

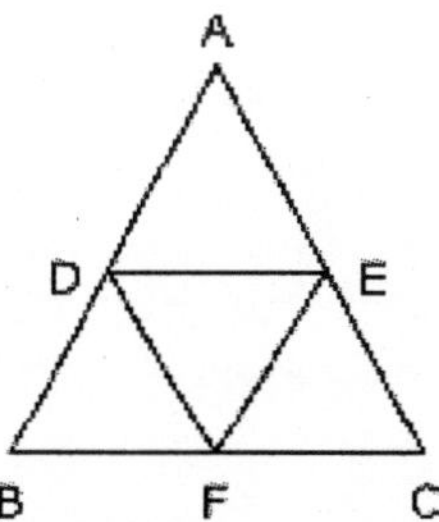

The simplest triangles are ADE, BDF, DEF and EFC i.e. 4 in number.

There is only one triangle ABC composed of four components.

Thus, there are 4 + 1 = 5 triangles in the given figure.

❐

Multiple Choice Questions

1. Find the number of triangles in the given figure.

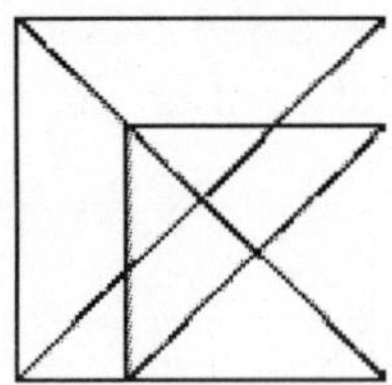

(a) 16 (b) 18
(c) 19 (d) 21

2. Find the number of triangles in the given figure.

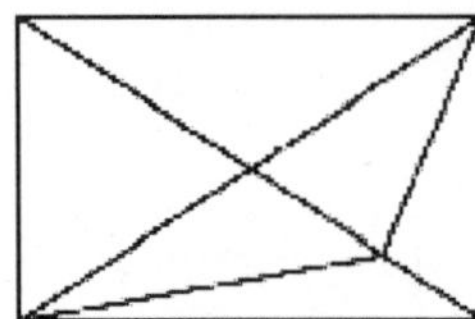

(a) 11 (b) 13
(c) 15 (d) 17

3. Find the number of triangles in the given figure.

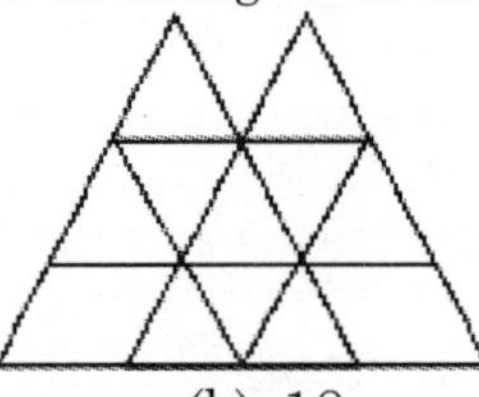

(a) 16 (b) 18
(c) 14 (d) 15

4. Find the number of triangles in the given figure.

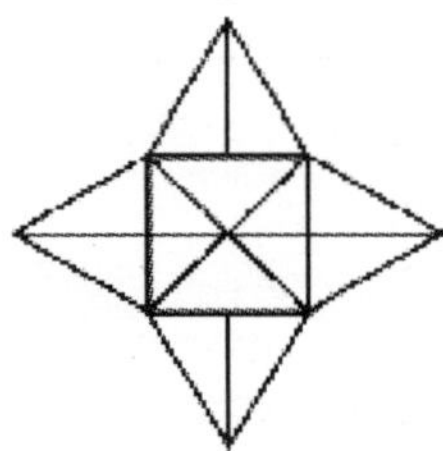

(a) 18 (b) 20
(c) 28 (d) 34

5. Find the number of triangles in the given figure.

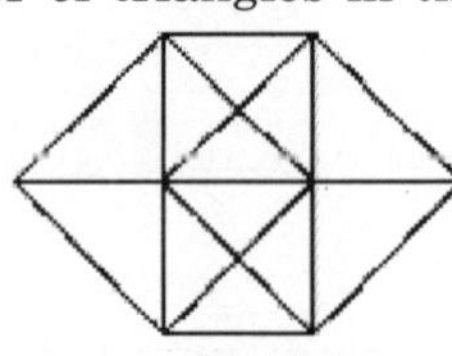

(a) 20 (b) 24
(c) 28 (d) 32

6. Find the minimum number of straight lines required to make the given figure.

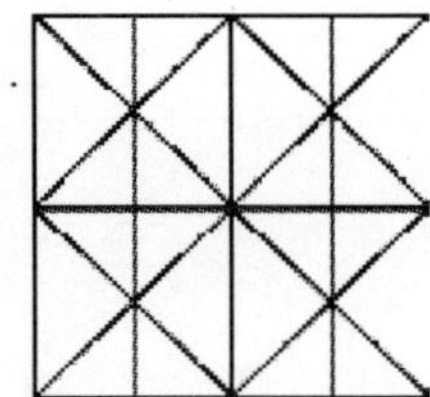

(a) 11 (b) 14
(c) 16 (d) 17

7. What is the number of straight lines and the number of triangles in the given figure?

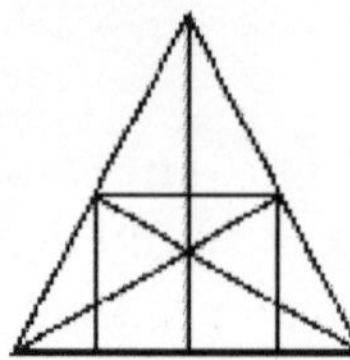

(a) 10 straight lines and 34 triangles
(b) 9 straight lines and 34 triangles
(c) 9 straight lines and 36 triangles
(d) 10 straight lines and 36 triangles

8. Find the number of triangles in the given figure.

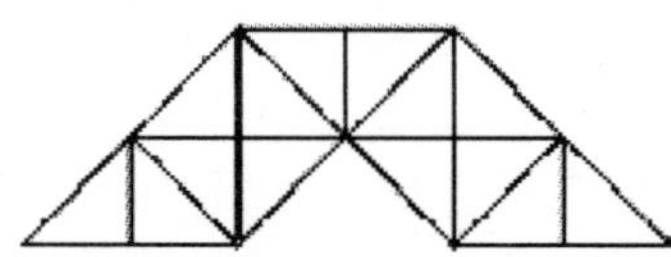

(a) 23 (b) 27
(c) 29 (d) 31

9. Find the number of triangles in the given figure.

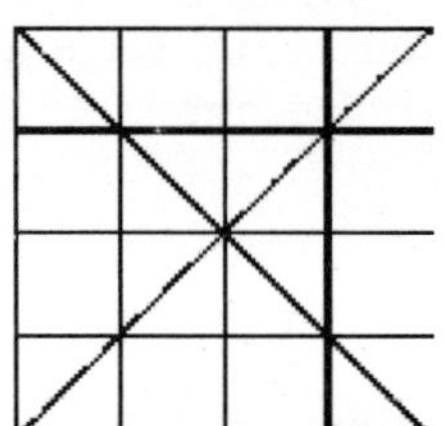

(a) 36 (b) 40
(c) 44 (d) 48

10. Find the number of triangles in the given figure.

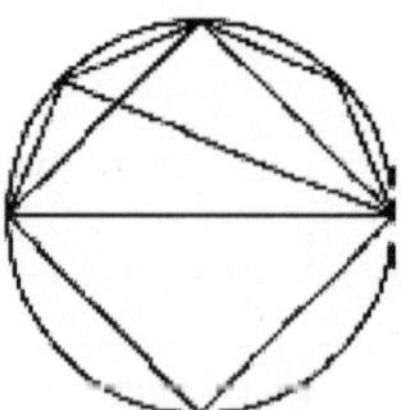

(a) 8 (b) 10
(c) 11 (d) 12

11. Find the number of triangles in the given figure.

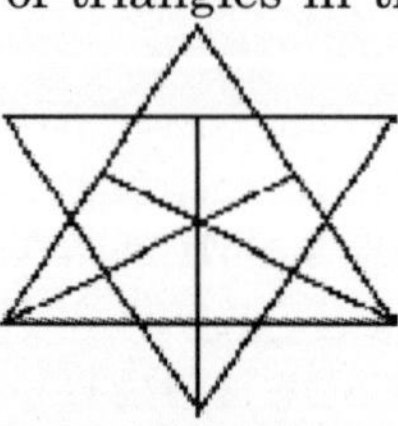

(a) 21 (b) 23
(c) 25 (d) 27

12. Find the number of triangles in the given figure.

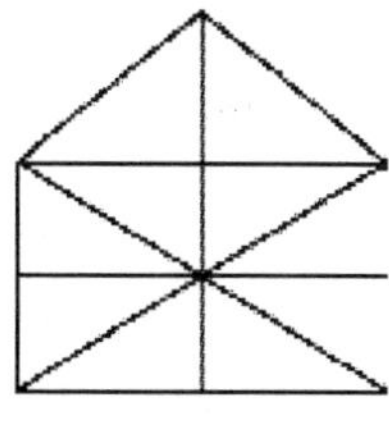

(a) 10 (b) 19
(c) 21 (d) 23

13. Find the minimum number of straight lines required to make the given figure.

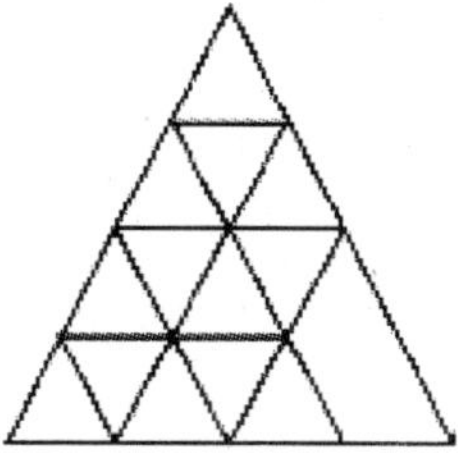

(a) 9 (b) 11
(c) 15 (d) 16

14. Find the number of triangles in the given figure.

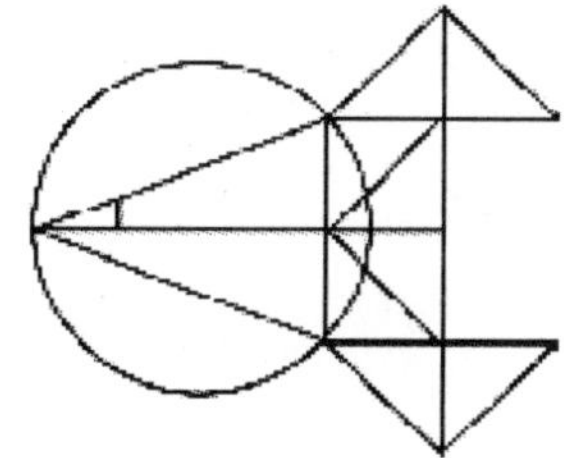

(a) 10 (b) 12
(c) 14 (d) 16

15. Find the minimum number of straight lines required to make the given figure.

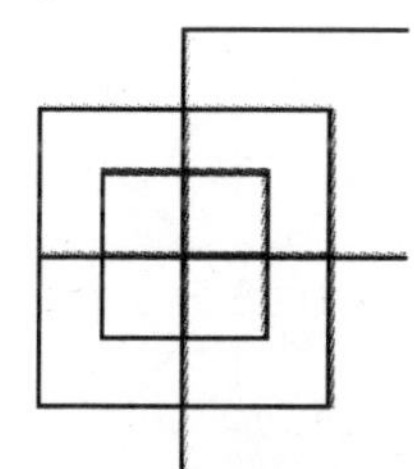

(a) 13 (b) 15
(c) 17 (d) 19

16. Find the number of triangles in the given figure.

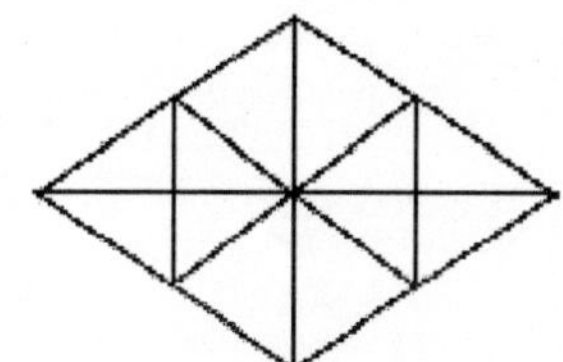

(a) 16 (b) 22
(c) 28 (d) 32

17. Find the number of triangles in the given figure.

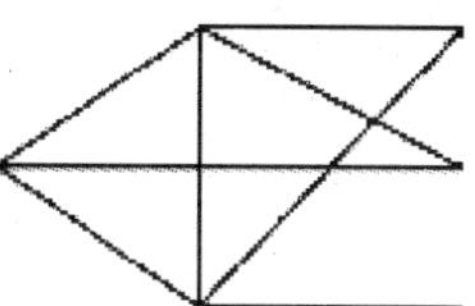

(a) 12 (b) 13
(c) 14 (d) 15

18. Find the number of quadrilaterals in the given figure.

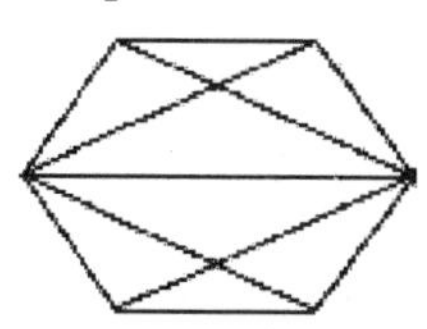

(a) 6 (b) 7
(c) 9 (d) 11

19. Count the number of squares in the given figure.

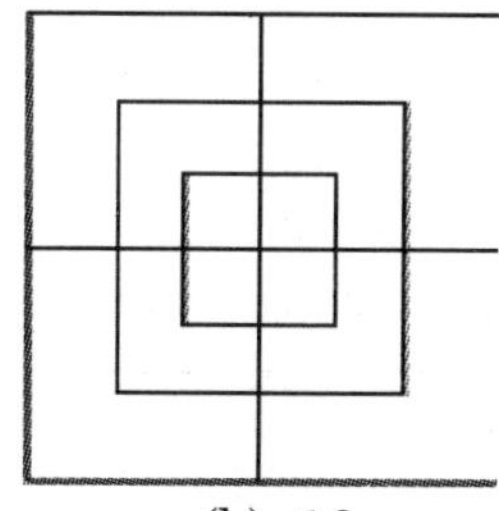

(a) 8 (b) 12
(c) 15 (d) 18

20. What is the minimum number of colours required to fill the spaces in the given diagram without any two adjacent spaces having the same colour?

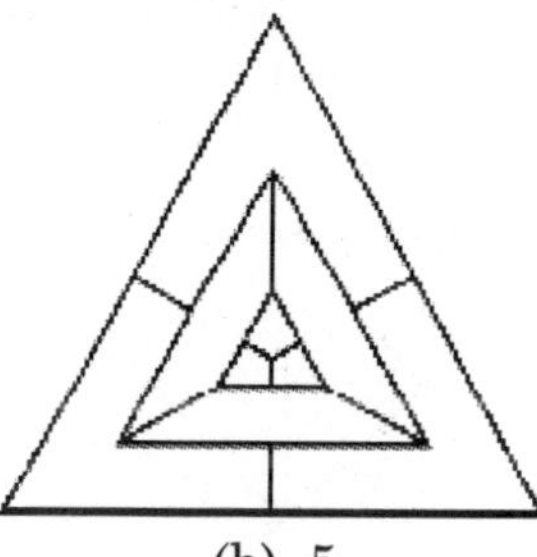

(a) 6 (b) 5
(c) 4 (d) 3

21. What is the minimum number of different colours required to paint the given figure such that no two adjacent regions have the same colour?

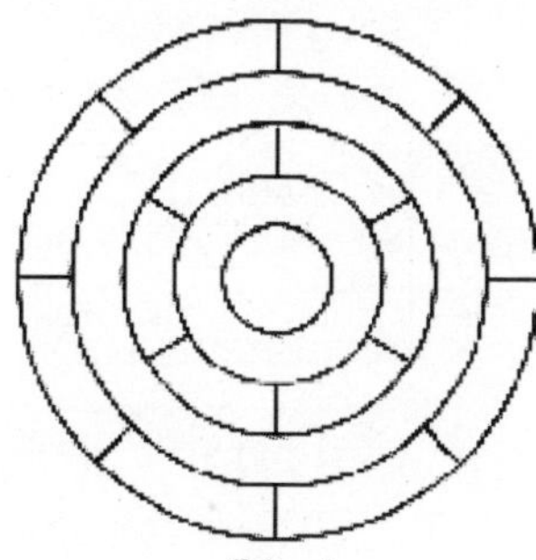

(a) 3 (b) 4
(c) 5 (d) 6

22. In the adjoining figure, if the centres of all the circles are joined by horizontal and vertical lines, then find the number of squares that can be formed.

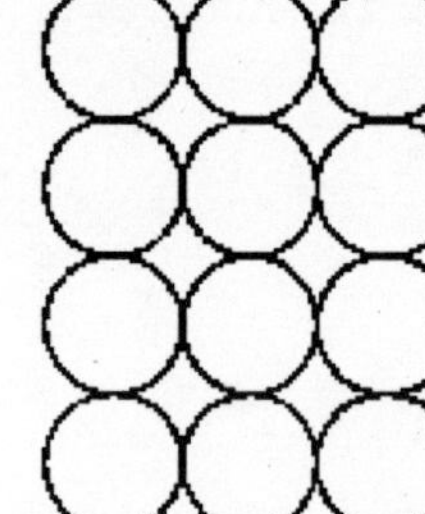

(a) 6 (b) 7
(c) 8 (d) 1

23. Count the number of triangles and squares in the given figure.

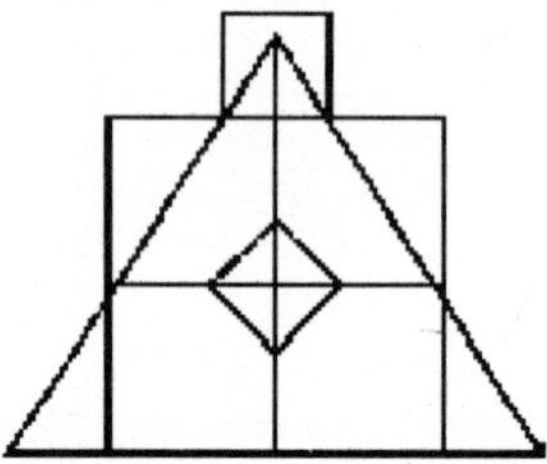

(a) 21 triangles, 7 squares
(b) 18 triangles, 8 squares
(c) 20 triangles, 8 squares
(d) 22 triangles, 7 squares

24. Count the number of squares in the given figure.

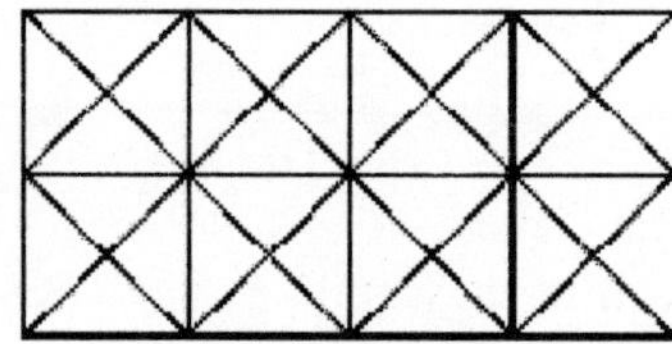

(a) 11 (b) 21
(c) 24 (d) 26

25. Count the number of squares in the given figure.

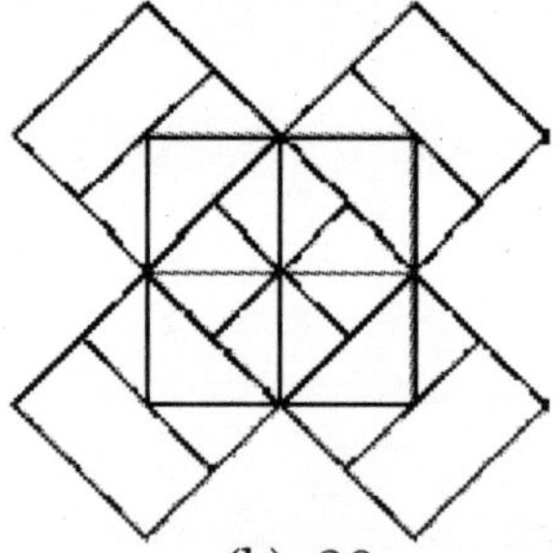

(a) 22 (b) 20
(c) 18 (d) 14

26. Count the number of rectangles in the given figure.

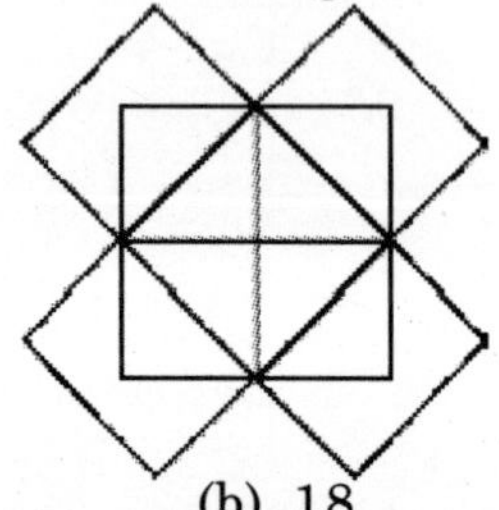

(a) 20 (b) 18
(c) 16 (d) 15

27. Count the number of parallelograms in the given figure.

(a) 47 (b) 45
(c) 41 (d) 39

28. What is the minimum number of straight lines that is needed to construct the figure?

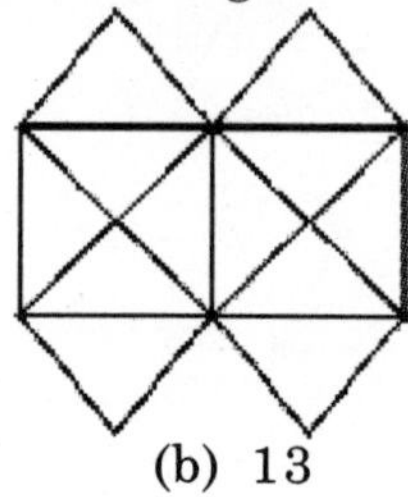

(a) 11 (b) 13
(c) 15 (d) 21

29. Determine the number of rectangles and hexagons in the given figure.

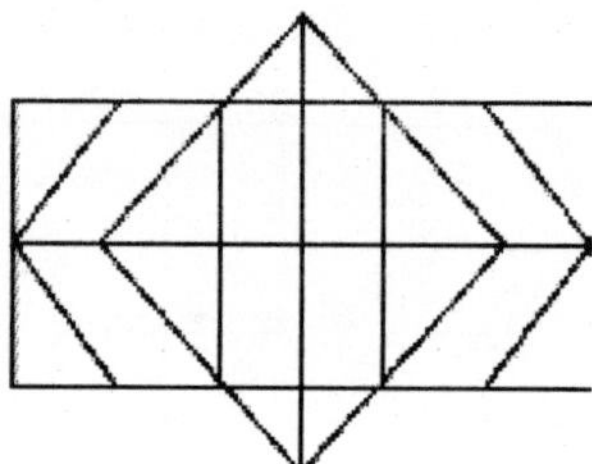

(a) 30, 5 (b) 32, 3
(c) 28, 5 (d) 30, 3

30. Count the number of triangles and squares in the given figure.

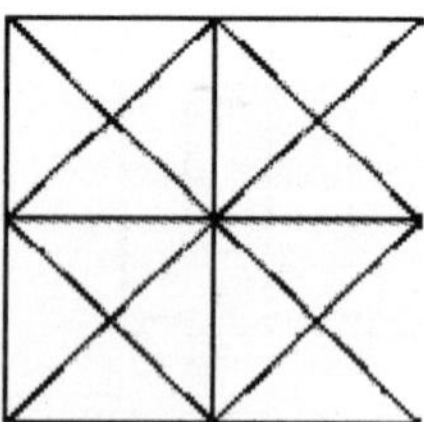

(a) 44 triangles, 10 squares
(b) 14 triangles, 16 squares
(c) 27 triangles, 6 squares
(d) 36 triangles, 9 squares

❐

Answer Key

1. (d)	**2.** (c)	**3.** (b)	**4.** (c)	**5.** (c)	**6.** (b)	**7.** (c)	**8.** (c)	**9.** (d)	**10.** (b)
11. (d)	**12.** (c)	**13.** (b)	**14.** (c)	**15.** (a)	**16.** (c)	**17.** (d)	**18.** (d)	**19.** (c)	**20.** (d)
21. (a)	**22.** (c)	**23.** (a)	**24.** (c)	**25.** (c)	**26.** (a)	**27.** (b)	**28.** (b)	**29.** (a)	**30.** (a)

Explanatory Notes

1. (d)
The figure may be labelled as shown.

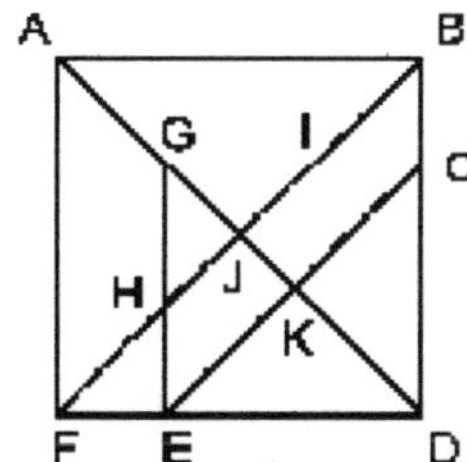

The simplest triangles are EFH, BIC, GHJ, GIJ, EKD and CKD i.e. 6 in number.

The triangles composed of two components each are ABJ, AFJ, GCK, GEK, CED arid GHI i.e. 6 in number.

The triangles composed of three components each are GCD, GED, DJB and DJF i.e. 4 in number.

The triangles composed of four components each are ABF and GCE i.e. 2 in number.

The triangles composed of five components each are ABD and AFD i.e. 2 in number.

There is only one triangle i.e. FBD composed of six components.

Total number of triangles in the figure
= 6 + 6 + 4 + 2 + 2 + 1 = 21

2. (c)
The figure may be labelled as shown.

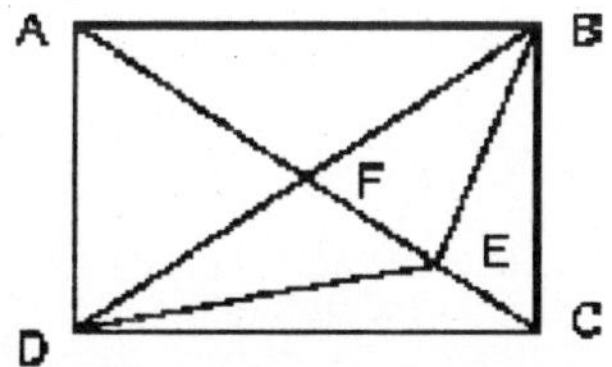

The simplest triangles are AFB, FEB, EBC, DEC, DFE and AFD i.e. 6 in number.

The triangles composed of two components each are AEB, FBC, DFC, ADE, DBE and ABD i.e. 6 in number.

The triangles composed of three components each are ADC and ABC i.e. 2 in number.

There is only one triangle i.e. DBC which is composed of four components.

Thus, there are 6 + 6 + 2 + 1 = 15 triangles in the figure.

3. (b)
The figure may be labelled as shown.

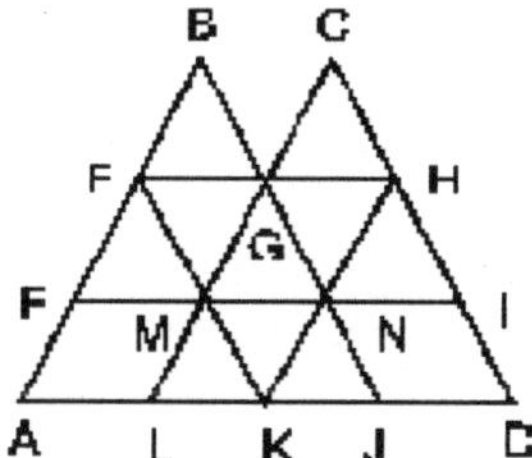

The simplest triangles are BFG, CGH, EFM, FMG, GMN, GHN, HNI, LMK, MNK and KNJ i.e. 10 in number.

The triangles composed of three components each are FAK and HKD i.e. 2 in number.

The triangles composed of four components each are BEN, CMI, GLJ and FHK i.e. 4 in number.

The triangles composed of eight components each are BAJ and OLD i.e. 2 in number.

Thus, there are 10 + 2 + 4 + 2 = 18 triangles in the given figure.

4. (c)
The figure may be labelled as shown.

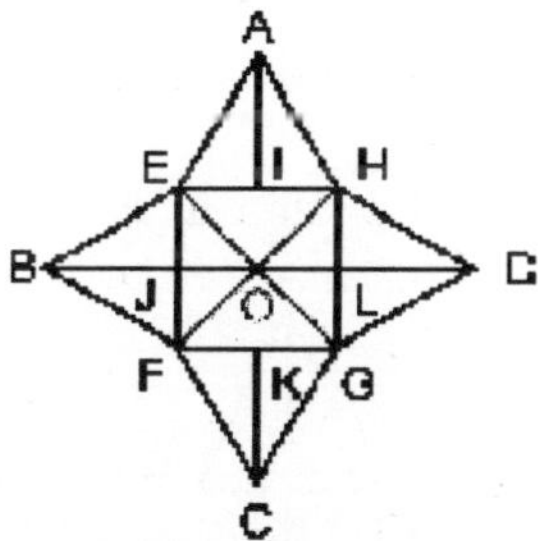

The simplest triangles are AEI, AIH, BEJ, BJF, CFK, CKG, DGL, DLH, EOJ, FOJ, FOG, LOG, HOL and HOE i.e. 14 in number.

The triangles composed of two components each are EAH, FBE, BEO, EOF, BFO, FCG, GDH, HOD, HOG and GOD i.e. 10 in number.

The triangles composed of three components each are EFH, EHG, FGH and EFG i.e. 4 in number.

Thus, there are 14 + 10 + 4 = 28 triangles in the given figure.

5. (c)
The figure may be labelled as shown.

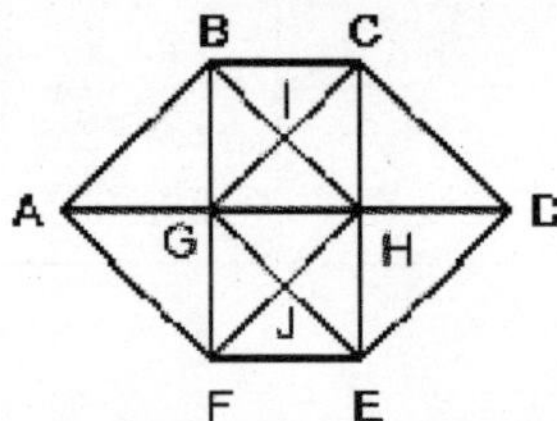

The simplest triangles are ABG, BIG, BIC, CIH, GIH, CDH, HED, GHJ, HJE, FEJ, GFJ and AGF i.e. 12 in number.

The triangles composed of two components each are ABF, CDE, GBC, BCH, GHG, BHG, GHF, GHE, HEF and GEF i.e. 10 in number.

The triangles composed of three components each are ABH, AFH, CDG and GDE i.e. 4 in number.

The triangles composed of four components each are BHF and CGE i.e. 2 in number.

Total number of triangles in the figure
= 12 + 10 + 4 + 2 = 28.

6. (b)
The figure may be labelled as shown.
The horizontal lines are AK, BJ, CI, DH and EG i.e. 5 in number.
The vertical lines are AE, LF and KG i.e. 3 in number.

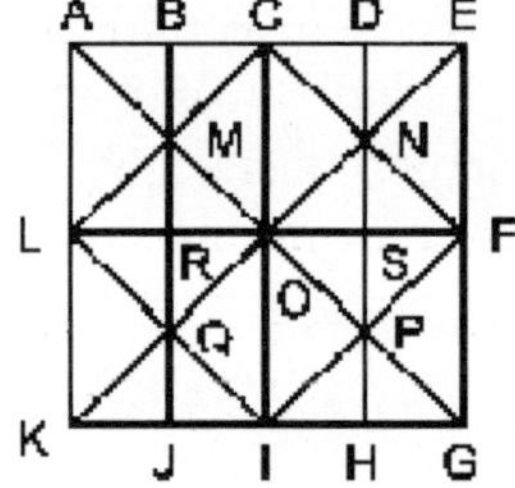

The slanting lines are LC, CF, FI, LI, EK and AG i.e. 6 in number.
Thus, there are 5 + 3 + 6 = 14 straight lines in the figure.

7. (c)
The figure may be labelled as shown.

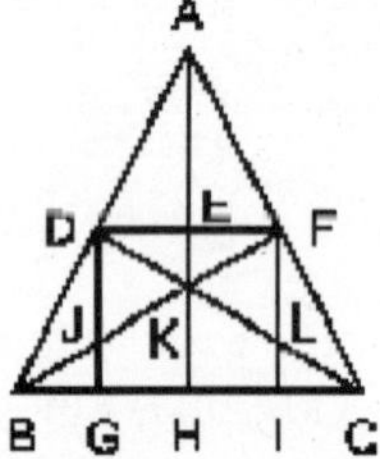

The Horizontal lines are DF and BC i.e. 2 in number.

The Vertical lines are DG, AH and FI i.e. 3 in number.

The Slanting lines are AB, AC, BF and DC i.e. 4 in number.

Thus, there are 2 + 3 + 4 = 9 straight lines in the figure.

Now, we shall count the number of triangles in the figure.

The simplest triangles are ADE, AEF, DEK, EFK, DJK, FLK, DJB, FLC, BJG and LIC i.e. 10 in number.

The triangles composed of two components each are ADF, AFK, DFK, ADK, DKB, FCK, BKH, KHC, DGB and FIC i.e. 10 in number.

The triangles composed of three components each are DFJ and DFL i.e. 2 in number.

The triangles composed of four components each are ABK, ACK, BFI, CDG, DFB, DFC and BKC i.e. 7 in number.

The triangles composed of six components each are ABH, ACH, ABF, ACD, BFC and CDB i.e. 6 in number.

There is only one triangle i.e. ABC composed of twelve components.

There are 10 + 10 + 2 + 7 + 6+ 1 = 36 triangles in the figure.

8. (c)
The figure may be labelled as shown.

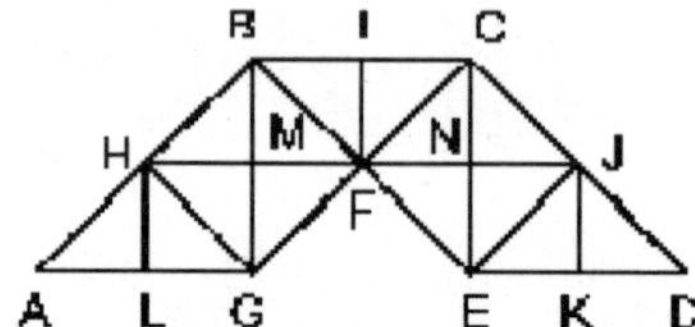

The simplest triangles are AHL, LHG, GHM, HMB, GMF, BMF, BIF, CIF, FNC, CNJ, FNE, NEJ, EKJ and JKD i.e. 14 in number.

The triangles composed of two components each are AGH, BHG, HBF, BFG, HFG, BCF, CJF, CJE, JEF, CFE and JED i.e. 11 in number.

The triangles composed of four components each are ABG, CBG, BCE and CED i.e. 4 in number.

Total number of triangles in the given figure
= 14 + 11 + 4 = 29

9. (d)
The figure may be labelled as shown.

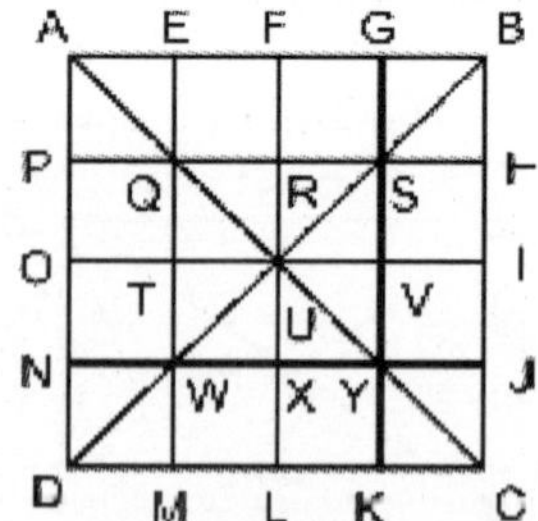

The simplest triangles are APQ, AEQ, QTU, QRU, BGS, BHS, RSU, SUV, TUW, UWX, NWD, WDM, UVY, UXY, JCY and YKC i.e. 16 in number.

The triangles composed of two components each are QUW, QSU, SYU and UWY i.e. 4 in number.

The triangles composed of three components each are AOU, AFU, FBU, BIU, UIC, ULC, ULD and OUD i.e. 8 in number.

The triangles composed of four components each are QYW, QSW, QSY and SYW i.e. 4 in number.

The triangles composed of six components each are AUD, ABU, BUC and DUC i.e. 4 in number.

The triangles composed of seven components each are QMC, ANY, EBW, PSD, CQH, AGY, DSK and BJW i.e. 8 in number.

The triangles composed of twelve components each are ABD, ABC, BCD and ACD i.e. 4 in number.

Thus, there are 16 + 4 + 8 + 4 + 4 + 8 + 4 = 48 triangles in the figure.

10. (b)

The figure may be labelled as shown.

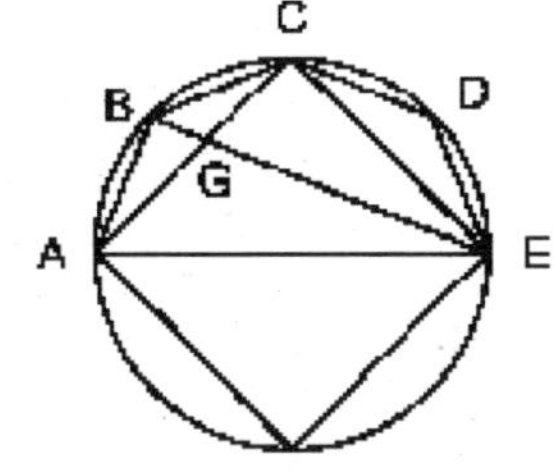

The simplest triangles are ABG, BCG, CGE, CDE, AGE and AEF i.e. 6 in number.

The triangles composed of two components each are ABE, ABC, BCE and ACE i.e. 4 in number.

There are 6 + 4 = 10 triangles in the figure.

11. (d)

The figure may be labelled as shown.

The simplest triangles are ABL, BCD, DEF, FGP, PGH, QHI, JQI, KRJ and LRK i.e. 9 in number.

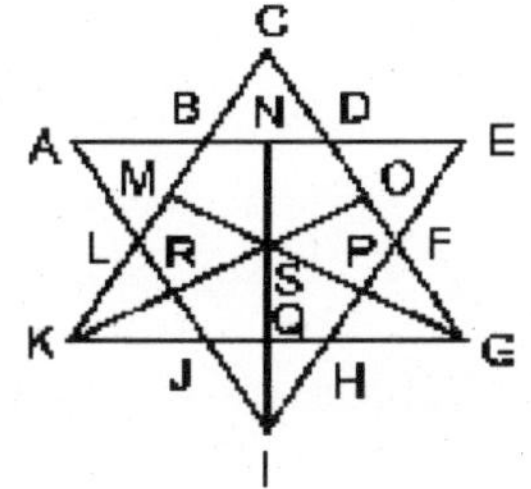

The triangles composed of two components each are OSG, SGQ, SPI, SRI, KSQ, KMS, FGH, JHI and JKL i.e. 9 in number.

There is only one triangle i.e. KSG which is composed of four components.

The triangles composed of five components each are NEI, ANI, MCG and KCO i.e. 4 in number.

The triangles composed of six components each are GMK and KOG i.e. 2 in number.

There is only one triangle i.e. AEI composed of ten components.

There is only one triangle i.e. KCG composed of eleven components.

Therefore, total number of triangles in the given figure = 9 + 9 + 1 + 4 + 2 + 1 + 1 = 27

12. (c)

The figure may be labelled as shown.

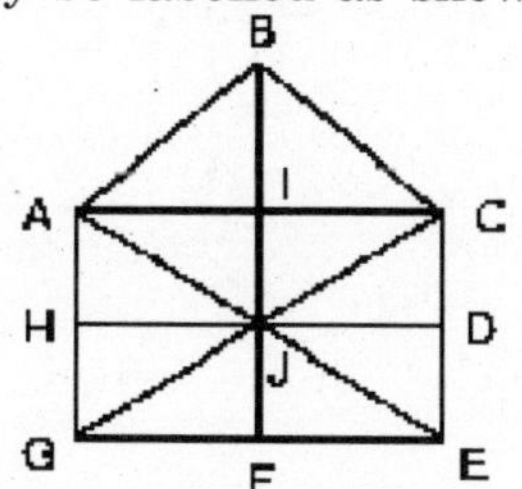

The simplest triangles are ABI, BIC, AIJ, CIJ, AHJ, CDJ, JHG, JDE, GJF and EJF i.e. 10 in number.

The triangles composed of two components each are ABC, BCJ, ACJ, BAJ, AJG, CJE and GJE i.e. 7 in number.

The triangles composed of four components each are ACG, ACE, CGE and AGE i.e. 4 in number.

Total number of triangles in the figure = 10 + 7 + 4 = 21

13. (b)

The figure may be labelled as shown.

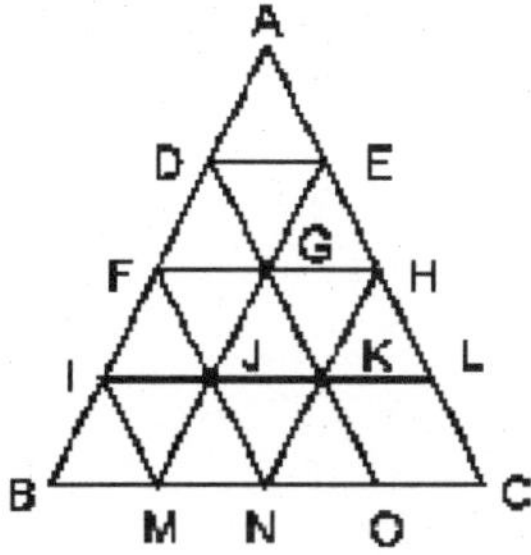

The horizontal lines are DE, FH, IL and BC i.e. 4 in number.

The slanting lines are AC, DO, FN, IM, AB, EM and HN i.e. 7 in number.

Thus, there are 4 + 7 = 11 straight lines in the figure.

14. (c)

The figure may be labelled as shown.

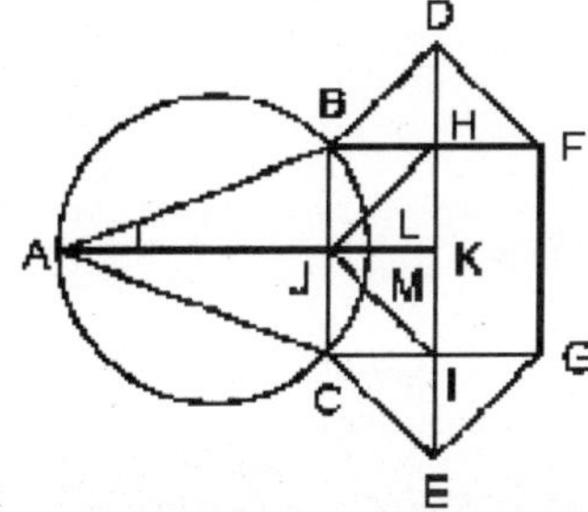

The simplest triangles are ABJ, ACJ, BDH, DHF, CIE and GIE i.e. 6 in number.

The triangles composed of two components each are ABC, BDF, CEG, BHJ, JHK, JKI and CJI i.e. 7 in number.

There is only one triangle JHI which is composed of four components.

Thus, there are 6 + 7 + 1 = 14 triangles in the given figure.

15. (a)

The figure may be labelled as shown.

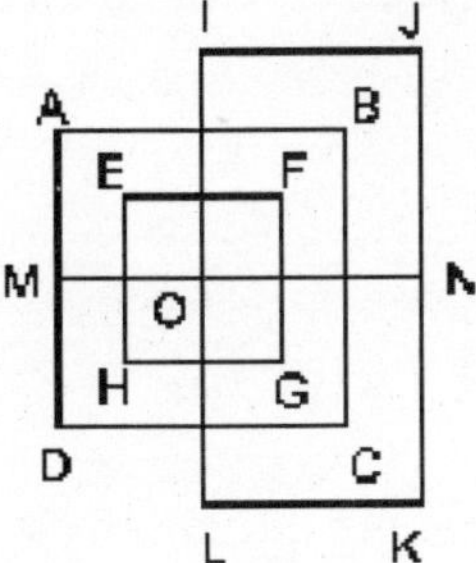

The horizontal lines are IJ, AB, EF, MN, HG, DC and LK i.e. 7 in number.
The vertical lines are AD, EH, IL, FG, BC and JK i.e. 6 in number.
Thus, there are 7 + 6 = 13 straight lines in the figure.

16. (c)
The figure may be labelled as shown.

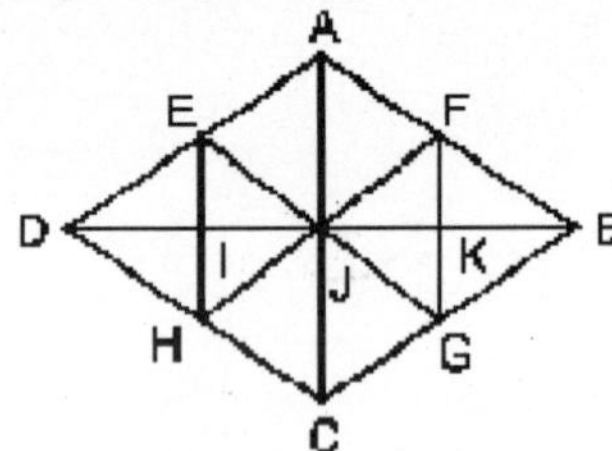

The simplest triangles are AFJ, FJK, FKB, BKG, JKG, JGC, HJC, HIJ, DIH, DEI, EIJ and AEJ i.e. 12 in number.

The triangles composed of two components each are JFB, FBG, BJG, JFG, DEJ, EJH, DJH and DEH i.e. 8 in number.

The triangles composed of three components each are AJB, JBC, DJC and ADJ i.e. 4 in number.

The triangles composed of six components each are DAB, ABC, BCD and ADC i.e. 4 in number.

Thus, there are 12 + 8 + 4 + 4 = 28 triangles in the figure.

17. (d)
The figure may be labelled as shown.

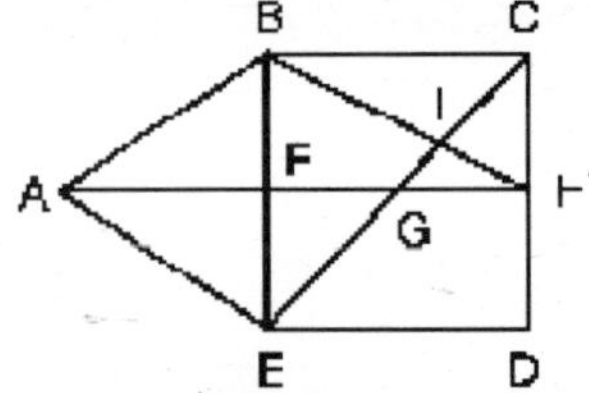

The simplest triangles are ABF, BIC, CIH, GIH, FGE and AFE i.e. 6 in number.

The triangles composed of two components each are ABE, AGE, BHF, BCH, CGH and BIE i.e. 6 in number.

The triangles composed of three components each are ABH, BCE and CDE i.e. 3 in number.

Hence, the total number of triangles in the figure
= 6 + 6 + 3 = 15

18. (d)
The figure may be labelled as shown.

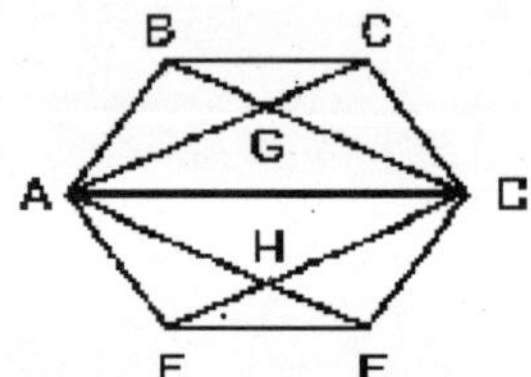

The quadrilaterals in the figure are ABCD, ABDE, ABDF, ABDH, CDHA, CDEA, CDFA, DEAG, DEFA, FAGD and AGDH.
The number of quadrilaterals in the figure is 11.

19. (c)
The figure may be labelled as shown.

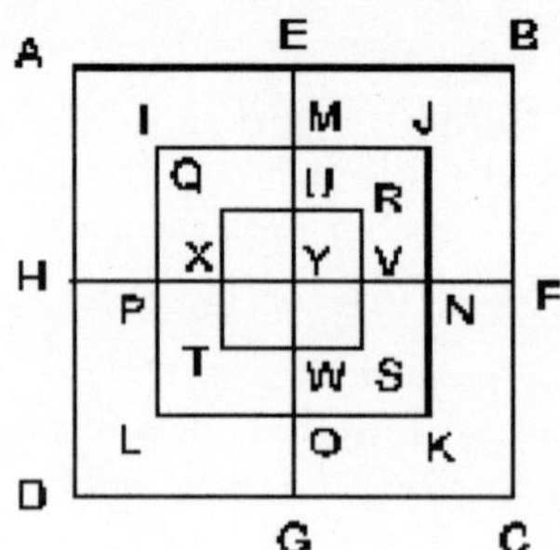

The simplest squares are QUYX, URVY, YVSW and XYWT i.e. 4 in number.

The squares composed of two components each are IMYP, MJNY, YNKO and PYOL i.e. 4 in number.

The squares composed of three components each are AEYH, EBFY, YFCG and HYGD i.e. 4 in number.

There is only one square i.e. QRST composed of four components.

There is only one square i.e. IJKL composed of eight components.

There is only one square i.e. ABCD composed of twelve components.

Total number of squares in the given figure
= 4 + 4 + 4 + 1 + 1 + 1 = 15

20. (d)
The figure may be labelled as shown.
The spaces P, Q and R have to be shaded by three different colours definitely (since each of these three spaces lies adjacent to the other two).
Now, in order that no two adjacent spaces be shaded by the same colour, the spaces T, U and S must be shaded with the colours of the spaces P, Q and R respectively.

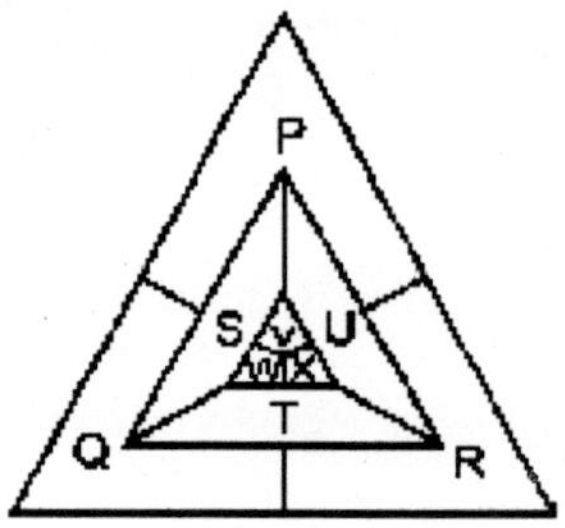

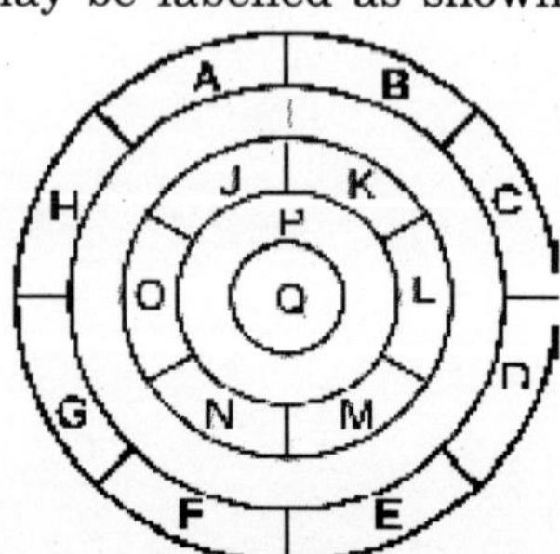

Also the spaces X, V and W must be shaded with the colours of the spaces S, T and U respectively i.e. with the colours of the spaces R, P and Q respectively. Thus, minimum three colours are required.

21. (a)
The figure may be labelled as shown.

The regions A, C, E and G can have the same colour say colour 1.

The regions B, D, F and H can have the same colour (but different from colour 1) say colour 2.

The region 1 lies adjacent to each one of the regions A, B, C, D, E, F, G and H and therefore it should have a different colour say colour 3.

The regions J, L and N can have the same colour (different from colour 3) say colour 1.

The regions K, M and O can have the same colour (different from the colours 1 and 3). Thus, these regions will have colour 2.

The region P cannot have any of the colours 1 and 2 as it lies adjacent to each one of the regions J, K, L, M, N and O and so it will have colour 3.

The region Q can have any of the colours 1 or 2.

Minimum number of colours required is 3.

22. (c)

The figure may be labelled as shown.

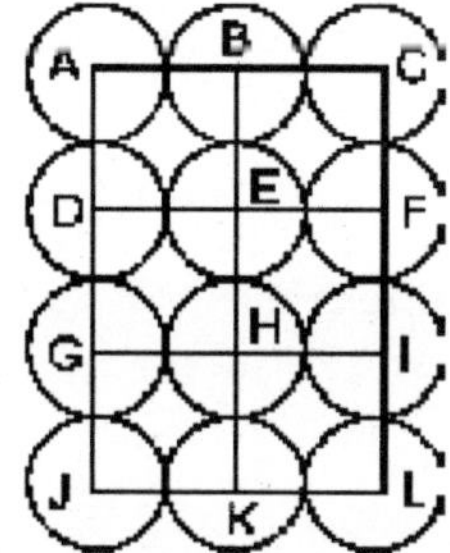

We shall join the centres of all the circles by horizontal and vertical lines and then label the resulting figure as shown.

The simplest squares are ABED, BCFE, DEHG, EFIH, GHKJ and HILK i.e. 6 in number.

The squares composed of four simple squares are ACIG and DFLJ i.e. 2 in number.

Thus, 6 + 2 = 8 squares will be formed.

23. (a)

The figure may be labelled as shown.

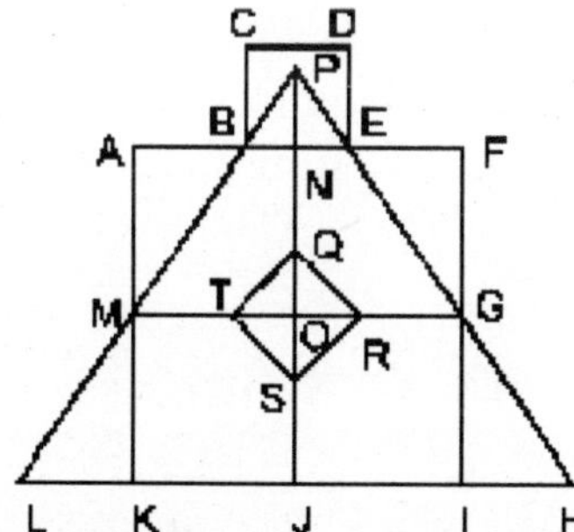

Triangles: The simplest triangles are BPN, PNE, ABM, EFG, MLK, GHI, QRO, RSO, STO and QTO i.e. 10 in number.

The triangles composed of two components each are BPE, TQR, QRS, RST and STQ i.e. 5 in number.

The triangles composed of three components each are MPO and GPO i.e. 2 in number.

The triangles composed of six components each are LPJ, HPJ and MPG i.e. 3 in number.

There is only one triangle LPH composed of twelve components.

Total number of triangles in the figure

= 10 + 5 – 2 + 3 + 1 = 21

Squares: The squares composed of two components each are KJOM and JIGQ i.e. 2 in number.

The squares composed of three components each are ANOM, NFGO and CDEB i.e.3 in number.

There is only one square i.e. QRST composed of four components.

There is only one square i.e. AFIK composed of ten components.

Total number of squares in the figure
= 2 + 3 + 1 + 1 = 7

24. (c)

The figure may be labelled as shown.

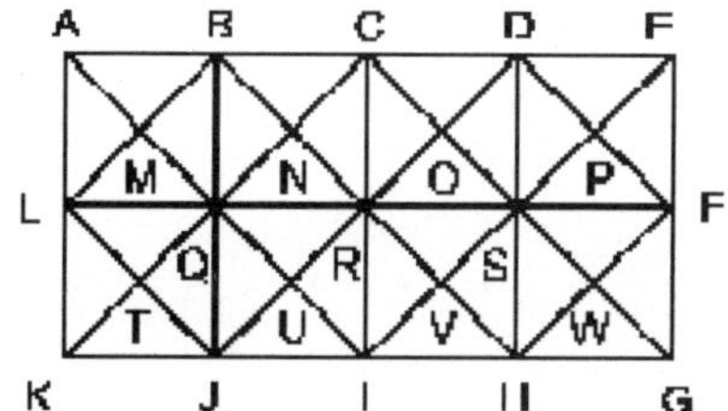

The squares composed of two components each are BNQM, CORN, DPSO, MQTL, NRUQ, OSVR, PFWS, QUJT, RVIU and SWHV i.e. 10 in number.

The squares composed of four components each are ABQL, BCRQ, CDSR, DEFS, LQJK, QRIJ, RSHI and SFGH i.e. 8 in number.

The squares composed of eight components each are BRJL, CSIQ and DFHR i.e. 3 in number.

The squares composed of sixteen components each are ACIK, BDHJ and CEGI i.e. 3 in number.

Thus, there are 10 + 8 + 3 + 3 = 24 squares in the figure.

25. (c)

The figure may be labelled as shown.

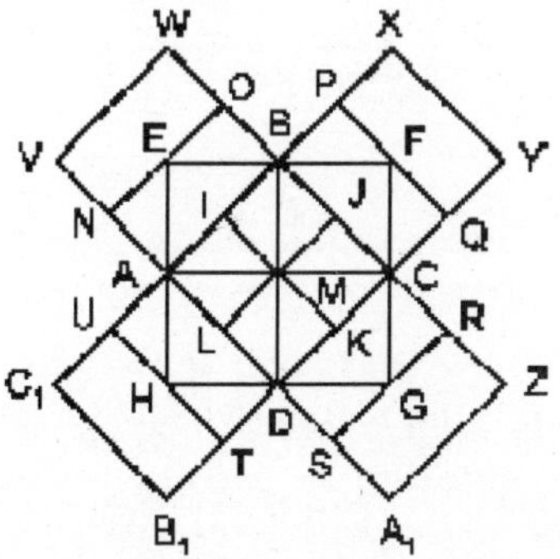

The squares composed of two components each are BJMI, CKMJ, DLMK and AIML i.e. 4 in number.

The squares composed of three components each are EBMA, BFCM, MCGD and AMDH i.e. 4 in number.

The squares composed of four components each are VWBA, XYCB, ZA_1DC and B_1C_1AD i.e. 4 in number.

The squares composed of seven components each are NOJL, PQKI, RSLJ and TUIK i.e. 4 in number.

There is only one square i.e. ABCD composed of eight components.

There is only one square i.e. EFGH composed of twelve components.

Total number of squares in the figure
= 4 + 4 + 4 + 4 + 1 + 1 = 18

26. (a)
The figure may be labelled as shown.

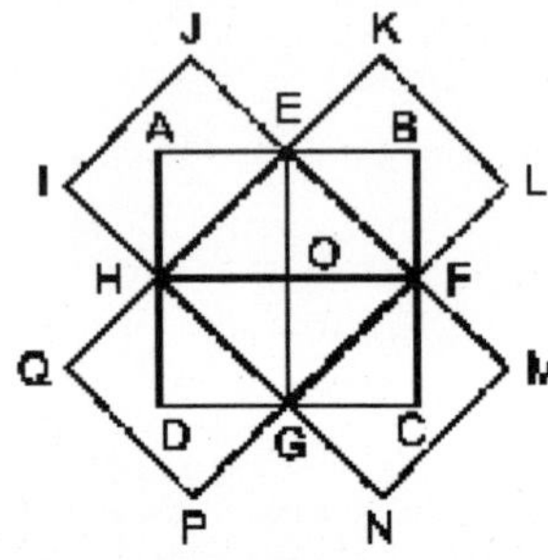

The rectangles composed of two components each are HUE, EKJF, FMNG, GPQH, AEOH, EBFO, OFCG and HOGD i.e. 8 in number.

The rectangles composed of four components each are ABFH, BCGE, CDHF, DAEG and EFGH i.e. 5 in number.

The rectangles composed of six components each are IJFG, KLGH, MNHE and PQEF i.e. 4 in number.

The rectangles composed of eight components each are IJMN, KLPQ and ABCD i.e. 3 in number.

Thus, there are 8 + 5 + 4 + 3 = 20 rectangles in the given figure.

(Note that the squares are also counted amongst rectangles)

27. (b)
The figure may be labelled as shown.

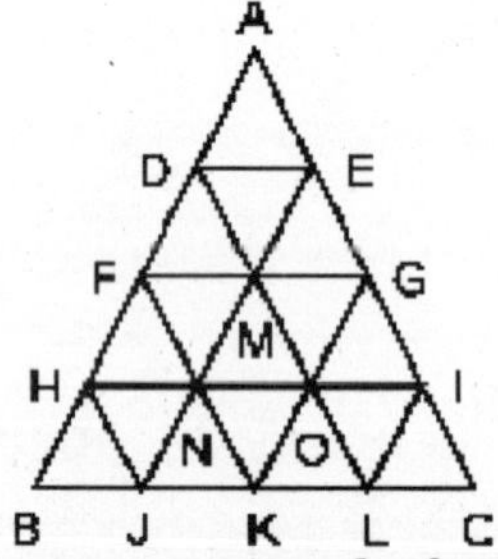

The parallelograms composed of two components each are ADME, DFNM, EMOG, FHJN, MNKO, GOLI, HBJN, NJKO, OKLI, FHNM, MNOG, DFME, HJKN, NKLO, OLCI, FNOM, MOIG and DMGE. i.e. 18 in number.

The parallelograms composed of four components each are HOKB, NILJ, FGOH, HOLJ, NICK, FGIN, FMJB, DENH, MGKJ, MGCL, DEIO, FMLK, AENF, AGOD, DMJH, DOKF, EILM and EGKN i.e. 18 in number.

The parallelograms composed of six components each are AEJH, DAIL, DECL, DEJB, HILB and HICJ i.e. 6 in number.

The parallelograms composed of eight components each are FGKB, FGCK and AGKF i.e. 3 in number.

Total number of parallelograms in the figure
= 18 + 18 + 6 + 3 = 45

28. (b)
The figure may be labelled as shown.

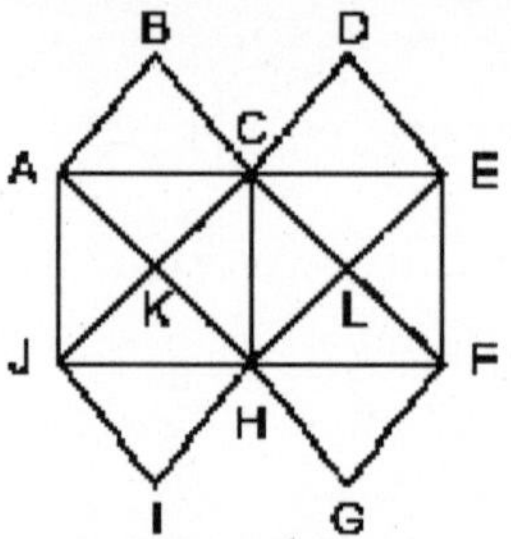

The horizontal lines are AE and JF i.e. 2 in number.
The vertical lines are AJ, CH and EF i.e. 3 in number.

The slanting lines are AG, BF, JD, IE, AB, DE, JI and FG i.e. 8 in number.

Total number of straight lines needed to construct the figure = 2 + 3 + 8 = 13

29. (a)
The figure may be labelled as shown.

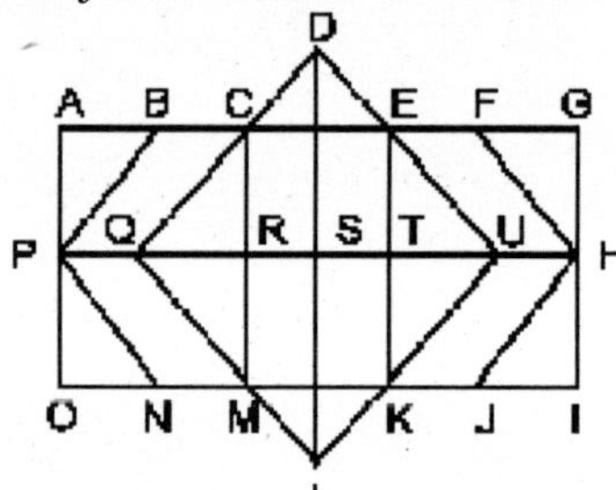

Rectangles: The simplest rectangles are CVSR, VETS, RSWM and STKW i.e. 4 in number.

The rectangles composed of two components each are CETR, VEKW, RTKM and GVWM i.e. 4 in number.

The rectangles composed of three components each are AQRP, PRMO, EGHT and THIK i.e. 4 in number.

The rectangles composed of four components each are CEKM, AVSP,TSWO, VGHS and SHIW i.e. 5 in number.

The rectangles composed of five components each are AETP, PTKO, CGHR and RHIM i.e. 4 in number.

The rectangles composed of six components each are ACMO and EGIK i.e. 2 in number.

The rectangles composed of eight components each are AGHP, PHIO, AVWO and VGIW i.e. 4 in number.

The rectangles composed of ten components each are AEKO and CGIM i.e. 2 in number.

AGIO is the only rectangle having sixteen components.

Total number of rectangles in the given figure
= 4 + 4 + 4 + 5 + 4 + 2 + 4 + 2 + 1 = 30.

Hexagons: The hexagons in the given figure are CDEKLM, CEUKMQ, CFHJMQ, BEUKNP and BFHJNP.

So, there are 5 hexagons in the given figure.

30. (a)

The figure may be labelled as shown.

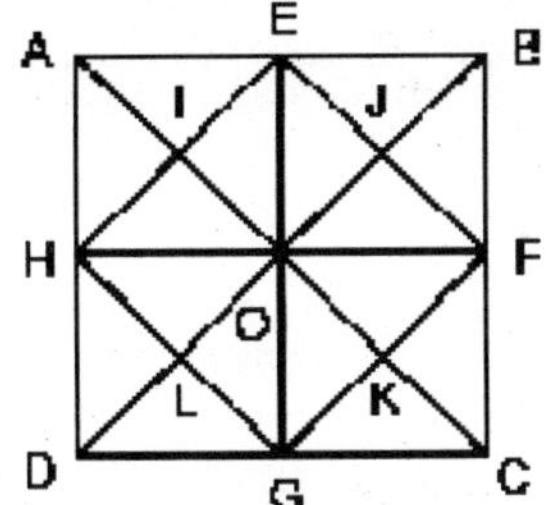

Triangles: The simplest triangles are AEI, EOI, OHI, HAI, EBJ, BFJ, FOJ, OEJ, HOL, OGL, GDL, DHL, OFK, FCK, CGK and GOK i.e. 16 in number.

The triangles composed of two components each are HAE, AEO, EOH, OHA, OEB, EBF, BFO, FOE, DHO, HOG, OGD, GDH, GOF, OFC, FCG and CGO i.e. 16 in number.

The triangles composed of four components each are HEF, EFG, FGH, GHE, ABO, BGO, CDO and DAO i.e. 8 in number.

The triangles composed of eight components each are DAB, ABC, BCD and CDA i.e. 4 in number.

Total number of triangles in the figure

= 16 + 16 + 8 + 4 = 44

Squares: The squares composed of two components are HIOL, IEJO, JFKO and KGLO i.e. 4 in number.

The squares composed of four components are AEOH, EBFO, OFGC and HOGD i.e.4 in number.

There is only one square EFGH which is composed of eight components.

There is only one square ABCD which is composed of sixteen components.

Total number of squares in the figure
= 4 + 4 + 1 + 1 = 10

❐

Previous Year Questions

1. Count the number of squares in the given figure.
[NTSE 2012 - Delhi first stage paper]

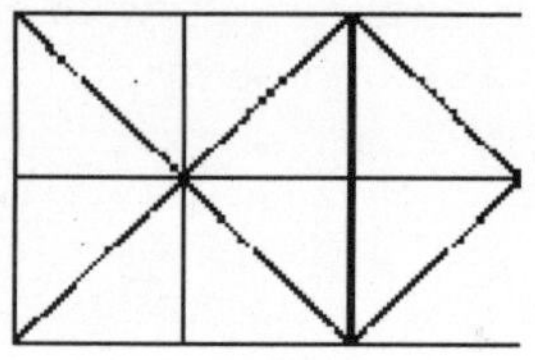

(a) 6 (b) 7
(c) 9 (d) 10

2. Count the number of squares in the given figure.
[NTSE 2004 – UP second stage paper]

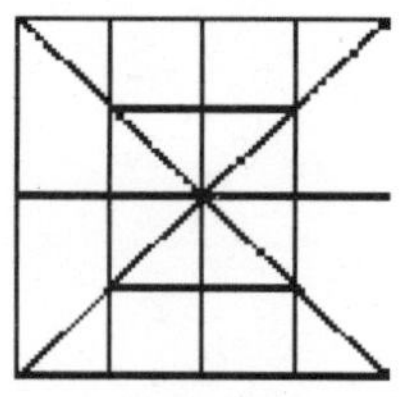

(a) 13 (b) 16
(c) 19 (d) 20

3. Find the number of triangles in the given figure.
[NTSE 2003 - Delhi first stage paper]

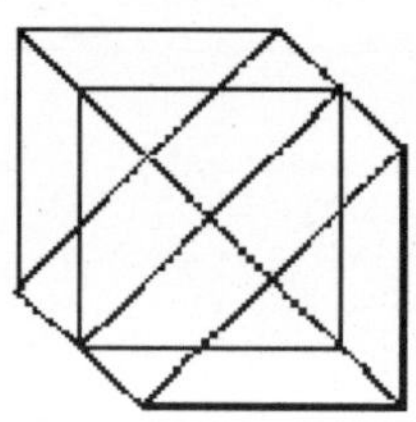

(a) 18 (b) 20
(c) 24 (d) 27

4. Find the number of triangles in the given figure.
[NTSE 1999 - Rajasthan Second stage Paper]

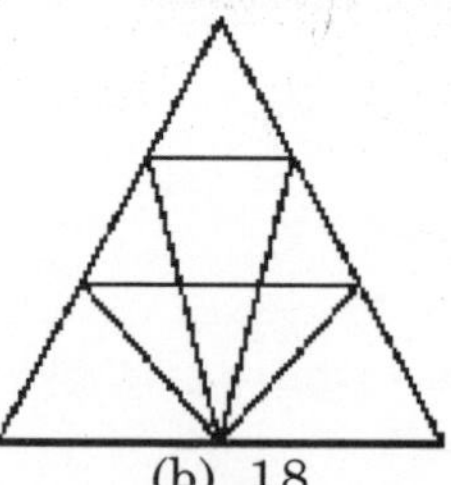

(a) 12 (b) 18
(c) 22 (d) 26

5. Find the number of triangles in the given figure.
[NTSE 2003 – Tamil Nadu first stage paper]

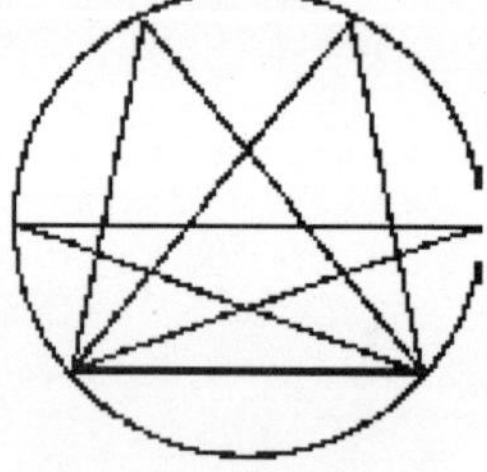

(a) 22 (b) 24
(c) 26 (d) 28

6. Find the minimum number of straight lines required to make the given figure.
[NTSE 2000 – Himachal Pradesh first stage paper]

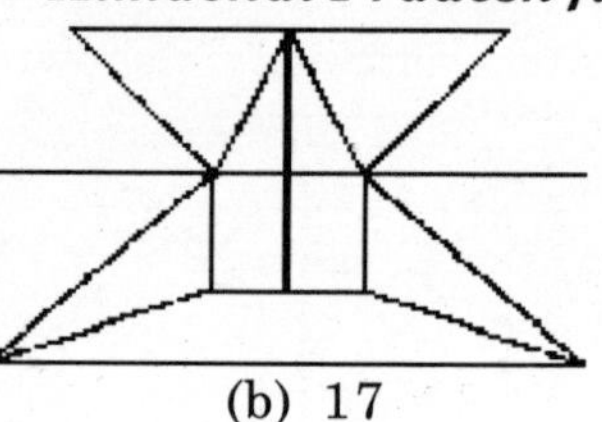

(a) 16 (b) 17
(c) 18 (d) 19

7. Count the number of rectangles in the given figure.
[NTSE 2002 Gujarat first stage paper]

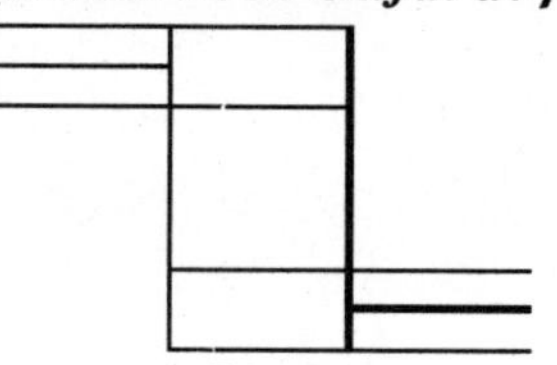

(a) 8 (b) 17
(c) 18 (d) 20

8. How many circles are there in the adjoining figure?
[NTSE 2003 - Haryana first stage paper]

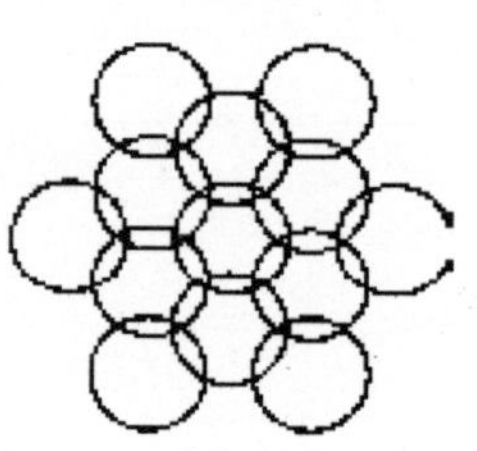

(a) 11 (b) 12
(c) 13 (d) 14

9. Count the number of squares in the given figure.
[NTSE 2005 – Jharkhand first stage paper]

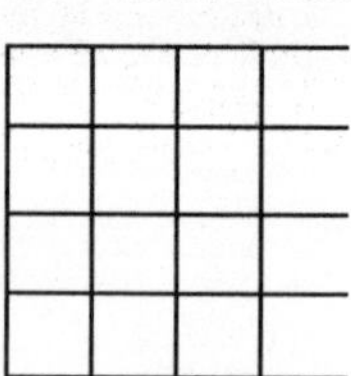

(a) 32 (b) 30
(c) 29 (d) 28

10. Count the number of triangles and squares in the given figure.
[NTSE 2003 - Assam first stage paper]

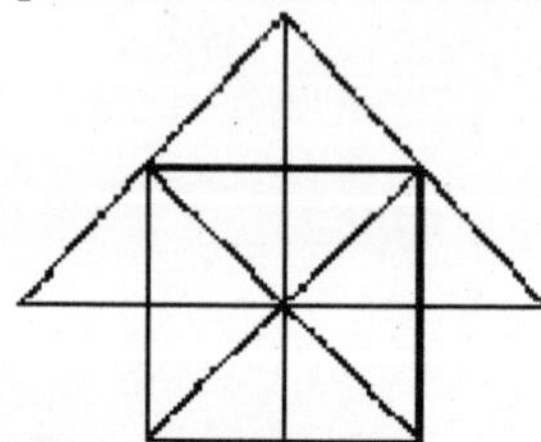

(a) 26 triangles, 5 squares
(b) 28 triangles, 5 squares
(c) 26 triangles, 6 squares
(d) 28 triangles, 6 squares

Answer Key

1. (c)	2. (b)	3. (c)	4. (b)	5. (d)	6. (b)	7. (c)	8. (c)	9. (b)	10. (d)

Explanatory Notes

1. (c)
The figure may be labelled as shown.

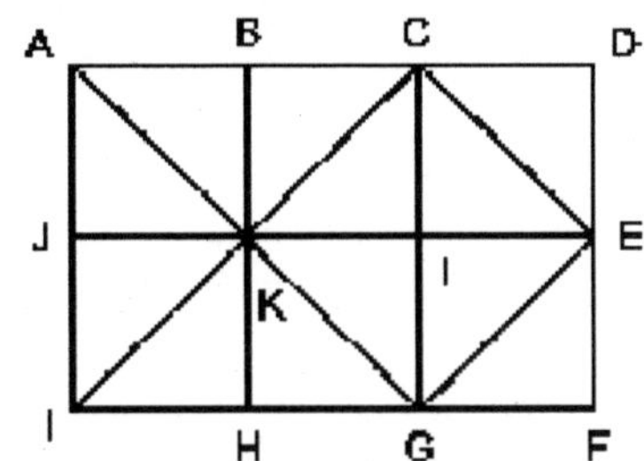

The squares composed of two components each are ABKJ, BCLK, CDEL, LEFG, KLGH and JKHI i.e. 6 in number.

There is only one square i.e. CEGK composed of four components.

The squares composed of eight components each are ACGI and BDFH i.e. 2 in number.

There are 6 + 1 + 2 = 9 squares in the figure.

2. (b)
The figure may be labelled as shown.

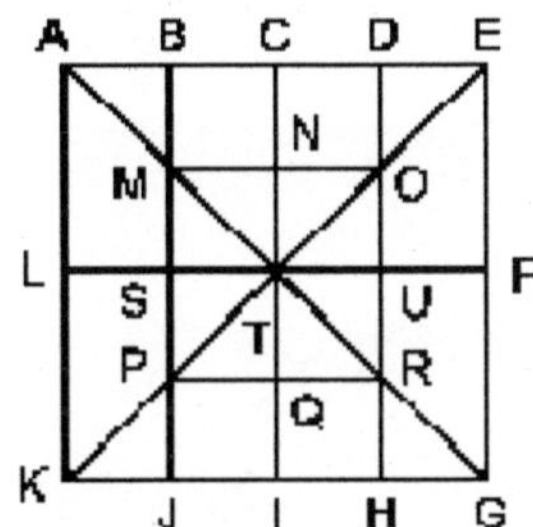

The simplest squares are BCNM, CDON, PQIJ and QRHI i.e. 4 in number.

The squares composed of two components each are MNTS, NOUT, STQP and TURQ i.e. 4 in number.

The squares composed of five components each are ACTL, CEFT, TFGI and LTIK i.e. 4 in number.

The squares composed of six components each are BDUS and SUHJ i.e. 2 in number.

There is only one square i.e. MORP composed of eight components.

There is only one square i.e. AEGK composed of twenty components.

Total number of squares in the figure
= 4 + 4 + 4 + 2+1 + 1 = 16.

3. (c)
The figure may be labelled as shown.

The simplest triangles are IJO, BCJ, CDK, KQL, MLQ, GFM, GHN and NIO i.e. 8 in number.

The triangles composed of two components each are ABO, AHO, NIJ, IGP, ICP, DEQ, FEQ, KLM, LCP and LGP i.e.10 in number.

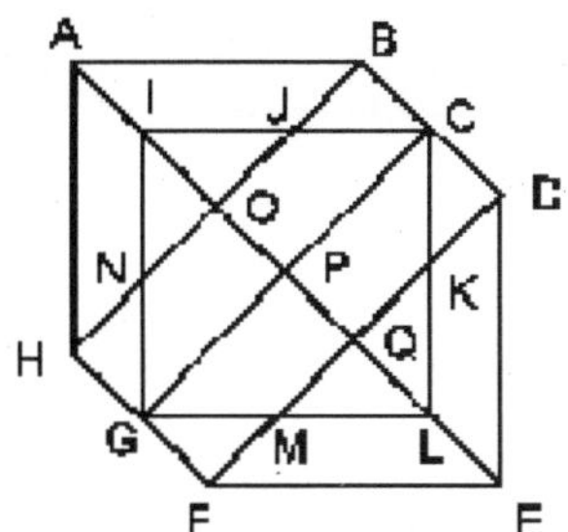

The triangles composed of four components each are HAB, DEF, LGI, GIC, ICL and GLC i.e. 6 in number.

Total number of triangles in the figure
= 8 + 10 + 6 = 24

4. (b)
The figure may be labelled as shown.

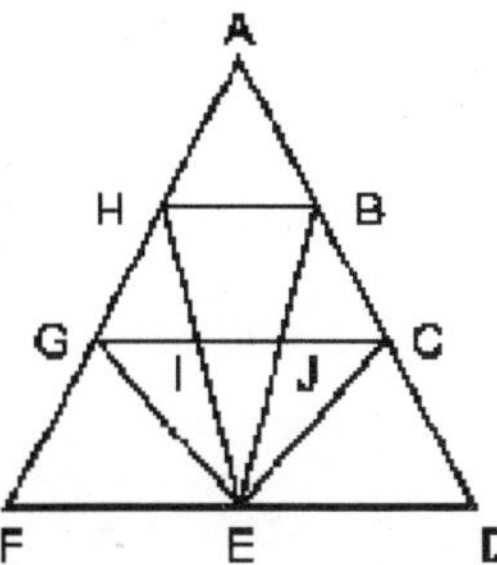

The simplest triangles are AHB, GHI, BJC, GFE, GIE, IJE, CEJ and CDE i.e. 8 in number.

The triangles composed of two components each are HEG, BEC, HBE, JGE and ICE i.e. 5 in number.

The triangles composed of three components each are FHE, GCE and BED i.e. 3 in number.

There is only one triangle i.e. AGC composed of four components.

There is only one triangle i.e. AFD composed of nine components.

Thus, there are 8 + 5 + 3 + 1 + 1 = 18 triangles in the given figure.

5. (d)
The figure may be labelled as shown.

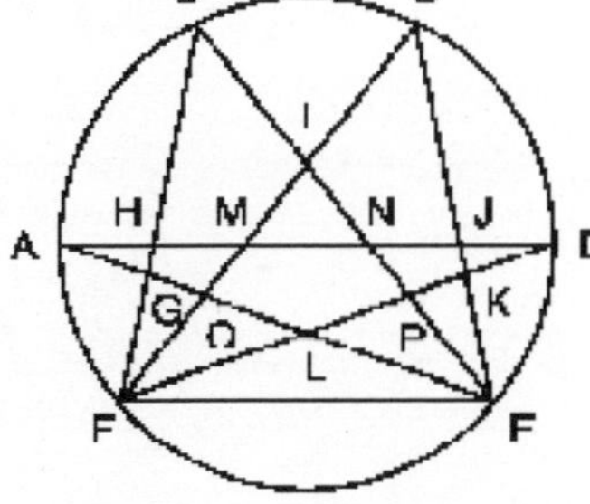

The simplest triangles are AGH, GFO, LFO, DJK, EKP, PEL and IMN i.e. 7 in number.

The triangles having two components each are GFL, KEL, AMO, NDP, BHN, CMJ, NEJ and HFM i.e. 8 in number.

The triangles having three components each are IOE, IFP, BIF and CEI i.e. 4 in number.

The triangles having four components each are ANE and DMF i.e. 2 in number.

The triangles having five components each are FCK, BGE and ADL i.e. 3 in number.

The triangles having six components each are BPF, COE, DHF and AJE i.e. 4 in number.

Total number of triangles in the figure

= 7 + 8 + 4 + 2 + 3 + 4 = 28

6. (b)

The figure may be labelled as shown.

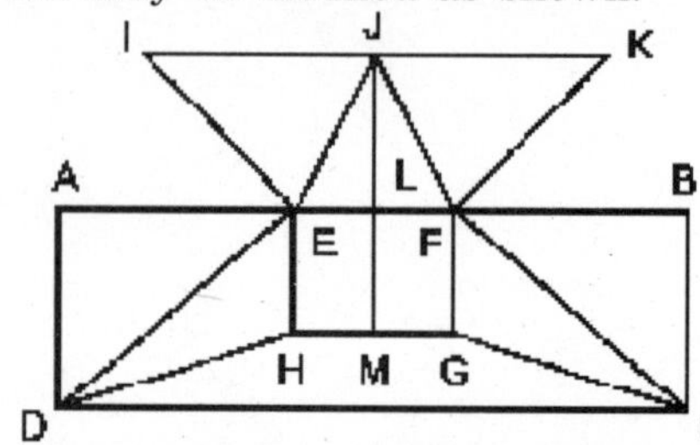

The horizontal lines are IK, AB, HG and DC i.e. 4 in number.

The vertical lines are AD, EH, JM, FG and BC i.e. 5 in number.

The slanting lines are IE, JE, JF, KF, DE, DH, FC and GC i.e. 8 is number.

Thus, there are 4 + 5 + 8 = 17 straight lines in the figure.

7. (c)

The figure may be labelled as shown.

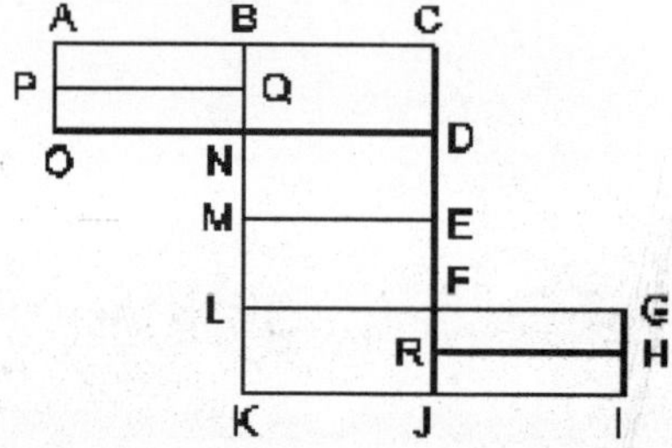

The simplest rectangles are ABQP, PQNO, BCDN, NDEM, MEFL, LFJK, FGHR and RHIJ i.e. 8 in number.

The rectangles composed of two components each are ABNO, BCEM, NDFL, MEJK and FGIJ i.e. 5 in number.

The rectangles composed of three components each are ACDO, BCFL, NDJK and LGIK i.e. 4 in number.

There is only one rectangle i.e. BCJK composed of four components.

Total number of rectangles in the figure

= 8 + 5 + 4 + 1 = 18

8. (c)

The figure may be labelled as shown.

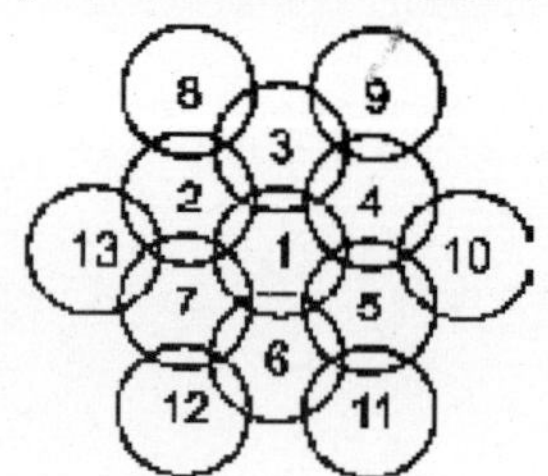

There are 13 circles in the given figure. This is clear from the adjoining figure in which the centres of all the circles have been numbered from 1 to 13.

9. (b)

The figure may be labelled as shown.

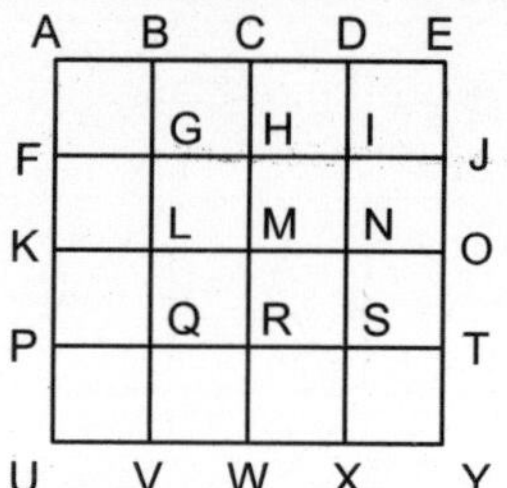

The simplest squares are ABGF, BCHG, CDIH, DEJI, FGLK, GHML, HINM, IJON, KLQP, LMRQ, MNSR, NOTS, PQVU, QRWV, RSXW and STYX i.e. 16 in number.

The squares composed of four components each are ACMK, BDNL, CEOM, FHRP, GISQ, HJTR, KMWU, LNXV and MOYW i.e. 9 in number.

The squares composed of nine components each are ADSP, BETQ, FIXU and GJYV i.e. 4 in number.

There is one square AEYU composed of sixteen components.

There are 16 + 9 + 4 + 1 = 30 squares in the given figure.

10. (d)

The figure may be labelled as shown.

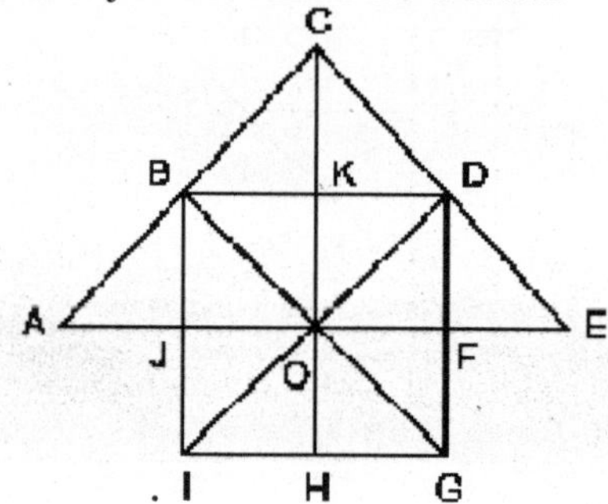

Triangles: The simplest triangles are JBO, BKO, KDO, DFO, FGO, GHO, HIO, IJO, ABJ, BCK, CKD and DEF i.e.12 in number.

The triangles composed of two components each are IBO, BDO, DGO, GIO, ABO, CDO, CBO, CBD and DEO i.e. 9 in number.

The triangles composed of four components each are IBD, BDG, DGI, GIB, ACO and COE i.e. 6 in number.

There is only one triangle i.e. ACE composed of eight components.

Thus, there are 12 + 9 + 6 + 1 = 28 triangles in the given figure.

Squares: The squares composed of two components each are BKOJ, KDFO, OFGH and JOHI i.e. 4 in number.

There is only one square i.e. CDOB composed of four components.

There is only one square i.e. BDGI composed of eight components.

Thus, there are 4 + 1 + 1 = 6 squares in the given figure.

❐

UNIT 14

Calendar and Clock

Features of a Calendar

- **Odd Days:**
  We are supposed to find the day of the week on a given date.
  For this, we use the concept of 'odd days'.
  In a given period, the number of days more than the complete weeks are called **odd days**.
- **Leap Year:**
  I. Every year divisible by 4 is a leap year, if it is not a century.
  II. Every 4th century is a leap year and no other century is a leap year.
  Note : A leap year has 366 days.
  Examples:
  I. Each of the years 1948, 2004, 1676 etc. is a leap year.
  II. Each of the years 400, 800, 1200, 1600, 2000 etc. is a leap year.
  III. None of the years 2001, 2002, 2003, 2005, 1800, 2100 is a leap year.
- **Ordinary Year:**
  The year which is not a leap year is called an ordinary year. An ordinary year has 365 days.
- **Counting of Odd Days:**
  I. 1 ordinary year = 365 days = (52 weeks + 1 day.) $\therefore$ 1 ordinary year has 1 odd day.
  II. 1 leap year = 366 days = (52 weeks + 2 days) $\therefore$ 1 leap year has 2 odd days.
  III. 100 years = 76 ordinary years + 24 leap years
  $= (76 \times 1 + 24 \times 2)$ odd days = 124 odd days = (17 weeks + days) $\equiv$ 5 odd days.
  $\therefore$ Number of odd days in 100 years = 5
  Number of odd days in 200 years = $(5 \times 2) \equiv 3$ odd days.
  Number of odd days in 300 years = $(5 \times 3) \equiv 1$ odd day.
  Number of odd days in 400 years = $(5 \times 4 + 1) \equiv 0$ odd day.
  Similarly, each one of 800 years, 1200 years, 1600 years, 2000 years etc. has 0 odd days.
- **Day of the Week Related to Odd Days:**

No. of Days	0	1	2	3	4	5	6
Day	Sun	Mon	Tues	Wed	Thurs	Fri	Sat

Solved Examples

1. What is the day on 1st January 1901?
(a) Monday (b) Wednesday
(c) Sunday (d) Tuesday
Solution: Option (d) is correct.
Explanation: 1st January 1901 means (1900 years and 1 day)
Now, 1600 years have 0 odd days
300 years have 1 odd day
1 day has 1 odd day
Total number of odd days = 0 + 1 + 1 = 2 days
Hence, the day on 1st January 1901 was Tuesday.

2. Today is Thursday. The day after 59 days will be:
(a) Monday (b) Tuesday
(c) Sunday (d) Wednesday
Solution: Option (c) is correct.
Explanation: Every day of the week is repeated after 7 days. Hence after 56 days it would be Thursday again and after 59 days it would be Sunday.

3. The year next to 1990 will have the same calendar as that of the year 1990 is:
(a) 1995 (b) 1996
(c) 1997 (d) 1999

Solution: Option (b) is correct.

Explanation: The year 1990 has 365 days i.e. 1 odd day, year 1991 has 365 days i.e. 1 odd day, year 1992 has 366 days i.e. 2 odd days.

Likewise years 1993, 1994, 1995, have 1 odd day each. The sum of odd days so calculated from year 1990 to 1995 (1 + 1 + 2 + 1 + 1 + 1) = 7 odd days ≡ 0 odd day.

Hence, the year 1996 will have the same calendar as that of the year 1990.

4. An application was received by inward clerk in the afternoon of a week day. Next day he forwarded it to the table of the senior clerk, who was on leave that day. The senior clerk put up the application to the desk officer next day in the evening. The desk officer studied the application and disposed off the matter on the same day i.e. Friday. Which day was the application received by the inward clerk?
   (a) Monday
   (b) Wednesday
   (c) Tuesday
   (d) Previous week's Saturday

   Solution: Option (b) is correct.

   Explanation: The senior clerk got the application on Friday. The inward clerk got the application on Wednesday.

Features of a Clock

- **Minute Spaces:**
  The face or dial of watch is a circle whose circumference is divided into 60 equal parts, called minute spaces.
- **Hour Hand and Minute Hand:**
  A clock has two hands; the smaller one is called the **hour hand** or **short hand** while the larger one is called **minute hand** or **long hand**.

I. In 60 minutes, the minute hand gains 55 minutes on the hour on the hour hand.

II. In every hour, both the hands coincide once.

III. The hands are in the same straight line when they are coincident or opposite to each other.

IV. When the two hands are at right angles, they are 15 minute-spaces apart.

V. When the hands are in opposite directions, they are 30 minute-spaces apart.

VI. Angle traced by hour hand in 12 hrs = 360°

VII. Angle traced by minute hand in 60 minute = 360°

VIII. If a watch or a clock indicates 8.15, when the correct time is 8, it is said to be 15 minutes **too fast**.

IX. On the other hand, if it indicates 7.45, when the correct time is 8, it is said to be 15 minutes **too slow**.

5. A clock is set right at 8 am. The clock gains 10 min in 24 hours. What will be the right time when the clock indicates 1 pm on the following day?
   (a) 11.40 pm (b) 12.48 pm
   (c) 12 pm (d) 10 pm

   Solution: Option (b) is correct.

   Explanation: Time from 8 am of a particular day to 1 pm on the following day = 29 hours. Now the clock gains 10 min in 24 hours, it means that 24 h 10 min of this clock is equal to 24 h of the correct clock.

   $\frac{145}{6}$ h of this clock= 24 h of the correct clock.

   29 h of this clock = $\frac{24}{145}\times 6\times 29$
   = 28 h, 48 min of the correct clock

   29 h of this clock = 28 h, 48 min of the correct clock.

   It means that the clock in question is 12 min faster than the correct clock. When clock indicated 1 pm, the correct time would be 48 min past 12.

6. A clock gaining 2 min every hour was synchronised at mid night with a clock losing 1 min every hour. How many minutes the clock (losing time) will be behind at eleven in the following morning?
   (a) 23 (b) 27
   (c) 22 (d) None of these

   Solution: Option (d) is correct.

   Explanation: Suppose both the clocks are at 12 pm. In the following morning 11 am, the gaining clock is 22 min ahead and losing clock is 11 min behind from the real time. The clock losing the time is 33 min behind the clock gaining the time.

7. At what time, in minutes, between 3 o'clock and 4 o'clock, both the needles will coincide each other?
   (a) $5\frac{1}{11}$ min (b) $12\frac{4}{11}$ min
   (c) $13\frac{4}{11}$ min (d) $16\frac{4}{11}$ min

   Solution: Option (d) is correct.

   Explanation: At 3 o'clock, the minute hand is 15 min. spaces apart from the hour hand.
   To be coincident, it must gain 15 min. spaces.
   55 min. are gained in 60 min.

   15 min. are gained in (60/55 × 15) = $16\frac{4}{11}$ min

   The hands are coincident at $16\frac{4}{11}$ min past 3.

8. How many times do the hands of a clock coincide in a day?
   (a) 20 (b) 21
   (c) 22 (d) 24

   Solution: Option (c) is correct.

   Explanation: The hands of a clock coincide 11 times in every 12 hours (Since between 11 and 1, they coincide only once, i.e., at 12 o'clock).
   The hands coincide 22 times in a day.

9. How many times in a day, the hands of a clock are straight?
   (a) 22 (b) 24
   (c) 44 (d) 48
   Solution: Option (c) is correct.
   Explanation: In 12 hours, the hands coincide or are in opposite direction 22 times.
   In 24 hours, the hands coincide or are in opposite direction 44 times a day.
10. A watch which gains uniformly is 2 minutes low at noon on Monday and is 4 min. 48 sec fast at 2 p.m. on the following Monday. When was it correct?
    (a) 2 p.m. on Tuesday
    (b) 2 p.m. on Wednesday
    (c) 3 p.m. on Thursday
    (d) 1 p.m. on Friday
    Solution: Option (b) is correct.
    Explanation: Time from 12 p.m. on Monday to 2 p.m. on the following Monday = 7 days 2 hours = 170 hours.
    $\therefore$ The watch gains $\left(2+4\frac{4}{5}\right)$ min in 170 hours
    Now, 34/5 min. are gained in 170 hrs.
    $\therefore$ 2 min. are gained in (170 × 5/34 × 2) hours = 50 hours
    $\therefore$ Watch is correct 2 days 2 hours after 12 p.m. on Monday i.e., it will be correct at 2 p.m. on Wednesday.

Multiple Choice Questions

1. It was Sunday on Jan 1, 2006. What was the day of the week Jan 1, 2010?
   (a) Sunday (b) Saturday
   (c) Friday (d) Wednesday
2. What was the day of the week on 28th May, 2006?
   (a) Thursday (b) Friday
   (c) Saturday (d) Sunday
3. What was the day of the week on 17th June, 1998?
   (a) Monday (b) Tuesday
   (c) Wednesday (d) Thursday
4. What will be the day of the week 15th August, 2010?
   (a) Sunday (b) Monday
   (c) Tuesday (d) Friday
5. Today is Monday. After 61 days, it will be:
   (a) Wednesday (b) Saturday
   (c) Tuesday (d) Thursday
6. If 6th March, 2005 is Monday, what was the day of the week on 6th March, 2004?
   (a) Sunday (b) Saturday
   (c) Tuesday (d) Wednesday
7. On what dates of April, 2001 did Wednesday fall?
   (a) 1st, 8th, 15th, 22nd, 29th
   (b) 2nd, 9th, 16th, 23rd, 30th
   (c) 3rd, 10th, 17th, 24th
   (d) 4th, 11th, 18th, 25th
8. How many days are there in x weeks x days?
   (a) $7x^2$ (b) $8x$
   (c) $14x$ (d) 7
9. The last day of a century cannot be
   (a) Monday (b) Wednesday
   (c) Tuesday (d) Friday
10. On 8th Feb, 2005 it was Tuesday. What was the day of the week on 8th Feb, 2004?
    (a) Tuesday (b) Monday
    (c) Sunday (d) Wednesday
11. The calendar for the year 2007 will be the same for the year:
    (a) 2014 (b) 2016
    (c) 2017 (d) 2018
12. Which of the following is not a leap year?
    (a) 700 (b) 800
    (c) 1200 (d) 2000
13. On 8th Dec, 2007 Saturday falls. What day of the week was it on 8th Dec, 2006?
    (a) Sunday (b) Thursday
    (c) Tuesday (d) Friday
14. January 1, 2008 is Tuesday. What day of the week lies on Jan 1, 2009?
    (a) Monday (b) Wednesday
    (c) Thursday (d) Sunday
15. January 1, 2007 was Monday. What day of the week lies on Jan. 1, 2008?
    (a) Monday (b) Tuesday
    (c) Wednesday (d) Sunday
16. If 11th January 1997 was a Sunday, then what day of the week was on 10th January 2000?
    (a) Tuesday (b) Wednesday
    (c) Thursday (d) Friday
17. An accurate clock shows 8 o'clock in the morning. Through how may degrees will the hour hand rotate when the clock shows 2 o'clock in the afternoon?
    (a) 144° (b) 150°
    (c) 168° (d) 180°
18. The reflex angle between the hands of a clock at 10.25 is:
    (a) 180° (b) 192.5°
    (c) 195° (d) 197.5°
19. A clock is started at noon. By 10 minutes past 5, the hour hand has turned through:
    (a) 145° (b) 150°
    (c) 155° (d) 160°
20. A watch which gains 5 seconds in 3 minutes was set right at 7 (a)m. In the afternoon of the same day, when the watch indicated quarter past 4 o'clock, the true time is:
    (a) 7 p.m. (b) 4 p.m.
    (c) 9 p.m. (d) 3 p.m.

Answer Key

1. (c)	2. (d)	3. (c)	4. (a)	5. (b)	6. (a)	7. (d)	8. (b)	9. (c)	10. (c)
11. (d)	12. (a)	13. (d)	14. (c)	15. (b)	16. (a)	17. (d)	18. (d)	19. (d)	20. (b)

Explanatory Notes

1. (c)
On 31st December, 2005 it was Saturday.
Number of odd days from the year 2006 to the year 2009 = (1 + 1 + 2 + 1) = 5 days.
∴ On 31st December 2009, it was Thursday.
Thus, on 1st Jan, 2010 it Friday.

2. (d)
28th May, 2006 = (2005 years + Period from 1.1.2006 to 28.5.2006)
Odd days in 1600 years = 0
Odd days in 400 years = 0
5 years = (4 ordinary years + 1 leap year)
= (4 × 1 + 1 × 2) ≡ 6 odd days
Jan. Feb. March April May
(31 + 28 + 31 + 30 + 28) = 148 days
∴ 148 days = (21 weeks + 1 day) ≡ 1 odd day.
Total number of odd days = (0 + 0 + 6 + 1) = 7 ≡ 0 odd day.
Given day is Sunday.

3. (c)
17th June, 1998 = (1997 years + Period from 1.1.1998 to 17.6.1998)
Odd days in 1600 years = 0
Odd days in 300 years = (5 × 3) ≡ 1
97 years has 24 leap years + 73 ordinary years.
Number of odd days in 97 years (24 x 2 + 73)
= 121 = 2 odd days.
Jan. Feb. March April May June
(31 + 28 + 31 + 30 + 31 + 17) = 168 days
∴ 168 days = 24 weeks = 0 odd day
Total number of odd days = (0 + 1 + 2 + 0) = 3
Given day is Wednesday.

4. (a)
15th August, 2010 = (2009 years + Period 1.1.2010 to 15.8.2010)
Odd days in 1600 years = 0
Odd days in 400 years = 0
9 years = (2 leap years + 7 ordinary years)
= (2 × 2 + 7 × 1) = 11 odd days ≡ 4 odd days.
Jan. Feb. March April May June July Aug.
(31 + 28 + 31 + 30 + 31 + 30 + 31 + 15) = 227 days
227 days = (32 weeks + 3 days) ≡ 3 odd days.
Total number of odd days = (0 + 0 + 4 + 3) = 7 ≡ 0 odd days.
Given day is Sunday.

5. (b)
Each day of the week is repeated after 7 days.
So, after 63 days, it will be Monday.
∴ After 61 days, it will be Saturday.

6. (a)
The year 2004 is a leap year. So, it has 2 odd days.
But, Feb 2004 not included because we are calculating from March 2004 to March 2005. So it has 1 odd day only.
∴ The day on 6th March, 2005 will be 1 day beyond the day on 6th March, 2004.
Given that, 6th March, 2005 is Monday.
∴ 6th March, 2004 is Sunday (1 day before to 6th March, 2005).

7. (d)
We shall find the day on 1st April, 2001.
1st April, 2001 = (2000 years + Period from 1.1.2001 to 1.4.2001)
Odd days in 1600 years = 0
Odd days in 400 years = 0
Jan. Feb. March April
(31 + 28 + 31 + 1) = 91 days ≡ 0 odd days.
Total number of odd days = (0 + 0 + 0) = 0
On 1st April, 2001 it was Sunday.
In April, 2001 Wednesday falls on 4th, 11th, 18th and 25th.

8. (b)
x weeks x days = $(7x + x)$ days = $8x$ days.

9. (c)
100 years contain 5 odd days.
∴ Last day of 1st century is Friday.
200 years contain (5 x 2) ≡ 3 odd days.
∴ Last day of 2nd century is Wednesday.
300 years contain (5 x 3) = 15 ≡ 1 odd day.
∴ Last day of 3rd century is Monday.
400 years contain 0 odd day.
∴ Last day of 4th century is Sunday.
This cycle is repeated.
∴ Last day of a century cannot be Tuesday or Thursday or Saturday.

10. (c)
The year 2004 is a leap year. It has 2 odd days.
∴ The day on 8th Feb, 2004 is 2 days before the day on 8th Feb, 2005.
Hence, this day is Sunday.

11. (d)
Count the number of odd days from the year 2007 onwards to get the sum equal to 0 odd day.

Year	**Odd day**
2007	1
2008	2
2009	1
2010	1
2011	1
2012	2
2013	1
2014	1
2015	1
2016	2
2017	1

Sum = 14 odd days ≡ 0 odd days.

∴ Calendar for the year 2018 will be the same as for the year 2007.

12. (a)
The century divisible by 400 is a leap year.
∴ The year 700 is not a leap year.

13. (d)
The year 2006 is an ordinary year. So, it has 1 odd day.
So, the day on 8h Dec, 2007 will be 1 day beyond the day on 8th Dec, 2006.
But, 8th Dec, 2007 is Saturday.
∴ 8th Dec, 2006 is Friday.

14. (c)
The year 2008 is a leap year. So, it has 2 odd days.
1st day of the year 2008 is Tuesday (Given)
So, 1st day of the year 2009 is 2 days beyond Tuesday. Hence, it will be Thursday.

15. (b)
The year 2007 is an ordinary year. So, it has 1 odd day.
1st day of the year 2007 was Monday.
1st day of the year 2008 will be 1 day beyond Monday. Hence, it will be Tuesday.

16. (a)
Total number of days between 11th January 1997 and 10th January 2000
= (365 – 11) in 1997 + 365 in 1998 + 365 in 1999 + 10 days in 2000
= (50 weeks + 4 odd days) + (52 weeks + 1 odd day) + (52 weeks + 1 odd day) + (1 week + 3 odd days)
Total number of odd days = 4 + 1 + 1 + 3 = 9 days = 1 week + 2 days
Hence, 10th January, 2000 would be 2 days ahead of Sunday i.e. it was on Tuesday.

17. (d)
Angle traced by the hour hand in 6 hours
$= (360/12 \times 6)° = 180°$

18. (d)
Angle traced by hour hand in 125/12 hrs
$= [(360/12) \times (125/12)]° = 312.5°$
Angle traced by minute hand in 25 min
$= (360/60 \times 25)° = 150°$
∴ Reflex angle $= 360° - (312.5° - 150°)$
$= 360° - 162.5° = 197.5°$

19. (c)
Angle traced by hour hand in 12 hrs = 360°.
Angle traced by hour hand in 5 hrs 10 min. i.e. 31/6 hrs
$= (360/12 \times 31/6)° = 155°$

20. (b)
Time from 7 a.m. to 4.15 p.m. = 9 hrs 15 minute = 37/4 hrs.
3 min. 5 sec. of this clock = 3 min. of the correct clock.
37/720 hrs of this clock =1/20 hrs of the correct clock.
37/4 hrs of this clock = (1/20 x 720/37 x 37/4) hrs of the correct clock.
= 9 hrs of the correct clock.
The correct time is 9 hrs after 7 a.m. i.e., 4 p.m.

❐

Previous Year Questions

1. How much does a watch lose per day, if its hands coincide every 64 minutes?
[NTSE 2012 - UP first stage paper]
(a) $32\frac{8}{11}$ min (a) $36\frac{5}{11}$ min
(c) 90 min (d) 96 min

2. At what time between 5.30 and 6 will the hands of a clock be at right angles?
[NTSE 2012 - West Bengal first stage paper]
(a) 44 min past 5 (b) $43\frac{7}{11}$ past 5
(c) 40 min past 5 (d) 45 min past 5

3. At what angle the hands of a clock are inclined at 15 minutes past 5?
[NTSE 2012 - Gujarat first stage paper]
(a) 58.5° (b) 64°
(c) 67.5° (d) 72.5°

4. The angle between the minute hand and the hour hand of a clock when the time is 8.30, is:
[NTSE 2006 - Karnataka first stage paper]
(a) 80° (b) 75°
(c) 60° (d) 105°

5. At what time between 4 and 5 o'clock will the hands of a watch point in opposite directions?
[NTSE 2012 - Delhi first stage paper]
(a) 45 min past 4 (b) 40 min past 4
(c) 52 min past 4 (d) $54\frac{6}{11}$ past 4

6. The day on the 5th March of a year is the same day on what date of the year?
[NTSE 2012 - Punjab first stage paper]
(a) 2nd April (b) 3rd September
(c) 4th October (d) 5th November

7. On what dates of January 1994 did Sunday fall?
[NTSE 2006 – Bihar first stage paper]
(a) 3 (b) 9
(c) 15 (d) 27

8. Today is Sunday. After 32 days it will be:
[NTSE 2002 - UP first stage paper]
(a) Monday (b) Thursday
(c) Wednesday (d) Saturday

9. What was the day of the week on 15th January, 1979?
[NTSE 2007 - Delhi first stage paper]
(a) Sunday (b) Monday
(c) Friday (d) Saturday

10. The first republic day of India was celebrated on 26th January 1950, it was:
[NTSE 2005 - Karnataka second stage paper]
(a) Tuesday (b) Monday
(c) Thursday (d) Friday

❐

Answer Key

1. (a)	**2.** (b)	**3.** (c)	**4.** (b)	**5.** (d)	**6.** (b)	**7.** (b)	**8.** (b)	**9.** (b)	**10.** (c)

Explanatory Notes

1. (a)
55 min. spaces are covered in 60 min.
60 min. spaces will be covered in (60/55 × 60) min.

$$= 65\frac{5}{11} \text{ min}$$

Loss in 64 min. = $65\frac{5}{11}\text{min}-64\text{min}=\frac{16}{11}\text{min}$

Loss in 24 hrs = (16/11 × 1/64 × 24 × 60) min

$$= 32\frac{8}{11} \text{ min.}$$

2. (b)
At 5 o'clock, the hands are 25 min. spaces apart.
To be at right angles and that too between 5.30 and 6, the minute hand has to gain (25 + 15)
= 40 min. spaces.
55 min. spaces are gained in 60 min.
40 min. spaces are gained in

$$(60/55 \times 40) = 43\frac{7}{11} \text{ min}$$

∴ Required time = $43\frac{7}{11}$ min past 5

3. (c)
Angle traced by hour hand in 21/4 hrs
= (360/12 × 21/4)° = 157.5°
Angle traced by min. hand in 15 min.
= (360/60 × 15)° = 90°
∴ Required angle = 157.5° – 90° = 67.5°

4. (b)
Angle traced by hour hand in 17/2 hrs
= (360/12 × 17/2)° = 255°
Angle traced by min. hand in 30 min.
= (360/60 × 30)° = 180°
∴ Required angle = (255 – 180) ° = 75°.

5. (d)
At 4 o'clock, the hands of the watch are 20 min. spaces apart.
To be in opposite directions, they must be 30 min. spaces apart.
∴ Minute hand will have to gain 50 min. spaces.
55 min. spaces are gained in 60 min.
50 in. spaces are gained in

$$(60/55 \times 50) \text{ min} = 54\frac{6}{11} \text{ min}$$

Thus, required time = $54\frac{6}{11}$ min past 4

6. (d)
Since any date in March is the same day of the week as the corresponding date in November of that year. So the same day falls on 5th November.

7. (b)
Number of odd days is (1600 + 300) years = 0 + 1 = 1
93 years = (23 leap year + 70 ordinary year)
= (46 + 70) odd days ≡ 4 odd days
January 1st = 1 odd day
∴ Day of the 1st January 1994 is 'Saturday'
Sunday was 2nd January
Thus Sunday fell on 2nd, 9th, 16th, 23rd, and 29th

8. (b)
Each day of the week is repeated after 7 days.
∴ After 35 days it will be 'Sunday'.
∴ After 32 days it will be 'Thursday'.

9. (b)
Number of odd days is (1600 + 300) years = 0 + 1 = 1
78 years = (19 leap year + 59 ordinary year)
= (38 + 59) odd days = 97 odd days ≡ 6 odd days
15 days of January have 1 odd day
Total number of odd days = (1 + 6 + 1) ≡ 1 odd days
The derived day was 'Monday'.

10. (c)
Number of odd days is (1600 + 300) years = 0 + 1 = 1
49 years = (12 leap years + 37 ordinary years)
= (24 + 37) odd days = 61 odd days ≡ 5 odd days
26th January have 5 odd days
Total number of odd days = (1 + 5 + 5) = 11 odd days
Required day is 'Thursday'

UNIT 15

Number, Ranking and Time Sequence Tests

- **Number Test :** In this type of test a series of number is given. The candidate has to find out how many times a number satisfying the conditions specified in the question occurs.
- **Ranking Test :** In this type of problems, generally the ranks of a person both from the top and bottom are given and the total number of persons is asked. In other type, the rank from either the top or the bottom and the total number of persons in a certain group are given, so the candidate has to tell the position/rank either from the top or bottom of an asked person.
- **Time sequence test :** In the time sequence test, you will be asked to find a day which falls between two pair of dates. From that you have to locate the exact day.
- **Important features about Calendar**
  - **Odd Days:**
    We are supposed to find the day of the week on a given date.
    For this, we use the concept of 'odd days'.
    In a given period, the number of days more than the complete weeks are called odd days.
  - **Leap Year:**
    I. Every year divisible by 4 is a leap year, if it is not a century.
    II. Every 4th century is a leap year and no other century is a leap year.

  Note : A leap year has 366 days.

Examples :

I. Each of the years 1948, 2004, 1676 etc. is a leap year.
II. Each of the years 400, 800, 1200, 1600, 2000 etc. is a leap year.
III. None of the years 2001, 2002, 2003, 2005, 1800, 2100 is a leap year.

- **Ordinary Year:**
  The year which is not a leap year is called an ordinary year. An ordinary year has 365 days.
- **Counting of Odd Days:**
  I. 1 ordinary year = 365 days = (52 weeks + 1 day.) $\therefore$ 1 ordinary year has 1 odd day.
  II. 1 leap year = 366 days = (52 weeks + 2 days) $\therefore$ 1 leap year has 2 odd days.
  III. 100 years = 76 ordinary years + 24 leap years
  = $(76 \times 1 + 24 \times 2)$ odd days = 124 odd days = (17 weeks + days) $\equiv$ 5 odd days.
  $\therefore$ Number of odd days in 100 years = 5
  Number of odd days in 200 years = $(5 \times 2) \equiv 3$ odd days.
  Number of odd days in 300 years = $(5 \times 3) \equiv 1$ odd day.
  Number of odd days in 400 years = $(5 \times 4 + 1) \equiv 0$ odd day.
  Similarly, each one of 800 years, 1200 years, 1600 years, 2000 years etc. has 0 odd days.
- **Day of the Week Related to Odd Days:**

No. of Days	0	1	2	3	4	5	6
Day	Sun	Mon	Tues	Wed	Thurs	Fri	Sat

Solved Examples

1. Which is the third number to the left of the number which is exactly in the middle of the following sequence of numbers?
1 2 3 4 5 6 7 8 9 2 4 6 8 9 7 5 3 1 9 8 7 6 5 4 3 2 1
(a) 3 (b) 4
(c) 5 (d) 7
Solution: Option (b) is correct.
Explanation: There are 27 numbers in the given sequence.
So, middle number = 14th number = 9.
Clearly, the third number to the left of this 9 is 4.

2. How many 3's are there in the following sequence which are neither preceded by 6 nor immediately followed by 9?
9 3 6 6 3 9 5 9 3 7 8 9 1 6 3 9 6 3 9
(a) 1 (b) 2
(c) 3 (d) 4
Solution: Option (b) is correct.
Explanation:
9 **3** 6 6 3 9 5 9 **3** 7 8 9 1 6 3 9 6 3 9

3. In a row of trees, one tree is fifth from either end of the row. How many trees are there in the row?
(a) 8 (b) 9
(c) 10 (d) 11
Solution: Option (b) is correct.
Explanation: Clearly, the number of trees in the row = (4 + 1 + 4) = 9.

4. In a queue, Amrita is 10th from the front while Mukul is 25th from behind and Mamta is just in the middle of the two. If there are 50 persons in the queue, then what position does Mamta occupy from the front?
(a) 20th (b) 19th
(c) 18th (d) 17th
Solution: Option (c) is correct.
Explanation: Number of persons between Amrita and Mukul = 50 – (10 + 25) = 15. Since Mamta lies in middle of these 15 persons, so Mamta's position is 8th from Amrita i.e. 18th from the front.

5. What is the day on 1st January 1901?
(a) Monday (b) Wednesday
(c) Sunday (d) Tuesday
Solution: Option (d) is correct.
Explanation:
1st January 1901 means (1900 year and 1 day)
Now, 1600 years have 0 odd days.
300 years have 1 odd day.
1 day has 1 odd day.
Total number of odd days = 0 + 1 + 1 = 2 days.
Hence, the day on 1st January 1901 was Tuesday.

6. Today is Thursday. The day after 59 days will be:
(a) Monday (b) Tuesday
(c) Sunday (d) Wednesday
Solution: Option (c) is correct.
Explanation: Every day of the week is repeated after 7 days. Hence after 56 days it would be Thursday again. And after 59 days it would be Sunday.

Multiple Choice Questions

1. Count each 7 which is not immediately preceded by 5 but is immediately followed by either 2 or 3.
How many such 7's are there?
5 7 2 6 5 7 3 8 3 7 3 2 5 7 2 7 3 4 8 2 6 7 8
(a) 2 (b) 3
(c) 4 (d) 5

2. How many 6's are there in the following series of numbers, which are preceded by 7 but not immediately followed by 9?
6 7 9 5 6 9 7 6 8 7 6 7 8 6 9 4 6 7 7 6 9 5 7 6 3
(a) 1 (b) 2
(c) 3 (d) 4

3. How many 7's are there in the following series which are not immediately followed by 3 but immediately preceded by 8?
8 9 8 7 6 2 2 6 3 2 6 9 7 3 2 8 7 2 7 7 8 7 3 7 7 9 4
(a) 10 (b) 3
(c) 2 (d) 0

4. Count each 1 in the following sequence of numbers that is immediately followed by 2, if 2 is not immediately followed by 3.
How many such 1's are there?
1 2 1 3 4 5 1 2 3 5 2 1 2 6 1 4 5 1 1 2 4 1 2 3 2 1 7 5 2 1 2 5
(a) 2 (b) 4
(c) 7 (d) 9

5. How many 7's are there in the following series which are preceded by 6, which is not preceded by 8?
8 7 6 7 8 6 7 5 6 7 9 7 6 1 6 7 7 6 8 8 6 9 7 6 8 7
(a) 0 (b) 1
(c) 2 (d) 3

6. In the following list of numerals, how many 2's are followed by 1's but not preceded by 4?
4 2 1 2 1 4 2 1 1 2 4 4 4 1 2 2 1 2 1 4 4 2 1 4 2 1 2 1 2 4 1 4 2 1 2 4 1 4 6
(a) 2 (b) 3
(c) 4 (d) 5

7. How many 7's are there in the following sequence which are preceded by 9 and followed by 6?
7 8 9 7 6 5 3 4 2 8 9 7 2 4 5 9 2 9 7 6 4 7
(a) 2 (b) 3
(c) 4 (d) 5

8. In the series : 7 8 9 7 6 5 3 4 2 8 9 7 2 4 5 9 2 9 7 6 4 7
Which figures have equal frequency ?
(a) 2, 5, 3 (b) 2, 4, 5
(c) 3, 7, 5 (d) 8, 6, 5

9. How many 6's are there in the following number sequence which are immediately preceded by 9 but not immediately followed by 4?
5 6 4 3 2 9 6 3 1 6 4 9 6 4 2 1 5 9 6 7 2 1 4 7 4 9 6 4 2
(a) 1 (b) 2
(c) 3 (d) 4

10. In the following series of numbers, find out how many times, 1, 3 and 7 have appeared together, 7 being in the middle and 1 and 3 on either side of 7?
2 9 7 3 1 7 3 7 7 1 3 3 1 7 3 8 5 7 1 3 7 7 1 7 3 9 0 6
(a) 3 (b) 4
(c) 5 (d) More than 5

11. In the series,
6 4 1 2 2 8 7 4 2 1 5 3 8 6 2 1 7 1 4 1 3 2 8 6
How many pairs of alternate numbers have a difference of 2 ?
(a) 1 (b) 2
(c) 3 (d) 4

12. How many even numbers are there in the following sequence of numbers which are immediately followed by an odd number as well as immediately preceded by an even number?
8 6 7 6 8 9 3 2 7 5 3 4 2 2 3 5 5 2 2 8 1 1 9
(a) 1 (b) 3
(c) 5 (d) None of these

13. **Series :** 5 1 4 7 3 9 8 5 7 2 6 3 1 5 8 6 3 8 5 2 2 4 3 4 9 6
How many odd numbers are there in the sequence which are immediately followed by an odd number ?
(a) 2 (b) 3
(c) 4 (d) More than 4

14. **Series :** 5 1 4 7 3 9 8 5 7 2 6 3 1 5 8 6 3 8 5 2 2 4 3 4 9 6
How many even numbers are there in the sequence, which are immediately preceded by an odd number but immediately followed by an even number ?
(a) 1 (b) 2
(c) 3 (d) 4

15. **Series :** 5 1 4 7 3 9 8 5 7 2 6 3 1 5 8 6 3 8 5 2 2 4 3 4 9 6
How many odd numbers are there in the sequence which are immediately preceded and also immediately followed by an even number ?
(a) 1 (b) 2
(c) 3 (d) 4

16. Raman ranks sixteenth from the top and forty ninth from the bottom in a class. How many students are there in the class?
(a) 63 (b) 64
(c) 65 (d) Cannot be determined

17. Sanjeev ranks seventh from the top and twenty eigh from the bottom in a class. How many students are there in the class?
(a) 37 (b) 36
(c) 35 (d) 34

18. If Atul finds that he is twelfth from the right in a line of boys and fourth from the left, how many boys should be added to the line such that there are 28 boys in the line?
(a) 12 (b) 13
(c) 14 (d) 20

19. Manisha ranked sixteenth from the top and twenty ninth from the bottom among those who passed an examination. Six boys did not participate in the competition and five failed in it. How many boys were there in the class?
(a) 40 (b) 44
(c) 50 (d) 55

20. Some boys are sitting in a row. P is sitting fourteenth from the left and Q is seventh from the right. If there are four boys between P and Q, how many boys are there in the row?
(a) 25 (b) 23
(c) 21 (d) 19

21. Aruna ranks twelfth in a class of forty-six. What will be her rank from the last?
(a) 33 (b) 34
(c) 35 (d) 37

22. Manoj and Sachin are ranked seventh and eleventh respectively from the top in a class of 31 students. What will be their respective ranks from the bottom in the class ?
(a) 20th and 24th (b) 24th and 20th
(c) 25th and 21st (d) 26th and 22nd

23. Ravi is 7 ranks ahead of Sumit in a class of 39. If Sumit's rank is seventeenth from the last, what is Ravi's rank from the start?
(a) 14th (b) 15th
(c) 16th (d) 17th

24. Kailash remembers that his brother Deepak's birthday falls after 20th May but before 28th May, while Geeta remembers that Deepak's birthday falls before 22nd May but after 12th May. On what date Deepak's birthday falls ?
(a) 20th May
(b) 21st May
(c) 22nd May
(d) Cannot be determined

25. Sangeeta remembers that her father‘s birthday was certainly after eighth but before thirteenth of December. Her sister Natasha remembers that their father‘s birthday was definitely after ninth but before fourteenth of December. On which date of December was their father‘s birthday?
    (a) 10th (b) 11th
    (c) 12th (d) Data inadequate
26. Standing on a platform, Amit told Sunita that Aligarh was more than ten kilometres but less than fifteen kilometres from there. Sunita knew that it was more than twelve but less than fourteen kilometres from there. If both of them were correct, which of the following could be the distance of Aligarh from the platform?
    (a) 11 (b) 12
    (c) 13 (d) 14
27. Ashish leaves his house at 20 minutes to seven in the morning, reaches Kunal's house in 25 minutes, they finish their breakfast in another 15 minute and leave for their office which takes another 35 minutes, At what time do they leave Kunal's houses to reach their office ?
    (a) 7.40 a.m. (b) 7.20 a.m.
    (c) 7.45 a.m. (d) 8.15 a.m.
28. Ajay left home for the bus stop 15 minutes earlier than usual. It takes 10 minutes to reach the stop. He reached the stop at 8.40 (a)m. What time does he usually leave home for the bus stop?
    (a) 8.30 a.m. (b) 8.45 p.m.
    (c) 8.55 a.m. (d) None of these
29. If 11th January 1997 was a Sunday then what day of the week was on 10th January 2000?
    (a) Tuesday (b) Wednesday
    (c) Thursday (d) Friday
30. An accurate clock shows 8 o'clock in the morning. Through how may degrees will the hour hand rotate when the clock shows 2 o'clock in the afternoon?
    (a) 144° (b) 150°
    (c) 168° (d) 180°

❐

Answer Key

1. (a)	**2.** (c)	**3.** (c)	**4.** (b)	**5.** (d)	**6.** (c)	**7.** (a)	**8.** (d)	**9.** (b)	**10.** (a)
11. (b)	**12.** (d)	**13.** (d)	**14.** (c)	**15.** (d)	**16.** (b)	**17.** (d)	**18.** (b)	**19.** (d)	**20.** (a)
21. (c)	**22.** (c)	**23.** (c)	**24.** (b)	**25.** (d)	**26.** (c)	**27.** (b)	**28.** (d)	**29.** (a)	**30.** (d)

Explanatory Notes

1. (a)
5 7 2 6 5 7 3 8 3 **7** 3 2 5 7 2 **7** 3 4 8 2 6 7 8

2. (c)
6 7 9 5 6 9 7 **6** 8 7 **6** 7 8 6 9 4 6 7 7 6 9 5 7 **6** 3

3. (c)
8 9 8 **7** 6 2 2 6 3 2 6 9 7 3 2 8 **7** 2 7 7 8 7 7 7 9 4

4. (b)
1 2 1 3 4 5 1 2 3 5 2 **1** 2 6 1 4 5 1 **1** 2 4 1 2 3 2 1 7 5 2 **1** 2 5

5. (d)
8 7 6 **7** 8 6 7 5 6 **7** 9 7 6 **1** 6 **7** 7 6 8 8 6 9 7 6 8 7

6. (c)
4 2 1 **2** 1 4 2 1 1 2 4 4 4 1 2 **2** 1 **2** 1 4 4 2 1 4 2 1 **2** 1 2 4 1 4 2 1 2 4 1 4 6

7. (a)
7 8 9 **7** 6 5 3 4 2 8 9 7 2 4 5 9 2 9 **7** 6 4 7

8. (d)
In the given series, 2 occurs 3 times; 3 occurs once; 4 occurs 3 times; 5 occurs 2 times; 6 occurs 2 times; 7 occurs 5 times; 8 occurs 2 times and 9 occurs 4 times.
Clearly, the frequency of 5, 6 and 8 is the same i.e. 2.

9. (b)
5 6 4 3 2 9 **6** 3 1 6 4 9 6 4 2 1 5 9 **6** 7 2 1 4 7 4 9 6 4 2

10. (a)
2 9 7 3 **1 7 3** 7 7 1 3 3 **1 7 3** 8 5 7 1 3 7 7 **1 7 3** 9 0 6

11. (b)
We proceed by checking the difference between pairs of alternate numbers i.e., (6,1), (4,2), (1,2), (2,8), (2,7), (8,4), (7,2) (4,1), (2,5), (1,3), (5,8), (3,6), (8,2), (6,1), (2,7), (1,1), (7,4), (1,1), (4,3), (1,2), (3,8), and (2, 6). Of these, the pairs with a difference of 2 are (4,2) and (1,3). Clearly, there are two such pairs.

12. (d)
8 **6** 7 6 **8** 9 3 2 7 5 3 4 2 **2** 3 5 5 2 2 **8** 1 1 9

13. (d)
5 1 4 **7 3** 9 8 **5** 7 2 6 **3 1** 5 8 6 3 8 5 2 2 4 3 4 9 6

14. (c)
5 1 4 7 3 9 8 5 7 **2** 6 3 1 5 **8** 6 3 8 5 **2** 2 4 3 4 9 6

15. (d)
5 1 4 7 3 9 8 5 7 2 6 3 1 5 8 6 **3** 8 **5** 2 2 4 **3** 4 **9** 6

16. (b)
Clearly, the number of students in the class
= (15 + 1 + 48) = 64

17. (d)
Clearly, the number of students in the class
= (6 + 1 + 27) = 34

18. (b)
Clearly, the number of boys in the line
= (11 + 1 + 3) = 15
∴ Number of boys to be added = 28 – 15 = 13

19. (d)
Number of boys who passed = (15 + 1 + 28) = 44
∴ Total number of boys in the class
= 44 + 6 + 5 = 55

20. (a)
Number of boys in the row = number of boys up till P + number of boys between P and Q + number of boys including Q and those behind Q
= 14 + 4 + 7 = 25

21. (c)
Number of students behind Aruna in rank = (46 – 12) = 34. So, Arun is 35th from the last.

22. (c)
Number of students behind Manoj in rank = (31 – 7) = 24. So, Manoj is 25th from the bottom. Number of students behind Sachin in rank = (31 – 11) = 20. So, Sachin is 21st from the bottom.

23. (c)
Sumit is 17th from the last and Ravi is 7 ranks ahead of Sumit. So, Ravi is 24th from the last. Number of students ahead of Ravi in rank = (39 – 24) = 15. So, Ravi is 16th from the start.

24. (b)
According to Kailash, Deepak's birthday falls on one of the day among 21st, 22nd, 23rd, 24th, 25th, 26th, and 27th May. According to Geeta, Deepak's birthday falls on one of the days among 13th, 14th, 15th, 16th, 17th, 18th, 19th, 20th, and 21st May. The day common to both the groups is 21st May.
∴ Deepak's birthday falls in 21st May.

25. (d)
According to Sangeeta, the father's birthday falls on one of the days among 9^{h}, 10th, 11th and 12th December. According to Natasha, the father's birthday falls on one of the day among 10th, 11th, 12th and 13th December. The days common to both the groups are 10th, 11th and 12th December. So, the father's birthday falls on any one of these days.

26. (c)
Clearly, according to Sunita, the distance was more than 12 km but less than 14 km, which is 13km.

27. (b)
Ashish leaves his house at 6.40 a.m. He reaches Kunal's in 25 minutes i.e. 7.05 a.m. Both leave for office 15 minutes after 7.05 a.m. i.e. at 7.20 a.m.

28. (d)
Clearly, Ajay left home 10 minutes before 8.40 a.m. i.e., at 8.30 a.m. But it was 15 minutes earlier than usual. So, he usually left for the stop at 8.45 a.m.

29. (a)
Total number of days between 11th January 1997 and 10th January 2000
= (365 – 11) in 1997 + 365 in 1998 + 365 in 1999 + 10 days in 2000
= (50 weeks + 4 odd days) + (52 weeks + 1 odd day) + (52 weeks + 1 odd day) + (1 week + 3 odd days)
Total number of odd days = 4 + 1 + 1 + 3
= 9 days = 1 week + 2 days
Hence, 10th January, 2000 would be 2 days ahead of Sunday i.e. it was on Tuesday.

30. (d)
Angle traced by the hour hand in 6 hours
$$= (360/12 \times 6)^\circ = 180^\circ$$

❐

Previous Year Questions

1. Reaching the place of meeting on Tuesday 15 minutes before 08.30 hours, Anuj found himself half an hour earlier than the man who was 40 minutes late. What was the scheduled time of the meeting?

   [NTSE 2012 - Chandigarh second stage paper]

   (a) 8.00 hrs (b) 8.05 hrs
   (c) 8.15 hrs (d) 8.45 hrs

2. The priest told the devotee, "The temple bell is rung at regular intervals of 45 minutes. The last bell was rung five minutes ago. The next bell is due to be rung at 7.45 a.m." At what time did the priest give this information to the devotee?

   [NTSE 20023 - Maharashtra second stage paper]

   (a) 7.40 a.m. (b) 7.05 a.m.
   (c) 7.00 a.m. (d) 6.55 a.m.

3. The train for Lucknow leaves every two and a half hours from New Delhi Railway Station. An announcement was made at the station that the train for Lucknow had left 40 minutes ago and the next train will leave at 18.00 hrs. At what time was the announcement made?

   [NTSE 2001 - Delhi second stage paper]

   (a) 17.10 hrs (b) 16.00 hrs
   (c) 15.50 hrs (d) None of these

4. There are twenty people working in an office. The first group of five works between 8.00 a.m. and 2.00 p.m. The second group of ten works between 10.00 a.m. and 4.00 p.m. And the third group of five works between 12 noon and 6.00 p.m. There are three computers in the office which all the employees frequently use. During which of the following hours the computers are likely to be used most?

   [NTSE 2000 - Orissa second stage paper]

   (a) 10.00 a.m. - 12 noon
   (b) 12 noon - 2.00 p.m.
   (c) 1.00 p.m. - 3.00 p.m.
   (d) 2.00 p.m. - 4.00 p.m.

5. A monkey climbs 30 feet before at the beginning of each hour and rests for a while when he slips back 20 feet before he again starts climbing in the beginning of the next hour. If he begins his ascent at 8.00 a.m., at what time will he first touch a flag at 120 feet from the ground?

   [NTSE 2001 - Rajasthan first stage paper]

   (a) 4 p.m. (b) 5 p.m.
   (c) 6 p.m. (d) None of these

6. The calendar for the year 2007 will be the same for the year: ***[NTSE 2004 - UP first stage paper]***

   (a) 2014 (b) 2016
   (c) 2017 (d) 2018

7. Which of the following is not a leap year?

   [NTSE 2003 - Delhi first stage paper]

   (a) 700 (b) 800
   (c) 1200 (d) 2000

8. On 8th Dec, 2007 Saturday falls. What day of the week was it on 8th Dec, 2006?

   [NTSE 2002 - Punjab second stage paper]

   (a) Sunday (b) Thursday
   (c) Tuesday (d) Friday

9. January 1, 2008 is Tuesday. What day of the week lies on Jan 1, 2009?

   [NTSE 2012 - Assam second stage paper]

   (a) Monday (b) Wednesday
   (c) Thursday (d) Sunday

10. January 1, 2007 was Monday. What day of the week lies on Jan. 1, 2008?

    [NTSE 2002 – Manipur second stage paper]

    (a) Monday (b) Tuesday
    (c) Wednesday (d) Sunday

❐

Answer Key

1. (b)	2. (b)	3. (d)	4. (b)	5. (c)	6. (d)	7. (b)	8. (d)	9. (c)	10. (b)

Explanatory Notes

1. (b)
Anuj reached the place at 0815 hours. Clearly, the man who was 40 minutes late would reach the place at 8.45 a.m. So, the scheduled time of meeting was at 08.05 hours.

2. (b)
Clearly, the last bell rang 45 minutes before 7.45 a.m. i.e. at 7.00 a.m. But it happened five minutes before he gave the information to the devotee. So, the information was given at 7.05 a.m.

3. (d)
Clearly, the last train left two and a half hours before 18.00 hours i.e. at 15.30 hours. But this happened 40 minutes before the announcement was made. So, the announcement was made at 16.10 hours.

4. (b)
Clearly, the computers would be used most when all the three groups are working simultaneously and this happens during the period 12 noon to 2 p.m.

5. (c)
Clearly, the monkey climbs 10 feet in one hour. So, it will climb up to a height of 90 feet in 9 hours i.e. at 5.00 p.m. It will then ascend a height of 30 feet in the next hour to touch the peak at 6.00 p.m.

6. (d)
Count the number of odd days from the year 2007 onwards to get the sum equal to 0 odd day.

Year	Odd day
2007	1
2008	2
2009	1
2010	1
2011	1
2012	2
2013	1
2014	1
2015	1
2016	2
2017	1

Sum = 14 odd days ≡ 0 odd days.
∴ Calendar for the year 2018 will be the same as for the year 2007.

7. (a)
The century divisible by 400 is a leap year.
The year 700 is not a leap year.

8. (d)
The year 2006 is an ordinary year. So, it has 1 odd day. So, the day on 8[h] Dec, 2007 will be 1 day beyond the day on 8th Dec, 2006.
But, 8th Dec, 2007 is Saturday.
8th Dec, 2006 is Friday.

9. (c)
The year 2008 is a leap year. So, it has 2 odd days.
1st day of the year 2008 is Tuesday (Given)
So, 1st day of the year 2009 is 2 days beyond Tuesday.
Hence, it will be Thursday.

10. (b)
The year 2007 is an ordinary year. So, it has 1 odd day.
1st day of the year 2007 was Monday.
1st day of the year 2008 will be 1 day beyond Monday.
Hence, it will be Tuesday.

❐

UNIT 16

Logical Reasoning

Introduction

In the questions based on 'Logical Reasoning', a statement is given followed by some conclusions. The candidate is required to go through the statements meticulously and then decide which of the given conclusion/s follows on the basis of it.

- **Statement:** A statement is a formal account of certain facts, views, problems or situations expressed in words.
- **Conclusion:** A conclusion is a belief or an opinion that is the result of reasoning out a given statement. It can also be defined as a proposition in an argument to which other propositions in the argument give support.
- **Keywords:** Words, such as all, no, few, most, must, had to, will be, always, never, should be, may, may not etc, help in evaluating the given conclusions.

Examples:

Statement: 'South-Asia will remain affected by global crises'- World Bank

Conclusion: Sri Lanka, a South- Asian country may or may not face the problem caused by global crises.

Solved Examples

☛ ***Directions (1 to 3) :*** *In each question below is given a statement followed by two conclusions numbered I and II. You have to assume everything in the statement to be true, then consider the two conclusions together and decide which of them logically follows beyond a reasonable doubt from the information given in the statement.*

Give answer:

- (A) If only conclusion I follows
- (B) If only conclusion II follows
- (C) If either I or II follows
- (D) If neither I nor II follows
- (E) If both I and II follow

1. Statement: Recent trends also indicate that the number of child migrants in large cities is increasing. These children leave their families to join the ranks of urban poor doing odd jobs in markets, workshops, hotels or in service sectors.

Conclusions:

I. Migration to big cities should be checked.

II. The plight of poor children should thoroughly be studied.

a. Only conclusion I follows
b. Only conclusion II follows
c. Either I or II follows
d. Neither I nor II follows
e. Both I and II follow

Solution: Option (c) is correct.

Explanation: The statement mentions the problem of increased migration of children to cities. But the ways to deal with the problem cannot be deduced from it. So, neither I nor II follows.

2. Statement: No country is absolutely self-dependent these days.

Conclusions:

I. It is impossible to grow and produce all that a country needs.

II. Countrymen in general have become lazy.

a. Only conclusion I follows
b. Only conclusion II follows
c. Either I or II follows
d. Neither I nor II follows
e. Both I and II follow

Solution: Option (a) is correct.

Explanation: Clearly, only I provide a suitable explanation to the given statement. So, only 'I' follows.

3. Statement: The percentage of the national income shared by the top 10 per cent of households in India is 35.

Conclusions:

I. When an economy grows fast, the concentration of wealth in certain pockets of population takes place.

II. The national income is unevenly distributed in India.

a. Only conclusion I follows
b. Only conclusion II follows

c. Either I or II follows
d. Neither I nor II follows
e. Both I and II follow

Solution: Option (b) is correct.

Explanation: Nothing about the growth of an economy is mentioned in the statement. So, 'I' does not follow. Also, it is given that 35 per cent of national income is shared by 10 per cent of households. This indicates unequal distribution of national income. So, II follows.

☛ ***Directions (4 to 5):*** *In each of the following questions, a statement/group of statements is given followed by some conclusions. Without resolving anything yourself, choose the conclusion which logically follows from the given statements.*

4. Statement: The Prime Minister emphatically stated that his government would make every possible effort for the upliftment of poor farmers and farmhands.

Conclusions:

I. Except poor farmers and farmhands, all others have got benefits of fruits of development.

II. No serious efforts have been made in the past for the upliftment of any section of the society.

a. Only conclusion I follows
b. Only conclusion II follows
c. Either I or II follows
d. Neither I nor II follows
e. Both I and II follow

Solution: Option (c) is correct.

Explanation: No other section of society except farmers has been talked about in the statement. So, neither I nor II follows.

5. Statements: A neurotic is a non-stupid person who behaves stupidly.

Conclusions:

I. Neuroticism and stupidity go hand in hand.

II. Normal persons behave intelligently.

a. Only conclusion I follows
b. Only conclusion II follows
c. Either I or II follows
d. Neither I nor II follows
e. Both I and II follow

Solution: Option (a) is correct.

Explanation:

It is mentioned in the statement that a neurotic is a person who behaves stupidly. So, I follows. The behaviour of normal persons cannot be deduced from the given statement. So, II does not follow.

Practice Exercise

☛ ***Directions (1 to 27):*** *In each question below is given a statement followed by two conclusions numbered I and II. You have to assume everything in the statement to be true, then consider the two conclusions together and decide which of them logically follows beyond a reasonable doubt from the information given in the statement.*

Give answer:

- (A) If only conclusion I follows
- (B) If only conclusion II follows
- (C) If either I or II follows
- (D) If neither I nor II follows
- (E) If both I and II follow

1. Statements: Players who break various records in a fair way get special prizes. Player X broke the world record but was found to be under the influence of a prohibited drug.

Conclusions:

I. X will get the special prize.

II. X will not get the special prize.

a. Only conclusion I follows
b. Only conclusion II follows
c. Either I or II follows
d. Neither I nor II follows
e. Both I and II follow

2. Statement: Company X has marketed the product. Go ahead; purchase it if the price and quality are your considerations.

Conclusions:

I. The product must be good in quality.

II. The price of the product must be reasonable.

a. Only conclusion I follows
b. Only conclusion II follows
c. Either I or II follows
d. Neither I nor II follows
e. Both I and II follow

3. Statement: Quality has a price tag. India is allocating lots of funds to education.

Conclusions:

I. Quality of education in India would improve soon.

II. Funding alone can enhance the quality of education.

a. Only conclusion I follows
b. Only conclusion II follows
c. Either I or II follows
d. Neither I nor II follows
e. Both I and II follow

4. Statement: Although we have rating agencies like CRISIL, ICRA, there is a demand to have a separate rating agency for IT companies to protect investors.

Conclusions:

I. Assessment of financial worth of IT companies calls for separate set of skills, insight and competencies.

II. Now, the investors investing in IT companies will get protection of their investment.

a. Only conclusion I follows
b. Only conclusion II follows
c. Either I or II follows
d. Neither I nor II follows
e. Both I and II follow

5. Statement: The standard of education in private schools is much better than Municipal and Zila Parishad-run schools.

Conclusions:

I. The Municipal and Zila Parishad should make serious efforts to improve standard of their schools.

II. All Municipal and Zila Parishad schools should be closed immediately.

a. Only conclusion I follows
b. Only conclusion II follows
c. Either I or II follows
d. Neither I nor II follows
e. Both I and II follow

6. Statement: All the organised persons find time for rest. Sunita, in spite of her very busy schedule, finds time for rest.

Conclusions:

I. Sunita is an organised person.

II. Sunita is an industrious person.

a. Only conclusion I follows
b. Only conclusion II follows
c. Either I or II follows
d. Neither I nor II follows
e. Both I and II follow

7. Statement: Domestic demand has been increasing faster than the production of indigenous crude oil.

Conclusions:

I. Crude oil must be imported.

II. Domestic demand should be reduced.

a. Only conclusion I follows
b. Only conclusion II follows
c. Either I or II follows
d. Neither I nor II follows
e. Both I and II follow

8. Statement: He stressed the need to stop the present examination system and its replacement by other methods which would measure the real merit of the students.

Conclusions:

I. Examinations should be abolished.

II. The present examination system does not measure the real merit of the students.

a. Only conclusion I follows
b. Only conclusion II follows
c. Either I or II follows
d. Neither I nor II follows
e. Both I and II follow

9. Statement: Fashion is a form of ugliness, so intolerable that we have to alter it every six months.

Conclusions:

I. Fashion designers do not understand the public mind very well.

II. The public by and large is highly susceptible to novelty.

a. Only conclusion I follows
b. Only conclusion II follows
c. Either I or II follows
d. Neither I nor II follows
e. Both I and II follow

10. Statement: Until our country achieves economic equality, the political freedom and democracy would be meaningless.

Conclusions:

I. Political freedom and democracy go hand in hand.

II. Economic equality leads to real political freedom and democracy.

a. Only conclusion I follows
b. Only conclusion II follows
c. Either I or II follows
d. Neither I nor II follows
e. Both I and II follow

11. Statement: People who speak too much against dowry are those who had taken it themselves.

Conclusions:

I. It is easier said than done.

II. People have double standards.

a. Only conclusion I follows
b. Only conclusion II follows
c. Either I or II follows
d. Neither I nor II follows
e. Both I and II follow

12. Statement: The national norm is 100 beds per thousand populations but in this state, 150 beds per thousand are available in the hospitals.

Conclusions:

I. Our national norm is appropriate.

II. The state's health system is taking adequate care in this regard.

a. Only conclusion I follows
b. Only conclusion II follows
c. Either I or II follows
d. Neither I nor II follows
e. Both I and II follow

13. Statement: Our securities investments carry market risk. Consult your investment advisor or agent before investing.

Conclusions:

I. One should not invest in securities.

II. The investment advisor calculates the market risk with certainty.

a. Only conclusion I follows
b. Only conclusion II follows
c. Either I or II follows
d. Neither I nor II follows
e. Both I and II follow

14. Statement: Money plays a vital role in politics.

Conclusions:

I. The poor can never become politicians.
II. All the rich men take part in politics.

a. Only conclusion I follows
b. Only conclusion II follows
c. Either I or II follows
d. Neither I nor II follows
e. Both I and II follow

15. Statement: Vegetable prices are soaring in the market.

Conclusions:

I. Vegetables are becoming a rare commodity.
II. People cannot eat vegetables.

a. Only conclusion I follows
b. Only conclusion II follows
c. Either I or II follows
d. Neither I nor II follows
e. Both I and II follow

16. Statement: The serious accident in which a person was run down by a car yesterday has again focused attention on the most unsatisfactory state of roads.

Conclusions:

I. The accident that occurred was fatal.
II. Several accidents have taken place so far because of unsatisfactory state of roads.

a. Only conclusion I follows
b. Only conclusion II follows
c. Either I or II follows
d. Neither I nor II follows
e. Both I and II follow

17. Statement: In a recent survey report, it has been stated that those who undertake physical exercise for at least half an hour a day are less prone to have any heart ailments.

Conclusions:

I. Moderate level of physical exercise is necessary for leading a healthy life.
II. All people who do desk-bound jobs definitely suffer from heart ailments.

a. Only conclusion I follows
b. Only conclusion II follows
c. Either I or II follows
d. Neither I nor II follows
e. Both I and II follow

18. Statement: A bird in hand is worth two in the bush.

Conclusions:

I. We should be content with what we have.
II. We should not crave for what is not.

a. Only conclusion I follows
b. Only conclusion II follows
c. Either I or II follows
d. Neither I nor II follows
e. Both I and II follow

19. Statement: This world is neither good nor evil; each man manufactures a world for himself.

Conclusions:

I. Some people find this world quite good.
II. Some people find this world quite bad.

a. Only conclusion I follows
b. Only conclusion II follows
c. Either I or II follows
d. Neither I nor II follows
e. Both I and II follow

20. Statement: The eligibility for admission to the course is minimum second class Master's degree. However, the candidates who have appeared for the final year examination of Master's degree can also apply.

Conclusions:

I. All candidates who have yet to get their Master's degree will be there in the list of selected candidates.
II. All candidates having obtained second class Master's degree will be there in the list of selected candidates.

a. Only conclusion I follows
b. Only conclusion II follows
c. Either I or II follows
d. Neither I nor II follows
e. Both I and II follow

21. Statement: Any student who does not behave properly in the school brings bad name to himself and for the school also.

Conclusions:

I. Such students should be removed from the school.
II. Stricter discipline does not improve the behaviour of students.

a. Only conclusion I follows
b. Only conclusion II follows
c. Either I or II follows
d. Neither I nor II follows
e. Both I and II follow

22. Statement: A Corporate General Manager asked four managers to either submit their resignations by the next day or face termination orders from service. Three of them had submitted their resignations by that evening.

Conclusions:

I. The next day, the remaining manager would also resign.
II. The General Manager would terminate his services the next day.

a. Only conclusion I follows
b. Only conclusion II follows
c. Either I or II follows
d. Neither I nor II follows
e. Both I and II follow

23. Statement: Only good singers are invited to the conference. No one without sweet voice is a good singer.

Conclusions:

I. All invited singers in the conference have sweet voice.

II. Those singers who do not have sweet voice are not invited in the conference.

a. Only conclusion I follows
b. Only conclusion II follows
c. Either I or II follows
d. Neither I nor II follows
e. Both I and II follow

24. Statement: To cultivate interest in reading, the school has made it compulsory from June this year for each student to read two books per week and submit a weekly report on the books.

Conclusions:

I. Interest in reading can be created by force.

II. Some students will eventually develop interest in reading.

a. Only conclusion I follows
b. Only conclusion II follows
c. Either I or II follows
d. Neither I nor II follows
e. Both I and II follow

25. Statement: Applications of applicants who do not fulfil eligibility criteria and/or who do not submit applications before last date will be summarily rejected and will not be called for the written test.

Conclusions:

I. Those who are called for the written test are the applicants who fulfil eligibility criteria and have submitted their applications before last date.

II. Written test will be held only after scrutiny of applications.

a. Only conclusion I follows
b. Only conclusion II follows
c. Either I or II follows
d. Neither I nor II follows
e. Both I and II follow

26. Statement: The manager humiliated Sachin in the presence of his colleagues.

Conclusions:

I. The manager did not like Sachin.

II. Sachin was not popular with his colleagues.

a. Only conclusion I follows
b. Only conclusion II follows
c. Either I or II follows
d. Neither I nor II follows
e. Both I and II follow

27. Statement: Women's organisations in India have welcomed the amendment of the Industrial Employment Rules 1946 to curb sexual harassment at the work place.

Conclusions:

I. Sexual harassment of women at work place is more prevalent in India as compared to other developed countries.

II. Many organisations in India will stop recruiting women to avoid such problems.

a. Only conclusion I follows
b. Only conclusion II follows
c. Either I or II follows
d. Neither I nor II follows
e. Both I and II follow

☛ ***Directions (28-47) :*** *In each of the following questions, a statement/group of statements is given followed by some conclusions. Without resolving anything yourself, choose the conclusion which logically follows from the given statements.*

28. Statement: We should inform all our officers not to read newspapers during office hours - Chief Manager tells. Chief Administrator.

Conclusions:

I. Reading newspapers during office hours is desirable.

II. Office efficiency will not increase by stopping this.

a. Only conclusion I follows
b. Only conclusion II follows
c. Either I or II follows
d. Neither I nor II follows
e. Both I and II follow

29. Statement: The Cabinet of State X took certain steps to tackle the milk glut in the state as the cooperatives and government dairies failed to use the available milk. - A news report.

Conclusions:

I. The milk production of State X is more than its need.

II. The Government and co-operative dairies in State X are not equipped in terms of resources and technology to handle such excess milk.

a. Only conclusion I follows
b. Only conclusion II follows
c. Either I or II follows
d. Neither I nor II follows
e. Both I and II follow

30. Statement: Video libraries are flourishing very much these days.

Conclusions:

I. People in general have got a video craze.

II. It is much cheaper to see as many movies as one likes on videos rather than going to the cinema hall.

a. Only conclusion I follows
b. Only conclusion II follows
c. Either I or II follows
d. Neither I nor II follows
e. Both I and II follow

31. Statement: The minister questioned the utility of the Space Research programme and suggested its replacement by other areas of felt national needs.

Conclusions:

I. Exploring the space does not contribute to critical national needs.

II. Research should be oriented to national needs.

a. Only conclusion I follows
b. Only conclusion II follows
c. Either I or II follows
d. Neither I nor II follows
e. Both I and II follow

32. Statement: The secret of success is constancy of purpose.

Conclusions:

I. Constant dripping wears the stone.

II. Single-minded devotion is necessary for achieving success.

a. Only conclusion I follows
b. Only conclusion II follows
c. Either I or II follows
d. Neither I nor II follows
e. Both I and II follow

33. Statement: Leaders, who raise much hue and cry about the use of Hindi, generally send their children to English medium schools.

Conclusions:

I. India lacks good Hindi medium schools.

II. There is a world of difference between preaching and practising.

a. Only conclusion I follows
b. Only conclusion II follows
c. Either I or II follows
d. Neither I nor II follows
e. Both I and II follow

34. Statement: Any young man, who makes dowry as a condition for marriage, discredits himself and dishonours womanhood.

Conclusions:

I. Those who take dowry in marriage should be condemned by society.

II. Those who do not take dowry in marriage respect womanhood.

a. Only conclusion I follows
b. Only conclusion II follows
c. Either I or II follows
d. Neither I nor II follows
e. Both I and II follow

35. Statement: The 'Official Secrets Act' (OSA) enacted by the ABC government during the war seems to be one of the major source of corruption in the country X.

Conclusions:

I. The OSA has to be abolished immediately to put an end to the corruption in the country X.

II. The ABC government had an intention of encouraging corruption in the government offices.

a. Only conclusion I follows
b. Only conclusion II follows
c. Either I or II follows
d. Neither I nor II follows
e. Both I and II follow

36. Statement: In India, more emphasis should be placed on areas such as agriculture, engineering and technology instead of basic and pure sciences.

Conclusions:

I. India has achieved sufficient progress in basic and pure sciences.

II. In the past, the productivity factor in our economy was neglected.

a. Only conclusion I follows
b. Only conclusion II follows
c. Either I or II follows
d. Neither I nor II follows
e. Both I and II follow

37. Statements: If all players play to their full potential, we will win the match. We have won the match.

Conclusions:

I. All players played to their full potential.

II. Some players did not play to their full potential.

a. Only conclusion I follows
b. Only conclusion II follows
c. Either I or II follows
d. Neither I nor II follows
e. Both I and II follow

38. Statement: In India, more emphasis should be placed on areas such as agriculture, engineering and technology instead of basic and pure sciences.

Conclusions:

I. India has achieved sufficient progress in basic and pure sciences.

II. In the past, the productivity factor in our economy was neglected.

a. Only conclusion I follows
b. Only conclusion II follows
c. Either I or II follows
d. Neither I nor II follows
e. Both I and II follow

39. Statement: If all players play to their full potential, we will win the match. We have won the match.

Conclusions:

I. All players played to their full potential.

II. Some players did not play to their full potential.

a. Only conclusion I follows
b. Only conclusion II follows
c. Either I or II follows
d. Neither I nor II follows
e. Both I and II follow

40. Statement: The Bank of England's move to auction 25 metric tons of gold drew plenty of bidders looking for a bargain, but was criticised by major gold producers worldwide.

Conclusions:

I. The Bank of England should not auction gold which it possesses to keep steady international prices of gold.

II. Bidders should quote higher gold prices to retain present value of gold in the international markets.

a. Only conclusion I follows
b. Only conclusion II follows
c. Either I or II follows
d. Neither I nor II follows
e. Both I and II follow

41. Statement: Good voice is a natural gift but one has to keep practising to improve and excel well in the field of music.

Conclusions:

I. Natural gifts need nurturing and care.

II. Even though your voice is not good, one can keep practising.

a. Only conclusion I follows
b. Only conclusion II follows
c. Either I or II follows
d. Neither I nor II follows
e. Both I and II follow

42. Statement: Adversity makes a man wise.

Conclusions:

I. The poor are wise.

II. Man learns from bitter experience.

a. Only conclusion I follows
b. Only conclusion II follows
c. Either I or II follows
d. Neither I nor II follows
e. Both I and II follow

43. Statement: The interview panel may select a candidate who neither possesses the desired qualifications nor does the values and attributes.

Conclusions:

I. The inclusion of specialists on the interview panel does not guarantee that the selection will be proper.

II. The interview test has certain limitations in the matter of selection of candidates.

a. Only conclusion I follows
b. Only conclusion II follows
c. Either I or II follows
d. Neither I nor II follows
e. Both I and II follow

44. Statement: The President of XYZ Party indicated that 25 independent Members of Legislative Assembly (MLA) are seriously considering various options of joining some political party. But in any case all of them collectively will join one party only.

Conclusions:

I. The 25 independent MLAs will join XYZ party in a short period of time.

II. The 25 independent MLAs will join some other political party in a short period of time.

a. Only conclusion I follows
b. Only conclusion II follows
c. Either I or II follows
d. Neither I nor II follows
e. Both I and II follow

45. Statement: I know nothing except the fact of my ignorance.

Conclusions:

I. Writer's knowledge is very poor.

II. The world of knowledge is too vast to be explored by a single person.

a. Only conclusion I follows
b. Only conclusion II follows
c. Either I or II follows
d. Neither I nor II follows
e. Both I and II follow

46. Statement: Company X has a record of manufacturing cameras of quality and the latest design so that you do not spoil even a single shot irrespective of the weather conditions.

Conclusions:

I. No other company except X is reputed in the camera industry.

II. Anyone can take an acceptable shot with camera X.

a. Only conclusion I follows
b. Only conclusion II follows
c. Either I or II follows
d. Neither I nor II follows
e. Both I and II follow

47. Statement: India's economy depends mainly on forests.

Conclusions:

I. Trees should be preserved to improve Indian economy.

II. India wants only maintenance of forests to improve economic conditions.

a. Only conclusion I follows
b. Only conclusion II follows
c. Either I or II follows
d. Neither I nor II follows
e. Both I and II followz

Answer Key

1. (b)	**2.** (e)	**3.** (a)	**4.** (a)	**5.** (a)	**6.** (e)	**7.** (c)	**8.** (b)	**9.** (b)	**10.** (b)
11. (e)	**12.** (b)	**13.** (b)	**14.** (d)	**15.** (d)	**16.** (e)	**17.** (a)	**18.** (e)	**19.** (e)	**20.** (d)
21. (d)	**22.** (c)	**23.** (e)	**24.** (b)	**25.** (e)	**26.** (d)	**27.** (d)	**28.** (d)	**29.** (e)	**30.** (e)
31. (e)	**32.** (e)	**33.** (c)	**34.** (e)	**35.** (a)	**36.** (b)	**37.** (a)	**38.** (b)	**39.** (a)	**40.** (d)
41. (a)	**42.** (b)	**43.** (e)	**44.** (c)	**45.** (b)	**46.** (b)	**47.** (a)			

Explanatory Notes

1. (b)
Clearly, X will not get the special prize because although he broke the world record, he was found to use unfair means. So, conclusion II follows while conclusion I does not.

2. (e)
It is mentioned in the statement that one who considers price and quality before buying a product should buy the product of company X. So, both conclusions follow.

3. (a)
According to the statement, funding is necessary to improve quality and India is allocating funds to education. This means that the quality of education will improve in India. So, conclusion I follows. But funding alone is sufficient to enhance quality, is not true. So, conclusion II does not follow.

4. (a)
The need for a separate rating agency for IT companies clearly indicates that such assessment requires a separate set of skills. So, conclusion I follows. However, the statement does not indicate only the need or demand and the future course of action nor its after-effects can be judged. So, conclusion II does not follow.

5. (a)
Clearly, the solution to the problem is not to close down the Municipal and Zila Parishad-run schools but to strive to improve the standard of education of these schools. So, only conclusion I follows while conclusion II does not.

6. (e)
Sunita has a very busy schedule. This means that she is industrious. But still she finds time for rest. This means that she is an organised person. So, both conclusions follow.

7. (c)
The statement mentions that demand for oil is increasing faster than the production. So, either the demand must be reduced or oil must be imported to fulfil the increasing demand. Thus, either conclusion I or conclusion II follows.

8. (b)
The statement stresses the need to adopt a new method of examination. So, conclusion I does not follow. However, conclusion II directly follows from the given statement.

9. (b)
The statement asserts that people cannot stand any particular trend for long and seek change quite often. So, only conclusion II follows.

10. (b)
Nothing about the relation between political freedom and democracy is mentioned in the statement. So, conclusion I does not follow. But conclusion II directly follows from the given statement.

11. (e)
The statement clearly implies that it is easier to say than to do something; and what people say is different from what they do. So, both conclusions follow.

12. (b)
Whether the national norm is appropriate or not cannot be said. So, conclusion I does not follow. However, more number of beds per thousand population are available in the hospital in the state. So, conclusion II follows.

13. (b)
Investment in securities involves risk. This does not mean that one should not invest in securities. So, conclusion I does not follow. Since the statement advises one to consult investment advisor before investing, so conclusion II follows.

14. (d)
Neither the poor nor the rich, but only the role of money in politics is being talked about in the statement. So, neither conclusion I nor conclusion II follows.

15. (d)
The availability of vegetables is not mentioned in the given statement. So, conclusion I does not follow. Also, conclusion II is not directly related to the statement and so it also does not follow.

16. (e)
Since the accident has caused concern, it must be fatal. So, conclusion I follows. The use of the word 'again' in the statement justifies the fact mentioned in conclusion II. So, conclusion II also follows.

17. (a)
The statement mentions that chances of heart ailments are greatly reduced by a regular half-hour exercise. So, conclusion I follows. However, it talks of only reducing the probability which does not mean that the persons involved in sedentary jobs shall definitely suffer from heart ailments. So, conclusion II does not follow.

18. (e)
Both the given conclusions clearly bring out the central theme of the proverb given in the statement. So, both conclusions follow.

19. (e)
The statement mentions that the world of a man is as he makes it himself. So, some people might find it good but some quite bad. Thus, both conclusions follow.

20. (d)
The statement mentions that the candidates who have obtained second class Master's degree or have appeared for the final year examination of Master's degree, can apply for admission. This implies that both types of candidates may be selected on certain grounds. Thus, some candidates of each type and not all candidates of any one type, may be selected. So, neither conclusion I nor II conclusion follows.

21. (d)
Clearly, conclusion I cannot be deduced from the statement. Also, nothing about discipline is mentioned in the statement. So, neither conclusion I nor conclusion II follows.

22. (c)
It is mentioned in the statement that either the managers should resign by the next day or their services would be terminated. So, either conclusion I or II conclusion follows.

23. (e)
The statement asserts that a good singer always has a sweet voice and only good singers are invited to the conference. This implies that all those invited in the conference have sweet voice and those who do not have sweet voice are not invited. So, both conclusions follow.

24. (b)
Clearly, the new scheme intends to develop interest in reading by incorporating the habit in their routine. So, only conclusion II follows while conclusion I does not.

25. (e)
The statement clearly mentions that fulfilling the eligibility criteria and submitting the application before the stipulated date are both essential to avoid rejection. So, conclusion I follows. Also, since it is given that the candidates whose applications are rejected shall not be called for written test, so conclusion II also follows.

26. (d)
The manager might have humiliated Sachin not because of his dislike but on account of certain negligence or mistake on his part. So, conclusion I does not follow. Also, nothing about Sachin's rapport with his colleagues can be deduced from the statement. So, conclusion II also does not follow.

27. (d)
The fact that a certain rule has been more welcomed in a certain country does not imply that the problem is more prevalent there. So, conclusion I does not follow. Also, the amendment seeks to discourage only sexual harassment of women and shall in no way discourage employment of women. So, conclusion II also does not follow.

28. (d)
Since the given statement talks of an order not to let the officers read newspapers during office hours, it implies that reading newspapers during office hours is undesirable. So, conclusion I does not follow. Also, the order has been issued with an intention to prevent loss to the office work due to officers' other indulgences. Thus, conclusion II also does not follow.

29. (e)
The use of the term 'milk glut' makes conclusion I implicit. Also, the fact that the cooperatives and Government dairies failed to use the available milk indicates that they lack the proper infrastructure to handle such quantities of milk. So, conclusion II also follows.

30. (e)
Since both conclusions provide suitable explanations to the given statement, so both follow.

31. (e)
Clearly, the statement stresses on the fact that heeding to national needs is much more important than Space Research programmes, which stray the concerned authorities from the former. So, both conclusions follow.

32. (e)
Both conclusions directly follow from the given statement.

33. (c)
Clearly, either conclusion I or conclusion II could be the reason for the situation expressed in the statement.

34. (e)
Clearly, the statement declares dowry as an evil practice and reflects its demerits. Thus, conclusion I follows. Also, it is given that those who take dowry dishonour womanhood. This implies that those who do not take dowry respect womanhood. So, conclusion II also follows.

35. (a)
The statement declares enactment of OSA as the direct cause of increase in corruption. So, conclusion I follows. However, the enactment of an act by a government is undertaken for betterment and not with the intention of encouraging corruption though whatever may be the outcome later on. So, conclusion II does not follow.

36. (b)
That more emphasis should be laid on productivity areas instead of sciences does not mean that the country has achieved sufficient progress in sciences. But it implies that the productivity factor was previously being neglected. So, conclusion II follows while conclusion I does not.

37. (a)
The statement asserts that match can be won only if all the players play to their full potential. So, only conclusion I follows while conclusion II does not.

38. (b)
That more emphasis should be laid on productivity areas instead of sciences does not mean that the country has achieved sufficient progress in sciences. But it implies that productivity factor was previously being neglected. So, conclusion II follows while conclusion I does not.
39. (a)
The statement asserts that match can be won only if all the players play to their full potential. So, only conclusion I follows while conclusion II does not.
40. (d)
The statement does not talk against the auction but only speaks of the response it received from the bidders and gold producers. So, conclusion I does not follow. The phrase 'plenty of bidders looking for a bargain' is quite contrary to conclusion II. So, conclusion II also does not follow.
41. (a)
Clearly, conclusion I follows directly from the given statement. However, conclusion II is not related to the given statement and so it does not follow.
42. (b)
The statement talks of 'adversity' in general and not of lack of money'. So, conclusion I does not follow. Conclusion II correctly explains the statement and hence it follows.
43. (e)
Clearly, both conclusions correctly explain the given statement. So, both follow.
44. (c)
The statement asserts that 25 independent M.L.As shall join one party only. Thus, they may join XYZ or any other party. So, either conclusion I or conclusion II follows.
45. (b)
The statement is a symbolic one and only conclusion II correctly explains it.
46. (b)
Clearly, the statement talks of Company X only, not of the other company. So, conclusion I does not follow. Also, it is mentioned that one can take a good shot even in bad weather conditions with a camera of Company X. So, conclusion II follows.
47. (a)
It is mentioned in the statement that India's economy depends mainly on forests. This means that forests should be preserved. So, conclusion I follows. But, that only preservation of forests can improve the economy cannot be said. So, conclusion II does not follow.

❒

RAPIDEX ENGLISH SPEAKING COURSE/EXCEL ENGLISH SPEAKING COURSE

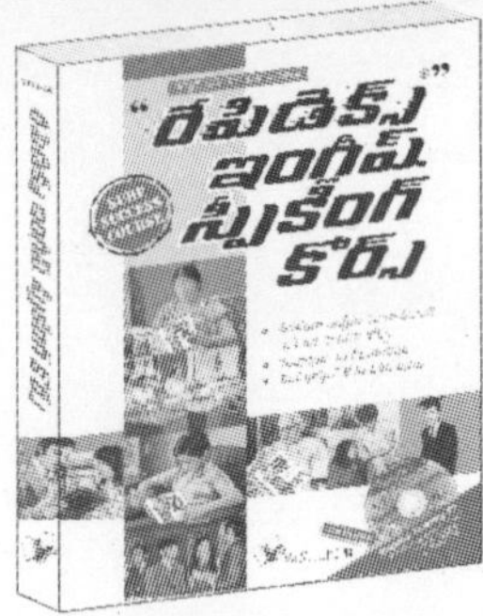
ISBN : 9789381448908
(Telugu)

ISBN : 9789381448915
(Bangla)

ISBN : 9789381448922
(Oriya)

ISBN : 9789381448939
(Assamese)

ISBN : 9789381448946
(Nepalese)

Published in sixte languages
Hindi, Malayalam, Tamil, Telugu, Kanna Marathi, Gujarati, Bangla, Ori Urdu, Assamese, Punjabi, Nepalese, Persian, Arabic and Sinhales

REGIONAL LANGUAGE/SPOKEN ENGLISH/LEARNING COURSES

ISBN : 9789357940054
(Bangla)

ISBN : 9789357940016
(Bangla)

ISBN :9789357940023
(Bangla)

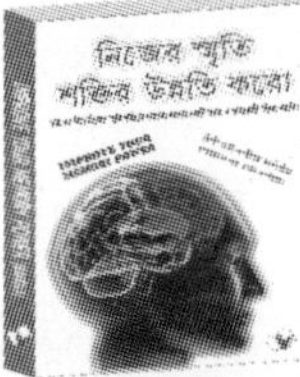
ISBN : 9789357940085
(Bangla)

ISBN : 9789357940825
(Bangla)

ISBN : 9789357940092
(Bangla)

ISBN : 9789357940009
(Bangla)

ISBN : 9789357940030
(Bangla)

ISBN : 9789357941
(2 Colour Book)

ISBN : 9789357940061
(Bangla)

ISBN : 9789357940047
(Bangla)

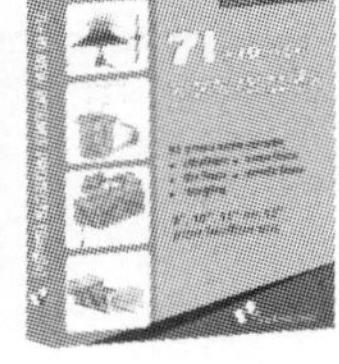
ISBN : 9788122310924
(Bangla)

ISBN : 9789357940078
(Bangla)

ISBN 9789350570357
(Kannada)

ISBN : 9789350571200
(Kannada)

ISBN : 9789350570340
(Kannada)

ISBN : 9789350570944
(Kannada)

(Coming Soon)

ISBN : 9789350570951
(Kannada)

ISBN : 9789350571309
(Kannada)

ISBN : 9789350571828
(Gujarati)

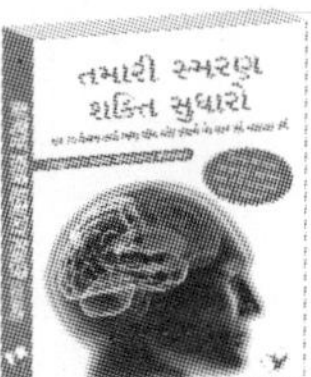
ISBN : 9789350571781
(Gujarati)

ISBN : 9789350571811
(Marathi)

ISBN : 9789350571804
(Marathi)

ISBN : 9789381384138
(Tamil)

ISBN : 9789381384121
(Tamil)

(Coming Soon)

ISBN : 9789357940153
(Eng.-Bangla)

ISBN : 9789357940399
(Eng.-Kannada)

ISBN : 9789357940375
(Eng.-Odia)

ISBN : 9789357940382
(Eng.-Telugu)

ISBN : 9789357941358
(Eng.-Malayalam)

ISBN : 9789357941327
(Eng.-Tamil)

ISBN : 9789357940856
(Eng.-Marathi)

ISBN : 9789357940849
(Eng.-Gujarati)

ISBN : 978935794l3
(Eng.-Assamese)

ISBN : 9789357941341
(Eng.-Urdu)

ISBN : 9789350570760
(Telugu)

ISBN : 9789350570098
(Telugu)

ISBN : 9789350571699
(Bangla)

ISBN : 9789350571125
(Bangla)

ISBN : 9789357940146
(Kannada)

ISBN : 9789357940139
(Kannada)

ISBN : 9789350571620
(Odia)

ISBN : 97893505711
(Odia)

STUDENT LEARNING/QUIZ/POPULAR SCIENCE/BIOGRAPHIES

ISBN : 9789357941310 ISBN : 9789357941495 ISBN : 9789381384053 ISBN : 9789381384060 ISBN : 9789381384121 ISBN : 9788122310924 ISBN : 9789381588468 ISBN : 9789381588604 ISBN : 97893505704

ISBN : 9789350570470 ISBN : 9789350570487 ISBN : 9789350570500 ISBN : 9789350570586 ISBN : 9789350571248 ISBN : 9789350571248 ISBN : 9789350571743 ISBN : 9789381384299 ISBN : 97893814480

ISBN : 9789381384305 ISBN : 9789381384954 ISBN : 9789381588819 ISBN : 9789350570371 ISBN : 9789350570388 ISBN : 9789350570395 ISBN : 9789350570401 ISBN : 9789350570364 ISBN : 978938158844

ISBN : 9789381448977 ISBN : 9789381384459 ISBN : 9789381384930 ISBN : 9789350571682 ISBN : 9789381588864 ISBN : 9789381588673 ISBN : 9789350570111 ISBN : 9789381384312 ISBN : 978938158868

ISBN : 9789350570258 ISBN : 9789350570227 ISBN : 9789381588499 ISBN : 9789381588338 ISBN : 9789381588345 ISBN : 9789381448656 ISBN : 9789381384558 ISBN : 9788192079639 ISBN : 97893505710

ISBN : 9789350571026 ISBN : 9789350571033 ISBN : 9789350571040 ISBN : 9789350571057 ISBN : 9789350570999 ISBN : 9789350571002 ISBN : 9789350571064 ISBN : 9789350571071 ISBN : 978935057108

ISBN : 9789350571101 ISBN : 9789381588321 ISBN : 9789381588307 ISBN : 9789381588567 ISBN : 9789350571163 ISBN : 9789350570517 ISBN : 9789381384183 ISBN : 9789381448625 ISBN : 978938138479

ISBN : 9789381384190 ISBN : 9789381448793 ISBN : 9789381588192 ISBN : 9789381588802 ISBN : 9789381588970 ISBN : 9789350570777 ISBN : 9789381448427 ISBN : 9789350570555 ISBN : 978935057054

All Books Available on Flipkart, Amazon, Infibeam, Snapdeal, Shopcluse • marketing@vspublishers.com

FUN. FACT & MAGIC/TALES & STORIES/LEISURE READING

SBN : 9788192079660 ISBN : 9788192079677 ISBN : 9789381588659 ISBN : 9789381588840 ISBN : 9789381588857 ISBN : 9789381588871 ISBN : 9789381588888 ISBN : 9789381384336 ISBN : 9789381448069

SBN : 9789381448090 ISBN : 9789381448083 ISBN : 9789381384343 ISBN : 9789381448076 ISBN : 9789381448809 ISBN : 9789381448885 ISBN : 9789350571248 ISBN : 9789350570210 ISBN : 9789381384329

SBN : 9789381448229 ISBN : 9789381448236 ISBN : 9789350570227 ISBN : 9789381588697 ISBN : 9788192079608 ISBN : 9789350571644 ISBN : 9789381588734 ISBN : 9789350570180 ISBN : 9789381448168

BN : 9789381588314 ISBN : 9789381588260 ISBN : 9788192079691 ISBN : 9789381588291 ISBN : 9789381588956 ISBN : 9789350570852 ISBN : 9789350570906 ISBN : 9789350570838 ISBN : 9789350570883

SBN : 9789350570845 ISBN : 9789350570890 ISBN : 9789350570869 ISBN : 9789350570913 ISBN : 9789350570821 ISBN : 9783950570876 ISBN : 9789350570920 ISBN : 9789350570937

BN : 9789381588987 ISBN : 9789350570005 ISBN : 9789350570012 ISBN : 9789350570029 ISBN : 9789381588994 ISBN : 9789350570036 ISBN : 9789350570043 ISBN : 9789350570050 ISBN : 9789381588406

N : 9789381448182 ISBN : 9789381448199 ISBN : 9789381448144 ISBN : 9789381384404 ISBN : 9789381588451 ISBN : 9789381588581 ISBN : 9789381588529 ISBN : 9789381448137 ISBN : 9789381448106

BN : 9789381448175 ISBN : 9789381448113 ISBN : 9789381448120 ISBN : 9789381448151 ISBN : 9789381384701 ISBN : 9789381384718 ISBN : 9789381384862 ISBN : 9788192079615 ISBN : 9789381384015

HEALTH & BEAUTY CARE/FAMILY & RELATIONS/LIFESTYLE

ISBN : 9789350570463

ISBN : 9789381588482

ISBN : 9789381448724

ISBN : 9789381448762

ISBN : 9789381448823

ISBN : 9789381384961

ISBN : 9789381384442

ISBN : 9789381448496

ISBN : 9789381588

ISBN : 9788122307511

ISBN : 9789381448502

ISBN : 9789381384633

ISBN : 9789381448489

ISBN : 9789381384251

ISBN : 9789350570593

ISBN : 9789381384831

ISBN : 9789381384800

ISBN : 9789350570

ISBN : 9789381384220

ISBN : 9789381384817

ISBN : 9789381384572

ISBN : 9789381448694

ISBN : 9789381384824

ISBN : 9789381384565

ISBN : 9789381384909

ISBN : 9789350570609

ISBN : 978938144

ISBN : 9789381448458

ISBN : 9789381384589

ISBN : 9788192079653

ISBN : 9789381384978

ISBN : 9789381448472

ISBN : 9789381448731

ISBN : 9789350571897

ISBN : 9789381448434

ISBN : 97893814

ISBN : 9789381384244

(also available in Hindi)

ISBN : 9789381384237

ISBN : 9789381384626

ISBN : 9789381448519

ISBN : 9789381384619

ISBN : 9789381448892

ISBN : 9789381384602

ISBN : 9789381588369

ISBN : 97893815

ISBN : 9789381588383

ISBN : 9789381588390

ISBN : 9789381448557

ISBN : 9789381588826

ISBN : 9789381384268

ISBN : 9788122305159

ISBN : 9789381448748

ISBN : 9789381384992

ISBN : 978938138

ISBN : 9789381448700

ISBN : 9789381588758

ISBN : 9789381384923

ISBN : 9789350570104

ISBN : 9789381448618

ISBN : 9789381448441

ISBN : 9789381384688

ISBN : 9789381384282

ISBN : 97881223

ISBN : 9789381448854

ISBN : 9789381384046

ISBN : 9789381384275

ISBN : 9789381384985

ISBN : 9789381448601

ISBN : 9789381448861

ISBN : 9789381384640

ISBN : 9789381384848

ISBN : 978938138

SUBJECT DICTIONARIES/IELTS/ACADEMIC/COMPUTER LEARNING

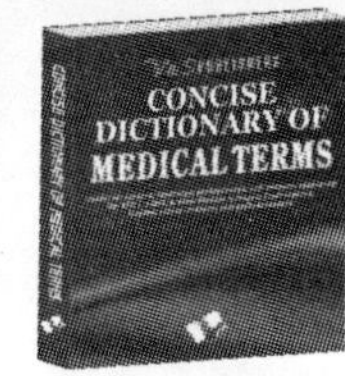

ISBN : 9789350571576 · ISBN : 9789350571583 · ISBN : 9789350571606 · ISBN : 9789350571590 · ISBN : 9789350571613

ISBN : 9789381588611 · ISBN : 9789381588628 · ISBN : 9789381588642 · ISBN : 9789381588635 · ISBN : 9789381588833 · ISBN : 9789350570326 · ISBN : 9789350570319 · ISBN : 9789350570333

ISBN : 9789350571507 · ISBN : 9789350571491 · ISBN : 9789350571521 · ISBN : 9789350571453

ISBN : 9789350571224 · ISBN : 9789350571231 · ISBN : 9789350571460 · ISBN : 9789350571453 · ISBN : 9789350571484 · ISBN : 9789350571477 · ISBN : 9789350571668 · ISBN : 9789350571538

ISBN : 9789350571392 · ISBN : 9789350571385 · ISBN : 9789350571408 · ISBN : 9789350571330 · ISBN : 9789350571347

ISBN : 9789350571415 · ISBN : 9789350571439 · ISBN : 9789350571422 · ISBN : 9789350571361 · ISBN : 9789350571354 · ISBN : 9789350571378 · ISBN : 9789350571149 · ISBN : 9789350571330

ISBN : 9789350571651 · ISBN : 9789350571286 · ISBN : 9789350571255 · ISBN : 9789350571262 · ISBN : 9789350571293 · ISBN : 9789350571279 · ISBN : 9789350571569 · ISBN : 9789357940368

ISBN : 9789350570241 · ISBN : 9789350570234 · ISBN : 9789350571965 · ISBN : 9789357941365 · ISBN : 9789357941549 · ISBN : 9789357941556 · ISBN : 9789357941563 · ISBN : 9789357941570 · ISBN : 9789350571934

ISBN : 9789357941501 · ISBN : 9789357941518 · ISBN : 9789357941525 · ISBN : 9789357941532 · ISBN : 9789357941747 · ISBN : 9789357941716 · ISBN : 9789357941709 · ISBN : 9789357941723

ISBN : 9789357941730 · ISBN : 9789350571693 · ISBN : 9789357941655 · ISBN : 9789357941662 · ISBN : 9789357941679 · ISBN : 9789357941686 · ISBN : 9789350570173 · ISBN : 9789381588895

ISBN : 9789350570142 · ISBN : 9789381588536 · ISBN : 9789350570159 · ISBN : 9789350570128 · ISBN : 9789350571316 · ISBN : 9789350571989 · ISBN : 9789350570135 · ISBN : 9789350570166